MOON HANDBOOKS®

ZION & BRYCE

© PAUL LEVY

Bryce Canyon

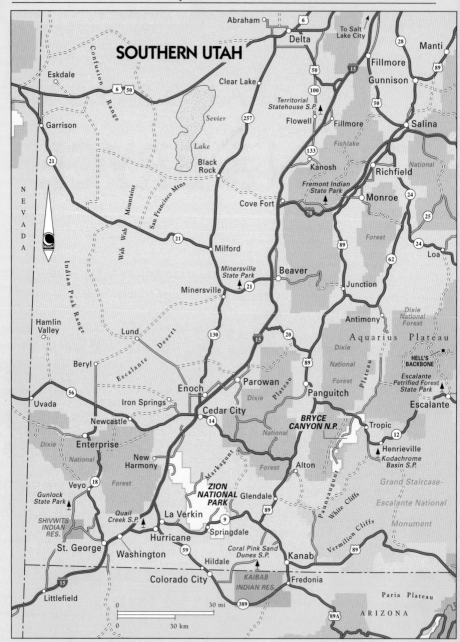

SOUTHERN UTAH

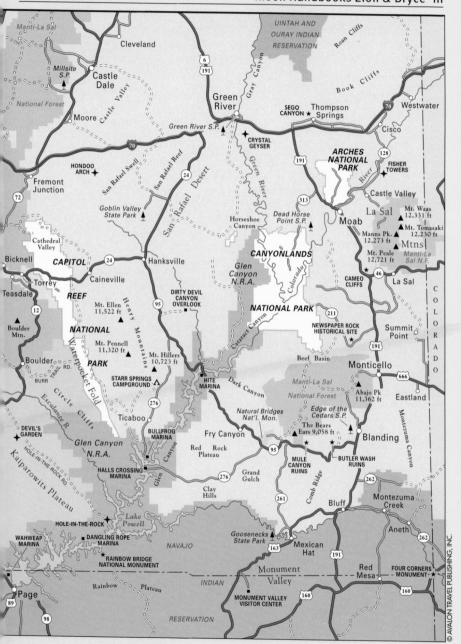

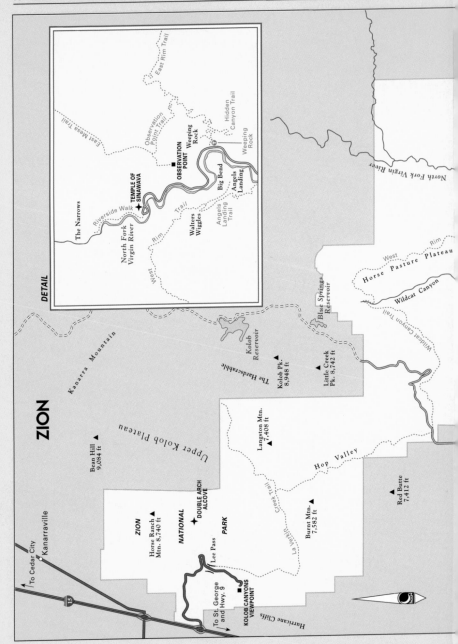

ZION

DETAIL

To Cedar City

Kanarraville

To St. George
and Hwy. 9

15

Kanarra Mountain

Upper Kolob Plateau

Bean Hill
9,084 ft ▲

ZION

Horse Ranch
Mtn. 8,740 ft ▲

DOUBLE ARCH
ALCOVE ✦

NATIONAL

Lee Pass

PARK

KOLOB CANYONS
VIEWPOINT ■

Hurricane Cliffs

La Verkin Creek Trail

Langston Mtn.
7,408 ft ▲

Hop Valley

Burnt Mtn.
7,582 ft ▲

Red Butte
7,412 ft ▲

The Hardscrabble

Kolob Pk.
8,948 ft ▲

Kolob
Reservoir

Little Creek
Pk. 8,742 ft ▲

Blue Springs
Reservoir

West Rim

Horse Pasture Plateau

Wildcat Canyon

Wildcat Canyon Trail

North Fork Virgin River

The Narrows

North Fork
Virgin River

Riverside Walk

TEMPLE OF
SINAWAVA ✦

OBSERVATION
POINT ■

Observation
Point Trail

East Rim Trail

East Mesa Trail

Weeping
Rock ●

Weeping
Rock

Hidden
Canyon Trail

Big Bend

Angels
Landing

Walters
Wiggles

Angels
Landing
Trail

West Rim Trail

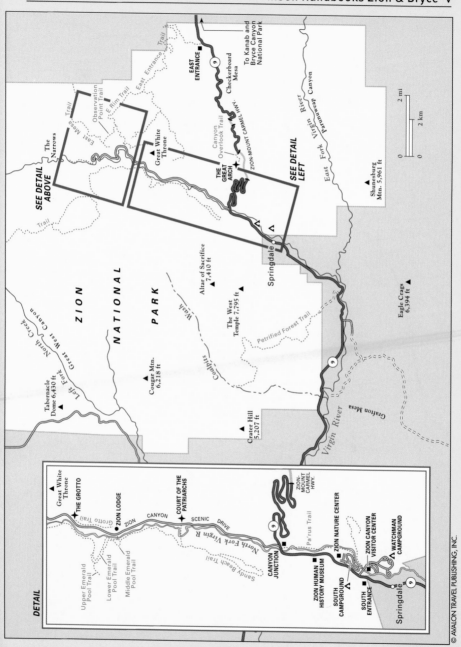

© AVALON TRAVEL PUBLISHING, INC.

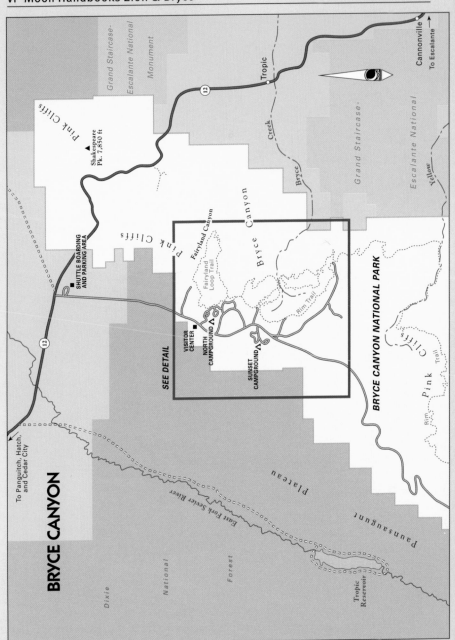

BRYCE CANYON

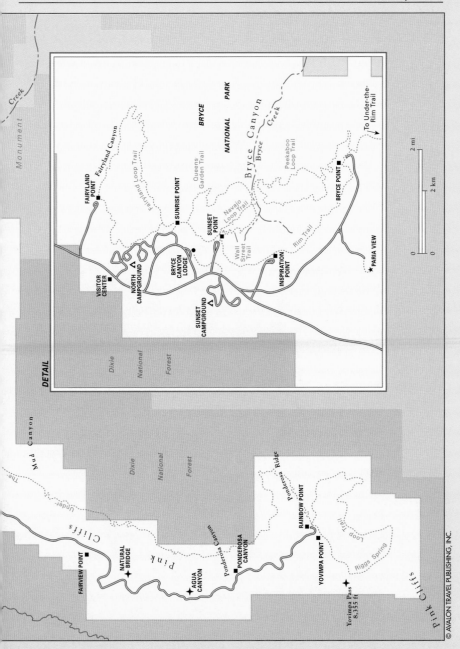

© AVALON TRAVEL PUBLISHING, INC.

Virgin River from Middle Emerald Pools Trail

© JUDY JEWELL

MOON HANDBOOKS®

ZION & BRYCE

INCLUDING ARCHES, CANYONLANDS, CAPITOL REEF, ESCALANTE, AND MOAB

FIRST EDITION

W. C. MCRAE

AVALON
TRAVEL

Moon Handbooks Zion & Bryce
First Edition

W. C. McRae

Published by
Avalon Travel Publishing
1400 65th St., Suite 250
Emeryville, CA 94608, USA

Printing History
1st edition—January 2003
5 4 3 2 1

Please send all comments, corrections,
additions, amendments, and critiques to:

Moon Handbooks Zion & Bryce

Avalon Travel Publishing
1400 65th St., Suite 250
Emeryville, CA 94608, USA
email: atpfeedback@avalonpub.com
www.moon.com

ISBN: 1-56691-551-1
ISSN: 1540-3823

Editor: Kevin McLain
Series Manager: Erin Van Rheenen
Copy Editor: Ginjer L. Clarke
Graphics Coordinator: Susan Mira Snyder
Production Coordinator: Amber Pirker
Cover Designer: Kari Gim
Interior Designers: Amber Pirker, Alvaro Villanueva, Kelly Pendragon
Map Editor: Olivia Solís
Cartographers: Kat Kalamaras, Mike Morgenfeld
Indexer: Vera Gross

Front cover photo: © Randy Wells

Distributed by Publishers Group West

Printed in the U.S.A. by R.R. Donnelley Norwest, Inc.

ABOUT THE AUTHOR
W. C. McRae

Bill McRae was born and raised in rural eastern Montana, on a traditional cattle and sheep ranch. Although he was brought up with one foot in the saddle, from an early age his real passion was for the culture of Europe, a taste that he evolved from stories of his grandparents' native Scotland. He made his first trip to the United Kingdom at 18, which awakened a serious urge to travel. This was the 1970s and much of the world seemed like a well-meaning and courteous place to have a party. And so he did. He used his college years as an excuse to travel, attending universities in England, Scotland, France, Canada, and the United States. He finished his education at the University of Kent, with an M.A. in Modern Literature. All of this traipsing about didn't make for much of an academic career, but it was a great education in life.

After university, Bill moved to Portland, Oregon, which is still his home. Since moving to Portland, Bill has supported his writing habit by working at a number of *real* jobs, including university teacher, caterer, journalist, and tile-setter. With his name on various travel guides, including *Moon Handbooks Montana* and *Moon Handbooks Utah,* Bill has also worked as an editor and contributor for Expedia.com, GORP.com, *National Geographic* and the Mobil Guide series. Between travel writing junkets, Bill makes his money writing about technology. You can always interest him in a hand of bridge, a camping trip, or cooking up something French and full of calories.

Bill has been traveling to Utah for a couple of decades, each time getting further off the road and digging deeper into the landscape. Every trip has a different focus, whether it's hiking into a new and more remote canyon, fixating on ancient rock art, or going deluxe at guest ranches. For Bill, Utah is the kind of place that gets under your skin, where you find yourself already planning your next adventure before you've finished up the current one.

Contents

SPECIAL TOPICS

BRYCE CANYON **151**

SPECIAL TOPICS

ZION **168**

Maps

MAP SYMBOLS

═══ Divided Highway	◉ State Capital	▲ Mountain
═══ Primary Road	○ City/Town	♠ State Park
─── Secondary Road	★ Point of Interest	⋀ Campground
······· Unpaved Road	• Accommodation	☮ Trailhead
············ Trail	▾ Restaurant/Bar	✦ Unique Natural Feature
	▪ Other Location	Dry Lake

Keeping Current

Travel information is constantly changing—sometimes so quickly that it's hard to keep up. We rely on our readers to keep us apprised of new developments. Find a restaurant that's too good to pass up, a hotel or campground that made a great trip that much better? We'd love to hear about them. Please also alert us to any information that may have changed since this book was published. If you want to sound off on this book, or Utah's National Parks in general, please drop us a line.

Moon Handbooks Zion & Bryce
Avalon Travel Publishing
1400 65th St., Suite 250
Emeryville, CA 94608, USA
atpfeedback@avalonpub.com

Introduction

Southern Utah is an extraordinary place, with landscapes so filled with staggering beauty, drama, and power that it seems a place of myth. The canyons, arches, and mesas of Utah could serve as the backdrop for a film of the Old Testament or the journeys of Gilgamesh. Five spectacular national parks and an enormous, wild national monument all lie within a day's drive of one another, sprawling over a highly eroded topography that's larger than many European countries. Yet within this high, dry area is surprising diversity, and each park has its own characteristic landscape. Find steep canyons and towering rock walls in Zion; red hoodoos in Bryce; rock arches and petrified sand dunes in Arches. Look to Canyonlands for slickrock and deeply carved river gorges; at Capitol Reef see a giant wrinkle in the earth, forming a colorful insight into geology; and hike dry washes and slot canyons in the huge Grand Staircase-Escalante National Monument. Each place is distinctive, but they're all characteristically southwestern. They all show different faces of the Colorado Plateau.

Many people first visit this area as part of a "grand tour" of the southwest. After getting a small glimpse of the magnificence and variety, some will latch onto one special place, and return year after year, growing to know it intimately.

Bryce Canyon

© PAUL LEVY

The Colorado Plateau

Utah's five national parks and the Grand Staircase-Escalante National Monument are all part of the Colorado Plateau, a high, broad physiographic province that includes southern Utah, northern Arizona, southwest Colorado, and northwest New Mexico. This roughly circular plateau, nearly the size of Montana, also contains the Grand Canyon, the Navajo Nation, and the Hopi Reservation.

Created by a slow but tremendous uplift, and carved by magnificent rivers, the plateau lies mostly between 3,000 and 6,000 feet, with some peaks reaching nearly 13,000 feet. Although much of the terrain is gently rolling, the Green and Colorado Rivers have sculpted remarkable canyons, buttes, mesas, arches, and badlands. Isolated uplifts and foldings have formed such features as the San Rafael Swell, Waterpocket Fold, and Circle Cliffs. The rounded Abajo, Henry, La Sal, and Navajo Mountains are examples of intrusive rock—an igneous layer that is formed below the earth's surface and later exposed by erosion.

The Colorado Plateau province is broken down into six physiographic sections: the Grand Canyon, Datil, Navajo, Uinta Basin, Canyon Lands, and High Plateaus. Utah's national parks are spread across the High Plateaus and Canyon Lands sections. The westernmost parks, Zion and Bryce, are in the High Plateaus; Capitol Reef, Arches, and Canyonlands are, not surprisingly, in the Canyon Lands section, and the Escalante River forms the dividing line between the two sections.

The High Plateaus (the Paunsagunt, Markagunt, and Aquarius Plateaus) are lava-topped uplands reaching above the main height of the Colorado Plateau, then dropping off to the south in a series of steps known as the Grand Staircase. Exposed layers range from the relatively young rocks of the Black Cliffs (lava flows) in the north to the increasingly older Pink Cliffs (visible at Bryce), Gray Cliffs (which include the Straight Cliffs of Grand Staircase-Escalante), White Cliffs (Zion's Navajo Sandstone), and Vermilion Cliffs (surrounding Kanab, Utah) toward the south.

The Canyon Lands section is noted for its synclines, anticlines, and folds—nongeologists can picture the rock layers as blankets on a bed, and then imagine how they look before the bed is made in the morning. This warping, which goes on deep beneath the earth's surface, has affected the overlying rocks, permitting the development of deeply incised canyons.

GEOLOGIC OVERVIEW

When you visit any one of Utah's national parks, the first things you're likely to notice are rocks. Vegetation is sparse and the soil is thin, so there's not much to hide geology here. Particularly stunning views are found where rivers have carved deep canyons through the rock layers.

By western U.S. standards, the rocks forming the Colorado Plateau have had it pretty easy. Although faults have cracked and uplifted rocks, and volcanoes have spewed lava across the plateau, it's nothing like the surrounding Rocky Mountains or Basin and Range provinces, both of which are the result of eons of violent geology. Mostly, sediments piled up, younger layers on top of older, then eroded, lifted up, and eroded some more.

The clean, orderly stairsteps from the young rocks in Bryce Canyon to the much older Grand Canyon show off the clearly defined layers of rock. Weird crenellations, hoodoos, and arches occur thanks to the way erosion acted on the various rocks making up this big Colorado Plateau layer cake.

Sedimentation

Water made this desert what it is today. Back before the continents broke apart and began drifting to their present-day locations, Utah was near the equator, just east of a warm ocean. Ancient seas washed over the land, depositing sand, silt, and mud. Layer upon layer, the soils piled up and were—over time—compressed into sandstones, limestones, and shales.

The ancestral Rocky Mountains rose to the east of the ocean, and, just to their west, a trough-like basin formed and was intermittently flushed with sea water. Evaporation caused salts and other minerals to collect on the basin floor; when the climate became wetter, more water rushed in.

As the ancestral Rockies eroded, their bulk washed down onto the basin. The sea level rose, washing in more mud and sand. When the seas receded, dry winds blew sand across the region, creating enormous dunes.

Over time, the North American continent drifted north, away from the equator, but it remained near the sea and was regularly washed by tides, leaving more sand and silt. Just inland, freshwater lakes filled, then dried, and the lakebeds consolidated into shales. During wet periods, streams coursed across the area, carrying then dropping their loads of muds, silts, and sands.

As the ancestral Rockies wore down to mere hills, other mountains rose, then eroded, contributing their sediments. A turn toward dry weather meant more dry winds, kicking up the sand and building it into massive dunes.

Uplift

About 15 million years ago the plateau began to lift, slowly, steadily, and, by geologic standards, in-

THE COLORADO PLATEAU

UTAH

Green River

70

70

Moab

15

Lake Powell

COLORADO

River

San Juan River

Colorado

40

17

40

ARIZONA

0   100 mi

0   100 km

NEW MEXICO

© AVALON TRAVEL PUBLISHING, INC.

credibly gently. Some areas were hoisted as high as 10,000 feet above sea level.

Along the western edge of the plateau, underlying faults—like those common in the Basin and Range area—shot through the sedimentary layers. Along these faults, the High Plateaus—the Markagunt, Paunsaugunt, and

© W.C. MCRAE

These tilted and vividly colored sedimentary layers near Bullfrog evince a complex geologic history.

NATURE'S PALETTE

In Utah, you'll get used to seeing a lot of colorful rock formations. The color of rock gives you clues to the composition and geologic history of the rock. In general:

• **Red rocks** are stained by rusty iron-rich sediments washed down from mountains, and are a clue that erosion has occurred.

• **Grey or brown rocks** were deposited by ancient seas.

• **White rocks** are colored by their "glue," the limey remains of dissolved seashells that leach down and harden sandstones.

• **Black rocks** are volcanic in origin.

• **Igneous rocks** are the odd rocks out. They are present in the La Sal, Abajo, and Henry Mountains near Canyonlands. These mountains are "laccoliths," formed by molten magma that pushed through the sedimentary layers, leaking deeper into some layers than others, and eventually forming broad dome-shaped protuberances, which were eroded into soft peaks, then carved by glaciers into the sharp peaks we see today.

A layer of lava also caps the Paunsaugant, Markagunt, and Aquarius Plateaus, which have lifted above the main level of the Colorado Plateau. This mostly basalt layer was laid down about 37 million years ago, before the Colorado Plateau began to uplift.

the Aquarius—rose above the height of the main Colorado Plateau.

Uplift is still occurring. A 1992 earthquake just outside Zion National Park was one strong reminder that the plateau continues to move.

Erosion

As the Colorado Plateau rose, its big rivers carved deep gorges through the uplifting rocks. Today, these rivers—the Green, Colorado, Escalante, Paria, and Virgin—are responsible for much of the dramatic scenery in Utah's national parks.

More subtle forms of erosion have also contributed to the plateau's present-day form. Water percolating down through the rock layers is one of the main erosive forces, washing away loose ma-

terial and dissolving ancient salts, often leaving odd formations, such as thin fins of resistant rock.

The many layers of sedimentary rocks forming the Colorado Plateau are all composed of different minerals and have varying densities, so it's not surprising that erosion affects each layer a bit differently. For instance, sandstones and limestones erode more readily than the harder mudstones or shales.

Erosion isn't limited to the force of water against rock. Rocks may be worn down or eaten away by a variety of forces, including wind, freezing and thawing, exfoliation (when sheets of rock peel off), oxidation, hydration and carbonation (chemical weathering), plant roots or animal burrows, and dissolving of soft rocks. Rockfalls in Zion, the ever-deepening channel of the Colorado River through Canyonlands, and the slow thinning of pedestals supporting Arches' balanced rocks are all clues that erosion continues unabated.

CLIMATE

The main thing for southern Utah travelers to remember is that they're in the desert.

The high-desert country of the Colorado Plateau lies mostly between 3,000–6,000 feet in elevation. Annual precipitation ranges from an extremely dry three inches in some areas to about 10 inches in others. Mountainous regions between 10,000–13,000 feet receive abundant rainfall in summer and heavy snows in winter.

Sunny skies prevail through all four seasons. Spring comes early to the canyon country with weather that's often windy and rapidly changing. Summer can make its presence known in April, although the real desert heat doesn't set in until late May or early June. Temperatures then soar into the 90s and 100s at midday, although the dry air makes the heat more bearable. Early morning is the choice time for travel in summer. A canyon seep surrounded by hanging gardens or a mountain meadow filled with wildflowers provides a refreshing contrast to the parched desert; other ways to beat the heat include hiking in the mountains and river-rafting.

Summer thunderstorm season begins anywhere from mid-June until August; huge billowing thunderstorm clouds bring refreshing rains and coolness. During this season, canyon hikers should be alert for flash flooding.

Autumn begins after the rains cease (usually October) and lasts into November or even December; days are bright and sunny with ideal temperatures, but nights become cold. In all of the parks, evenings will be cool even in midsummer. Think of southern Utah as the lunar surface: as soon as the sun goes down, all the heat of the day escapes into the atmosphere. Even if the day was baking hot, you'll need a jacket and a warm sleeping bag for the night.

Elevation matters: Bryce Canyon National Park is at 8,000 feet, and will be significantly cooler than nearby Zion, at about 4,000 feet. Bryce is the only park to regularly be covered with enough snow for cross-country skiing or snowshoeing. It's also the park where, during the early spring, a motel room will seem like a good idea to all but the most hardy tent campers. Winter lasts only about two months at the lower elevations. Light snows on the canyon walls add new beauty to the rock layers. Nighttime temperatures commonly dip into the teens, which is too cold for most campers. Otherwise, winter can be a fine time for travel. Heavy snows rarely occur below 8,000 feet.

Flash Floods

Rainwater runs quickly off the rocky desert surfaces and into gullies and canyons. A summer thunderstorm or a rapid late-winter snowmelt can send torrents of mud and boulders rumbling down dry washes and canyons. Backcountry drivers, horseback riders, and hikers need to avoid hazardous locations when storms threaten or unseasonably warm winds blow on the winter snowpack.

Flash floods can sweep away anything in their path, including boulders, cars, and campsites. Do not camp or park in potential flash-flood areas. If you come to a section of flooded road-

A canyon seep surrounded by hanging gardens or a mountain meadow filled with wildflowers provides a refreshing contrast to the parched desert; other ways to beat the heat include hiking in the mountains and river-rafting.

way—a common occurrence on desert roads after storms—wait until the water goes down before crossing (it shouldn't take long). Summer lightning causes forest and brush fires, posing a danger to hikers who are foolish enough to climb mountains when storms threaten.

The bare rock and loose soils so common in the canyon country do little to hold back the flow of rain or meltwater. In fact, slickrock is effective at shedding water as fast as it comes in contact. Logs and other debris wedged high on canyon walls give proof enough of past floods.

FLORA

Within the physiographic province of the Colorado Plateau, several different life zones are represented.

In the low desert, shrubs eke out a meager existence. Climbing higher you'll pass through

© W.C. MCRAE

Spikey *Yucca utahensis* produce late spring stalks of flowers attractive to butterflies.

grassy steppe, sage, and piñon-juniper woodlands, to ponderosa pine. Of all these zones, the piñon-juniper is most common.

But it's not a lock-step progression of plant A at elevation X and plant B at elevation Z. Soils are an important consideration, with sandstones being more hospitable than shales. Plants will grow wherever the conditions will support them, and Utah's parks have many microenvironments that can lead to surprising plant discoveries. Look for different plants in these different habitats: slickrock (where cracks can gather enough soil to host a few plants), riparian (moist areas with the greatest diversity of life), and terraces and open space (the area between riverbank and slickrock, where shrubs dominate). With more than 800 native species, Zion has the greatest plant diversity of any of Utah's parks.

How Plants Survive in the Desert

Most of the plants you'll see in Utah's national parks are well adapted to desert life. Many are succulents, which have their own water-storage systems in their fleshy stems or leaves. Cacti are the most obvious succulents; they swell with stored moisture during the spring, then slowly shrink and wrinkle as the stored moisture is used.

Other plants have different strategies for making the most of scarce water. Some, such as yucca, have deep roots, taking advantage of what moisture exists in the soil. The leaves of desert plants are often vertical, exposing less surface area to the sun. Leaves may also have very small pores, slowing transpiration, or stems coated with a resinous substance, which also slows water loss. Hairy or light-colored leaves help reflect sunlight.

Desert wildflowers are annuals; they bloom in the spring, when water is available, then form seeds, which can survive the dry, hot summer, and die back. A particularly wet spring means a bumper crop of wildflowers.

Even though mosses aren't usually thought of as desert plants, they are found growing in seeps along canyon walls and in cryptobiotic soils. When water is unavailable, mosses dry up; when the water returns, the moss quickly plumps up again.

Junipers have a fairly drastic way of dealing

hanging garden, Zion National Park

with water shortage. During a prolonged dry spell, a juniper tree can shut off the flow of water to one or more of its branches, sacrificing these branches to keep the tree alive.

Hanging Gardens

Look along Zion's Virgin River canyon for clumps of ferns and mosses lit with maidenhair ferns, shooting stars, monkeyflowers, columbine, orchids, and bluebells. These unexpectedly lush pockets are called "hanging gardens," gem-like islands of plant life nestled into canyon walls.

Hanging gardens take advantage of a unique microclimate created by the meeting of two rock layers: Navajo Sandstone and Kayenta Shale. Water percolates down through porous sandstone and, when it hits the denser shale layer, travels laterally along the top of the harder rock and emerges at cliff's edge. These little springs support lush plant life.

Tamarisk

One of the Colorado Plateau's most common trees, the non-native tamarisk is also one of the peskiest. Imported from the Mediterranean and widely planted along the Colorado River to control erosion, the tamarisk has spread wildly, and its dense stands have crowded out native trees such as cottonwoods. Tamarisks are notoriously thirsty trees, sucking up vast amounts of water, but they give back little in the way of food or habitat for local wildlife. Their thick growth also increases the risk of fire. The National Park Service is taking steps to control tamarisk.

Cryptobiotic Soil

Over much of the Colorado Plateau, the soil is alive. What looks like a grayish-brown crust is actually a dense network of filament-forming blue-green algae intertwined with soil particles, lichens, moss, green algae, and microfungi. This slightly sticky, crusty mass holds the soil together, slowing erosion. Its sponge-like consistency allows it to soak up water and hold it. Plants growing in cryptobiotic soil have a great advantage over plants rooted in dry, sandy soil.

Crytobiotic soils are extremely fragile. Make every effort to avoid stepping on them—stick to trails, slickrock, or rocks instead.

FAUNA

Although they're not thought of as great "wildlife parks" like Yellowstone or Denali, Utah's national parks are home to plenty of animals. Desert animals are often nocturnal and unseen by park visitors.

Rodents

Rodents include squirrels, packrats, kangaroo rats, chipmunks, and porcupines, most of which spend their days in burrows.

One of the few desert rodents out foraging during the day is the white-tailed antelope squirrel, which looks much like a chipmunk. Its white tail reflects the sunlight, and, when it needs to cool down a bit, an antelope squirrel smears its face with saliva (yes, that probably *would* work for you, too, but that's why you have sweat glands). The antelope squirrel lives at lower elevations; higher up you'll see golden-mantled ground squirrels.

Look for rabbits—desert cottontails and jackrab-

bits—at dawn and dusk. If you're rafting the Green or Colorado Rivers, keep an eye out for beavers.

Kangaroo rats are particularly well adapted to desert life. They spend their days in cool burrows, eat only plants, and never drink water! Instead, a kangaroo rat metabolizes dry food in a way that produces water.

Utah prairie dogs have been given a new lease on life in Bryce National Park. In 1973 the animals were listed as an endangered species and reintroduced to Bryce. Today about 130 animals live in the park—the largest protected population of Utah prairie dogs. Prairie dogs live together in social groups called colonies or towns, which are laced with burrows, featuring a network of entrances for quick pops in and out of the ground. Prairie dogs are preyed on by badgers, coyotes, hawks, and snakes, so a colony will post lookouts, who are constantly searching for danger. When threatened, the lookouts "bark" to warn the colony. Utah prairie dogs hibernate during the winter and emerge from their burrows to mate furiously in early April.

Piñon seeds are fodder for desert birds and rodents.

Porcupines are common in Capitol Reef and Zion; although they prefer to live in forested areas, especially the piñon-juniper zone, they sometimes forage in streamside brush. These nocturnal creatures have also been known to visit campsites, where they like to gnaw on sweaty boots or backpack straps.

Bats

As night falls in canyon country, bats emerge from the nooks and crannies that protect them from the day's heat and begin to feed on mosquitoes and other insects. The tiny gray western pipistrelle is common. It flies early in the evening, feeding near streams, and can be spotted by its somewhat erratic flight. The pallid bat spends a lot of its time creeping across the ground in search of food and is a late-night bat (look for it after 10 P.M. in the summer at Capitol Reef). Another common bat (here and across the United States) is the prosaically named big brown bat.

Large Mammals

Mule deer are common in all of the parks, as are coyotes. Other large mammals include the predators: mountain lions and coyotes. If you're lucky, you'll get a glimpse of a bobcat or a fox.

If you're hiking the trails of Bryce Canyon early in the morning and see something that looks like a small dog in a tree, it's probably a gray fox. These small (5–10-pound) foxes live in forested areas and have the cat-like ability to climb trees. They're most commonly seen on the connecting trail between the Queens Garden and Navajo Loop trails. Kit foxes, which are even tinier than gray foxes, with prominent ears and a big bushy tail, are common in Arches and Canyonlands. Red foxes also live across the plateau.

Desert bighorn sheep live in Arches, Canyonlands, and Capitol Reef; look for them trotting across steep, rocky ledges. In Arches, they're frequently sighted along Highway 191 south of the visitors center. They also roam the talus slopes and side canyons near the Colorado River. Desert bighorns have also been reintroduced in Zion and can occasionally be spotted in steep, rocky areas on the park's east side.

Reptiles

Reptiles are well-suited to desert life. As cold-blooded, or ectothermic, animals, their body temperature depends on the environment, rather than on internal metabolism, and it's easy for them to keep warm in the desert heat. When it's cold, reptiles hibernate or drastically slow their metabolism.

The western whiptail lizard is common in Arches. You'll recognize it because its tail is twice as long as its body. Also notable is the western collared lizard, with a bright green body set off by a black collar.

Less flashy but particularly fascinating are the several species of parthenogenic lizards. All of

KNOW YOUR TRACKS

Here's the scenario: You're hiking down a trail and notice fresh, large paw prints. Mountain lion or Labrador retriever? Here's the way to tell the difference. Mountain lions usually retract their claws when they walk. Dogs, of course, can't do this. So if close inspection of the print reveals toenails, it's most likely from a canine's paw.

But about those mountain lions . . . in recent years incidents of mountain lion–human confrontations have increased markedly and received much publicity. These ambush hunters usually prey on sick or weak animals, but will occasionally attack people, especially children and small adults. When hiking or camping with children in mountain lion territory (potentially all of Utah's national parks), it's important to keep them close to the rest of the family.

If you are stalked by a mountain lion, make yourself look big by raising your arms, waving a big stick, or spreading your coat. Maintain direct eye contact with the animal, and do not turn your back to it. If the mountain lion begins to approach, throw rocks and sticks, and continue to look large and menacing as you slowly back away. In case of an attack, fight back; do not "play dead."

To put things in perspective, it's important to remember that mountain lions are famously elusive. If you do see one, it will probably be a quick glimpse of the cat running away from you.

these lizards are female, and they reproduce by laying eggs that are clones of themselves. Best-known is the plateau striped whiptail, but six of the 12 species of whiptail present in the area are all-female.

The northern plateau lizard is common in areas from about 3,000–6,000 feet. It's not choosy about its habitat—juniper-piñon woodlands, prairies, riparian woodlands, and rocky hillsides are all perfectly acceptable. This is the lizard you'll most often see scurrying across your campsite in Zion or Capitol Reef.

Rattlesnakes are present across the area, but, given a chance, they'll get out of your way rather than strike. (Still, it's another good reason to wear sturdy boots.) The midget faded rattlesnake, a small subspecies of the western rattlesnake, lives in burrows and rock crevices and is mostly active at night. Although this snake has especially toxic venom, full venom injections occur in only one-third of all bites.

Amphibians

Although they're not usually thought of as desert animals, a variety of frogs and toads live on the Colorado Plateau. Tadpoles live in wet springtime potholes as well as in streams and seeps. If you're camping in a canyon, you may be lucky enough to be serenaded by a toad chorus.

Bullfrogs are not native to the western United States, but since they were introduced in the early 1900s, they have flourished, very likely at the expense of native frogs and toads, whose eggs and tadpoles they eat.

The big round toes of the small, spotted canyon treefrog make it easy to identify—that is, if you can see this well-camouflaged frog in the first place! They're most active at night, spending their days on streamside rocks or trees.

Toads present in Utah's parks include the Great Basin spadefoot, red spotted toad, and western woodhouse toad.

Birds

Have you ever seen a bird pant? Believe it or not, that's how desert birds expel heat from their bodies. They allow heat to escape by drooping their wings away from their bodies, exposing thinly feathered areas (sort of like pulling up your shirt and using it to fan your torso).

The variety of habitats across the Colorado Plateau, such as piñon-juniper, perennial streams, dry washes, and rock cliffs, allow many species of bird to find homes. Birders will find the greatest variety of birds near rivers and streams. Other birds, such as golden eagles, kestrels (small falcons), and peregrine falcons nest high on cliffs and patrol open areas for prey. Common hawks include the red-tailed hawk and northern harrier; late-evening strollers may see great horned owls. California condors were reintroduced in 1996 to Zion, and while they're still not abundant, their population is steadily increasing.

People usually notice the canyon wren by its lovely song; this small, long-beaked bird nests in cavities along cliff faces. The related rock wren is—as its name implies—a rock collector: it paves a trail to its nest with pebbles, and the nest itself is lined with rocks. Another canyon bird, the white-throated swift, swoops and calls as it chases insects and mates, rather dramatically, in flight. They're often seen near violet-green swallows

JUDY JEWELL ©

This sculpture may be the best sighting you'll get of the canyon wren, which is more often heard than seen.

(which are equally gymnastic fliers) in Canyonlands, Arches, and Grand Staircase-Escalante.

Chukar—chunky game birds introduced for the benefit of hunters in the 1930s—are common at Capitol Reef, where they're often seen on or near the ground, foraging in low-lying shrubs and grasses.

Several species of hummingbird (mostly black-chinned, but also broad-tailed and rufous) are often seen in the summer. Woodpeckers are also common, including the northern flicker and red-naped sapsucker, and flycatchers like Say's phoebe, western kingbird, and western wood-pewee can be spotted too. Two warblers—the yellow and the yellow-rumped—are common in the summer, and Wilson's warbler stops in during spring and fall migrations. Horned larks are present year-round.

Mountain bluebirds are colorful, easy for a novice to identify, and common in Canyonlands and Arches. Look for the American dipper along the Virgin River in Zion. This small, gray bird distinguishes itself from other similar birds by its habit of plunging headfirst into the water in search of insects.

Both the well-known scrub jay and its local cousin, the piñon jay, are noisy visitors to almost every picnic. Other icons of western avian life—the turkey vulture, the raven, and the magpie—are widespread and easily spotted.

Fish

Obviously, deserts aren't particularly known for their aquatic life, and the big rivers of the Colorado Plateau are now dominated by non-native species such as channel catfish and carp. Many of these fish were introduced as game fish. Native fish, like the six-foot, 100-pound Colorado pikeminnow, are now uncommon.

Spiders and Scorpions

Tarantulas, black widow spiders, and scorpions all live across the Colorado Plateau, and all are objects of many a parkgoer's phobias. Although the black widow spider's venom is toxic, tarantulas deliver only a mildly toxic bite (and rarely bite humans), and a scorpion's sting is about like that of a bee.

ENVIRONMENTAL ISSUES

Utah's national parks have generally been shielded from the environmental issues that play out in the rest of the state, which has always been business-oriented, with a heavy emphasis on extractive industries such as mining and logging.

The main environmental threats to the parks are the consequences of becoming too popular. During the summer, auto and RV traffic can clog park roads, with particularly bad snarls at viewpoint parking areas. Both Zion and Bryce have made attempts to control park traffic by running shuttle buses along scenic drives. At Zion, it's mandatory to ride the bus (or your bike) during summer, and it's made a significant difference.

Hikers also have an impact, especially when they tread on fragile cryptobiotic soil. Killing this living soil crust drastically increases erosion in an already easily eroded environment.

Non-native Species

Non-native species don't respect park boundaries, and several non-native animals and plants have established strongholds in Utah's national parks, altering the local ecology by outcompeting native plants and animals.

Particularly invasive plants include tamarisk (salt cedar), cheat grass, Russian knapweed, and Russian olive. Tamarisk is often seen as the most troublesome invader. This thirsty Mediterranean plant was imported in the 1800s as an ornamental shrub and was later planted by the Department of Agriculture to slow erosion along the banks of the Colorado River in Arizona. It rapidly took hold, spreading upriver at roughly 12 miles per year, and is now firmly established on all of the Colorado's tributaries, where it grows in dense stands. Tamarisk consumes a great deal of water and rarely provides food and shelter necessary for the survival of wildlife. It also outcompetes cottonwoods because tamarisk shade inhibits the growth of cottonwood seedlings.

Courthouse Wash in Arches is one of several sites where the National Park Service has made an effort to control tamarisk. Similar control experiments have been established in nearby areas, mostly in small, tributary canyons of the Colorado River.

History

PREHISTORY

Beginning about 15,000 years ago, nomadic groups of Paleo-Indians traveled across the Colorado Plateau in search of game animals and wild plants, but they left few traces.

Nomadic bands of hunter-gatherers roamed the Colorado Plateau for at least 5,000 years. The climate was probably cooler and wetter when these first Indians arrived, with both food plants and game animals more abundant than today.

Agriculture was introduced from the south about 2,000 years ago and brought about a slow transition to a settled village life. The Fremont culture emerged in the northern part of the region (including present-day Capitol Reef and Arches National Parks and Grand Staircase-Escalante National Monument) and the Anasazi in the southern part (there was a settlement in present-day Zion National Park). In some areas, including Escalante and Arches, both groups lived contemporaneously. Although both groups made pots, baskets, bowls, and jewelry, only the

Anasazi constructed masonry villages. Thousands of stone dwellings, ceremonial kivas, and towers built by the Anasazi still stand. Both groups left behind intriguing rock art, either pecked in (petroglyphs) or painted (pictographs).

The Anasazi and Fremont departed from this region about 800 years ago, perhaps because of drought, warfare, or disease. Some of the Anasazi moved south and joined the Pueblo tribes of present-day Arizona and New Mexico. The fate of the Fremont Indians remains a mystery.

After the mid-1200s and until white settlers arrived in the late 1800s, small bands of nomadic Ute and Paiute moved through southern Utah. The Navajo began to enter Utah in the early 1800s. None of the three Indian groups established firm control of the region north of the San Juan River, where present-day national parks are located.

AGE OF EXPLORATION

In 1776, Spanish explorers of the Dominguez-Escalante Expedition were the first Europeans to visit and describe the region. They had given up partway through a proposed journey from Santa Fe to California and returned to Santa Fe along a route passing through the sites of present-day Cedar City and Hurricane, crossing the Colorado River in a place that is now covered by Lake Powell.

The Old Spanish Trail, used from 1829–1848, ran through Utah to connect New Mexico with California, crossing the Colorado River near present-day Moab. Fur trappers and mountain men, including Jedediah Smith, also traveled southern Utah's canyons in search of beaver and other animals during the early 1800s; inscriptions carved into the sandstone record their passage. In 1859, the U.S. Army's Macomb Expedition made the first documented description of what is now Canyonlands National Park. Major John Wesley Powell's pioneering river expeditions down the Green and Colorado Rivers in 1869 and 1871–1872 filled in many blank areas on the maps.

ANASAZI OR ANCESTRAL PUEBLOAN?

As you travel through the Southwest, you may hear reference to the "ancestral Puebloans." In this book, we've chosen to use the more familiar name for these people—the Anasazi. The word *Anasazi* is actually a Navajo term that archaeologists chose, thinking it meant "old people." A more literal translation is "enemy ancestors." For this reason, some consider the name inaccurate. The terminology is in flux, and which name you hear depends on who you're talking to or where you are. The National Park Service now uses the more descriptive term ancestral Puebloan. These prehistoric people built masonry villages and eventually moved south to Arizona and New Mexico, where their descendants, such as the Acoma, Cochiti, Santa Clara, Taos, and Hopi Mesas, live in modern-day pueblos.

MORMON SETTLEMENT

In 1849–1850, Mormon leaders in Salt Lake City took the first steps toward colonizing southern Utah. Parowan, now a sleepy community along I-15, became the first Mormon settlement in southern Utah, and Cedar City the second—both established in 1851. In 1855, a successful experiment in growing cotton along Santa Clara Creek near present-day St. George aroused considerable interest among the Mormons. New settlements soon arose in the Virgin River Valley; however, poor roads hindered development, and floods, droughts, disease, and hostile Indians discouraged some Mormon pioneers, but many of those who stayed prospered by raising food crops and livestock.

Also in 1855, the Elk Ridge Mission was founded near present-day Moab. It lasted only a few months before Ute Indians killed three Mormon settlers and sent the rest fleeing for their lives. Church members had better success during the 1870s in the Escalante area (1876) and Moab (1877).

RELIGION IN UTAH

Quick, a little free-association test. When you say "Utah," what do you think?

Most people, unsurprisingly, respond "Mormon." And Mormonism is inescapable for anyone traveling around Utah with eyes even half-open. Just as sensitive travelers would not denigrate Catholicism in Ireland or Buddhism in Thailand, travelers in Utah would do well to keep an open mind about Utah's predominant religion.

Remember that the church's proper title is the Church of Jesus Christ of Latter-Day Saints, and that members prefer to be called "Latter-day Saints," "Saints" (usually this term is just used amongst church members), or "LDS." While calling someone a Mormon isn't *wrong*, it's not quite as respectful.

The religion is based in part on the Book of Mormon, the name given to a text derived from a set of "golden plates" found by Joseph Smith in 1827 in western New York. Smith claimed to have been led by an angel to the plates, which were covered with a text written in "reformed Egyptian." A farmer by upbringing, Smith translated the plates and published an English-language version of the Book of Mormon in 1830.

The Book of Mormon tells the story of the lost tribes of Israel which, according to Mormon teachings, migrated to North America and became the ancestors of today's Native Americans. According to the Book of Mormon, Jesus also journeyed to North America, and the book includes teachings and prophecies that Christ supposedly gave to the ancient Indians.

The most stirring and unifying aspect of Mormon history is the incredible westward migration made by the small, fiercely dedicated band of Mormon pioneers in the 1840s. Smith and his followers were persecuted in New York and then in their newly founded utopian communities in Ohio, Missouri and Illinois. After Smith was murdered near Carthage, Illinois in 1844, the group decided to press even further westward toward the frontier, led by church president Brigham Young. The journey across the then very Wild West to the Great Salt Lake basin was made by horseback, wagon or handcart - hundreds of Mormon pioneers pulled their belongings across the Great Plains in four foot by four foot carts. The first group of Mormon pioneers reached the Salt Lake City area in 1847. The bravery and tenacity of the group's two-year migration forms the basis of many Utah residents' fierce pride in their state and religion.

Most people know that LDS members are clean-living, family people who eschew alcohol, tobacco, and stimulants, including caffeine. This can make it a little tough for visitors to feed their own vices (and indeed, it may make what formerly seemed like a normal habit feel a little more sinister). But Utah has loosened up a lot in the past few years, largely thanks to hosting the 2002 Winter Olympics, and it's really not too hard to find a place to have a beer with dinner, though you may have to make a special request. Towns near the national parks are particularly used to hosting non-Saints, and attach virtually no stigma to waking up with a cup of coffee or settling down with a glass of wine.

For sheer effort and endurance, it's hard to beat the efforts of the Hole-in-the-Rock Expedition of 1879–1880. Sixty families with 83 wagons and more than 1,000 head of livestock crossed some of the West's most rugged canyon country in an attempt to settle at Montezuma Creek on the San Juan River. They almost didn't make it: a journey expected to take six weeks turned into a six-*month* ordeal. The exhausted company arrived on the banks of the San Juan River on April 5, 1880. Too tired to continue just 20 easy miles to Montezuma Creek, they stayed and founded the town of Bluff. The Mormons established other towns in southeastern Utah, too, relying on ranching, farming, and mining for their livelihoods. None of the communities in the region ever reached a large size; Moab is the biggest with a population of 4,500.

NATIONAL PARK MOVEMENT IN UTAH

In the early 1900s, people other than Native Americans, Mormon settlers, and government explorers began to notice that southern Utah was a remarkably scenic place and that it might be developed for tourism.

In 1909, a presidential Executive Order designated Mukuntuweap (now Zion) National Monument, in Zion Canyon. Roads were built to improve the access, and by 1917, a tent camping resort was operating in the canyon. Two years later, Congress passed a bill forming Zion National Park. In the 1920s, the Union Pacific completed a rail line to Cedar City and Zion; Zion Lodge was built; and the technically challenging construction of the Zion–Mt. Carmel Highway, including its impressive 5,613-foot tunnel, began.

Early homesteaders around Bryce took visiting friends and relatives to see the incredible rock formations, and pretty soon they found themselves in the tourism business. In 1923, when Bryce Canyon National Monument was dedicated, the Union Pacific Railroad took over the fledgling tourist camp and began building Bryce Lodge. Tours of the hoodoos proved to be spectacularly popular, and Bryce became a national park in 1928.

Like Bryce and Zion, Arches was also helped along by railroad executives looking to develop their own businesses. In 1929, President Herbert Hoover signed the legislation creating Arches National Monument.

Capitol Reef became a national monument in 1937, thanks largely to one vigorous and enthusiastic local, and for years it was loved passionately by a handful of Utah archaeology buffs, but largely ignored by the federal government, who put it under the administrative control of Zion National Park.

During the 1960s, the National Park Service responded to a huge increase in park visitation nationwide by expanding facilities, spurring Congress to change the status of several national monuments to national parks. Canyonlands became a national park in the 1960s; after a spate of uranium prospecting in the nuclear-giddy 1950s, Capitol Reef and Arches gained national park status in 1971.

As visitors continued to flood the parks during the 1980s and 1990s, park managers realized they needed to develop strategies to deal with the crowds and, especially, the traffic. New trails, campgrounds, and visitors centers were built, and Zion and Bryce have both made attempts to control traffic on their scenic roads.

In 1996, President Bill Clinton used provisions of the National Antiquities Act to establish the Grand Staircase-Escalante National Monument. This vast tract of land, which totals more than 1.8 million acres, is the largest national monument land grouping in the lower 48 states, bringing under federal Interior Department management tracts of land previously administered by the Bureau of Land Management, the National Forest Service, and the state of Utah. Designation as a national monument means that the land is off-limits to specific kinds of development and that the land will be managed to preserve its wilderness characteristics as much as possible. The timing of the designation was apparently motivated by plans to develop a large strip coal mine in the slickrock Escalante River canyons, a well-loved destination for long-distance hikers and adventurers.

On the Road

Although the national parks of Utah are located in a geographically compact area, connecting the dots and visiting each of them isn't as straightforward as it might seem. The extremely rugged topography of the area has made road building difficult, so visiting all of the parks requires a lot of driving. Maps often show unpaved backroads that can serve as shortcuts. Many of these are fine if you have a high-clearance vehicle, but check locally before setting out to determine current conditions: rainstorms and snowmelt can render these roads impassible. Otherwise, sit back and enjoy the ride. These are some of the world's most scenic landscapes, and if you're in a hurry, you should stick to the freeway.

In general, the parks attract two kinds of visitors: tourists who come mostly to look and outdoor enthusiasts who come mostly to do. This book provides information for both kinds of traveler, but advocates a middle ground between the two archetypes. Southern Utah has plenty of eye-popping scenery, and you'll want to see as much as possible, especially on your first trip through these desert canyons. This book also makes it easy to get out of the car and explore these landscapes up close and personal. For each park, you'll find a selection of hikes rated from easy to challenging, plus information on

Zion Road

© PAUL LEVY

mountain biking, horseback riding, four-wheel-drive exploring, white-water rafting, and other forms of recreation that let you get outdoors to explore the unique geology, natural history, and archeology of these parks.

The parks are all open year-round, although spring (Apr.–June) and fall (Sept.–Oct.) are the best times to visit—you'll avoid the heat and crowds of high summer in July and August. The entry fee for the national parks has gone up greatly in the past few years; admission to Zion is now $20 per vehicle. If you're planning on making the rounds of the Utah national parks, it's an excellent idea to purchase the park system's Golden Eagle Passport ($65) or the National Parks Pass ($50), both of which cover admission costs at all national parks and monuments.

Travel Strategies

The primary challenge of planning a trip to this part of the world is allocating enough time to explore everything there is to see and do. Although distances are not huge, traveling between—and in many cases, within—the parks takes more time than a casual glance at the map might indicate. Also, some parks are more easily experienced during a short excursion than others. The highlights of Arches National Park can be seen in one day, whereas it may take a week to get to the wilderness heart of Grand Staircase-Escalante National Monument or the Maze District of Canyonlands National Park.

There are a couple of ways to plan a trip to this area. If you basically want to see the parks and the desert landscapes of southern Utah by car, you'll need at least a week; a suggested itinerary follows. It's worth noting that the North Rim of the Grand Canyon is less than a two-hour drive from the Utah–Arizona border in southeast Utah, and if you're in road trip mode, this will be an irresistible addition to your vacation.

If you're planning a trip to Utah that entails driving from vista to vista on paved roads, then you should plan on visiting Arches National Park, Moab, the Island in the Sky District of Canyonlands, and Bryce Canyon. Stop in Zion and take the shuttle up the North Fork of the Virgin River canyon. Link these scenic high points with a drive along Highway 12 through Grand Staircase-Escalante National Park, and you'll touch the surface of what southern Utah offers.

A second way to plan a trip to Utah (alternately, the way to plan your *second* trip to Utah) is to focus on recreation. Choose to focus on hiking and explore the backcountry of Capitol Reef's Waterpocket Fold or the canyons of the Escalante River. Moab is a world-famous center for slickrock mountain biking (biking is restricted in the national parks themselves, but hundreds of miles of trails wind through adjacent public lands). Moab is also the center for white-water rafting trips down the Colorado River's Cataract Canyon, a multiday trip that offers all the drama and adventure of a Grand Canyon expedition. There are other ways to focus a trip to southeastern Utah. The area is rich in prehistoric rock art and Anasazi remains. Planning a trip to visit these remote and fascinating sites will take you into haunting and mysterious corners of the area, such as Horseshoe and Sego Canyons, and the rock tower ruins at Hovenweep National Monument.

TRAVEL HUBS

Public transportation, including regularly scheduled air flights, is almost nonexistent in southern Utah and the parks. Unless you're on a bicycle, you will need your own vehicle to explore southern Utah.

If you're driving from other points in North America, Utah is easy to reach. The parks are east of I-15, which runs from Canada to Mexico, parallel to the Rocky Mountains. The parks are south of I-70, which links Denver to I-15.

International travelers are flying into the region have numerous options. Salt Lake City is convenient as a terminus for travelers who want to make a loop tour through the parks. For other travelers, the Utah national parks are part of a longer American road trip. Many European travelers fly into Denver, rent vehicles or RVs, cross the Rocky Mountains, and explore southern Utah (and perhaps the Grand Canyon) on the way to Las Vegas, from whence they return.

SUGGESTED ROUTES

From Salt Lake City, it's a long 238-mile drive to Moab, the center for exploring Arches and Canyonlands National Parks. The fastest route takes you south from Salt Lake City on I-15, cutting east at Spanish Fork on Highway 6/U.S. 89 to Price, and south to Green River and I-70, and then to Moab on U.S. 191. Dramatic scenery highlights the entire length of this four-hour drive.

From Denver, follow I-70 west, up over the Continental Divide along the Rocky Mountains, and down onto the Colorado River. Cross into Utah and take I-70 exit 212 at Cisco. From Denver to Cisco is 297 miles, all of which is on freeway. From Cisco, follow Highway 128 for 37 highly scenic miles through red-rock canyons to Moab. Allow 5.5 hours of driving time between Moab and Denver.

From Las Vegas, it's just 120 miles northeast on I-15 to St. George. From St. George, use the Denver itinerary above, but in reverse order.

The following itinerary would take around 10 days to complete. Most travelers will have less time than this to devote to Utah's national parks, so use this itinerary to focus your trip according to your interests and timeline.

Moab is a major center for recreation in southeast Utah. This small town is also the most convenient hub for visiting both Arches and Canyonlands National Parks. You can tour **Arches** in half a day if you take only short hikes to viewpoints; if you want to visit all of the sites

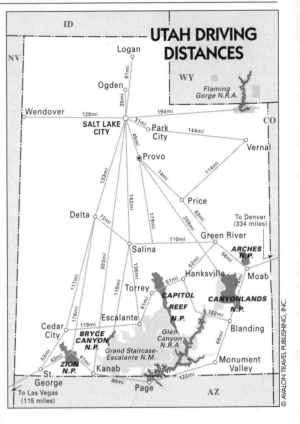

along the park road and hike to famed Delicate Arch, you'll devote most of a day to the park. Even if you're short on time, you'll want to make the half-day journey to the vista points in **Canyonlands' Island in the Sky District.** Between raft trips, mountain biking, exploring the parks, hiking the backcountry, and enjoying Moab's fine restaurants and brewpubs, you can easily pass three days in these parks and the Moab area.

From Moab, you have a choice of routes. The fastest route to the rest of Utah's national parks is to return north along I-70 to Green River, then south on Highway 24 to **Capitol Reef National Park.** Along this route, the distance from Moab to Capitol Reef is 145 miles.

Alternately, if you desire a more leisurely and scenic route to Capitol Reef, continue south on

U.S. 191 from Moab. Taking the long way to Capitol Reef will cost you an extra day but will give you the opportunity to pass several less frequently visited parks and beautifully remote landscapes. Be aware that there's a dearth of lodgings along this route. Some advance planning is a good idea: you'll either need to camp, reserve a hotel room at Bullfrog Marina, or spend a long day driving to do this loop comfortably. Some of the parks worth exploring are the **Needles District** of Canyonlands (78 miles south of Moab off U.S. 191), with incredible slickrock landscapes that are best seen from short hikes, and the **Natural Bridges National Monument,** west of Blanding on Highway 95. Natural Bridges is 120 miles south of Moab, off U.S. 191 and Highway 95.

At this point, you'll have another choice of how and where to cross the Colorado River. The most amusing option is to follow Highway 276 to Hall Crossing (40 miles) and take the **car ferry across Lake Powell** to Bullfrog Marina, where the region's top hotel awaits. From Bullfrog, you can follow the well-maintained Notom-

Bullfrog backcountry road to Highway 24 and the entrance to Capitol Reef National Park (80 miles), or you can follow Highway 276 and Highway 95 to Hanksville and enter the park along Highway 24 (117 miles). From Natural Bridges, you can also stay on Highway 95, vault the Colorado River by bridge, and continue on through Hanksville and Capitol Reef by the most direct route (84 miles). **Torrey,** a small town just west of the park, has a profusion of hotels and is the best destination for exploring the Capitol Reef area.

Capitol Reef National Park will require at least half a day to explore. You'll want to explore the old pioneer town of Fruita, hike to see the petroglyphs, and drive the scenic park road. Add a hike up along the Chimney Rock Trail or along Capitol Wash, and you can easily spend a day in the park.

From Torry, follow Highway 12 south through the **Grand Staircase-Escalante National Monument.** The 118-mile trip between Torrey and Bryce Canyon National Park is one of the most scenic routes in all of Utah. Allow a

Zion's shuttle buses transport visitors along the once-jammed park roads.

TOURIST INFORMATION

G eneral tourist literature and maps are available from the **Utah Travel Council,** Council Hall/Capitol Hill, Salt Lake City, UT 84114-7420, 801/538-1030, fax 801/538-1399, website: www.utah.com.

Call, email, or write in advance of your visit to obtain maps and brochures from the parks.

Arches National Park
P.O. Box 907
Moab, UT 84532-0907
435/719-2299
website: www.nps.gov/arch
email: archinfo@nps.gov

Capitol Reef National Park
HC 70 Box 15
Torrey, UT 84775-9602
435/425-3791
website: www.nps.gov/care
email: CARE_interpretation@nps.gov

Bryce Canyon National Park
P.O. Box 170001
Bryce Canyon, UT 84717-0001
435/834-5322
website: www.nps.gov/brca
email: Brca_reception _ area@nps.gov

Grand Staircase-Escalante National Monument
318 North 100 East
Kanab, UT 84741
435/644-4600
website: www.ut.blm.gov/monument
email: escalant@ut.blm.gov

Canyonlands National Park
2282 S. West Resource Blvd.
Moab, UT 84532-3298
435/719-2313
website: www.nps.gov/cany
email: canyinfo@nps.gov

Zion National Park
SR 9
Springdale, UT 84767-1099
435/772-3256
website: www.nps.gov/zion
email: ZION_park_information@nps.gov

full day to take in all the scenery and sights, including a visit to the prehistoric ruins at **Anasazi State Park** and hike up dramatic **Lower Calf Creek Falls Trail.** If you have another day in your itinerary and you're up for more exploring, head 12.5 miles south from Highway 12 on the Hole-in-the-Rock Road and traipse around **Devil's Garden** and go canyoneering in the canyons of **Dry Fork of Coyote Gulch,** 26 miles south of Highway 12. Spend the night in the town of Escalante at a motel or at the Escalante Petrified Forest State Park campground.

Continue west on Highway 12 to **Bryce Canyon National Park.** Park the car and spend the day riding the park shuttle to vista points and explore the hoodoos from trailheads along the scenic park road. Camp in the park or stay at the historic park lodge or at one of the motels just outside the park entrance.

Get up in time to see the rising sun light up the hoodoos, then drive west to U.S. 89. From here you can continue south to Kanab (61 miles). A three-day loop out of Kanab (following U.S. 89A, AZ 57, and U.S. 89) will give you an express tour of the Grand Canyon's North Rim and the southern reaches of the Grand Staircase-Escalante National Monument. From Kanab to the North Rim is 74 miles.

From U.S. 89 south of Bryce, you can also turn west on Highway 9 and enter Zion National Park via the dramatic Zion–Mt. Carmel Highway (from Bryce to Zion is 84 miles), then find a campsite or check into the lodge or a motel in Springdale. Ride the park shuttle for a quick overview of Zion Canyon. Spend a second day exploring the canyon and its many enchanting hikes, including the Riverside Walk or the Emerald Pools trails.

Make your way west to St. George on I-15.

From here, you have a choice of returning north to Salt Lake City on the freeway (300 miles but less than five hours of driving if you drive at typical Utah speeds) or continuing south on I-15 to Las Vegas, a short two hours and 115 miles away.

From Salt Lake City

Many tours of Utah's national parks begin in Salt Lake City. Its busy airport and plethora of hotels make it an easy place to begin and end a trip to the Utah national parks.

AIRPORT

Salt Lake City is a hub for Delta Airlines, and most other major airlines have regular flights into Salt Lake City International Airport, website: www.slcairport.com. The airport is an easy seven miles west of downtown; reach it via I-80 or North Temple.

SkyWest Airlines, 800/453-9417, Delta's commuter line, flies to Cedar City and St. George in Utah and to towns in adjacent states. There is currently no scheduled air transportation between Moab and Salt Lake City.

The airport has three terminals; in each you'll find a ground-transportation information desk, a cafeteria, motel/hotel courtesy phones, auto rentals (Hertz, Avis, National, Budget, and Dollar), the Morris Travel office, and a ski-rental shop. Terminal 1 also houses Zion's First National Bank (currency exchange), an ice-cream parlor, and gift shops. The Utah Information Center (Salt Lake Convention and Visitors Bureau) is upstairs in Terminal 2 and is open 24 hours daily (but staffed only during the day), 801/575-2800. Terminal 3 is dedicated to foreign arrivals and departures.

TRAIN

The only passenger train through Salt Lake City is Amtrak's *California Zephyr*, which heads west to Reno and Oakland and east to Denver and Chicago four times a week. The Amtrak depot is at 340 S. 600 West. Amtrak prices tickets as airlines do, with advance-booking, special seasonal, and other discounts available. Amtrak office

hours (timed to meet the trains) are irregular, so call first, 800/872-7245 (information and reservations), website: www.amtrak.com.

LONG-DISTANCE BUS

Salt Lake City sits at a crossroads of several major freeways and has good **Greyhound** bus service. Generally speaking, buses go north and south along I-15 and east and west along I-80; you won't be able to take the bus to any of Utah's national parks. The Greyhound station is downtown at 160 W. South Temple, 800/231-2222 or 801/355-9579.

CAR RENTALS

You'll find all of the major companies and many local outfits eager to rent you a set of wheels. Many agencies have an office or delivery service at the airport: Avis, Salt Lake International Airport, 800/331-1212 or 801/575-2847; Budget, 641 N. 3800 West, 800/527-0700 or 801/575-2500; Dollar, 601 N. 3800 West, Salt Lake International Airport, 800/421-9849 or 801/575-2580; Enterprise, 151 E. 5600 South, 801/266-3777, 801/534-1888 or 800/RENT-A-CAR; Hertz, Salt Lake International Airport, 775 North Terminal Dr., 800/654-3131 or 801/575-2683; National, Salt Lake City International Airport, 800/227-7368 or 801/575-2277; Thrify, just outside the airport at 15 S. 2400 West, 800/847-4389 or 801/265-6677; and Payless, 1974 West North Temple, 800/327-3631 or 801/596-2596.

RV AND MOTORCYCLE RENTALS

Access RV Rental, 300 S. U.S. 89, North Salt Lake City, 800/327-6910 or 801/936-1200, website: www.accessrvrental.com, is a local company with relatively good rates on RV rentals. Cruise America is a larger company, with both RV and motorcycle rentals available from their office at 4125 South State St., 801/288-0930, website: www.cruiseamerica.com. Let's Go America rents large RVs, 4221 S. 500 West, 801/263-3100 or 877/263-3100. El Monte RV provides rentals out of A-1 Pioneer Moving and Storage, 2001 Warm Springs Rd., 888/337-2214, website: www.elmonterv.com.

Expect to pay from $750–1,400 per week to rent an RV, depending on the season and the size of the RV. Motorcycles run $80–150 per day.

ACCOMMODATIONS

With the exception of the two hostels, these lodgings are all convenient to the airport, and nearly all will offer some form of transportation to and from the airport. Hotels with the smallest address on West North Temple are closest to downtown.

If you're driving into town and just want to find a hotel room *fast,* head south and west of downtown, where chain hotels proliferate. The area around 600 South and 200 West is especially fertile ground for midpriced hotels.

Less than $50

In order to find budget accommodations, you'll have to leave the airport area. **The Avenues Hostel,** one mile east of Temple Square, offers dorm rooms with use of a kitchen, TV room, and laundry. Information-packed bulletin boards list city sights and goings-on, and you'll meet travelers from all over the world. Year-round rates for the dorm are $14 per person (cost includes sheets), while private rooms are $25–45 (only half have private baths). Reservations (with first-night's deposit) are advised in the busy summer-travel and winter-ski seasons. The hostel is on the corner of 107 F St. and 2nd Ave., Salt Lake City, UT 84103, 801/363-3855; open 8 A.M.–10 P.M. year-round. From downtown, head east on South Temple Street to F Street, then turn north two streets.

Directly south of downtown a couple miles is the **International Ute Hostel,** 21 East Kelsey Ave., 801/595-1645. Beds in dorm-style rooms

are $15; private rooms are $35; and there's full access to kitchen facilities and common areas. Kelsey Avenue is the equivalent of 1160 South, just east off State Street.

$50–75

Although it's on the road to the airport, the **Econo Lodge,** 715 W. North Temple, 801/363-0062 or 800/BE-ECONO, is also convenient to downtown because it's located just west of the railroad overpass. The motel offers a courtesy car to downtown or the airport and has a pool and guest laundry. Of the many older motorcourt motels along North Temple, the best maintained is the **Overniter Motor Inn,** 1500 W. North Temple, 800/914-8301 or 801/533-8300, with an outdoor pool and clean rooms. Moderately priced rooms are also available at **Days Inn,** 1900 W. North Temple, 800/329-7466 or 801/539-8538, and at the **Motel 6 Airport,** 1990 W. North Temple, 801/364-1053, where there's a pool. Closer to the airport, the **Airport Inn,** 2333 W. North Temple, 801/539-0438, has a pool and guest laundry.

$75–100

Comfortable rooms, an outdoor pool, and a better-than-average free continental breakfast make the **Comfort Inn Airport,** 200 N. Admiral Byrd Rd., 800/535-8742 or 801/537-7444, an appealing place to spend a night.

Practically next door to the terminal are the **Holiday Inn & Suites,** 5575 W. Amelia Earhart Dr., 800/522-5575 or 801/537-7020, with a pool and spa. At the **Airport Hilton,** 5151 Wiley Post Way, 800/999-3736 or 801/539-1515, rooms are spacious and nicely furnished, and facilities include two pools, a putting green, a sports court, and an exercise room and spa. The hotel even has its own lake.

More than $100

The **Radisson Hotel Salt Lake City Airport,** 2177 W. North Temple, 800/333-3333 or 801/364-5800, is an attractive, lodge-like building with nicely furnished rooms. Guests receive a complimentary continental breakfast and newspaper, and in the evenings there's a manager's reception with free beverages. Facilities include a pool, spa, and fitness room. Suites come with a loft bedroom area. There's quite a range in room rates, and package rates and promotions can bring the rates down dramatically.

If you want to really do Salt Lake City in style, two downtown hotels are good places to splurge. **Hotel Monaco,** 15 West 200 South, 801/595-0000 or 877/294-9710, occupies a grandly renovated historic office building in a convenient spot in the middle of downtown; on the main floor is **Bambara,** one of the most sophisticated restaurants in Utah. Rooms are sumptuously furnished with real élan: this is no anonymous upscale hotel in beige and mauve. Expect wild colors and contrasting fabrics, lots of flowers, and excellent service. Facilities include an on-site fitness center, meeting rooms, plus concierge and valet services. Each room comes with two-line phones, a CD stereo, in-room fax, printer, and copier, plus an iron and board. Pets are welcome, and if you forgot your own pet, the hotel will deliver a companion goldfish to your room.

A new addition to the Salt Lake hotel scene, the gigantic **Grand America Hotel and Suites,** 75 E. 600 South, 800/533-3525, is Salt Lake City's take on the Vegas fantasy hotel. A block square (that's 10 acres in this land of long blocks), its 24 stories contains 775 rooms, more than half of them suites. Rooms have luxury-level amenities; expect all the perks and niceties that modern hotels can offer.

CAMPING

Of the several commercial campgrounds around the periphery of Salt Lake City, **Camp VIP** is the most convenient. The campground is located between downtown and the airport at 1350 W. North Temple, 801/328-0224, and offers tent and RV sites year-round with showers, swimming pool, gameroom, playground, store, and laundry. From I-15 northbound, take Exit 311 for I-80, go west 1.3 miles on I-80, exit north one-half mile on Redwood Rd. (Highway 68), then turn right another one-half mile on North Temple. From I-15 southbound, take Exit 313 and turn south 1.5 miles on 900 West,

then turn right 0.8 mile on North Temple. From I-80 either take the North Temple exit or exit on Redwood Rd. (Highway 68) and go north one-half mile, then right one-half mile on North Temple.

There are two good Forest Service campgrounds in Big Cottonwood Canyon about 15 miles southeast of downtown Salt Lake City and another two up Little Cottonwood Canyon, about 19 miles southeast of town. All have drinking water, and all prohibit pets (because of local watershed regulations).

In Big Cottonwood Canyon, **Spruces Campground** (elevation 7,400 feet, 9.1 miles up the canyon) is open early June–mid-October. Some sites can be reserved by calling 877/444-6777 or online at www.reserveusa.com. The season at **Redman Campground** (elevation 8,300 feet) lasts mid-June–early October. It's located between Solitude and Brighton, 13 miles up the canyon.

Little Cottonwood Canyon's **Tanners Flat Campground** (elevation 7,200 feet, 4.3 miles up the canyon) is open mid-May–mid-October. Reserve a site at 877/444-6777 or www.reserveusa.com. **Albion Basin Campground** lies high in the mountains a few miles past Alta Ski Area (elevation 9,500 feet) and is open early July–late September; go 11 miles up the canyon (the last 2.5 miles are gravel).

STOCKING UP

If you're going to be camping on your trip through Utah's national parks, you may want to pick up some provisions in Salt Lake City before hitting the road south. Just east of I-15, off I-80 in the Sugar House district, the large **Wild Oats** store, 1131 E. Wilmington Ave., 801/359-7913, has a good deli, lots of organic produce, bulk foods, and good bread (likely the last you'll see for a while). It's in a complex that also contains some good restaurants, a camping supply store, and the brightest, shiniest tattoo parlor you'll ever lay eyes on.

Downtown, stop at **Tony Caputo Market & Deli,** 308 W. Broadway, 801/531-8669, is an old-style Italian deli brimming with delicious sausages, cheeses, and olives. Don't forget a sandwich to go!

From Las Vegas

Just because you're going to Utah, don't assume it's best to fly into Salt Lake City. If you're traveling to Zion, Bryce, and/or Grand Staircase-Escalante, consider flying into Las Vegas rather than Salt Lake City. Not only is it closer to these parks, but car rentals are usually about $100 a week cheaper. Even if you have absolutely no interest in gambling, many casino hotels have very good midweek rates.

AIRPORT

McCarran International Airport, 5757 Wayne Newton Blvd., 702/261-5743, website: www .mccarran.com, is just a few minutes south of The Strip (aka Las Vegas Boulevard South, the four-mile stretch of casinos and hotels).

Las Vegas is well served by all the major airlines, and also by smaller or "no-frills" carriers such as Frontier Airlines, 800/432-1359, and Southwest Airlines, 800/435-9792, whose bargain prices keep all the other airlines competitive.

The airport has two terminals—Terminal 1 has most of the domestic traffic, and Terminal 2 serves international and charter flights—linked by a shuttle. Exchange foreign currency in Terminal 2; find full-service banking and check-in for some of the larger casino hotels in Terminal 1. Slot machines, of course, are everywhere.

LONG-DISTANCE BUS

The Greyhound depot is at 220 S. Main St., 702/384-9561or 800/231-2222.

CAR RENTALS

It's relatively inexpensive to rent a car in Las Vegas; an economy car will run about $120 per week, before taxes. At the airport, find Avis, 800/331-1212 or 702/261-5591; Budget, 800/527-0700 or 702/736-1212; Dollar, 800/800-4000 or 702/739-8403; Hertz, 800/654-3131 or 702/736-4900; National, 800/227-7368 or 702/261-5391; Payless, 800/327-3631 or 702/736-6147; Sav-mor, 800/634-6779 or 702/736-1234; and Thrifty, 800/847-4389 or 702/896-7600. Alamo is near the airport at 6855 Bermuda Road, 702/263-8411; a shuttle runs between the airport and the rental office.

RV RENTALS

Rent an RV from Cruise America, 6070 Boulder Highway, 702/456-6666, website: www.cruise america.com. El Monte RV, 13001 Las Vegas Blvd., 888/337-2214 or 702/269-8000, website: www.elmonterv.com, is another good bet. Rates typically start at about $800 a week during the spring, fall, and winter; $1,000 per week during the summer. American RV Rental, 562/266-1814, website: www.americanrvrentals.com, is a Los Angeles–based company that will deliver an RV to you in Las Vegas, then pick it up when you're done with it—for an extra $200. Because their rental rates are somewhat lower than their Vegas-based competitors, this may be an option worth considering.

For its sheer number of hotel rooms, Las Vegas can't be beat. Even if you have no desire to visit Vegas, it may make sense to spend the first and/or final nights of your trip here. It's relatively easy to find a bargain rate at a casino hotel.

ACCOMMODATIONS

For its sheer number of hotel rooms, Las Vegas can't be beat. Even if you have no desire to visit Vegas, it may make sense to spend the first and/or final nights of your trip here. During the week, it's relatively easy to find a bargain rate at a casino hotel. Reservation services, such as **Las Vegas Hotels Reservation Service,** 800/968-2352, website: www.lasvegasnevadahotels; **Reservations Plus,** 800/805-9528, website: www.resplus.com; or the **Las Vegas Convention and Visitor Authority,** 800/332-5334, website: www.lasvegas24hours.com, may be able to help you find a good deal on a room.

Less than $50

If you're looking for someplace to call home in Las Vegas, try the **Las Vegas International Hostel,** a friendly place in a slightly dodgy neighborhood between downtown and The Strip at 1208 Las Vegas Blvd. S., 702/385-9955. Dorm beds start at $12, private rooms at $26.

If you can stand the frenzied atmosphere, **Circus Circus,** on the North Strip at 2880 Las Vegas Blvd. S., 800/444-2472 or 702/734-0410, has great weekday rates starting at about $40 per day, going up by about $20 on weekends.

$50–75

About one mile from the airport, and not too far off the south end of The Strip, find the **Airport Inn Travelodge,** 5075 Koval Lane, 888/844-3131 or 702/736-3600. This motel with an outdoor pool and free continental breakfast is a good alternative to a casino hotel. In the same price range and also off The Strip near the airport is the **Best Western McCarran Inn,** 4970 Paradise Rd., 800/626-7575 or 702/798-5530.

More than $100

If you're looking for lodging that's quintessentially Las Vegas, a bit of a splurge, and convenient to the airport, consider basking in the hip luxury of **Mandalay Bay Resort and Casino,** at the south end of The Strip, 3950 Las Vegas Blvd. S., 702/632-7777 or 877/632-7400.

From Denver

Although it may not seem intuitive to start your tour of Utah's national parks in Denver, that's exactly what works best for many folks, especially Europeans who fly nonstop from European capital cities to Denver International Airport. From there, it's easy to rent a car or RV and begin a tour of western national parks, typically including Rocky Mountain National Park, Utah's five national parks, and the Grand Canyon.

AIRPORT

Locals joke that Denver International Airport (DIA), 8500 Peña Blvd., 303/342-2000, website: www.flydenver.com, is in Kansas; it's actually 23 miles northeast of downtown Denver on CO 470 north of I-70. Major airlines using DIA include American, British Airways, Continental, Delta, and United.

DIA's Jeppesen Terminal has a giant atrium and three concourses connected by a lightrail train. Car rental counters are in the central terminal atrium between security-screening areas.

CAR RENTALS

The following companies have car rentals at DIA or immediately adjacent to it: Advantage, 800/777-5500 or 303/342-0990; Avis, 800/331-1212 or 303/342-5500; Alamo, 24530 E. 78th Ave, 800/462-5266 or 303/342-7373; Budget, 800/527-0700; Dollar, 800/800-4000 or 866/434-2226; Hertz, 800/654-3131 or 303/753-8800; National, 800/227-7368 or 303/342-0717; Payless, 800/729-5377 or 303/342-9444; and Thrifty, 800/367-2277 or 303/342-9400.

RV RENTALS

B&B RV is a local company, 6960 Smith Rd., 303/322-6013, website: www.bb-rv.com; Moturis Inc. is located northeast of downtown Denver at 5300 Colorado Blvd in Commerce City, 888/295-6837 or 303/295-6837, website: www.moturis.com, and rents both RVs and motorcycles (French, Italian, and German are spoken here); Colorado's Ride the West RV Rentals is at 1207 S. Platte River Dr., 888/673-6878 or 303/806-0132. Larger companies include Cruise America, 8950 North Federal Blvd., 303/650-2865; and El Monte RV, operating out of Holidays on Wheels RV at 6570 N. Federal Blvd., 888/337-2214, website: www.elmonterv.com.

ACCOMMODATIONS

Chain hotels have set up shop in the area surrounding DIA. Almost all of these hotels offer a shuttle to and from the airport. Expect to pay about $75 per night for a standard hotel room.

The closest lodgings are about six miles from the airport. Here you'll find **Comfort Suites,** 6210 Tower Rd., 303/371-9300, where all rooms are suites; and the **Fairfield Inn Denver Airport,** 6851 Tower Rd., 303/576-9640.

About 12 miles south of the airport, near the intersection of I-70 and Peña Boulevard, is another cluster of motels, including **Comfort Inn,** 16921 East 32nd Ave., 303/367-5000; and the

Hilton Garden Inn Denver Airport, 16475 East 40th Circle, 303/371-9393.

If you're looking for the classic swank downtown Denver hotel, try the **Brown Palace,** 321 17th St., 800/321-2599 or 303/297-3111. A room at this historic and ornate hotel will set you back more than $200.

At the other end of the spectrum is the **Hostelling International Denver Hostel of the Rocky Mountains,** in an old apartment building at 1530 Downing St., 303/861-7777, with dorm beds for $15. Next door, the hostel owners run a European-style B&B, with simple rooms for about $40. Breakfast is included in both hostel and B&B rates.

Sightseeing Highlights

ARCHES

Just up the road from Moab is Arches National Park, with its famous rock bridges. Arches is a great family park: it's not too large, and there are lots of medium-length, medium-difficulty hikes to explore. Unlike other Utah national parks, there's still plenty to see even if you can't get out and hike: you'll be able to see some of the good stuff even if you're in a car. Be sure to hike to the **Windows Section,** a series of arches and rock fins at the center of the park, and to **Delicate Arch,** overlooking the Colorado River.

CANYONLANDS

Canyonlands National Park is remote and otherworldly, with a wealth of rock art, Anasazi ruins, and vertical desert landscapes—a perfect place for a multiday backpacking trip. There are four sections to the park: the **River District,** containing the canyons of the Colorado and Green Rivers; the **Needles District,** with a wealth of hiking trails and backcountry roads leading through a standing rock desert; the **Maze District,** an extremely remote area filled with geologic curiosities and labrynthine canyons; and the **Island in the Sky District,** a flat-topped mesa that overlooks all the rest. A separate area, the **Horseshoe**

Canyon Unit, lies to the west and contains a significant cache of prehistoric rock art. Only the Island in the Sky and Needles districts are easily accessible to casual travelers. The vistas from **Grand View Overlook** at the the Island in the Sky survey hundreds of miles of canyon country. It's a strenuous trail and the route to the trailhead is long and dusty, but the hike to the **Grand**

Sunrise and sunset provide vivid contrasts for photographers.

ON THE ROAD

© W.C. MCRAE

Meeks Mesa and the western entrance to Capitol Reef National Park

Gallery in Horseshoe Canyon leads to astonishingly powerful pictographs and petroglyphs; this was clearly a sacred site for Native Americans.

CAPITOL REEF

Through no fault of its own, Capitol Reef National Park draws fewer crowds than Utah's other national parks. The park preserves a vast wrinkle of rock called **Waterpocket Fold** that buckles up into a vertical barricade across more than 100 miles of southeast Utah. Of the few canyons that penetrate Waterpocket Fold, the Fremont River Canyon is easily accessable along Highway 24. Ancient petroglyphs, pioneer farms and orchards, and soaring rock formations extend the length of the canyon. A paved scenic highway explores more canyons along the fold's western face. The rest of the park is remote backcountry—just the way hikers and backpackers like it.

GRAND STAIRCASE-ESCALANTE

Grand Staircase-Escalante National Monument preserves some of the Southwest's best canyon hiking. Numerous long-distance hiking trails

and an assortment of day hikes follow **the slot canyons of the Escalante River system.** Mountain bikers can head down the **Hole-in-the-Rock Road** or the **Burr Trail** to visit some of the same landscape via jeep road; even cruising scenic Highway 12 across Escalante country in a car is an eye-popping experience.

BRYCE CANYON

Bryce Canyon National Park has famous vistas across an eroded amphitheater of **pink sandstone hoodoos.** One of the most popular parks, it's often just considered an extended photo opportunity for shutterbugs; however, you'll have quite a different experience from the amateur photographers along the rim if you venture into the park's backcountry. Short trails lead down from the canyon edge into a wonderland of fanciful formations and outcrops.

ZION

Zion National Park is one of the most popular in the park system: hiking trails lead up narrow canyons cut into massive stone cliffs, passing

SAY IT RIGHT!

The following place names are easy to mispronounce. Say it like a local!

Tooele	Too-WIL-a
Kanab	Ke-NAB
Uinta	u-INT-a
Lehi	LEE-hi
Nephi	NEE-fi
Hurricane	HUR-aken
Manti	MAN-tie
Ephraim	E-from
Weber	WE-ber
Duchesne	du-SHANE
Monticello	mon-ta-SELL-o
Panguitch	PAN-gwich

Escalante poses an unusual problem. Utahans from northern parts of the state pronounce the name of the town and the famous river canyons as es-ka-LAN-tay; however, citizens of the town pronounce it without the final long E, as es-ka-LANT.

along quiet pools of water and groves of willows. Zion is so breathtaking and awe-inspiring that the early Mormons named these canyons for their vision of heaven. The park's main canyon, carved by the Virgin River, is a much quieter place to visit now that access is by shuttle bus; however, the rest of the park's canyons are the province of long-distance hikers.

STATE PARKS AND NATIONAL MONUMENTS

Don't ignore the areas outside national park boundaries. Chances are good that you'll drive right past these parks and monuments as you explore southern Utah. These areas are often less thronged than the national parks, but equally as compelling. **The Cedar Breaks National Monument** preserves an area with formations similar to Bryce Canyon, but without the crowds. Just below Bryce Canyon, **Kodachrome Basin State Park** is ringed by remarkable pink cliffs, plus odd rock pillars called sand pipes. **Red Canyon,** a national recreation area administered by the U.S. Forest Service, is located immediately west of Bryce Canyon and shares its geology, but because it's not a national park, you can mountain bike and ride horses amid the red-rock formations. **Hovenweep National Monument** contains the ruins of ancient Anasazi stone villages. **Natural Bridges National Monument** contains formations that rival Arches National Park, but without the crowds. Plus there are abundant Indian ruins, petroglyphs, and good hiking trails. **Dead Horse State Park** provides an eagle's-eye point of view over the Colorado River Canyon near Moab.

Recreation Highlights

HIKING AND BACKPACKING

Utah offers lots of backcountry adventure for those interested in exploring the scenery on foot. One increasingly popular activity is canyoneering—exploring mazelike slot canyons. Hundreds of feet deep but sometimes only wide enough for a hiker to squeeze through, these canyons are found in the southern part of the state, particularly near Escalante and in the Paria River area. You'll need to be fit and watch the weather carefully for flash floods in order to explore these regions.

Much of the canyonlands of southern and southeastern Utah are accessible only by foot; visits to remote Anasazi ruins and petroglyphs reward the long-distance hiker. Hiking the deserts of southern Utah requires extra precautions: even fit and experienced hikers can find these trails challenging. Be sure to carry *lots* of water and wear a hat, a thin long-sleeved shirt, and sunscreen to protect your skin. Heat exhaustion and dehydration are the most common sources of medical emergency in the national parks.

CAMPING

All of Utah's national parks have campgrounds, with each park keeping at least one campground

CLIMBING IN UTAH'S NATIONAL PARKS

Most visitors to Utah's national parks enjoy spotting rock climbers scaling canyon walls and sandstone pillars. But for a few, the whole reason to visit southern Utah is to climb. These folks will need a climbing guide, either the classic and rather hard-to-find *Desert Rock* by Eric Bjørnstad, or *Rock Climbing Utah*, by Stewart M. Green.

Prospective climbers should take note: Just because you're the star of the local rock gym, don't think that climbing Zion's high, exposed big walls or Canyonlands' remote sandstone towers is going to be simple. Sandstone poses its own set of challenges; it weakens when wet, so it's wise to avoid climbing in damp areas or after rain. Arches' Entrada Sandstone is particularly tough to climb.

Climbers in the national parks should take care to use clean climbing techniques. Approach climbs via established trails to prevent further erosion of slopes. Camp in park campgrounds or, on multiday climbs, get a backcountry permit. Because white chalk leaves unsightly marks on canyon walls, add red pigment to your chalk. Do not disturb vegetation growing in cracks along your route. Tube or bag human waste and carry it out. Remove all old, worn rope and equipment, but do not remove fixed pins. Make sure your climb is adequately protected by visually inspecting any preexisting bolts or fixed pins. It is illegal to use a power drill to place bolts. Never climb directly above trails, where hikers may be hit by dislodged rocks.

In Canyonlands, even stricter regulations are in place. Here, no new climbing hardware may be left in a fixed location; protection may not be placed with the use of a hammer except to replace existing belay and rappel anchors and bolts on existing routes, or for emergency self-rescue; and unsafe slings must be replaced with an earth-colored sling.

Plan to climb in the spring or fall. During the summer, the walls become extremely hot. Some climbing areas may be closed during the spring to protect nesting raptors. Check at the visitors centers for current closures.

© W.C. MCRAE

rock climbing near Needles District

open year-round. With the exception of Zion's Watchman Campground, no reservations are taken for campsites; it's all first-come, first-served. During the summer and on holiday weekends during the spring and fall, it's best to arrive at the park early in the day and select a campsite immediately. Don't expect to find hookups or showers at National Park Service campgrounds. For these comforts, look just out-side the park entrance, where you'll generally find a full-service commercial campground.

Backcountry campers in national parks will need to stop by the park visitors center for a backcountry permit. Backcountry camping may be limited to specific sites in order to spread people out a bit; if so, a park ranger will consult with you and assign you a campground.

BACKCOUNTRY TRAVEL

Before heading into the backcountry, check with a ranger about weather, water sources, fire danger, trail conditions, and regulations. Backpacking stores are also good sources of information. Here are some tips for traveling safely and respectfully in the backcountry:

HOW TO SELECT AN OUTFITTER

Utah has several outfitters, guides, trail drive operators, and guest ranches, all of whom promise to get you outdoors and into an Old West adventure, but all outfitting and recreational services are not created equal. The most important consideration in choosing an outfitter is safety, the second is your comfort. Make sure you feel confident on both counts before signing on.

Here are some points to ponder while you plan your adventure vacation.

All outfitters should be licensed or accredited by the state and be happy to provide you with proof. This means that they are bonded, carry the necessary insurance, and have money and organizational wherewithal to register with the state. This rules out fly-by-night operations and college students who've decided to set up business for the summer. If you're just starting to plan an excursion, contact the Utah Travel Council at Capital Hill, Salt Lake City, 800/200-1160 or 801/538-1030. The council's website, www.utah.com, contains an extensive network of outfitters and guides.

Many outfitters offer similar trips. When you've narrowed down your choice, call and talk to the outfitters on your short list. Ask lots of questions, and try to get a sense of who these people are; you'll be spending a lot time with them, so make sure you feel comfortable. If you have special interests, like bird or wildlife watching, be sure to mention them to your potential outfitter. A good outfitter will take your interests into account when planning a trip.

If there's a wide disparity in prices between outfitters for the same trip, find out what makes up the difference. The cheapest trip may not be the best choice for you. Food is one of the most common areas to economize in. If you don't mind having cold cuts each meal for your five-day pack trip, then maybe the cheapest outfitter is okay. If you prefer a cooked meal, or alcoholic beverages, or a choice of entrées, then be prepared to pay more. On a long trip, it might be worth it. Also be sure you know what kind of accommodations are included in multiday trips. You may pay more to have a tent or cabin to yourself, but again, it may be worth it.

Ask how many years an outfitter has been in business and how long your particular escort has guided this trip. Although a start-up outfitting service can be perfectly fine, you should know what level of experience you are buying. If you have questions, especially for longer or more dangerous trips, ask for referrals.

Most outfitters will demand that you pay a portion (usually half) of your fee well in advance to secure your place, so be sure to ask about your outfitter's cancellation policy. Some lengthy float trips can cost thousands of dollars; if cancellation means the forfeiture of the deposit, then you need to know that. Also, find out what the tipping or gratuity policy is for your outfitter. Sometimes 15 or 20 percent extra is added to your bill as a tip for the "hands." Although this is undoubtedly nice for the help, you should be aware that your gratuities for a week's stay can run into the hundreds of dollars.

- Tell rangers or other reliable people where you are going and when you expect to return; they'll alert rescuers if you go missing.
- Travel in small groups for the best experience (group size may also be regulated).
- Avoid stepping on—or camping on—fragile cryptobiotic soils.
- Use a portable stove to avoid leaving fire scars.
- Resist the temptation to shortcut switchbacks; this causes erosion and can be dangerous.
- Avoid digging tent trenches or cutting vegetation.
- Help preserve old Indian and historic ruins.

- Camp at least 300 feet away from springs, creeks, and trails. Camp at least a quarter-mile from a *sole* water source to avoid scaring away wildlife and livestock.
- Avoid camping in washes at any time; be alert to thunderstorms.
- Take care not to throw or kick rocks off trails—someone might be underneath you.
- Don't drink water directly from streams or lakes, no matter how clean the water appears; it may contain the parasitic protozoan *Giardia lamblia,* which causes giardiasis. Boiling water for several minutes will kill giardia as

well as most other bacterial or viral pathogens. Chemical treatments and water filters usually work, too, although they're not as reliable as boiling (giardia spends part of its life in a hard shell that protects it from most chemicals).

- Bathe and wash dishes away from lakes, streams, and springs. Use biodegradable soap and scatter your wash water.
- Bring a trowel for personal sanitation; dig 6–8 inches deep and cover your waste.
- Pack out all your trash, including toilet paper and feminine hygiene items.
- Bring plenty of feed for your horses and mules.
- Leave dogs at home; they're not permitted on national park trails.
- If you realize you're lost, find shelter. If you're sure of a way to civilization and plan to walk out, leave a note with your departure time and planned route.
- Visit the Leave No Trace website, www .lnt.org, for more details on responsible back-country travel.

BIKING

More than any other single recreational activity, mountain biking has put Utah on the map. Trails in the Slickrock Canyon Country near Moab attract more than 150,000 biking enthusiasts annually, and now nearly all corners of the state promote their old Forest Service or mining roads as a biking paradise.

Although mountain bikes are prohibited on national park trails, there's almost always great biking just outside the park boundaries. Both Canyonlands and Grand Staircase-Escalante are laced with dirt roads and jeep tracks that are ideal for mountain biking.

Although mountain bikes are prohibited on national park trails, there's almost always great biking just outside the park boundaries. Both Canyonlands and Grand Staircase-Escalante are laced with dirt roads and jeep tracks that are ideal for mountain biking.

A good general resource is the *Bicycle Utah Vacation Guide,* which gives general information about biking paths throughout Utah and listings of tour operators, related organizations, and businesses, available free from P.O. Box 738, Park City, UT 84060, 435/649-5806, or online at www.bicycleutah.com.

In general, Utah summers are too hot for mountain biking. The peak season in Moab runs from Mar.–May and again from Sept.–Nov.

RAFTING AND BOATING

The most notable float trip in Utah is down the Colorado River between Moab and the backwaters of Lake Powell. This multiday trip passes through Cataract Canyon, and for spectacular adventure it's second only to trips through the Grand Canyon. The Green River, above its confluence with the Colorado, has many spectacular—although quieter—stretches, both within the park and upstream from it. For these trips, you'll need to plan well in advance because spaces are limited and demand more than outstrips availability. In towns like Moab and Green River, several outfitters provide exciting day trips that can usually take people with only a day's notice. Ask state tourist offices for their *Utah Rivers* magazine or check out the official website at www.utah.com/raft.

ON THE ROAD

Health and Safety

ON THE ROAD

DRIVING THE PARKS

During the summer, patience is the key to driving in Utah's national parks. Roads are often crowded with slow-moving RVs, and traffic jams are not uncommon. At Zion, shuttle buses have replaced private vehicles along the scenic Zion Canyon Road, and a voluntary shuttle runs through the main Bryce Canyon amphitheater.

If you're traveling on backroads, especially in the Grand Staircase-Escalante National Monument, make sure you have plenty of gas, even if it means paying top dollar at a small-town gas pump.

Summer heat in the desert puts an extra strain on both cars and drivers. It's worth double-checking your vehicle's cooling system, engine oil, transmission fluid, fan belts, and tires to make sure they are in top condition. Carry several gallons of water in case of a breakdown or radiator trouble. Never leave children or pets in a parked car during warm weather because temperatures inside can cause fatal heatstroke in minutes.

At times the desert has *too much* water, when late-summer storms frequently flood low spots in the road. Wait for the water level to subside before crossing. Dust storms can completely block visibility but tend to be short-lived. During such storms, pull completely off the road, stop, and turn off your lights so as not to confuse other drivers. Radio stations carry frequent weather updates when weather hazards exist.

If stranded, stay with your vehicle unless you're *positive* of where to go for help, then leave a note explaining your route and departure time. Airplanes can easily spot a stranded car (tie a piece of cloth to your antenna), but a person walking is more difficult to see. It's best to carry emergency supplies: blankets or sleeping bags, a first-aid kit, tools, jumper cables, a shovel, traction mats or chains, a flashlight, rain gear, water, food, and a can opener.

Maps

The Utah Department of Transportation prints and distributes a free, regularly updated map of Utah. Ask for it when you call for information or when you stop at a visitors information office. Benchmark Maps' *Utah Road and Recreation Atlas* is loaded with beautiful maps, recreation information, and global positioning system (GPS) grids. If you're planning on extensive backcountry exploration, be sure to ask locally about conditions.

Off-Road Driving

Here are some tips for safely traversing the backcountry in a vehicle (preferably one with four-wheel drive):

- Drive slowly enough to choose a safe path and avoid obstacles such as rocks or giant potholes, but keep up enough speed to propel you through sand or mud.
- Keep an eye on the route ahead of you. If there are obstacles, stop, get out of your vehicle, and survey the situation.
- Reduce the tire pressure if you're driving across sand.
- Drive directly up or down the fall line of a slope. Cutting across diagonally may seem less frightening, but it puts you in a position to slide or roll over.

If you really want to learn to drive your four-wheel-drive rig, consider signing up for a class. Bill Burke's 4-Wheeling America, 970/858-3468, website: www.bb4wa.com, runs Moab-based classes at several times a year.

HEAT AND WATER

Southern Utah in summer is a *very* hot place. Be sure to use sunscreen, or else you risk having an uncomfortable vacation. Wearing a wide-brimmed hat and good sunglasses, with full UV-protection, can shield you from the sun's harmful effects. Heat exhaustion can also be a problem if you're hiking in the hot sun. In midsummer, try to get an early start if you're hiking in full sun. If you're out during the heat of the afternoon, look for a shady spot and rest until the sun begins to drop.

Drink steadily throughout the day, whether you are thirsty or not, rather than gulping huge amounts of water once you feel thirsty. For hikers, one of the best ways to drink enough is to carry water in a hydration pack (the two top brands are Camelbak and Platypus). These collapsible plastic bladders come with a hose and a mouthpiece, so you can carry your water in your pack, thread the hose out the top of the pack and over your shoulder, keeping the mouthpiece handy for frequent sips of water. One easy way to tell if you're getting enough to drink is to monitor your urine output. If you're only urinating a couple of times a day, and the color and odor of your urine are both strong, it's time to start drinking more water.

HYPOTHERMIA

Don't think that just because you're in the Utah desert you're immune to hypothermia. This lowering of the body's temperature below 95°F causes disorientation, uncontrollable shivering, slurred speech, and drowsiness. The victim may not even realize what's wrong. Unless corrective action is taken immediately, hypothermia can lead to death. Thus, hikers should travel with companions and always carry wind and rain protection.

ON THE ROAD

THINGS THAT BITE OR STING

Although travelers in Utah's national parks are not going to get attacked by a grizzly bear, and encounters with mountain lions are rare, there are a few animals to watch out for.

Snakes, scorpions, and spiders are all present in considerable numbers, and there are a few key things to know about dealing with this phobia-inducing trio.

Rattlesnakes, including the particularly venomous midget-faded rattlesnake, are present throughout southern Utah. The midget-faded snakes live in Arches and Canyonlands, where they frequent burrows and rock crevices and are mostly active at night. Even though their venom is toxic, full venom injections are relatively uncommon and, like all rattlesnakes, they pose little threat unless they're provoked.

If you see a rattlesnake, observe it at a safe distance. Be careful where you put your hands when canyoneering or scrambling—it's not a good idea to reach above your head and blindly plant your hands on a sunny rock ledge. Hikers should wear sturdy boots, minimizing the chance that the snake fangs will reach the skin if a bite occurs. Do not walk barefoot outside after dark because this is when snakes are out hunting for prey.

First aid for rattlesnake bites is an area full of conflicting ideas: to suck or not to suck; to apply a constricting bandage or not; or to take time treating in the field versus rushing to the hospital. Most people who receive medical treatment after being bitten by a rattlesnake live to tell the story. Prompt administration of antivenin is the most important treatment, and the most important aspect of first aid is to arrange transportation of the victim to a hospital as quickly as possible.

A scorpion's sting isn't as painful as you'd expect (it's about like a bee sting), and the venom is insufficient to cause any real harm. Still, it's not what you'd call pleasant, and experienced desert campers know to shake out their boots every morning because scorpions and spiders are attracted to warm, moist, dark places.

Tarantulas and black widow spiders are present across much of the Colorado Plateau. Believe it or not, a tarantula's bite does not poison humans; the enzymes secreted when they bite do turn the insides of frogs, lizards, and insects to a soft mush, allowing the tarantula to suck the guts from its prey. Another interesting tarantula fact: while males live about as long as you'd expect a spider to live, female tarantulas can live for up to 25 years. (Females *do* sometimes eat the males, which may account for some of this disparity in longevity.)

Black widow spiders, on the other hand, have a toxic bite. Although the bite is usually painless, it delivers a potent neurotoxin, which quickly causes pain, nausea, and vomiting. It is important to seek immediate treatment for a black widow bite; although few people actually die from these bites, recovery is helped along considerably by antivenin.

Space blankets are lightweight and cheap and offer protection against the cold in emergencies. Remember that temperatures can plummet rapidly in Utah's dry climate—a drop of 40°F between day and night is common. Be especially careful at high elevations, where summer sunshine can quickly change into freezing rain or a blizzard. Simply falling into a mountain stream can also lead to hypothermia and death unless proper action is taken. If you're cold and tired, don't waste time! Seek shelter and build a fire, change into dry clothes, and drink warm liquids. If a victim isn't fully conscious, warm him or her by skin-to-skin contact in a sleeping bag. Try to keep the victim awake and offer plenty of warm liquids.

GIARDIA

Giardia, a protozoan that has become common in even the most remote mountain streams, is carried in animal or human waste that is deposited or washed into the water. When ingested, it begins reproducing, causing intense cramping and diarrhea in the host that can become serious and may not be cured without medical attention.

No matter how clear a stream looks, it's best to assume that it is contaminated and to take precautions against giardia by filtering, boiling, or treating water with chemicals before drinking it. A high-quality filter will remove giardia and a host of other things you don't want to be drinking. (Spend a bit extra for one that removes particles down to one micrometer in size.) It's also effective to simply boil your water; 2–5 minutes at a rolling boil will kill giardia even in the cyst stage. Because water boils at a lower temperature as elevation increases, increase the boiling time to 15 minutes if you're at 9,000 feet. Two drops of bleach left in a quart of water for 30 minutes will remove most giardia, although some microorganisms are resistant to chemicals.

HANTAVIRUS

Hantavirus is an infectious disease agent that was first isolated during the Korean War and then discovered in the Americas in 1993 by a task force of scientists in New Mexico. This disease agent occurs naturally throughout most of North and South America, especially in dry desert conditions. The infectious agent is airborne, and in the absence of prompt medical attention, its infections are usually fatal. This disease is called hantavirus pulmonary syndrome (HPS). It can affect anyone, but given some fundamental knowledge, it can also be easily prevented.

The natural host of the hantavirus appears to be rodents, especially mice and rats. The virus is not usually transmitted directly from rodents to humans; rather, the rodents shed hantavirus particles in their saliva, urine, and droppings. Humans usually contract HPS by inhaling particles that are infected with the hantavirus. The virus becomes airborne when the particles dry out and get stirred into the air (especially from sweeping a floor or shaking a rug). Humans then inhale these particles, which leads to the infection.

HPS is not considered a highly infectious disease, so people usually contract HPS from long-term exposure. Because transmission usually occurs through inhalation, it is easiest for a human being to contract hantavirus within a contained environment, where the virus-infected particles are not thoroughly dispersed. Being in a cabin or barn where rodents can be found poses elevated risks for contracting the infection.

Simply traveling to a place where the hantavirus is known to occur is not considered a risk factor. Camping, hiking, and other outdoor activities also pose low risks, especially if steps are taken to reduce rodent contact. If you happen to stay in a rodent-infested cabin, thoroughly wet any droppings and dead rodents with a chlorine bleach solution (1 cup per gallon of water) and let them stand for a few minutes before cleaning them up. Be sure to wear rubber gloves for this task, and double-bag your garbage.

The first symptoms of HPS can occur anywhere between five days and three weeks after infection. They almost always include fever, fatigue, aching muscles (usually in the back, shoulders, and/or thighs), and other flu-like conditions. Other early symptoms may include headaches, dizziness, chills, and abdominal discomfort (such as vomiting, nausea, and/or diarrhea). These symptoms are shortly followed by intense coughing and shortness of breath. If you have these symptoms, seek medical help immediately. Untreated infections of hantavirus are almost always fatal.

Tips for Travelers

FOREIGN VISITORS

Entering the United States
There are three different levels of passport, identification, and visa requirements for foreign visitors. Canadian citizens entering the United States must have proof of Canadian citizenship, such as a citizenship card with photo or a Canadian passport.

Citizens of 28 other countries can enter under a reciprocal visa waiver program. These citizens can enter the United States for up to 90 days for tourism or business with a valid passport; however, no visa is required. These countries include most of Western Europe, plus Japan, Australia, New Zealand, and Singapore. For a full list of reciprocal visa countries, check out the website at www.travel.state.gov/vwp.html. Visitors on this program who arrive by sea or air must show round-trip tickets back out of the United States within 90 days, and must be able to present proof of financial solvency (credit cards are usually sufficient). If citizens of these countries are staying longer than 90 days, they must apply for and present a visa.

Citizens of countries not covered by the reciprocal visa program are required to present both a valid passport and a visa to enter the United States. These are obtained from U.S. embassies and consulates. These travelers are also required to offer proof of financial solvency and provide a round-trip ticket out of the United States within the timeline of the visa.

Customs
U.S. Customs allows each person over the age of 21 to bring in one liter of liquor and 200 cigarettes duty free into the country. Non-U.S. citizens can bring in $100 worth of gifts without paying duty. If you are carrying more than $10,000 in cash or travelers checks, you are required to declare it.

Traveling in the United States
Once in the United States, foreign visitors can travel freely among states without restrictions. A few states maintain agricultural checkpoints at state borders to prevent transport of fruit or plants, but Utah is not one of these states.

Currency Exchange and Banking
Outside of Salt Lake City, there are few opportunities to exchange foreign currency or travelers checks in non-U.S. funds at banks or exchanges. Travelers checks in U.S. dollars are accepted at face value in most businesses without additional transaction fees.

By far the best way to keep yourself in cash is by using bank, debit, or cash cards at **ATMs** (automated teller machines). Not only does withdrawing funds from your own home account save in fees, but you also often get a better rate of exchange. Nearly every town in Utah will have an ATM. Most ATMs at banks require a small fee to dispense cash. Most grocery stores allow you to use a debit or cash card to purchase food, with the option for a cash withdrawal. These transactions are free.

Credit Cards
Credit cards are accepted nearly everywhere in Utah. The most common are Visa and MasterCard. American Express, Diners Club, and Discover are also used, although these aren't as ubiquitous.

Electricity
As in all of the United States, electricity is 110 volts. Plugs have either two flat or two-flat-plus-one-round prongs. Older homes and hotels may have outlets that only have two-prong outlets, and you may well be traveling with computers or appliances that have three-prong plugs. Ask your hotel or motel manager for an adapter;

ON THE ROAD

if necessary, you may need to buy a three-prong adapter, but the cost is small.

ACCESSIBILITY

Travelers with disabilities will find Utah progressive when it comes to accessibility. All of the parks (except Grand Staircase-Escalante National Monument) have all-abilities trails and services. All five national parks have reasonably good facilities for visitors with limited mobility. Visitors centers are all-accessible, and at least a couple of trails in each park are paved or smooth enough for a wheelchair user to navigate with some assistance. Each park has a few accessible campsites.

Most hotels also offer some form of barrier-free lodging. It's best to call ahead and inquire what these accommodations are, however, because these services can vary quite a bit from one establishment to another.

Because the Grand Staircase-Escalante National Monument is almost entirely undeveloped, trails are generally inaccessible to wheelchair users.

SENIOR TRAVELERS

The parks and Utah in general are hospitable for senior travelers. The Golden Age Passport is issued by the National Parks Department and allows U.S. citizens 62 years of age and older to have free admission to national parks and to camp at the parks for half off. The card costs $10 per person and is available from any park office. There is a similar discount program at Utah state parks.

GAY AND LESBIAN TRAVELERS

Utah is not the most enlightened place in the world when it comes to gay issues, but that shouldn't be an issue for travelers to the national parks. Needless to say, a little discretion is a good idea in most public situations, and don't expect to find much of a gay scene anywhere in southern Utah. Moab is notably more progressive than anywhere else in this part of the state, but there are no gay bars or gathering places.

© W.C. MCRAE

A good example of small-town life in Utah, Green River has changed little since the 1940s.

ALCOHOL AND NIGHTLIFE

Observant Mormons don't drink alcoholic beverages, and state laws have been drafted to make purchasing alcohol relatively awkward. If going out for drinks and nightclubbing is part of your idea of entertainment, you'll find that only Moab offers much in the way of nightspots. Most towns have a liquor store; outside Moab, don't even expect restaurants to have liquor licenses.

SMOKING

Smoking is taboo for observant Mormons, and smoking is prohibited in almost all public places. You're also not allowed to smoke on church grounds. Obviously, take care when smoking in national parks and pick up your own butts. Besides the risk of fire, there's nothing that ruins a natural experience more that wind-blown piles of cigarette filters.

PETS IN THE PARKS

Unless you really have no other option, it's best not to bring your dog (or cat, or bird, or ferret) along on a national park vacation. Dogs are prohibited on most trails, and for most of the year it's far too hot to leave an animal locked in a car. Additionally, in Zion, private cars are prohibited on the scenic canyon drive, and no pets are allowed on the shuttle buses that drive this route.

ON THE ROAD

UTAH'S DRINKING LAWS

The state's liquor laws are rather confusing and peculiar. Some of Utah's drinking laws were revised in preparation for the 2002 Winter Olympics, but in more remote parts of Utah, don't expect to find it easy to get a drink.

Several different kinds of establishments are licensed to sell alcoholic beverages.

Taverns, which include brewpubs, can only sell 3.2 percent beer (not wine, which is classed as hard liquor in Utah). You don't need to purchase food or be a member of a private club to have a beer in a tavern. With the exception of brewpubs, taverns are usually fairly derelict and not especially cheery places to hang out.

Licensed restaurants are able to sell beer, wine, and hard liquor but only with food orders. Before the Olympics came to town, servers were not able to ask you if you cared for a drink; such solicitation was barred by law. Old habits die hard: in many parts of Utah, you'll need to specifically ask for a drink or the drink menu in order to begin the process. In Salt Lake City, Moab, and Park City, most restaurants have liquor licenses. In other cities and towns, few eating establishments offer alcohol.

Private clubs are essentially the same as bars in other parts of the United States. You can have drinks with or without food during opening hours; however, you must be a member in order to eat or drink in a private club. For travelers, this doesn't present an insurmountable hurdle because you can buy temporary memberships (a two-week membership usually costs around $5). If you're fond of a drink and nightlife, it might well be worth it. Most live music clubs are private clubs, for instance. Also, club members are able to sign in up to five friends on a nightly basis. You can either ask a friendly-looking stranger to sign you in, or, if you're part of a group, one of you can become a member and sign in the others.

A long-standing Utah law forbids the advertising of alcohol. No signs or notices are allowed to indicate that alcohol is available: you won't see many neon Spud McKenzies in Utah. (The law is only spottily enforced these days.) Although it's pretty obvious that a brewpub will have beer, you won't know whether drinks are served at a restaurant until you ask.

Nearly all towns will have a state-owned liquor store, and 3.2 percent beer is available in most grocery stores. Many travelers find that carrying a bottle of your favorite beverage to your room is the easiest way to enjoy an evening drink.

The state drinking age is 21.

SMALL-TOWN UTAH

If you've never traveled in Utah before, you may find that Utahans don't initially seem as welcoming and outgoing as people in other western states. In many smaller towns, visitors from outside the community are a relatively new phenomenon, and not everyone in the state is anxious to have their towns turned into tourist or recreational meccas. The Mormons are very family- and community-oriented, and if certain individuals initially seem insular and uninterested in travelers, don't take it as unfriendliness.

Mormons are also orderly and socially conservative people. Brash displays of rudeness or use of foul language in public will not make you popular.

Arches

A concentration of rock arches of marvelous variety has formed within the maze of sandstone fins at this park, one of the most popular in the United States. Balanced rocks and tall spires add to the splendor. Paved roads and short hiking trails provide easy access to some of the more than 1,500 arches in the park. If you're short on time, a drive to the Windows Section (23.5 miles round-trip) affords a look at some of the largest and most spectacular arches. To visit all the stops and hike a few short trails would take all day.

Most of the early settlers and cowboys that passed through the Arches area paid little attention to the scenery. In 1923, however, a prospector by the name of Alexander Ringhoffer interested officials of the Rio Grande Railroad in the scenic attractions at what he called Devils Garden (now known as Klondike Bluffs). The railroad men liked the area and contacted Stephen Mather, first director of the National Park Service. Mather started the political process that led to designating two small areas as a national monument in 1929, but Ringhoffer's Devils Garden wasn't included until later. The monument grew in size over the years and became Arches National Park in 1971. The park now comprises 76,519 acres—small enough to be appreciated in one day, yet large enough to warrant extensive exploration.

© JUDY JEWELL

Devils Garden

ARCHES

Long Valley

Eagle Park

Salt

Valley

Klondike Bluffs

Yellow

Cat Flat

ARCHES

DARK ANGEL

Devils Garden

PRIVATE ARCH

DOUBLE O ARCH

LANDSCAPE ARCH

DEVILS GARDEN

MARCHING MEN

SKYLINE ARCH

BROKEN ARCH

Salt

SAND DUNE ARCH

Valley

Wash

Salt Wash

Winter Camp Ridge

Fiery Furnace

WOLFE RANCH

DELICATE ARCH

DELICATE ARCH VIEWPOINT

ARCHES

PANORAMA POINT

Dry Mesa

NATIONAL PARK

Garden of Eden

COVE OF CAVES

Rock Pinnacles

BALANCED ROCK

NORTH/SOUTH WINDOW

Windows Section

Courthouse

The Great Wall

Petrified Dunes

Mat Martin Point

Sevenmile Canyon

313

Wash

191

SHEEP ROCK

THREE GOSSIPS

Courthouse Towers

COURTHOUSE TOWERS VIEWPOINT/ THE ORGAN

PARK AVENUE

128

Colorado River

VISITOR CENTER

Arths Pasture

MOAB

0   2 mi

0   2 km

279

191

Moab

© AVALON TRAVEL PUBLISHING, INC.

Natural History

GEOLOGY

An unusual combination of geologic forces created the arches. About 300 million years ago, evaporation of inland seas left behind a salt layer more than 3,000 feet thick in the Paradox Basin of this region. Sediments, including those that later became the arches, then covered the salt. Unequal pressures caused the salt to gradually flow upward in places, bending the overlying sediments as well. These upfolds, or anticlines, later collapsed when ground water dissolved the underlying salt. The faults and joints caused by the uplift and collapse opened the way for erosion to carve hundreds of freestanding fins. Alternate freezing and thawing action and exfoliation (flaking caused by expansion when water or frost penetrates the rock) continued to peel away more rock until holes formed in some of the fins. Rockfalls within the holes helped enlarge the arches. Nearly all arches in the park eroded out of Entrada Sandstone.

Eventually all the present arches will collapse, but we should have plenty of new ones by the time that happens. The fins' uniform strength and hard upper surfaces have proved ideal for arch formation. Not every hole in the rock is an arch. The opening must be at least three feet in one direction, and light must be able to pass through. Although the term *windows* often refers to openings in large walls of rock, windows and arches are really the same. Water seeping through the sandstone from above has created a second type of arch—the pothole arch. You may also come across a few natural bridges cut from the rock by perennial water runoff.

FLORA AND FAUNA

Elevation at the park ranges from 3,960 feet along the Colorado River to 5,653 feet in the Windows area. Annual precipitation averages only 10–11 inches. Even so, plants and wildlife have found niches in this rugged high-desert country. Shrubs and grasslands cover most of the land not

ARCHES' EPONYMOUS ROCK FORMATIONS

Arches' geological formations result from a combination of underground shifting and buckling of rocks, and aboveground erosion.

Beneath the visible rocks at Arches is an underground salt bed, laid down about 300 million years ago when seas washed over the area and then evaporated. The salt bed is not particularly stable, and the weight of many layers of rock on top of it have caused it to buckle and warp, shifting and cracking the overlying layers.

The rocks that lie on top of the salt beds—the rocks you actually *see* at Arches—are mostly Entrada Sandstone, which is a pretty general category of rock. Within this Entrada formation are three distinct types of sandstone. The

the Windows in Arches National Park

formation's dark red base layer is known as the Dewey Bridge member. It's softer than the formation's other sandstones and erodes easily.

Dewey Bridge rocks are topped by the pinkish orange Slick Rock member, the park's most visible rocks. The Slick Rock layer is much harder than the Dewey Bridge, and the combination of the two layers—softer rocks overlaid by harder—is responsible for the differential erosion that forms hoodoos and precariously balanced rocks. The thin top layer of Entrada Sandstone is called the Moab Tongue, a white rock similar to Navajo Sandstone.

© W.C. MCRAE

ARCHES

occupied by barren rock. Cottonwood trees grow along some of the washes, while piñon pine and juniper form pygmy forests at higher elevations. Specially adapted plant communities thrive in the dark cryptobiotic crusts on the soil. Hanging gardens surround springs and seeps.

Tracks across the sands show the presence of shy or nocturnal wildlife. Animals include mule deer, coyote, gray fox, porcupine, bobcat, ringtail cat, kangaroo rat, antelope ground squirrel, collared lizard, and midget faded rattlesnake.

Exploring the Park

VISITORS CENTER

Located just past the entrance booth, the visitors center provides a good introduction to what to expect ahead. Exhibits identify the rock layers, describe the geologic and human history, and illustrate some of the wildlife and plants of the park. Staff members present a short slide program upon request and answer your questions. Look for the posted list of special activities; rangers host campfire programs and lead a wide variety of guided walks from Apr.–Sept. You'll also find checklists, pamphlets, books, maps, posters, postcards, and film here for purchase. See the ranger for advice and the free backcountry permit required for overnight trips. The easy 0.2-mile **Desert Nature Trail** begins in front of the visitors center and identifies some of the native plants. Picnic areas lie outside the visitors center and at Balanced Rock and Devils Garden.

A road guide to Arches National Park, available at the visitors center, has detailed descriptions that correspond to place names along the main road. Be sure to stop only in parking lots and designated pullouts. Watch out for others who are sight-seeing in this popular park. With less than 30 miles of paved road in the park, the traffic density can be surprisingly high in the summer high season.

The entrance fee of $10 per vehicle ($5 bicyclists) is good for seven days at Arches only. The park brochure available at the entrance station and visitors center has a map of major scenic features, drives, trails, and back roads.

The park is open all year; visitors center hours are daily 8 A.M.–4:30 P.M., with extended hours in summer. Arches National Park is five miles north of downtown Moab on U.S. 191. For more information, see www.nps.gov/arch, write P.O. Box 907, Moab, UT 84532, or call 435/719-2299.

MOAB FAULT

The park road begins a long but well-graded climb from the visitors center up the cliffs to the northeast. A pullout on the right after 1.1 miles gives a good view of Moab Canyon and its geology. The rock layers on this side of the canyon have slipped down more than 2,600 feet in relation to the other side. Movement took place about six million years ago along the Moab Fault, which follows the canyon floor. Rock layers at the top of the far cliffs are nearly the same age as those at the *bottom* on this side! If you could stack the rocks of this side on top of rocks on the other side, you'd have a complete stratigraphic column of the Moab area—more than 150 million years' worth.

PARK AVENUE

South Park Avenue Overlook and Trailhead are on the left 2.1 miles from the visitors center. Great sandstone slabs form a "skyline" on each side of this dry wash. A trail goes north one mile down the wash to North Park Avenue Trailhead (1.3 miles ahead by road). Arrange to be picked up there or backtrack to your starting point. The large rock monoliths of Courthouse Towers rise north of Park Avenue. Only a few small arches exist now, although major arches may have formed in the past.

BALANCED ROCK

This gravity-defying formation is on the right 8.5 miles from the visitors center. A boulder more than 55 feet high rests precariously atop a

EDWARD ABBEY: "RESIST MUCH, OBEY LITTLE"

Edward Abbey spent two summers in the late 1950s living in a trailer in Arches National Park. From this experience, he wrote *Desert Solitaire*, which, when it was published in 1968, introduced many readers to the beauties of Utah's slickrock country, and the need to preserve it. In the introduction to this book, he gives a word of caution to slickrock pilgrims:

Do not jump into your automobile next June and rush out to the Canyon country hoping to see some of that which I have attempted to evoke in these pages. In the first place you can't see anything from a car; you've got to get out of the goddamned contraption and walk, better yet crawl, on hands and knees, over the sandstone and through the. . . cactus. When traces of blood begin to mark your trail you'll see something, maybe.

This sense of letting the outdoors affect you—right down to the bone—pervades Abbey's writing. He advocated responding to assaults on the environment in an equally raw, gutsy way. Convinced that the only way to confront rampant development in the American West was by preserving its wilderness, he was a pioneer of radical environmentalism, a "desert anarchist." Long before Earth First!, Abbey's fictional characters blew up dams and created a holy environmentalist ruckus in *The Monkeywrench Gang*. Some of his ideas were radical, others reactionary, and he seemed deeply committed to raising a stir. Abbey's writing did a lot to change the way people think about the American West, its development, and staying true to values derived from the natural world.

Two recent biographies, *Edward Abbey: A Life*, by James M. Cahalan, and the less academic *Adventures with Ed*, by Abbey's good friend Jack Loeffler, help readers see the person behind the icon.

Cahalan, James M. *Edward Abbey: A Life.* Tucson: University of Arizona Press, 2001; 357 pages; $27.95.

Loeffler, Jack. *Adventures with Ed: A Portrait of Abbey.* Albuquerque: University of New Mexico Press, 2002; 308 pages; $24.95.

ARCHES

73-foot pedestal. Chip Off the Old Block, a much smaller version of Balanced Rock, stood nearby until it collapsed in the winter of 1975–1976. For a closer look at Balanced Rock, take the 0.3-mile trail encircling it. There's a picnic area across the road. Author Edward Abbey lived in a trailer near Balanced Rock during a season as a park ranger in the 1950s; his journal became the basis for the classic *Desert Solitaire*.

WINDOWS SECTION

Turn right 2.5 miles on a paved road past Balanced Rock. Short trails (.25–1 mile long one-way) lead from the road's end to some massive arches. Windows Trailhead is the start for North Window (an opening 51 feet high and 93 feet wide), South Window (66 feet high and 105 feet wide), and Turret Arch (64 feet high and 39 feet wide). Double Arch, a short walk from a second trailhead, is an unusual pair of arches; the larger opening—105 feet high and 163 feet wide—is best appreciated by walking inside. The smaller opening is 61 feet high and 60 feet wide. Together, the two arches frame a large opening overhead, but this isn't considered a true arch.

Garden of Eden Viewpoint, on the way back to the main road, has a good panorama of Salt Valley to the north. Under the valley, the massive body of salt and gypsum that's responsible for the arches comes close to the surface. Tiny Delicate Arch can be seen across the valley on a sandstone ridge. Early visitors to the Garden of Eden saw rock formations resembling Adam (with an apple) and Eve. Two other viewpoints of the Salt Valley area lie farther north on the main road.

DELICATE ARCH AND THE WOLFE RANCH

Drive north 2.5 miles on the main road from the Windows junction and turn right 1.8 miles to the Wolfe Ranch, where a bit of pioneer history survives. John Wesley Wolfe came to this spot in 1888, hoping the desert climate would provide relief for health problems he had related to a Civil War injury. He found a good spring high in the rocks, grass for cattle, and water in Salt Wash to irrigate a garden. The ranch that he built provided a home for him and some of his family for more than 20 years, and cattlemen later used it as a line ranch. Then sheepherders brought in their animals, which so overgrazed the range that the grass has yet to recover. A trail guide available at the entrance tells about the Wolfe family and features of their ranch. The weather-beaten cabin built in 1906 still survives. A short trail leads to petroglyphs above Wolfe Ranch; figures of horses indicate that Ute Indians did the artwork. Park staff can give directions to other rock-art sites; great care should be taken not to touch the fragile artwork.

Delicate Arch stands in a magnificent setting atop gracefully curving slickrock. Distant canyons and the La Sal Mountains lie beyond. The span is 45 feet high and 33 feet wide. A moderately strenuous three-mile round-trip hike leads to the arch. Another perspective on Delicate Arch can be obtained by driving 1.2 miles beyond Wolfe Ranch. Look for the small arch high above. A steep trail (one-half-mile round-trip) climbs a hill for the best panorama.

FIERY FURNACE

Return to the main road and continue three miles to the Fiery Furnace Viewpoint and Trailhead on the right. Closely packed sandstone fins form a maze of deep slots, with many arches and at least one natural bridge inside. The Fiery Furnace can be fun to explore, either on your own with a permit or on a ranger-guided hike; a fee and ticket are required for the latter.

The Fiery Furnace gets its name from sandstone fins that turn flaming red on occasions when thin cloud cover at the horizon reflects the warm light

The Fiery Furnace gets its name from sandstone fins that turn flaming red on occasions when thin cloud cover at the horizon reflects the warm light of sunrise or sunset.

© W.C. MCRAE

Skyline Arch

of sunrise or sunset. Actually, the shady recesses provide a cool respite from the hot summer sun.

SKYLINE ARCH

This arch is located on the right one mile past Sand Dune/Broken Arch Trailhead. In desert climates, erosion may proceed imperceptibly for centuries until a cataclysmic event happens. In 1940, a giant boulder fell from the opening of Skyline Arch, doubling the size of the arch in just seconds. The hole is now 45 feet high and 69 feet wide. A short trail leads to the base of the arch.

DEVILS GARDEN AREA

The Devils Garden trailhead, picnic area, and campground all lie near the end of the main park road. Devils Garden offers fine scenery and more arches than any other section of the park. The hiking trail leads past large sandstone fins to Landscape and six other named arches. Carry water if the weather is hot or if you might want to continue past the one-mile point at Landscape Arch. Adventurous hikers could spend days exploring the maze of canyons among the fins.

KLONDIKE BLUFFS AND TOWER ARCH

Relatively few visitors come to the spires, high bluffs, and fine arch in this northwestern section of the park. A fair-weather dirt road turns off the main drive 1.3 miles before Devils Garden Trailhead, winds down into Salt Valley, and heads northwest. After 7.5 miles, turn left one mile on the road signed Klondike Bluffs to the Tower Arch Trailhead. These roads may be washboarded but are usually okay in dry weather for cars; don't drive on them if storms threaten. The trail to Tower Arch winds past the Marching Men and other rock formations; the distance is three miles round-trip. Alexander Ringhoffer, who discovered the arch in 1922, carved an inscription on the south column. The area can also be fun to explore off-trail (map and compass needed). Those with four-wheel-drive vehicles can drive close to the arch on a separate jeep road. Tower Arch has an opening 34 feet high by 92 feet wide. A tall monolith nearby gave the arch its name.

FOUR-WHEEL-DRIVE ROAD

A rough road near Tower Arch in the Klondike Bluffs turns southeast past **Eye of the Whale Arch** in Herdina Park to Balanced Rock on the main park road, 10.8 miles away. The road isn't particularly difficult for four-wheel-drive enthusiasts, although normal backcountry precautions should be taken. A steep sand hill north of Eye of the Whale Arch is difficult to climb for vehicles coming from Balanced Rock; it's better to drive from the Tower Arch area instead.

ARCHES

Recreation

HIKING

Established hiking trails lead to many fine arches and overlooks that can't be seen from the road. You're free to wander cross-country, too, but please stay on rock or in washes to avoid damaging the fragile cryptobiotic soils. Wear good walking shoes with rubber soles for travel across slickrock. The summer sun can be especially harsh on the unprepared hiker—don't forget water, a hat, and sunscreen. The desert rule is to carry at least one gallon of water per person for an all-day hike. Take a map and compass for off-trail hiking. Be cautious on the slickrock because the soft sandstone can crumble easily. Also, remember that it's easier to go up a steep slickrock slope than it is to come back down!

You can reach almost any spot in the park on a day hike, although you'll also find some good overnight possibilities. Areas for longer trips include Courthouse Wash in the southern part of the park and Salt Wash in the eastern part. All backpacking is done off-trail. A backcountry permit must be obtained from a ranger before camping in the backcountry.

Backcountry regulations include no fires, no pets, and camping out of sight of any road (at least one mile away) or trail (at least one-half-mile away) and at least 300 feet from a recognizable archaeological site or nonflowing water source.

Park Avenue

Get an eyeful of massive stone formations and a feel for the natural history of the park on the easy to moderate Park Avenue trail. This mile-long hike leaves from the Park Avenue Trailhead, just past the crest of the switchbacks that climb up into the park. The vistas from here are especially dramatic: the Courthouse Towers, the Three Gossips, and other fanciful rock formations loom above a natural amphitheater. The trail drops into a narrow wash before traversing the park highway at the North Park Avenue trailhead.

Hikers can be dropped off at one trailhead and picked up a half hour later at the other.

The Windows

Ten miles into the park, just past the impossible-to-miss Balanced Rock, follow signs and a paved road to the Windows Section. Two sandy trails lead to clusters of enormous arches that are impossible to see from the road. These easy trails are good for family groups because younger or more ambitious hikers can scramble to their hearts' content along rocky outcrops. A one-mile roundtrip loop leads to the Windows, including the **North** and **South Windows** and **Turret Arch.** Unmarked trails lead to vistas and scrambles along the stone faces that comprise the ridge. A second trail leaves from just past the Windows parking area, leading to **Double Arch.** This short, half-mile-long trail leads to two giant spans that are joined at one end.

Delicate Arch

If you don't have the time or the endurance for the strenuous hike to Delicate Arch, you can view this astonishing arch from a distance at the **Delicate Arch Viewpoint,** located one mile passed the Wolfe Ranch area. From the viewing area, hikers can scramble one-quarter mile up a sometimes steep trail to a rim with views across Cache Valley.

For those who are able, the three-mile roundtrip hike to the base of **Delicate Arch** is one of the park's highlights. The trail leaves from the Wolfe Ranch, crosses a swinging bridge, climbs a slickrock slope, follows a gully, then contours across steep slickrock to the main overlook. The round-trip distance is three miles with an elevation gain of 500 feet; carry water.

This hike is one of the most scenic in the park. Just before the end of the trail, walk up to a small arch for a framed view of the final destination. The classic photo of Delicate Arch is taken late in the afternoon when the sandstone glows with golden hues. Standing at the base of Delicate Arch is a magical moment: the arch rises out of the barren, almost lunar rock face, yet it seems ephemeral. Views from the arch over the Colorado River valley are amazing.

Fiery Furnace

The Fiery Furnace area is open only to hikers with free permits or to those joining a ranger-led hike. During summer, rangers offer daily two- to three-hour hikes into this unique area from Apr.–Oct.; $6 adult fee and ticket are required. In-person reservations are obtained at the visitors center up to one week in advance.

The Fiery Furnace is a maze of narrow sandstone canyons, and the route through the area is sometimes challenging, requiring hands-and-knees scrambling up cracks and ledges. Navigation is difficult: Route-finding can be tricky because what look like obvious paths often lead to dead ends. Drop-offs and ridges make straight-line travel impossible. It's easy to get disoriented! If you're uncertain about your hiking or directional skills, the ranger-led hikes provide the best way to see the wonders of the Fiery Furnace.

For those who are able, the three-mile round-trip hike to the base of Delicate Arch is one of the park's highlights. Standing at the base is a magical moment: the arch rises out of the barren, almost lunar rock face, yet it seems ephemeral.

Broken and Sand Dune Arches

The trailhead is on the right 2.4 miles past the Fiery Furnace turnoff. A short trail leads to small Sand Dune Arch (opening is eight feet high and 30 feet wide) tucked within fins. A longer trail (one mile round-trip) crosses a field to Broken Arch, which you can also see from the road. The opening is 43 feet high and 59 feet wide. Up close, you'll see that the arch isn't really broken. These arches can also be reached by trail from near comfort station number three at Devils Garden Campground. Low-growing Canyonlands biscuitroot, found only in areas of Entrada Sandstone, colonizes sand dunes. Hikers can protect the habitat of the biscuitroot and other fragile plants by keeping to washes or rock surfaces.

Hikes from Devils Garden

From the end of the paved park road, a 7.2-mile round-trip hike leads to eight named arches and a vacation's-worth of scenic wonders. The first two arches lie off a short side trail to the right. **Tunnel Arch** has a relatively symmetrical opening 22 feet high and 27 feet wide. The nearby **Pine Tree Arch** is named for a piñon pine that once grew inside; the arch has an opening 48 feet high and 46 feet wide. Continue on the main trail to **Landscape Arch,** which has an incredible 306-foot span (six feet longer than a football field!) and is 106 feet high. This is one of the longest unsupported rock spans in the world. The thin arch looks ready to collapse at any moment. A rockfall from the arch on September 1, 1991, worries some people who fear the end may be near. Distance from the trailhead is two miles round-trip, an easy one-hour walk.

The trail narrows past Landscape Arch and continues one-quarter mile to **Wall Arch,** in a long wall-like fin. The opening is 41 feet high and 68 feet wide. A short side trail branches off to the left beyond Wall Arch to **Partition Arch** (26 feet high and 28 feet wide) and **Navajo Arch** (13 feet high and 41 feet wide). Partition was so named because a piece of rock divides the main opening from a smaller hole eight feet high and 8.5 feet wide. Navajo Arch is a rock-shelter type; perhaps prehistoric Indians camped here. The main trail continues northwest and ends at **Double O Arch** (four miles round-trip from the trailhead). Double O has a large oval-shaped opening (45 feet high and 71 feet wide) and a smaller hole (nine feet high and 21 feet wide) underneath. **Dark Angel** is a distinctive rock pinnacle one-quarter mile northwest; cairns mark the way. Another primitive trail loops back to Landscape Arch via **Fin Canyon.** The route goes through a different area of Garden but adds about one mile to (three miles back to the trailhead instead of two). Pay careful attention to the trail markers to keep on the correct route.

BIKING

Cyclists *must* stick to established roads in the park. They also have to contend with heavy traffic on the narrow paved roads and dusty, washboarded surfaces on the dirt roads. Beware of the deep sand on the four-wheel-drive roads. Nearby, Bureau of Land Management (BLM) and Canyonlands National Park areas offer much better mountain biking.

CLIMBING

Rock climbers don't need a permit, although they should first discuss their plans with a ranger. Most features named on U.S. Geological Survey maps are *closed* to climbing.

Although the rock in Arches is sandy, climbers find the landscapes worth the challenge. The most commonly climbed faces are along the sheer stone faces of Park Avenue. For more information, consult the guidebook *Desert Rock*, by Eric Bjørnstad.

CAMPGROUNDS

The **Devils Garden Campground** is located near the end of the 18-mile scenic drive, although in summer you must preregister at the visitors center. The campground is open all year with water; $10. Try to arrive early during the busy Easter–October season; only groups can reserve spaces. Elevation here is 5,355 feet. During summer evenings, rangers at the Campfire Circle tell about the park's geology, history, wildlife, flora, and environment.

Moab

By far the largest town in southeastern Utah, Moab (pop. 5,500) makes an excellent base for exploring Arches and Canyonland National Parks and the surrounding canyon country. Moab lies near the Colorado River in a green valley enclosed by high sandstone cliffs. The biblical Moab was a kingdom at the edge of Zion, and early settlers must have felt themselves at the edge of their world, too, being so isolated from Salt Lake City—the Mormon city of Zion. Moab's existence on the fringe of Mormon culture and the sizable gentile population gave the town a unique character.

In recent years, Moab has become nearly synonymous with mountain biking. The slickrock canyon country seems made for exploration by bike, and people come from all over the world to pedal the backcountry. River trips on the Colorado River are nearly as popular, and a host of other outdoor recreational diversions—from horseback riding to four-wheel jeep exploring to hot-air ballooning—combine to make Moab one of the most popular destinations in Utah.

Moab is also one of the most youthful and vibrant communities in the state; thousands of young people travel to Moab for the recreation, while hundreds of others work here as guides and outfitters. Call them recreationals, funpigs, gearheads, or even *yummies* (for Young Urban Macho Men Into Extreme Sports), but the fact is that tanned, fit, and Lycra-covered bodies are the norm here, and the town's brewpubs, bike shops, and cafés do a booming trade.

© W.C. MCRAE

one of Moab's original trading posts, now devoted to tourist curios

MOAB

To Colorado River, Arches National Park, Dead Horse Point, Canyonlands National Park, and I-70

Negro Bill Canyon

BUCK'S GRILL HOUSE

THE RANCH HOUSE

SLICKROCK COUNTRY CAMPGROUND/ WESTERN RIVER EXPEDITIONS

Swiss Cheese Ridge

Mt. View Cave

ECHO POINT

191

SUPER 8 MOTEL

SUNSET GRILL

MI VIDA DR.

McGIL

500

CLIFFVIEW

MOAB ROCK SHOP

ABYSS VIEW POINT

Practice Loop

0   0.25 mi

0   0.25 km

CANYON COUNTRY BED & BREAKFAST

100 W. ST.

BANDITOS GRILL

TAG-A-LONG EXPEDITIONS

DAYS INN

Start One Way Loop

400 N. ST.

W. ST.

ALLEN MEMORIAL HOSPITAL

CITY PARK AND SWIMMING POOL

PARK DR.

DESERT GARDENS

ECLECTICAFE

200 N. ST.

SUNFLOWER HILL BED & BREAKFAST

MOAB SLICKROCK BIKE TRAIL

ST.

BOWEN MOTEL

LANDMARK MOTEL

100 N. ST.

Swiss Cheese Ridge

JAILHOUSE CAFE

RED ROCK LODGE MOTEL

CENTER CAFE

CENTER ST.

CEDAR BREAKS CONDOS

100
200
300

RIO COLORADO RESTAURANT

SEE DETAIL

100 S. ST.

CITY DUMP

Mill Creek

ARROYO RD.

KANE

BEST WESTERN GREENWELL MOTEL

SZECHUAN RESTAURANT

MOAB DINER & ICE CREAM SHOPPE

S. ST

TUSHIE ST.

FAT CITY SMOKEHOUSE

GONZO INN

200 ST.

To Colorado River, Kane Creek Canyon, and Moab's Skyways

VIRGINIAN MOTEL

300 S. ST.

LOCUST LN.

Moab Rim

CREEK BLVD

MILL CREEK DR.

400 E. ST.

SAND FLATS RD.

Moab Rim Trail

RED STONE MOAB VALLEY INN

CANYONLANDS CAMPARK

BAR M CHUCKWAGON SUPPER

Mill Creek

SLICKROCK CINEMAS

BIG HORN LODGE

MOUNTAINVIEW AVE.

MILLER'S SHOPPING CENTER

POWERHOUSE LN.

MOAB BREWERY

COMFORT SUITES

191

Pack Creek

BUREAU OF LAND MANAGEMENT DISTRICT OFFICE

Moab Rim

LAZY LIZARD HOSTEL

HOLYOAK LN.

To KOA Campground, Golf Course, National Parks Service, USFS Offices, and Monticello

Detail inset:

SUNSET MOTEL

POPLAR PLACE PUB & EATERY

100
200

MAIN ST.

100 N. ST.

MOAB INFORMATION CENTER

POST OFFICE

BREAKFAST AT TIFFANY'S

SLICK ROCK CAFE

HOTEL OFF CENTER/ DESERT BISTRO

CENTER ST.

BEST WESTERN CANYONLANDS INN

MOAB MUSEUM AND GRAND COUNTY PUBLIC LIBRARY

EDDIE MCSTIFF'S/ MONDO CAFE

© AVALON TRAVEL PUBLISHING, INC.

As Moab's popularity has grown, so have concerns that the town and the surrounding countryside is simply getting loved to death. The landscape has always been a staple in car ads (remember those Chevy pickups balanced on a red-rock pinnacle?); now the landscape sells the "Just Do It" lifestyle for MTV, Nike, and other merchandisers of youth culture. On a busy day, hundreds of mountain bikers form queues to negotiate the trickier sections of the famed Slick Rock Trail, and more than 20,000 people crowd into town on busy weekends to bike, hike, float, and party. As noted in an article in *Details* magazine, "Moab is pretty much the Fort Lauderdale of the intermountain West." Whether this old Mormon town and the delicate desert environment can endure such an onslaught of popularity is a question of increasing concern.

History

Prehistoric Fremont and Anasazi Indians once lived and farmed in the bottoms of the canyons around Moab. Their rock art, granaries, and dwellings can still be seen here. Nomadic Ute Indians had replaced the earlier groups by the time the first white settlers arrived. The Old Spanish Trail, opened in 1829 between New Mexico and California, passed through Spanish Valley and crossed the Colorado River near present-day Moab.

Mormon missionaries tried to establish the Elk Mountain Mission here in 1855. They managed to plant some fields, build a stone fort, and convert some of the Utes before a series of attacks killed three missionaries and sent the others fleeing back to civilization. The valley

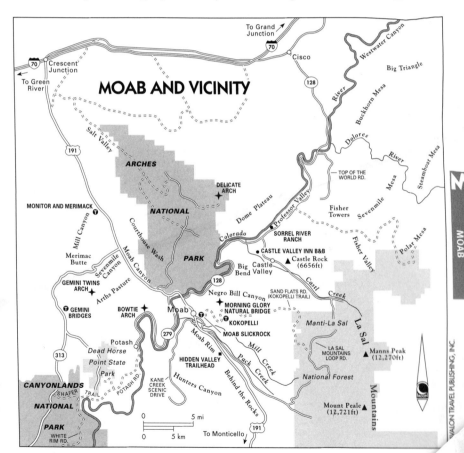

© W.C. MCRAE

Downtown Moab is a hybrid of early 20th-century storefronts and trendy new businesses.

reverted to the Indians and small numbers of explorers, outlaws, ranchers, and trappers for the next 20 years. Settlers with better success founded Moab in the 1870s. Indian troubles ceased after 1881, and the community became a quiet farming and ranching center.

Oil exploration in the 1920s caused some excitement, but nothing like that of the uranium boom that began in 1952. Moab's population tripled in just three years as eager prospectors swarmed into the canyons. One of these hopefuls, Charlie Steen, did hit it big. Experts had laughed at Charlie's efforts until he discovered the Mi Vida uranium bonanza about 30 miles south of town. An instant multimillionaire, he built a large mansion overlooking Moab and hosted lavish parties attended by Hollywood celebrities. Charlie Steen and most of the prospectors have moved on, but Moab has never been the same since.

Sights

DAN O'LAURIE MUSEUM

This regional museum tells the story of Moab's and Grand County's past, from prehistoric and Ute Indian artifacts to the explorations of Spanish missionaries. Photos and tools show pioneer Moab life, much of which centered around ranching or mining; here, too, you'll find displays of rocks and minerals, as well as bones of huge dinosaurs that once tracked across this land. Ask for a *Moab Area Historic Walking Tour* leaflet to learn about historic buildings in town. Located at 118 E. Center, 435/259-7985; open in summer Mon.–Sat. 1–8 P.M.; rest of the year Mon.–Thurs. 3–7 P.M. and Sat. 1–7 P.M.; free.

HOLE 'N THE ROCK

Albert Christensen worked 12 years to excavate his dream home within a sandstone monolith south of town. When he died in 1957, his wife Gladys worked another eight years to complete the project. The interior has notable touches like a 65-foot chimney drilled through the rock ceiling, paintings, taxidermy exhibits, and a lapidary room. The 5,000-square-foot, 14-room home is open for tours daily 8 A.M.–dusk in summer and daily 9 A.M.–5 P.M. the rest of the year; $2.50 adults, $1.50 ages 6–12. It also has a gift shop, 435/686-2250. A picnic area and snack bar are outside. Located 15 miles south of Moab on U.S. 191.

MOAB'S SKYWAY

One of Moab's new tourist attractions is this 12-minute tramway, which lifts you up 1,000 feet to the top of the red-rock rims that flank the city to the southwest. Once on top of the rims, you can relax with refreshments or hike along trails. An easy one-mile trail follows the rims; more adventurous hikers can use the skyway as a shortcut to Hidden Canyon (see the Hiking section). Bicycles are carried free on the skyway; from on top, you'll have nowhere to go but down on several biking trails. Tickets are $9 adults, $8 seniors, and $7 children 12 and under. Open daily,

9 A.M.–late evening (lighted night rides available in warm weather). The skyway is one mile west of

Moab off Kane Creek Boulevard (turn west at the McDonald's), 435/259-7799.

Recreation

Moab sits at the center of some of the most picturesque landscapes in North America. Even the most casual visitor will want to get outdoors and explore the river canyons, natural arches, and mesas. Mountain biking and river tours are the recreational activities that get the most attention in the Moab area, although hikers, climbers, and horseback riders will find plenty to do. If you're less physically adventurous, you can explore the landscape on scenic flights or on hot-air balloon trips, or follow old mining roads in four-wheel-drive vehicles to remote backcountry destinations.

Contact the Moab Information Center, 800/635-6622 or 435/259-8825, for full information about the area's recreational options; the center, located at Main and Central streets in the center of town, has representatives of the National Park Service, the Bureau of Land Management (BLM), and the U.S. Forest Service on staff, and they can direct you to the adventure of your liking. The offices also have literature, books, and maps. BLM officials can also give locations of the developed and undeveloped designated campsites near the Moab Slickrock Bike Trail, Kane Creek, and along the Colorado River; you must use the designated sites in these areas.

Sports and Equipment Rentals

Rim Cyclery, 94 W. 100 North, 435/259-5333, offers mountain bikes and cross-country skis, as well as mountain-bike tours. Mountain-bike rentals and tours are also available at **Moab Cyclery,** 391 S. Main, 435/259-7423; **Poison Spider Bicycles,** 497 N. Main, 435/259-7882; and **Western Spirit Cycling,** 38 S. 100 West, 435/259-8969. Expect to pay about $45 per day to rent a mountain bike.

Canyon Voyages, 401 N. Main St., 435/259-6007, and **Tag-A-Long Expeditions,** 452 N. Main St., 435/259-8946, are two local rafting companies that rent rafts and kayaks for those

who would rather organize their own river adventure. Canoe rental from **Red River Canoe Company,** 497 N. Main St., 435/259-7722, costs $18–25 per person and includes necessary equipment and transportation.

You can rent jeeps and other four-wheel-drive vehicles at **Farabee 4X4 Adventures,** 83 S. Main, 435/259-7494, or **Slickrock Jeep Rentals,** 284 N. Main, 435/259-5678.

HIKING

To reach most of Moab's prime hiking trails requires a short drive to trailheads; these routes are all picturesque and are fully described as follows. For more options, pick up the brochure "Moab Area Hiking Trails" at the visitors center, and turn to the chapters on Arches and Canyonlands National Parks.

Trails from Kane Creek Scenic Drive and Highway 191 South

The high cliffs just southwest of town provide fine views of the Moab Valley, highlands of Arches National Park, and the La Sal Mountains. The **Moab Rim Trail** turns off Kane Creek Boulevard 1.5 miles downriver from Moab. The total driving distance from the junction of Main Street and Kane Creek Boulevard is 2.6 miles; look for the trailhead on the left 0.1 mile after a cattle guard.

You can see the sky through Little Arch across the river from the trailhead. Four-wheel-drive vehicles can also ascend the Moab Rim Trail, although the rough terrain is considered difficult for them; the first 200 yards will give drivers a feel for the difficulty. The trail climbs northeast 1.5 miles along tilted rock strata of the Kayenta Formation to the top of the plateau. This hike is moderately difficult, with a gain of 940 feet and good views nearly all the way. Once on top, hikers can follow jeep roads southeast to Hidden

MOAB

Valley Trail and descend on a hiking trail to U.S. 191 south of Moab—a 5.5-mile trip one-way. Experienced hikers can also head south from the rim to **Behind the Rocks,** a fantastic maze of sandstone fins.

You'll see not only a "hidden valley" from the **Hidden Valley Trail** but also panoramas of the Moab area and Behind the Rocks. The moderately difficult trail ascends 500 feet in a series of switchbacks to a broad shelf below the Moab Rim, then follows the shelf (hidden valley) to the northwest. It then crosses a low pass and follows a second shelf in the same direction. Near the end of the second shelf, the trail turns left to a divide, where you can see a portion of the remarkable fins of Behind the Rocks. This divide is one mile from the start and 680 feet higher in elevation. The trail continues one-third mile from the divide down to the end of the Moab Rim Trail, which is a jeep road and hiking trail. Instead of turning left to the divide, you can make a short side trip (no trail) to the right for views of Moab.

To reach the Hidden Valley Trailhead, drive south three miles on U.S. 191 from Moab, turn right 0.4 mile on Angel Rock Road to its end (the turnoff is just south of Milepost 122), then right 0.3 mile on Rimrock Lane.

A look at the topographic map will show that something strange is going on at the area called **Behind the Rocks.** Massive fins of Navajo Sandstone 100–500 feet high, 50–200 feet thick, and up to one-half-mile long cover a large area. Narrow vertical cracks, sometimes only a few feet wide, separate the fins. Archaeological sites and several arches are in the area. No maintained trails exist here, and some routes require technical climbing skills. The maze offers endless exploration routes. If you get lost (which is very easy to do), remember that the fins are oriented east-west; the rim of the Colorado River Canyon is reached by going west, and Spanish Valley is reached by going east. Bring plenty of water, a topographic map (Moab 71/2-minute), and a

A look at the topographic map will show that something strange is going on at the area called Behind the Rocks. Massive fins of Navajo Sandstone 100–500 feet high, 50–200 feet thick, and up to one-half-mile long cover a large area.

compass. Access routes are Moab Rim and Hidden Valley Trails (from the north and east) and Pritchett Canyon (from the west and south). Although it is only a couple of miles from Moab, Behind the Rocks seems a world away. The BLM is studying a possible wilderness designation to protect the solitude and character of this strange country.

Hikers along **Hunters Canyon** enjoy seeing a rock arch and other rock formations in the canyon walls and the lush vegetation along the creek. Off-road vehicles have made tracks a short way up, then you'll be walking, mostly along the creekbed. Short sections of trail lead around thickets of tamarisk and other water-loving plants. Look for Hunters Arch on the right about one-half mile up. Most of the water in Hunters Canyon comes from a deep pool surrounded by hanging gardens of maidenhair fern. A dry fall and a small natural bridge lie above the pool. This pretty spot marks the hike's three-mile point and an elevation gain of 240 feet. At this point the hike becomes very brushy. To reach the trailhead from Moab, drive eight miles on Kane Creek Boulevard along the Colorado River and up Kane Creek Canyon. The road is asphalted where it fords Hunter Creek, but the asphalt is usually covered with dirt washed over it by the creek.

You can make a longer hike by going up Hunters Canyon and descending on Pritchett Canyon Road. The road crosses the normally dry creekbed just upstream from the deep pool. To bypass the dry fall above the pool, backtrack 300 feet down the canyon and rock-scramble up a short, steep slope—on your right heading upstream. At a junction just east of there, a jeep road along the north rim of Hunters Canyon meets Pritchett Canyon Road. Walk northeast one-half mile on Pritchett Canyon Road to a spur trail on the left leading to Pritchett Arch. Then continue 4.5 miles on Pritchett Canyon Road to Kane Creek Boulevard. This country is more open and desertlike than Hunters Canyon.

A 3.2-mile car shuttle or hike is needed to return to Hunters Canyon Trailhead.

Trails from Highway 279

The **Portal Overlook Trail** switchbacks up a slope, then follows a sloping sandstone ledge of the Kayenta Formation to an overlook. A panorama takes in the Colorado River, Moab Valley, Arches National Park, and the La Sal Mountains. The hike is 1.5 miles (one-way), with an elevation gain of 980 feet. This trail is a twin of the Moab Rim Trail across the river. Begin from the Jaycee Park Campground on the right, 3.8 miles from the turnoff at U.S. 191; mulberry trees shade the attractive spot. Expect to share this trail with many mountain bikers.

The 1.5-mile (one-way) **Corona Arch and Bowtie Arch Trail** leads across slickrock country to these impressive arches. You can't see them from the road, although a third arch—Pinto—is visible. The signed trailhead is on the right 10 miles from U.S. 191 (midway between mileposts 5 and 6); you'll see railroad tracks just beyond the trailhead. The trail climbs up from the parking area, crosses the tracks, and follows a bit of a jeep road and a small wash to an ancient gravel bar. Pinto (or Gold Bar) Arch stands to the left, although there's no trail to it. Follow cairns to Corona and Bowtie. Handrails and a ladder help in the few steep spots.

Despite being only a few hundred yards apart, each arch has a completely different character and history. Bowtie formed when a pothole in the cliffs above met a cave underneath. It used to be called Paul Bunyan's Potty before that name was appropriated for an arch in Canyonlands National Park. The hole is about 30 feet in diameter. Corona Arch, reminiscent of the larger Rainbow Bridge, eroded out of a sandstone fin. The graceful span is 140 feet long and 105 feet high. Both arches are composed of Navajo Sandstone. If you have time for only one hike in the Moab area, this one is especially recommended.

Trails off Highway 128

Negro Bill Canyon is one of the most popular hiking destinations in the Moab Area. The route follows a lively stream pooled by beavers and surrounded by abundant greenery and sheer canyon cliffs. The high point of the hike is Morning Glory Natural Bridge, the sixth-longest natural rock span in the country at 243 feet. The trailhead is on the right just after crossing a concrete bridge three miles from U.S. 191. A trail leads upcanyon, along the creek in some places, high on the banks in others.

To see Morning Glory Natural Bridge, head two miles up the main canyon to the second side canyon on the right, then follow a good side trail one-half mile up to the long, slender bridge. The spring and small pool underneath keep the air cool even in summer; ferns, columbines, and poison ivy grow here. The elevation gain is 330 feet. William "Nigger Bill" Granstaff was a mulatto who lived in the area from about 1877–1881. Modern sensibilities have changed his nickname to "Negro Bill."

Experienced hikers can continue up the main canyon about eight miles and rock-scramble (no trail) up the right side, then drop into Rill Creek, which leads to the North Fork of Mill Creek and into Moab. The total distance is about 16 miles one-way; you'll have to find your own way between canyons. The upper Negro Bill and Rill Canyons can also be reached from Sand Flats Road. The Moab and Castle Valley 15-minute and Moab 1:100,000 topographic maps cover the route. This would be a good overnight trip, although fast hikers have done it in a day. Expect to do some wading and rock-scrambling. Water from the creeks and springs is available in both canyon systems, but be sure to purify it first.

A car shuttle is necessary between the Negro Bill and Mill Creek trailheads. You can reach Mill Creek from the end of Powerhouse Lane on the east edge of Moab (see the Moab map), but *don't park here*. Vehicle break-ins are a serious problem. Either have someone meet or drop you off here or park closer to town near houses. A hike up the North Fork offers very pretty scenery. A deep pool and waterfall lie three-quarters of a mile upstream; follow Mill Creek upstream and take the left (north) fork. Negro Bill and Mill Creek Canyons are BLM wilderness study areas.

You can't miss the **Fisher Towers** as you drive Highway 128. These spires of dark red sandstone rise 900 feet above Professor Valley. You can hike around the base of these needle rocks on a trail accessed from the BLM picnic area. Titan, the third and highest rock tower, stands one mile from the picnic area; you'll find a viewpoint overlooking Onion Creek 1.1 miles farther along. Carry water for this moderately difficult hike.

Trails North of Moab, off Highway 191

The short **Mill Creek Dinosaur Trail,** with numbered stops, identifies the bones of dinosaurs who lived here 150 million years ago. You'll see fossilized wood, too. Pick up the brochure from the Moab Information Center or at the trailhead. From Moab, go 14 miles north on U.S. 191 (or four miles north of the Dead Horse Point turnoff) and turn left two miles on a dirt road, keeping right at a fork 1.1 miles in.

You'll find many other points of interest nearby. A copper mill and tailings dating from the late 1800s lie across the canyon. Halfway Stage Station ruins, where travelers once stopped on the Thompson-to-Moab run, are a short distance down the other road fork. Jeepers and mountain bikers can do a 13- to 14-mile loop to Monitor and Merimac Buttes (an information sign just in from U.S. 191 has a map and details).

BIKING

Moab is the West's most noted mountain-bike destination. In addition to the famed and challenging slickrock trails (slickrock is the exposed sandstone that composes much of the land's surface here) that wind through astonishing desert landscapes, cyclists can pedal through alpine meadows in the La Sal Mountains, while nearly abandoned four-wheel-drive tracks open up the backcountry to the adventurous. Be aware that the most famous trails, like the Slickrock Bike Trail, are not for beginning mountain bikers. You'll need to be fit, as well as expert in fat-tire technique to enjoy and, in some cases, make it all the way through these trails. Other trails are better matched to the skills of novices.

It's a good idea to read up on Moab-area trails before planning a trip here (heaps of books and pamphlets are available; see the Suggested Reading). You can also hire an outfitter to teach you about the special skills needed to mountain-bike in slickrock country, or join a guided tour. A good place to start is the Trails Illustrated *Bike Map #501* of the Moab area, which has mountain-bike routes color-coded according to difficulty. Or pick up a *Moab Area Mountain Bike Trails* map at the Moab Information Center.

Most people come to Moab to mountain-bike between mid-March and late May, and then again in fall, from mid-September to the end of October. Unless you are an early riser, summer is simply too hot for extended bike touring in these desert canyons. Be prepared for crowds, especially in mid-March, during spring break. In 1999, the Slickrock Trail alone attracted more than 150,000 riders.

If you've never biked on slickrock or in the desert, here are a few basic guidelines. Take care if venturing off a trail—it's a long way down some of the sheer cliff faces! A trail's steep slopes and sharp turns can be tricky, so a helmet is a must. Knee pads and riding gloves also protect from scrapes and bruises. Fat bald tires work best on the rock; partially deflated knobby tires do almost as well. Carry plenty of water—one gallon in summer, half a gallon in cooler months. Tiny plant associations, which live in fragile cryptobiotic soil, don't want you tearing through their homes; stay on the rock and avoid sand areas.

Dozens of trails thread the Moab area; some of the best and most noted are described as follows.

Slickrock Bike Trail

Undulating slickrock just east of Moab challenges even the best mountain-bike riders; this is not an area in which to learn mountain-bike skills. Originally, motorcyclists laid out this route, although now about 99 percent of riders rely on leg and lung power. The practice loop near the beginning allows first-time visitors a chance to get a feel for the slickrock. The "trail" consists only of painted white lines. Riders following it have less chance of getting lost or finding themselves in hazardous areas. Plan on about five hours to do the 9.6-mile main loop, and expect to do some walking.

Side trails lead to viewpoints overlooking

Moab, the Colorado River, and arms of Negro Bill Canyon. Panoramas of the surrounding canyon country and the La Sal Mountains add to the pleasure of biking.

To reach the trailhead from Main Street in Moab, turn east 0.4 mile on 300 South, turn right 0.1 mile on 400 East, turn left (east) 0.5 mile on Mill Creek Drive, then left 2.5 miles on Sand Flats Road.

The practice loop also makes an enjoyable 2.5-mile hike. Steep drop-offs into the tributaries of Negro Bill Canyon offer breathtaking views. It's best to walk off to the side of the white lines marking the route. You'll reach the practice loop one-quarter mile from the trailhead.

Kokopelli's Trail

Mountain bikers have linked together a series of back roads through the magical canyons of eastern Utah and western Colorado. You can start on Sand Flats Road in Moab and ride east to Castle Valley (21.1 miles), Fisher Valley (44.9 miles), Dewey Bridge (62.9 miles), Cisco Boat Landing (83.5 miles), Rabbit Valley (108 miles), and Loma (140 miles). Lots of optional routes and access points allow for many possibilities. Campsites along the trail have tables, grills, and outhouses. See the small book *The Utah-Colorado Mountain Bike Trail System, Route 1—Moab to Loma*, by Peggy Utesch, for detailed descriptions. An excellent brochure, *Kokopelli's Trail Map*, is available free at the Moab Information Center.

Gimini Bridges (Bull Canyon) Trail

This 14-mile trail passes through tremendous natural rock arches and the slickrock fins of the Wingate Formation, making this one of the most scenic of Moab-area trails; it's also one of the more moderate trails in terms of necessary skill and fitness. The trail begins 12.5 miles up Highway 313 (the access road to Dead Horse Point

> *Moab is the West's most noted mountain-bike destination. In addition to the famed and challenging slick-rock trails that wind through astonishing desert landscapes, cyclists can pedal through alpine meadows in the La Sal Mountains, while nearly abandoned four-wheel-drive tracks open up the backcountry to the adventurous.*

State Park), a total of 21 miles—all uphill—from Moab, so a shuttle or drop-off is a good idea.

Monitor and Merimack Trail

A good introduction to the varied terrains in the Moab area, the 13.2-mile Monitor and Merimack Trail also includes a trip to a dinosaur fossil bed. The trail climbs through open desert and up Tusher Canyon, then explores red sandstone towers and buttes across slickrock before dropping down Mill Canyon. At the base of the canyon, you can leave your bike and hike the Mill Canyon Dinosaur Trail before completing the loop to the parking area. Reach the trailhead by traveling 15 miles north of Moab on U.S. 191.

Guided Tours

Multiday tours vary in price depending on the difficulty of the trail and the degree of comfort involved. The charge for these trips is usually between $125–150 per day, including food and shuttles. Be sure to inquire whether rates include bike rental. **Dreamrides Mountainbike Tours,** 435/259-6419, website: www.dreamride.com, focuses on leading small, customized group tours. Most packages are three- or five-day tours at roughly $120 per day, accommodations extra. **Rim Tours,** 1233 S. U.S. 191, Moab, UT 84532, 800/626-7335 or 435/259-5223, website: www.rimtours.com, and **Kaibab Mountain Bike Tours,** operated out of Moab Cyclery at 391 S. Main, Moab, UT 84532, 800/451-1133 or 435/259-7423, website: www.kaibabtours.com, lead several half-day (around $60–75), full-day ($75–120), and multiday trips on mountain bikes; some of their tours combine cycling with rafting and/or hiking.

Western Spirit Cycling, P.O. Box 411, Moab, UT 84532, 435/259-8969 or 800/845-BIKE (845-2453), website: www.westernspirit.com, offers 25 different bicycle tours in the western

United States, with about one-third in Utah. Moab-area trips include the White Rim, the Maze, and the Kokopelli Trail.

Nichols Expeditions, 497 N. Main, 800/635-1792 or 435/259-7882, website: www.nicholsexpeditions.com, goes to all three districts of Canyonlands National Park and offers combination biking/kayaking trips that feature trips down the Colorado River.

Shuttle Services

Many mountain-bike trails are essentially one-way, and unless you want to cycle back the way you came, you'll need to arrange a shuttle service to pick you up and return you to Moab or to your vehicle. Also, if you don't have a vehicle or a bike rack, you will need to use a shuttle service to get to more distant trailheads. **Roadrunner Shuttle,** 435/259-9402, and **Acme Bike Shuttle,** 435/260-2534, both operate shuttle services; the usual fare is $12 per person. Both companies will also shuttle hikers to trailheads or pick up rafters. Roadrunner also serves as a taxi service for groups.

RAFTING AND BOAT TOURS

Even a visitor with a tight schedule can get out and enjoy the canyon country on rafts and other watercraft. Outfitters offer both laid-back and exhilarating day trips, which usually require little advance planning. Longer, multiday trips include gentle canoe paddles along the placid Green River and thrilling expeditions down the Colorado River.

You'll need to reserve well in advance for most of the longer trips because the BLM and the National Park Service limit the numbers of trips through the backcountry, and space, especially in high season, is at a premium. Experienced rafters can also plan their own unguided trips, although you'll need a permit for all areas except for the day-long Fisher Towers float upstream from Moab.

The rafting season runs Apr.–Sept., and jetboat tours run Feb.–Nov. Contact the Moab Information Center and the National Park Service office for lists or brochures of tour operators; independent river-runners can also visit the center for Colorado River infomation, although you

MOUNTAIN-BIKE ETIQUETTE

When mountain biking in the Moab area, don't expect an instant wilderness experience. Because of the popularity of the routes, the fragile desert environment is under quite a bit of stress, and you'll need to be considerate of the thousands of other people who share the trails. By keeping these rules in mind, you'll help keep Moab from being loved to death.

• *Ride only on open roads and trails.* Much of the desert consists of extremely fragile plant and animal ecosystems, and riding recklessly through cryptobiotic soils can destroy desert life and lead to erosion. If you pioneer a trail, chances are someone else will follow the tracks, leading to ever more destruction.

• *Protect and conserve scarce water sources.* Don't wash, swim, walk, or bike through potholes, and camp well away from isolated streams and waterholes. The addition of your insect repellent, body oils, suntan lotion, or lubrication from your bike can destroy the thronging life of

a pothole. Camping right next to a remote stream can deprive shy desert wildlife of life-giving water access.

• *Leave all Native American sites and artifacts as you find them.* First, it's against the law to disturb antiquities; second, it's stupid. Enjoy looking at rock art, but don't touch the images—body oils hasten their deterioration. Don't even think about taking pot shards, arrowheads, or artifacts from where you find them. Leave them for others to enjoy or for archaeologists to decipher.

• *Dispose of human solid waste thoughtfully.* The desert can't easily absorb human fecal matter. Desert soils have few microorganisms to break down organic material, and, simply put, mummified turds can last for years. Be sure to bury human solid waste at least 6–12 inches deep in sand and at least 200 feet away from streams and water sources. Pack out toilet paper in resealable bags.

need to pick up permits from the BLM or National Parks offices. Most river-runners obtain their permits by applying in January and February for a March drawing; the Moab Information Center BLM Ranger can advise on this process and provide the latest information about available cancellations.

Moab-Area Outfitters

Moab is full of river-trip companies, and most offer a variety of day and multiday trips; in addition, many will combine raft trips with biking, horseback riding, hiking, or four-wheel-drive excursions. Call for brochures or check out the many websites at www.discovermoab.com/tour.htm. Listed as follows are major outfitters that offer a variety of rafting options. Most of them offer trips to the major river destinations on the Colorado and Green Rivers as well as other rivers in Utah and the West. Inquire about special natural history or petroglyph tours, if these specialty trips interest you.

- **Western River Expeditions,** 800/453-7450 or 801/942-6669, website: www.westernriver.com
- **Tag-A-Long Expeditions,** 452 N. Main, 800/453-3292 or 435/259-8946, website: www.tagalong.com
- **Navtec Expeditions,** 321 N. Main (P.O. Box 1267, Moab, UT 84532), 800/833-1278 or 435/259-7983, website: www.navtec.com
- **Canyon Voyages,** 800/733-6007 or 435/259-6007, website: www.canyonvoyages.com
- **Adrift Adventures,** 378 N. Main, 800/874-4483 or 435/259-8594, website: www.adrift.net
- **Moki-Mac,** 800/284-7280 or 435/564-3361, website: www.mokimac.com
- **Sheri Griffith Expeditions,** 800/332-2439 or 503/259-8229, website: www.griffithexp.com

Moab Rafting and Kayaking Destinations

For most of the following, full-day rates include lunch and beverages, while part-day trips include just lemonade and soft drinks. On overnight trips, you will sleep in tents in backcountry campgrounds.

The **Colorado River** offers several exciting options. The most popular day-run near Moab starts upstream on the Colorado River near Fisher Towers and bounces through several moderate rapids on the way back to town. Full-day raft trips from Fisher Towers to near Moab generally cost $45–50 per person. Half-day trips run over much the same stretch of river (no lunch, though) and cost around $35 per adult.

For a more adventurous rafting day trip, the Colorado's rugged **Westwater Canyon** offers lots of white water and several class III–IV rapids near the Utah–Colorado border. These long day trips are more expensive, typically $120–135 a day. The Westwater Canyon is also often offered as part of multiday adventure packages. The **Dolores River** joins the Colorado about two miles upstream from Dewey Bridge, near the Colorado border. The Dolores River offers exciting white water in a narrow canyon during the spring runoff; the season is short, though, and the river is too low to run by mid-June. With plenty of Class III and IV rapids, this trip usually takes three days and costs around $500 per person.

The **Cataract Canyon** section of the Colorado River, which begins south of the river's confluence with the Green River and extends to the backwater of Lake Powell, usually requires four days of rafting to complete. This is the wildest white water in the Moab area, with big, boiling Class III and IV rapids. Costs range between $550–750, depending on what kind of craft, the number of days, and whether you fly, hike, or drive out at the end of the trip.

The **Green River** also offers rafting (and canoeing, see following section) opportunities, although they are milder than the Colorado. Trips on the Green make good family outings. Most trips require five days, leaving from the town of Green River and taking out at Mineral Bottom, just above the Canyonlands National Park boundary. Highlights of the Green River include Labyrinth Canyon and Bowknot Bend. Costs are usually between $500–600 for a five-day trip.

Rafting on Your Own

The Fisher Towers section of the Colorado is gentle enough for amateur rafters to negotiate on their own. Rent a raft or kayak from one of the rafting outfitters listed previously. A popular one-day raft trip with mild rapids begins from the Hittle Bottom Recreation Site, 23.5 miles up Highway 128 near Fisher Towers and ends 14 river miles downstream at Take-Out Beach, 10.3 miles up Highway 128 from U.S. 191. You can rent rafts and the mandatory life jackets in Moab, and you won't need a permit on this section of river.

Experienced white-water rafters with permits can put in at the BLM's Westwater Ranger Station in Utah or at the Loma boat launch in Colorado. A start at Loma adds a day or two to the trip and the sights of Horsethief and Ruby Canyons. Normal takeout is at Cisco, although it's possible to continue 16 miles on slow-moving water through open country to Dewey Bridge.

Daily raft rentals begin at $85 or so; kayaks rent for $35.

Canoe Trips

Canoeists can also sample the calm waters of the Green River on multiday excursions with **Red River Canoe Company,** 800/753-8216, website: www.redrivercanoe.com. They run scheduled trips to four sections of the river. Red River Canoe also offers trips to calmer stretches of the Colorado and Delores rivers. The company also conducts white-water canoe workshops on the Colorado's Professor Valley and combination canoe and mountain-bike trips. Cost ranges from $110–140 per person per day.

Jetboat Tours

Guided jetboat excursions through Canyonlands National Park start at around $50 for a half-day trip. **Tex's Riverways,** 435/259-5101, website: www.texsriverways.com, offers trips of various lengths on the Green and Colorado Rivers. **Tag-A-Long Expeditions,** and **Adrift Adventures,** see previous list for contact information, both offer half-day trips and full-day combination jetboat/jeep excursions.

Motorboat Tours

Canyonlands by Night tours leave at sunset in an open motorboat and go several miles upstream on the Colorado River; a guide points out canyon features. The sound and light show begins on the way back; music and historic narration accompany the play of lights on canyon walls. Cost is $26 adults, $16 ages 4–12; boats run Apr.–mid-Oct. Dinner cruises are available. **Canyonlands by Day** trips go downriver into the Colorado River Canyon near Dead Horse Point. Of the two trips offered, one goes 60 miles downstream ($58 adults, $45 ages 4–12) and the other travels 30 miles ($38 adults, $28 ages 4–12). Tours operate Mar.–Oct.; reservations are a good idea because the boat fills up fast. Trips depart from the Spanish mission–style office just north of Moab, across the Colorado River, 435/259-5261, website: www.canyonlandsbynight.com.

FOUR-WHEEL TOURING

Road tours offer visitors a special opportunity to view unique canyonland arches and spires, indigenous rock art, and wildlife. An interpretive brochure at the Moab Information Center outlines the Moab Area Rock Art Auto Tour, which routes motorists to petroglyphs tucked away behind golf courses and ranches. You might also pick up a map of Moab-area four-wheel-drive trails: four rugged, 15- to 54-mile loop routes through the desert, which take from 2.5–4 hours to drive. Those who left their trusty four-by-four and off-road driving skills at home can take an off-road jeep tour through a private operator. Both **Tag-A-Long Tours,** 452 N. Main, Moab, UT 84532, 800/453-3292 or 435/259-8946, website: www.tagalong.com, and **Adrift Adventures,** 378 N. Main (P.O. Box 577, Moab, UT 84532), 800/874-4483 or 435/259-8594, website: www.adrift.net, have half-day (around $50) and full-day jeep tours (around $90) with combination jetboat or hiking options. Full-day tours include lunch.

Lin Ottinger's Tours, 600 N. Main, Moab, UT 84532, 435/259-7312, offers backcountry driving trips from mid-April to mid-October. Lin has been poking around the canyons of this area since the uranium boom of the 1950s, and he knows the best places; frequent stops allow plenty of time to walk around for a look at Indian art and scenic and geologic features. Half-day trips are $65, full-day $80.

You can also rent four-by-fours from **Farabee 4X4 Adventures,** 401 N. Main, 800/806-5337 or 435/259-7494, or **Slick Rock Jeep Rental,** 284 N. Main, 435/259-5678.

AIR TOURS

You'll have a bird's-eye view of southeastern Utah's incredible landscape from Moab or Green River Airport with **Redtail Aviation,** P.O. Box 515, Moab, UT 84532, 435/259-7421 (Moab), or 800/842-9251. Flights include Arches National Park ($53) and Canyonlands National Park (Needles, Island in the Sky, and Maze Districts; $99). Longer tours are available, too. Rates are based on two or more persons. Flights operate all year. **Slickrock Air Guides,** 2231 S. U.S. 191, Moab, UT 84532, 435/259-6216 or 866/259-1626, website: www.slickrockairguides.com, offers a one-hour tour over the Canyonlands area for $99 per person, and $295 for 3.5 hours over Canyonlands, Natural Bridges, Lake Powell, and the Capitol Reef area with a stop for lunch at the Marble Canyon Lodge.

Entertainment and Events

NIGHTLIFE

A lot of Moab's nightlife focuses on Moab's two brewpubs, the rowdy and well-loved **Eddie Mc-Stiff's,** 57 S. Main in Western Plaza, 435/259-BEER (435/259-2337), and the newer and posher **Moab Brewery,** 686 S. Main St., 435/259-6333. For live music, try the **Outlaw Saloon,** 44 W. 200 North, 435/259-2654, the **Club Río,** 100 W. Center St., 435/259-6666, or the **Sportsman's Lounge,** 1991 S. Hwy. 191, 435/259-9972.

For a selection of movies, head for **Slickrock Cinemas,** 580 Kane Creek Blvd., 435/259-4441.

EVENTS

To find out about local happenings, contact the Moab Information Center, 435/259-8825. Major annual events include the **Moab Half Marathon** in late **March** (third Sat.). **April** brings the **Cannondale Cup Bicycle Race.**

Over Memorial Day weekend in **May** is the **Green River to Moab Friendship Cruise** on the Green and Colorado Rivers.

June kicks up dust at the fairgrounds with two rodeos: the professional **P.R.C.A. Rodeo** early in the month, and the **Canyonlands Rodeo,** with rodeo, parade, dance, horse racing, and 4-H gymkhana toward the end of the month.

August means it's time for the **Grand County Fair,** with agricultural displays, crafts, and arts judging. The **Moab Music Festival** keeps getting larger, with several weekends of music by jazz, bluegrass, and other groups, plus outdoor chamber music.

SHOPPING

Main Street, between 200 North and 200 South has nearly a dozen galleries and gift shops with Native art and other gifts. **Perpendicular to the Wind Gallery,** 37 E. Center, and **Overlook Gallery,** 83 E. Center, feature local artists and photographers.

Back of Beyond Books, 83 N. Main, 435/259-5154, features an excellent selection of regional books and maps. A good selection of books and maps is also sold at **Times Independent Maps,** 5 E. Center St., 435/259-7525.

MOAB

Accommodations

Moab has been a tourist destination for generations and offers a wide variety of lodging choices, ranging from older motels to new upscale resorts. Luckily, lodgings are relatively inexpensive. The only time when Moab isn't busy is in the dead of winter, from Nov.–Feb. At all other times, be sure to make reservations well in advance.

If you're having trouble finding a room, **Moab/Canyonlands Central Reservations,** 435/259-5125, 800/748-4386, or 800/505-5343, website: www.moabutahlodging.com/reservations, can make bookings at 85 percent of Moab's accommodations, which include area bed-and-breakfasts, motels, condos, cabins, private houses, and luxury vacation homes. Summer rates are shown; those in winter typically drop 40 percent.

LESS THAN $50

The **Lazy Lizard Hostel,** 1213 S. U.S. 191, 435/259-6057, costs just $8 per night for simple dorm-style accommodations. You won't need a hostel card, and all guests share access to a hot tub, kitchen, barbecue, coin-operated laundry, and common room with cable TV. Camping ($6 per person), showers for nonguests ($2), and private rooms ($24 double occupancy) are offered, too. New log cabins here can sleep two ($30) to four ($45) people. The Lazy Lizard sits one mile south behind A-1 Storage; the turnoff is about 200 yards south of Moab Lanes.

For just a few more dollars, you can stay at the vintage **Hotel Off Center,** 96 E. Center, 800/237-4685 or 435/259-4244, which has basic rooms (bath down the hall) or bunks in a dorm.

$50–75

The **Sunset Motel,** 41 W. 100 North, 800/421-5614 or 435/259-5191, offers kitchenettes, a pool, and a hot tub, and pets are okay. The motel also offers a fully furnished apartment and a 12-sleeper with two bathrooms, four bedrooms, and a kitchen. The **Red Rock Lodge Motel,** 51 N. 100 West, 435/259-5431, has rooms with re-

frigerators and coffee makers; there's a hot tub and locked bicycle storage facilities. At the **Virginian Motel,** 70 E. 200 South, 800/261-2063 or 435/259-5951, more than half the rooms have kitchenettes; pets are okay.

The **Red Stone Inn,** 535 S. Main St., 800/772-1972 or 435/259-3500, is a newer, one-story motel; most rooms have efficiency kitchens. Other amenities include a bicycle maintenance area, covered patio with gas barbecue grill, and guest laundry. Pets are okay in smoking rooms only with a $5-per-night fee. The **Days Inn,** 426 N. Main, 800/329-7466 or 435/259-4468, has a pool. The **Big Horn Lodge,** 550 S. Main, 800/325-6171 or 435/259-6171, has a pool and a restaurant.

$75–100

The local **Super 8 Motel,** 889 N. Main, 800/800-8000 or 435/259-8868, has a pool and a hot tub. The **Landmark Motel,** located right in the center of Moab at 168 N. Main, 800/441-6147 or 435/259-6147, has a pool and a small waterslide, a hot tub, a guest laundry room, and three family units. Right across the street, the **Bowen Motel,** 169 N. Main, 800/874-5439 or 435/259-7132, is a pleasant, homey motel with an outdoor pool and free continental breakfast.

The **Best Western Canyonlands Inn,** 16 S. Main, 800/528-1234 or 435/259-2300, is also in the heart of Moab, with suites, a pool, a fitness room and spa, a restaurant, and a bike storage area.

Canyon Country Bed & Breakfast, 590 N. 500 West, 800/350-5262 or 435/259-5262, is a large Southwestern-style ranch home just north of downtown. The four guest rooms have both private and shared baths; guests share a hot tub and can rent kayaks and mountain bikes.

If you want seclusion and a wilderness setting, stay at the **Castle Valley Inn B&B,** located in Castle Valley, 18 miles east of Moab, 888/272-8181 or 435/259-7830, website: www.castlevalleyinn.com. The inn adjoins a wildlife refuge in a stunning landscape of red-rock mesas and needle-pointed buttes. You can stay in one of the main house's five guest rooms or in one of the three bungalows with kitchens. For an additional fee and with advance notice, dinner is available for guests. Facilities include a hot tub; no children or pets are allowed; two-night minimum is required on weekends. To reach Castle Valley Inn, follow Highway 128 east from Moab for 16 miles and turn south 2.3 miles toward Castle Valley. Open Feb. 15–Dec. 15.

The three two-bedroom cottages that compose **Desert Gardens,** 123–127 W. 200 North, 800/505-5343 or 435/259-5125, each contain a full kitchen, bath, and living room. The cottages sit in a large shaded yard with access to a hot tub, barbecue, and nicely maintained gardens. Two-night minimum stay is required.

$100–125

The **Best Western Greenwell Motel,** 105 S. Main, 800/528-1234 or 435/259-6151, has a pool, an on-premises restaurant, and some kitchenettes. The **Ramada Inn,** 182 S. Main, 888/989-1988 or 435/259-7141, has nicely appointed rooms (some with balconies) and a pool, spa, and facilities for small meetings. South of downtown is the **Comfort Suites,** 800 S. Main, 800/228-5150 or 435/259-5252, an all-suites motel with large, nicely furnished rooms complete with microwaves and refrigerators. Facilities include an indoor pool, a spa, an exercise room, locked bike storage, and a guest laundry room.

One of the newest and most unique-looking accommodations in Moab is the **Gonzo Inn,** 100 W. 200 South, 800/791-4044 or 435/259-2515. With a look somewhere between an adobe inn and a postmodern warehouse, the Gonzo doesn't try to appear anything but young and hip. Expect large rooms with Day-Glo colors, a pool, and a friendly welcome.

Located in an old residential area, the **Sunflower Hill Bed & Breakfast,** 185 N. 300 East, 800/662-2786 or 435/259-2974, website: www .sunflowerhill.com, offers high-quality lodgings in one of Moab's original farmhouses and in a newly built garden cottage with patios and bal-

conies. All 12 rooms have private baths, air conditioning, and queen-size beds; there are also two suites. Guests share access to an outdoor hot tub, bike storage, patios, and large gardens. Children are welcome from age eight; open year-round.

If you're looking for a bit more room or a longer-term stay, consider the **Cedar Breaks Condos,** 10 S. 400 East, 888/272-8181 or 435/259-7830, with six two-bedroom units with living rooms and full kitchens. Daily maid service is provided and breakfast food is stocked daily in the refrigerator.

CAMPGROUNDS

Spanish Trail RV Park, 2980 S. U.S. 191, 800/787-2751 or 435/259-2411, has showers, laundry, and restrooms and is open year-round. Sites range from $19 for tents to $24 for hookups. **Canyonlands Campground,** 555 S. Main St., 800/522-6848 or 435/259-6848, is open all year; it has showers, a laundry room, a store, and a pool; sites run $18–23. **Slickrock Campground,** one mile north of Moab at 1301 1/2 N. U.S. 191, 800/448-8873 or 435/259-7660, remains open year-round; it has showers, a store, an outdoor café, a pool, and cabins with air conditioning and heat; $18 tents or RVs without hookups, $23 with basic hookup, and $30 for cabins.

Moab Valley RV & Campark, two miles north of Moab at 1773 N. U.S. 191 (opposite the turnoff for Highway 128), 435/259-4469, is also open all year; it has showers; sites for tents or RVs start at $22. **Moab KOA,** four miles south of Moab at 3225 S. U.S. 191, 800/562-0372 or 435/259-6682, is open Mar.–Nov.; it has showers, a laundry room, a store, mini-golf, and a pool; $26 tents or RVs without hookups, $29 with hookups; kamping kabins go for $42.

The BLM now requires that all camping along the Colorado River (accessible by road above and below Moab), Kane Creek, and near the Moab Slickrock Bike Trail *must* be in developed designated sites (with toilets) or undeveloped designated sites (your own porta-potty required; no restrooms or fee). The following four camping areas are available along Highway 128 for a $10 fee. From the U.S. 191/Highway 128 junction,

MOAB

the lodge at the Sorrel River Ranch

you'll find Jay Cee Park at 4.2 miles, Hal Canyon at 6.6 miles, Oak Grove at 6.9 miles, and Big Bend Recreation Site at 7.4 miles. Contact the Moab Information Center for locations of additional campgrounds. You'll also find campgrounds farther out at Arches and Canyonlands National Parks, Dead Horse Point State Park, La Sal Mountains, and Canyon Rims Recreation Area.

GUEST RANCHES

A short drive from Moab along the Colorado River's red-rock canyon is the region's premium luxury guest ranch, the **Sorrel River Ranch,** 17 miles northeast of Moab on Highway 128, 435/259-4642 or 877/359-2715, website: www.sorrelriver.com. The ranch sits on 240 acres in some of the most dramatic landscapes in the Moab area—located just across the river from Arches National Park and beneath the soaring mesas of Castle Valley. Accommodations are in a series of beautifully furnished wooden lodges, all tastefully fitted with Old West–style furniture. All units have kitchenettes and a patio with porch swing or back deck overlooking the river (some rooms have both). Horseback rides are offered into the *arroyos* (dry river beds) behind the ranch; kayaks and bicycles can be rented. The ranch's restaurant, the River Grill Restaurant, has some of the best views in Utah and an adventurous menu that ranges from steaks to grilled duck breast.

Food

Moab has the best restaurants in all of southern Utah; no matter what else the recreational craze has produced, it has certainly improved the food. Several Moab-area restaurants are closed for annual vacation in February.

BREAKFAST AND LIGHT MEALS

Start the day at **Breakfast at Tiffany's,** 90 E. Center, 435/259-2553, a happening coffee shop with fresh pastries and a deli. For a traditional breakfast, try the **Jailhouse Cafe,** 101 N. Main St., 435/259-3900. Another favorite is the **Mondo Café,** 59 S. Main St., in McStiff's Plaza, 435/259-5551; they serve fresh baked goods, espresso drinks, and sandwiches for lunch. The **Moab Diner & Ice Cream Shoppe,** 189 S. Main St., 435/259-4006, is a good place to know about—you'll find the breakfasts old-fashioned and abundant, a Southwestern green chili edge to the food, and the best ice cream in town; open for breakfast, lunch, and dinner. **EclectiCafe,** 352 N. Main, 435/259-6896, has a good selection of organic and vegetarian dishes, mostly with ethnic roots. Open for three meals daily.

CASUAL DINING

Unless otherwise noted, each of the following establishments has a full liquor license. Entrées range from $8–15.

For light meals and snacks, try the **Poplar Place Pub & Eatery,** Main and 100 North, 435/259-6018, which serves pizza, pasta, and deli sandwiches in a pub atmosphere; open daily for lunch and dinner. The **Slick Rock Cafe,** 5 N. Main, 435/259-8004, is another versatile restaurant. Open for breakfast, lunch, and dinner in a historic building downtown, the Slick Rock serves up-to-date food at reasonable prices, all with a spicy Southwestern or Caribbean kick.

The **Rio Colorado Restaurant,** 100 W. Center St., 435/259-6666, can fill the bill for almost any appetite—sandwiches, Mexican food, steak, seafood, chicken, pasta, and salads; open Sat. and Sun. for breakfast and daily for lunch and dinner. Moab's best Mexican restaurant is **Bandito's Grill,** 467 N. Main, 435/259-3894, with a large selection of excellent house specialties and outdoor seating.

Only one restaurant in town serves Asian food: the **Szechuan Restaurant,** 105 S. Main, 435/259-8984. Fortunately, the food is good, spicy, and inexpensive. **Fat City Smokehouse,** 36 S. 100 West, 435/259-4302, specializes in Texas-style pit barbecue for lunch and dinner; open Mon.–Sat. Beer only.

For a Western night out, consider **Bar M Chuckwagon Supper,** located on the banks of Mill Creek at 541 S. Mulberry Ln., just southeast of town, 435/259-2276. Tasty cowboy-style cooking is served up from chuck wagons, followed by a variety of live Western entertainment; open for dinner only (call to check on times) Apr.–Oct. Mon.–Sat.; beer only. The meal plus entertainment costs $20 for everyone 11 years and older, $10 for younger children.

BREWPUBS

After a hot day out on the trail, who can blame you for thinking about a cold brew and a good meal at a brewpub? Luckily, Moab has two excellent pubs to fill the bill. **Eddie McStiff's,** 57 S. Main in Western Plaza, 435/259-BEER (435/259-2337), was the first brewpub in Moab and is an extremely popular place to sip a cool one or eat a hearty meal of pasta, pizza, steaks, salads, chicken, and Mexican food. The pub is a convivial place to meet like-minded travelers; in good weather there's seating in a nice courtyard. You'll have to try hard not to have fun here; open daily for lunch and dinner.

There's more good beer and maybe better food at the **Moab Brewery,** 686 S. Main St., 435/259-6333, although this more recent restaurant has yet to attract the kind of scene you'll find at Eddie McStiff's. The atmosphere is light and airy, and the food is good—steaks, sandwiches, burgers, and a wide selection of salads. There's deck seating when weather permits.

MOAB

© W.C. MCRAE

In Moab, bicycles are welcome at the local brewpub.

FINE DINING

The **Ranch House** serves elegant meals in an 1896 pioneer house at 1266 N. U.S. 191 on the north edge of town, 435/259-5753; specialties are regional Mountain West cuisine. Expect to pay $20–27 for entrées. Open daily for dinner; reservations recommended. The **Sunset Grill,** 900 N. U.S. 191, 435/259-7146, is located in uranium king Charlie Steen's mansion situated high above Moab, with "million-dollar" sweeping views of the valley. Chefs offer steaks, fresh seafood, and a selection of modern pasta dishes ($17–28). Open Mon.–Sat. for dinner.

Buck's Grill House, 1393 N. U.S. 191, 435/259-5201, is a steakhouse with a difference. The restaurant features a pleasant Western atmosphere, and the food seems familiar enough— steaks, prime rib, roast chicken, seafood, grilled pork loin—but the quality of the preparation and the side dishes makes the difference. The butter spice rub on the cowboy steaks or prime rib is excellent. Entrées range between $12–23.

The **River Grill** at Sorrel River Ranch, 17 miles northeast of Moab on Highway 128, has a lovely dining room that overlooks spires of red rock and the dramatic cliffs of the Colorado River. The scenery is hard to top, and the food is excellent, with a focus on prime beef and Continental specialties (the chef is French-born). Fresh fish and seafood are flown in daily and forms the basis for nightly specials.

Moab has two restaurants that feature the most up-to-the-moment cuisine. The **Center Cafe,** a long-time Moab favorite for its international menu and excellent service, has moved to 60 N. 100 West, 435/259-4295. The menu is eclectic, with a wide selection of pasta dishes (including several vegetarian choices) and other inventive fare that feature Continental influences and free-range and organic ingredients ($15–28). At its new location, the Center Café is now open for lunch and dinner Tues.–Sun. The new location also features a market for homemade breads, cheeses, and gourmet takeout.

The **Desert Bistro,** 92 Center St., 435/259-0756, is Moab's newest restaurant, featuring sophisticated cuisine in a spare but comfortable dining room. The focus of the seasonal menu is on local meats and game plus fresh fish and seafood cooked with Rocky Mountain regional aplomb ($14–23). Highly recommended.

Information and Services

INFORMATION

The **Moab Information Center,** Main and Center, 435/259-8825 or 800/635-MOAB (635-6622), is the place to start for nearly all local and area information. The National Park Service, the BLM, the U.S. Forest Service, the Grand County Travel Council, and the Canyonlands Natural History Association all are represented in this multiagency facility. Visitors needing help from any of these agencies should start at the information center rather than at the agency offices. Free literature is available, and a large selection of books and maps are sold. Especially useful is the free *Southeastern Utah Travel Guide,* which describes features of and opportunities for recreation in the Arches and Canyonlands National Parks. Included are comprehensive lists of tour operators, places to rent and purchase recreation equipment, and campgrounds. The office is open daily from 8 A.M.–9 P.M. in summer (reduced hours the rest of the year). There are several Moab-related travel websites; probably the best is at www.discovermoab.com.

The **National Park Service office** in Moab, 2282 Southwest Resource Blvd., Moab, UT 84532 (three miles south of downtown), 435/259-7164, is headquarters for Canyonlands and Arches National Parks and Natural Bridges National Monument. Open Mon.–Fri. 8 A.M.–4:30 P.M., the **Manti-La Sal National Forest office** is also at 2282 Southwest Resource Blvd., 435/259-7155; open Mon.–Fri. 8 A.M.–noon and 12:30–4:30 P.M. The **BLM District office** is at 82 E. Dogwood on the south side of town behind Comfort Suites; mailing address is P.O. Box 970, Moab, UT 84532; 435/259-8193 (general information); open Mon.–Fri. 7:45 A.M.–4:30 P.M. Some land-use maps are sold; this is where you pick up your river-running permits.

SERVICES

The **Grand County Public Library,** 25 S. 100 East (next to the Dan O'Laurie Museum), 435/259-5421, is a good place for local history and general reading; open Mon.–Thurs. 1–9 P.M., Fri. 1–5 P.M., and Sat. 10 A.M.–2 P.M. The library is for local residents, but others can use the services on a daily basis.

The **post office** is downtown at 50 E. 100 North, 435/259-7427. **Allen Memorial Hospital** provides medical care at 719 W. 400 North, 435/259-7191. For **emergencies** (ambulance, sheriff, police, or fire), dial 911.

PARKS AND RECREATION

The **city park,** 181 W. 400 North, 435/259-8226, has shaded picnic tables, a playground, and an outdoor swimming pool. **Lions Park** offers picnicking along the Colorado River two miles north of town. **Rotary Park,** on Mill Creek Drive, is family-oriented and has lots of activities for kids. **Moab Arts and Recreation,** 111 E. 100 North, 435/259-6272, sponsors year-round activities for kids; you don't need to be a resident to take part.

Moab Golf Club, 2705 S. East Bench Rd., 435/259-6488, features an 18-hole course, a driving range, and a pro shop. Go south five miles on U.S. 191, turn left two miles on Spanish Trails Road, then right one-quarter mile on Murphy Lane.

TRANSPORTATION

There are currently no commercial flights between Moab and Salt Lake City. The only commercial flights to Moab are to and from Denver and Phoenix on Great Lakes Airlines, 800/554-5111, which is a regional partner of United Airlines. The Moab/Canyonlands Airfield is 16 miles north of Moab on Highway 191.

The only other public transport option to Moab is the ARK Shuttle run by Bighorn Express, 888/655-7433, website: www.bighornexpress.com, which makes one minibus run daily between Moab and Salt Lake City. Advance reservations are required. One-way fare is $50.

MOAB

For rental cars, contact **Certified Ford,** 500 S. Main, 435/529-6107, or **Thrifty,** 400 N. Main, 435/259-7317, which has an office at the Moab airport. **Taxi** service includes shuttles for bicyclists and river-runners, 435/259-TAXI (435-259-8294).

Scenic Drives and Excursions from Moab

Each of the following routes is at least partly accessible to standard low-clearance highway vehicles. If you have a four-wheel-drive vehicle, you'll have the option of additional, off-road exploring.

You'll find detailed travel information on these and other places in the books and separate maps by F.A. Barnes, *Canyon Country Off-Road Vehicle Trails: Island Area* (north of Canyonlands National Park) and *Canyon Country Off-Road Vehicle Trails: Arches & La Sals Areas* (around Arches National Park). The BLM takes care of nearly all of this land; staff in the Moab offices may know current road and trail conditions.

UTAH SCENIC BYWAY 279

Utah 279 goes downstream through the Colorado River Canyon on the other side of the river from Moab. Pavement extends 16 miles past fine views, prehistoric rock art, arches, and hiking trails. A potash plant marks the end of the highway; a rough dirt road continues to Canyonlands National Park. From Moab, head north 3.5 miles on U.S. 191, then turn left on Highway 279. The highway enters the canyon at the Portal, 2.7 miles from the turnoff. Towering sandstone cliffs rise on the right, and the Colorado River drifts along just below on the left.

Stop at a signed pullout on the left 0.6 mile past the canyon entrance to see **Indian Ruins Viewpoint,** a small prehistoric Indian ruin tucked under a ledge across the river. The stone structure was probably used for food storage.

Groups of **petroglyphs** cover cliffs along the highway 5.2 miles from U.S. 191. These may not be signed; they are 0.7 mile beyond Milepost 11. Look across the river to see The Fickle Finger of Fate among the sandstone fins of Behind the Rocks. A petroglyph of a bear is 0.2 mile farther down the highway. Archaeologists think that Fremonts and the later Ute Indians did most of the artwork in this area.

A signed pullout on the right 6.2 miles from U.S. 191 points out **dinosaur tracks** and petroglyphs visible on rocks above. Sighting tubes help locate the features. It's possible to hike up the steep hillside for a closer look.

The aptly named **Jug Handle Arch,** with an opening 46 feet high and three feet wide, is close to the road on the right, 13.6 miles from U.S. 191. Ahead the canyon opens up. Underground pressures of salt and potash have folded the rock layers into an anticline.

At the **Moab Salt Plant,** mining operations inject water underground to dissolve the potash and other chemicals, then pump the solution to evaporation ponds. The ponds are dyed blue to hasten evaporation, which takes about a year. You can see these colorful solutions from Dead Horse Point and Anticline Overlook on the canyon rims.

High-clearance vehicles can continue on the unpaved road beyond the plant. The road passes through varied canyon country, with views overlooking the Colorado River. At a road junction in Canyonlands National Park (Island in the Sky District), you have a choice of turning left for the 100-mile White Rim Trail (four-wheel drive only past Musselman Arch), continuing up the steep switchbacks of the Shafer Trail Road (four-wheel drive recommended) to the paved park road, or returning the way you came.

UTAH SCENIC BYWAY 128

Utah 128 turns northeast from U.S. 191 just south of the Colorado River Bridge, two miles north of Moab. This exceptionally scenic canyon route follows the Colorado for 30 miles upstream before crossing at Dewey Bridge and turning north to I-70. The entire highway is paved.

SEGO CANYON ROCK ART

If you approach Moab along I-70, consider a sidetrip to one of premier rock art galleries in Utah, just a short distance from the freeway junction with US 191 to Moab. Sego Canyon is just three miles passed Thompson, reached by taking exit 185 off I-70. Drive through the slumbering little town, and continue up the canyon behind town (BLM signs also point the way). A side road leads to a parking area when the canyon walls close in. Sego Canyon is a showcase of prehistoric rock art—it preserves rock drawings and images that are thousands of years old. The Barrier Canyon Style drawings may be 8,000 years old; the more recent Fremont Style images were created in the last thousand years. Compared to these ancient pictures, the Ute etchings are relatively recent; experts speculate that they may have been drawn in the 1800s, when Ute villages still lined Sego Canyon. Interestingly, the newer petroglyphs and pictographs are more representational than the older ones. The ancient Barrier Canyon figures are typically horned ghost-like beings that look like aliens from early Hollywood sci-fi thrillers. The Fremont Style images depict stylized human figures made from geometric shapes; the crudest figures are the most recent. The Ute images are of buffaloes and hunters on horseback.

© W.C. MCRAE

Sego Canyon's rock art ranges from the ghostly and symbolic (Barrier Canyon era) to the abstract (from the later Fremont and Ute periods).

In 1986, a new bridge replaced the narrow Dewey suspension bridge that once caused white knuckles on drivers of large vehicles. The Lions Park picnic area at the turnoff from U.S. 191 is a pleasant stopping place. Big Bend Recreation Site is another good spot 7.5 miles up Highway 128.

A network of highly scenic jeep roads branches off Castle Valley and Onion Creek roads into side canyons and the **La Sal Mountains Loop Road,** described in the book and separate map *Canyon Country Off-Road Vehicle Trails: Arches & La Sals Areas,* by F.A. Barnes. This paved scenic road goes through Castle Valley, climbs high into the La Sals, then loops back to Moab. Allow at least three hours to drive the 62-mile loop. The turnoff from Highway 128 is 15.5 miles up from U.S. 191.

A graded county road, **Onion Creek Road,** turns southeast off the highway 20 miles from U.S. 191 and heads up Onion Creek, crossing it many times. *Avoid this route if storms threaten.* The unpleasant-smelling creek contains poisonous arsenic and selenium. Colorful rock formations of dark red sandstone line the creek, and you'll cross an upthrusted block of crystalline gypsum. After about eight miles, the road climbs steeply out of Onion Creek to upper Fisher Valley and a junction with Kokopelli's Trail, which follows a jeep road over this part of its route.

The Gothic spires of **Fisher Towers** soar as high as 900 feet above Professor Valley. The BLM has a picnic area nearby and a hiking trail that skirts the base of the three main towers; Titan, the tallest, is the third one.

In 1962, three climbers from Colorado made the first ascent of Titan Tower. The almost vertical rock faces, overhanging bulges, and sections of rotten rock made for an exhausting 3.5 days of climbing (the party descended to the base for two of the nights). Their final descent from the summit took only six hours. See the November 1962 issue of *National Geographic* magazine for the story and photos. Supposedly, the name Fisher is not that of a

MOAB

pioneer, but a corruption of the geologic term *fissure* (a narrow crack). An unpaved road turns southeast off Highway 128 near Milepost 21 (21 miles from U.S. 191) and continues two miles to the picnic area.

The modern two-lane concrete **Dewey Bridge** has replaced the picturesque wood-and-steel suspension bridge built in 1916. Here, the BLM has built the Dewey Bridge Recreation Site with a picnic area, trailhead, boat launch, and a small campground. Bicyclists and hikers can still use the old bridge; an interpretive sign explains its history. Drivers can continue on the highway to I-70 through rolling hills nearly devoid of vegetation.

Upstream from Dewey Bridge are the wild rapids of **Westwater Canyon.** The Colorado River cut this narrow gorge into dark metamorphic rock. You can raft or kayak down the river in one day or a more leisurely two days. Camping is limited to a single night. Unlike most desert rivers, this section of the Colorado also offers good river-running at low water levels in late summer and autumn. Westwater Canyon's inner gorge, where boaters face their greatest challenge, is only about 3.5 miles long; however, you can enjoy scenic sandstone canyons both upstream and downstream.

The bumpy four-wheel-drive route, the **Top-of-the-World Road,** climbs to an overlook with outstanding views of Fisher Towers, Fisher Valley, Onion Creek, and beyond. Turn right (east) on the Entrada Bluffs Road (just before crossing Dewey Bridge). After 5.5 miles, keep straight on a dirt road when the main road curves left, then immediately turn right (south) and go uphill 100 yards through a gate (gateposts are railroad ties) and continue about 4.5 miles on the Top-of-the-World Road to the rim. Elevation here is 6,800 feet, nearly 3,000 feet higher than the Colorado River.

KANE CREEK SCENIC DRIVE

This road heads downstream along the Colorado River on the same side as Moab. The four miles through the Colorado River Canyon are paved, followed by six miles of good dirt road through Kane Springs Canyon. This route also leads to

several hiking trails (see previous section). People with high-clearance vehicles or mountain bikes can continue across a ford of Kane Springs Creek to Hurrah Pass and an extensive network of four-wheel-drive trails. The book and separate map *Canyon Country Off-Road Vehicle Trails: Canyon Rims & Needles Areas,* by F.A. Barnes, has detailed back-road information.

LA SAL MOUNTAINS LOOP ROAD

This paved road on the west side of the range provides a good introduction to the high country. Side roads and trails lead to lakes, alpine meadows, and old mining areas. Viewpoints overlook Castle Valley, Arches and Canyonlands National Parks, Moab Rim, and other scenic features. Vegetation along the drive runs the whole range from cottonwoods, sage, and rabbitbrush of the desert to forests of aspen, fir, and spruce. The 62-mile loop road can easily take a full day with stops for scenic overlooks, a picnic, and a bit of hiking or fishing. Because of the high elevations, the loop's season usually lasts May–Oct. Stock up on supplies in Moab because you won't find any stores or gas stations after leaving town. Before venturing off the Loop Road, it's a good idea to check current back-road conditions with the U.S. Forest Service office in Moab, where you should ask for a road log of sights and side roads.

NEEDLES AND ANTICLINE OVERLOOKS

These viewpoints atop the high mesa east of Canyonlands National Park offer magnificent panoramas of the surrounding area. Now part of the **BLM's Canyon Rims Recreation Area,** these easily accessed overlooks provide the kind of awe-inspiring vistas over the Needles District that you'll need to hike to find in the park itself. The turnoff for both overlooks is at Milepost 93 on U.S. 191, 32 miles south of Moab and seven miles north of the Highway 211 junction for the Needles District.

For the **Needles Overlook,** follow the paved road 22 miles west to its end (turn left at the junction 15 miles in). The BLM has a picnic area and

ISLANDS IN THE DESERT: ALPINE ECOSYSTEMS

Rising high above the desert are the La Sal, Henry, and Abajo Mountains. At elevations between 7,000 and 8,500 feet, the desert gives way to forests of aspen, Gambel oak, ponderosa pine, and mountain mahogany. Conifers dominate up to the treeline, at about 12,000 feet. Alpine flowering plants, grasses, sedges, and mosses cling to the windy summits of these mountains. Wildlife of the forests includes many of the desert dwellers, as well as elk, bear, mountain lion, marmot, and pika. A herd of bison roams freely in the Henry Mountains; the surrounding desert keeps them from going elsewhere. These high meadows, where temperatures rarely top 80°F, can be re-vivifying after broiling under the desert sun in the Colorado River Canyon. Best of all, the high country of the La Sals and the Abajos are less than an hour's drive from Moab, Arches or Canyonlands parks.

the La Sal Mountains
from Arches National Park

© W.C. MCRAE

interpretive exhibits here. A fence protects visitors from the sheer cliffs that drop off more than 1,000 feet. You can see much of Canyonlands National Park and southeastern Utah. Look south for Six-Shooter Peaks and the high country of the Abajo Mountains; southwest for the Needles (thousands of spires reaching for the heavens); west for the confluence area of the Green and Colorado Rivers, the Maze District, the Orange Cliffs, and the Henry Mountains; northwest for the lazy bends of the Colorado River Canyon and the sheer-walled mesas of Island in the Sky and Dead Horse Point; north for the Book Cliffs; and northeast for the La Sal Mountains. The changing shadows and colors

of the canyon country make for a continuous show throughout the day.

For the **Anticline Overlook,** continue straight north at the junction with the Needles road, and drive 17 miles on a good gravel road to the fenced overlook at road's end. Here you're standing 1,600 feet above the Colorado River. The sweeping panorama over the canyons, the river, and the twisted rocks of the Kane Creek Anticline is nearly as spectacular as that from Dead Horse Point, only 5.5 miles west as the crow flies. Salt and other minerals of the Paradox Formation pushed up overlying rocks into the dome visible below. Downcutting by the Colorado River has revealed the twisted rock layers. The Moab Salt Mine across the river to the north uses a solution technique to bring up potash from the Paradox Formation several thousand feet underground. Pumps then transfer the solution to the blue-tinted evaporation ponds. Look carefully on the northeast horizon to see an arch in the Windows Section of Arches National Park, 16 miles away.

You can reach **Pyramid Butte Overlook** by a gravel road that turns west off the main drive two miles before Anticline Overlook; the road goes around a rock monolith to viewpoints on the other side (1.3 miles round-trip). Four-wheel-drive vehicles can go west out to **Canyonlands Overlook** (17 miles round-trip) on rough, unmarked roads. The turnoff, which may not be signed, is about 0.3 mile south of the Hatch Point Campground turnoff.

There are two campgrounds along the access road; each has water (mid-Apr.–mid-Oct.), tables, grills, and outhouses and charges a $10 fee. **Windwhistle Campground,** backed by cliffs to the south, has fine views to the north and a nature trail; follow the main road from U.S. 191 for six miles and turn left. At **Hatch Point Campground,** in a piñon-juniper woodland, you can enjoy views to the north; water available Apr.–mid-Oct. Go 24 miles in on the paved and gravel roads toward Anticline Overlook, then turn right one mile.

Canyonlands

The canyon country of southeastern Utah puts on its supreme performance in this vast park, which spreads across 527 square miles. The deeply entrenched Colorado and Green Rivers meet in its heart, then continue south as the mighty Colorado through tumultuous Cataract Canyon Rapids. The park is divided into five districts. The Colorado and the Green rivers form the **River District** and divide Canyonlands National Park into three other regions. **Island in the Sky** lies north between the rivers, the **Maze** is to the west, and **Needles** is to the east. The **Horseshoe Canyon Unit** lies farther to the west. This small parcel of land preserves a canyon on Barrier Creek, a tributary of the Green River, in which astounding petroglyphs and other ancient rock paintings are preserved.

Each district has its own distinct character. No bridges or roads directly connect the three land districts and the Horseshoe Canyon Unit, so most visitors have to leave the park to go from one region to another. The huge park can be seen in many ways and on many levels. Paved roads reach a few areas, four-wheel-drive roads go to more places, and hiking trails reach still more, yet much of the land shows no trace of human passage. To get the big picture, you can fly over this incredible complex of canyons (see Air Tours under Recreation in the Moab chapter); however, only a river trip or a hike lets you experience the solitude and detail of the land.

The park can be visited in any season of the year, with spring and autumn the best choices. Summer temperatures can get into the 100s, Carrying (and drinking) water becomes critical then; carry at least one gallon per person per day. Arm yourself with insect repellent from late spring to midsummer. Winter days tend to be bright and sunny, although nighttime temperatures can dip into the teens or subzeros. Visitors coming in winter should inquire about travel conditions because snow and ice occasionally close roads and trails at higher elevations.

Needles punctuate the horizon.

Natural History

GEOLOGY

Deep canyons of the Green and Colorado Rivers have sliced through rocks representing 150 million years of deposition. The Paradox Formation, exposed in Cataract Canyon, contains salt and other minerals responsible for some of the folded and faulted rock layers in the region. Under the immense pressure of overlying rocks, the Paradox flows like plastic, forming domes where the rock layers are thinnest and causing cracks or faults as pressures rise and fall. Each of the overlying formations has a different color and texture; they're the products of ancient deserts, rivers, and seas that once covered this land. Views from any of the overlooks reveal that an immense quantity of rock has already been washed downriver toward California. Not so evident, however, is the 10,000 vertical feet of rock that geologists say once lay across the high mesas. The dry climate and sparse vegetation allow clear views of the remaining rock layers and the effects of erosion and deformation. You can read the geologic story at Canyonlands National Park in the 3,500 feet of strata that remain, from the bottom of Cataract Canyon to the upper reaches of Salt Creek in the Needles District.

FLORA AND FAUNA

Extremes of flash flood and drought, hot summers, and cold winters discourage all but the most hardy and adaptable life. Desert grasses, small flowering plants, cacti, and shrubs like blackbrush and saltbush survive on the mostly thin soils and meager 8–9 inches of annual precipitation. Trees either grow in cracks that concentrate rainfall and nutrients or rely on springs or canyon streams for moisture. Piñon pine and juniper prefer the higher elevations of the park, while cottonwoods live in the canyon bottoms that have permanent subsurface water. Tamarisk, an exotic streamside plant, and willows often form dense thickets on sandbars along the Green and Colorado Rivers. The hanging gardens of lush vegetation that surround cliffside springs or seeps seem oblivious to the surrounding desert.

The fragile desert ecology can easily be upset. Cattle, especially in the Needles District, once overgrazed the grasslands and trampled cryptobiotic crusts and other vegetation. Increased

POTHOLE ECOSYSTEMS

At Canyonlands it's easy to be in awe of the deep canyons and big desert rivers. But the little details of Canyonlands geology and ecology are pretty wonderful, too. Consider the potholes: shallow depressions dusted with wind-blown dirt. These holes, which range from less than an inch to several feet deep, fill after rainstorms and bring entire little ecosystems to life.

Pothole dwellers must be able to survive long periods of dryness, and then pack as much living as possible into the short wet periods. Some creatures, like the tadpole shrimp, live only for a couple of weeks. Others, like the spadefoot toad, hatch from drought-resistant eggs when water is present, quickly pass through the critical tadpole stage, then move onto dry land, returning to mate and lay eggs in potholes.

Though pothole dwellers are tough enough to survive in a dormant form during the long dry spells, most are very sensitive to sudden water chemistry changes, temperature changes, sediment input, being stepped on, and being splashed out onto dry land. Humans should never use pothole water for swimming, bathing, or drinking, as this can change the salinity or pH of a pool drastically. Organisms are unable to adapt to these human-generated changes, which occur suddenly, unlike slow, natural changes. While the desert pothole ecosystems may seem unimportant, they act as an indicator of the health of the larger ecosystems in which they occur.

CANYONLANDS

CANYONLANDS

To I-70 and
Green River

To I-70 and Moab

279

313

Potash

POTASH RD.

Dead Horse
State Park

VISITOR
CENTER

DEAD HORSE
POINT OVERLOOK

SHAFER

SHAFER
TRAIL

MINERAL RD.

MINERAL
BOTTOM

VISITOR CENTER

NECK
SPRING

Lathrop Trail

Taylor
Canyon

Alcove Spring
Trail

Syncline Trail

TAYLOR

Taylor

WHALE ROCK

UPHEAVAL
DOME

ISLAND
IN THE SKY
DISTRICT

AZTEC
BUTTE

MESA
ARCH

AIRPORT

WHITE RIM ROAD

GOOSEBERRY

WHITE RIM
OVERLOOK

GRAND VIEW
POINT OVERLOOK

WHITE CRACK

CANYONLANDS

NATIONAL

Colorado River

Rim

WILLOW FLAT
CAMPGROUND

GREEN RIVER
OVERLOOK

Murphy
Point

CANDLESTICK

WHITE RIM ROAD

MURPHY
HOGBACK

White

Green River

PARK

LABYRINTH

HARDSCRABBLE

POTATO
BOTTOM

Glen Canyon

National

HORSESHOE
CANYON UNIT

GREAT GALLERY
PETROGLYPHS

HANS FLAT RANGER
STATION

© AVALON TRAVEL PUBLISHING, INC.

COLORADO RIVER OVERLOOK

NEEDLES OUTPOST

ROADSIDE RUIN
CAVE SPRING
WOODEN SHOE ARCH OVERLOOK
SQUAW FLAT CAMPGROUND/TRAILHEAD

VISITOR CENTER

SLICKROCK

BIG SPRING CANYON OVERLOOK

POTHOLE POINT

ELEPHANT HILL

Elephant

CONFLUENCE OVERLOOK

Confluence

Lower Red Lake Trail

Chesler Park

Horse Canyon

CASTLE ARCH

FORTRESS ARCH

ANGEL ARCH

Salt Creek Canyon

Lost Canyon

Squaw Canyon

Big Spring Cyn.

DRUID ARCH

Canyon

NEEDLES DISTRICT

Davis Canyon

Lavender Canyon

Manti-La Sal National Forest

Beef Basin

Bobbys Hole

THE MAZE DISTRICT

MAZE OVERLOOK

The Fins

Colorado River

Elaterite Basin

North Trail Canyon

Flint Trail

Recreation Area

Orange Cliffs

BAGPIPE BUTTE OVERLOOK

Waterhole Flat

N

5 mi

5 km

0

0

CANYONLANDS

erosion and growth of undesirable exotic plants like cheatgrass have been the result. Scars left by roads and mines during the uranium frenzy of the 1950s can still be seen, most commonly in the Island in the Sky District.

Fewer than 10 species of fish evolved in the canyons of the Colorado and the Green. These fish developed streamlined bodies and strange features, such as humped backs, to cope with the muddy and varying river waters. Species include Colorado squawfish, humpback chub, bonytail chub, and humpback sucker; most of these live nowhere else. All have suffered greatly reduced populations and restricted ranges as a result of recent dam-building.

Of the approximately 65 mammal species living in the park, about one-third are rodents and another third are bats. You're most likely to see chipmunks, antelope ground squirrels, and rock squirrels, which are often active during the day. Most other animals wait until evening to come out and feed; in the morning, look for tracks of mule deer, bighorn sheep, coyote, gray fox, badger, porcupine, spotted skunk, beaver, black-tailed jackrabbit, wood rat, kangaroo rat, and many species of mice.

Visiting the Park's Many Districts

There are four districts and a noncontiguous unit to the park, each affording great views, spectacular geology, a chance to see wildlife, and endless opportunities to explore. You won't find crowds or elaborate park facilities because most of Canyonlands remains a primitive backcountry park.

The **Island in the Sky District** has paved roads on its top to impressive belvederes such as **Grand View Overlook** and to Upheaval Dome, a strange geologic feature. If you're short on time or don't want to make a rigorous backcountry trip, you'll find this district the best choice. It is easily visited as a half-day trip from Moab. The "Island," which is actually a large mesa, is much like Dead Horse Point on a giant scale; a narrow neck of land connects the north side with the "mainland." Hikers and those with suitable vehicles can drop off the Island in the Sky and descend about 1,300 feet to the **White Rim 4WD Road,** which follows cliffs of the White Rim around most of the island.

Few visitors make it over to the **Maze District,** which is some of the wildest country in the United States. Only the rivers and a handful of four-wheel-drive roads and hiking trails provide access. Experienced hikers can explore the "maze" of canyons on unmarked routes. **Horseshoe Canyon Unit,** a detached section of the park northwest of the Maze District, is equally remote. It protects the **Great Gallery,** a group of pictographs left by prehistoric Native Americans.

This ancient artwork is reached at the end of a series of long, unpaved road and down a canyon on a moderately challenging hiking trail.

Colorful rock spires prompted the name of the **Needles District,** which is easily accessed from Highway 211 and U.S. 191 south of Moab. Splendid canyons contain many arches, strange rock formations, and archaeological sites. Overlooks and short nature trails can be enjoyed from the paved scenic drive in the park. Hikers enjoy day hikes and backpack treks on the network of trails and routes within the district. Drivers with four-wheel-drive vehicles have their own challenging roads through canyons and other highly scenic areas.

The **River District** includes long stretches of the Green and the Colorado. River-running provides one of the best ways to experience the inner depths of the park. Boaters can obtain helpful literature and advice from park rangers. Groups planning their own trip through Cataract Canyon need a river-running permit. Flat-water permits are also required, and payment of a fee is necessary.

VISITORS CENTERS AND INFORMATION

There are visitors centers at the entrance to the Island in the Sky District, 435/259-4712, and the Needles District, 435/259-4711. The Hans Flat Ranger Station is located on a remote plateau above the even more isolated canyons of the Maze District and the Horseshoe Canyon Unit, 435/259-2652. The River District is administered out of the National Park Service Office, 2282 S. West Resource Blvd., Moab, UT 84532, 435/719-2313. This office can generally handle inquiries for all districts of the park.

If you are in Moab, it is most convenient to stop at the Moab Information Center, at the corner of Main and Center, 435/259-8825 or 800/635-MOAB (635-6622), where a National Park ranger is usually on duty. Any of the offices has brochures, maps, and books, as well as someone to answer your questions. The website www.nps.gov/cany is a good source for current information and permit applications.

Admission to the park is $10 per vehicle, or $5 per bicyclist or pedestrian. Admission is good for one week in any district of the park. In addition, a complex system of fees is charged for backcountry camping, four-by-four exploration, and river-rafting, detailed as follows.

Front-country camping is allowed only in established campgrounds and designated backcountry campsites. Except for the main campgrounds at Willow Flat (Island in the Sky) and Squaw Flat (Needles), you'll need a permit for **backcountry camping.** There is a $15 fee for a backpacking permit and a $30 fee for a vehicle site permit. Each of the three major districts has a different policy for backcountry vehicle camping, so it's a good idea to make sure that you understand the details. Backcountry permits will also be needed for any trips with stock; check with a ranger for details.

Rock-climbing is allowed in the park, and permits are not required (unless the trip involves overnight camping); however, it's always a good idea to check in at district visitors centers for advice and information, and to learn where climbing is restricted. Climbing is not allowed within 300 feet of cultural sites.

Pets aren't allowed on trails and must always be leashed. No firewood collecting is permitted in the park; backpackers need stoves for cooking. Vehicle and boat campers can bring in firewood but must use grills or fire pans.

The best maps for the park are a series of topographic maps printed on waterproof paper by Trails Illustrated; these have the latest trail and road information. A giant U.S. Geological Survey (USGS) topographic map, Canyonlands National Park and Vicinity, has the same 1:62,500 scale at a lower cost, but without the updated information and fancy paper. Handouts from the ranger offices describe natural history, travel, and other aspects of the park.

Back-road travel is a popular method of exploring the park. Canyonlands National Park offers hundreds of miles of exceptionally scenic jeep roads, favorites both with mountain bikers and four-by-four enthusiasts. Park regulations require all motorized vehicles to have proper registration and licensing for highway use (all-terrain vehicles are prohibited); drivers must be licensed. Normally you must have a vehicle with both four-wheel drive and high clearance. It's essential for both motor vehicles and bicycles to stay on existing roads to prevent damage to the delicate desert vegetation. Carry tools, extra fuel, water, and food in case of breakdown in a remote area.

Before making a trip, drivers and cyclists should talk with a ranger to register and to learn of current road conditions, which can change drastically from one day to the next. Also, the rangers will be more knowledgeable about where to seek help in case you become stuck. Primitive campgrounds are provided on most of the roads, but you'll need a backcountry permit from a ranger. Books on backcountry exploration include local author F.A. Barnes' *Canyon Country Off-Road Vehicle Trails: Island Area* and *Canyon Country Off-Road Vehicle Trails: Canyon Rims & Needles Areas* and Jack Bikers' *Canyon Country Off-Road Vehicle Trails: Maze Area* (see Suggested Reading for all titles).

CANYONLANDS

Island in the Sky

Panoramic views from the "Island" can be enjoyed from any point along the rim; you'll see much of the park and southeastern Utah. Short hiking trails lead to overlooks, Mesa Arch, Aztec Butte, Whale Rock, Upheaval Dome, and other features. Longer trails make steep, strenuous descents from the island to the White Rim 4WD Road below. Elevations on the island average about 6,000 feet. *Bring water for all hiking, camping, and travel in Island in the Sky.* No services are available, except at the visitors center in emergencies (bottled water is sold).

EXPLORING ISLAND IN THE SKY
Visitors Center

Stop here for information about Island in the Sky and to see some exhibits on geology and history; books and maps are available for purchase. The visitors center is open daily 8 A.M.–4:30 P.M. with reservations made from 12:30–4:30 P.M. Mon.–Sat. (may close from noon–1 P.M. in winter), 435/259-4351. A bulletin board outside has park information. The visitors center is located just before crossing "the neck" to Island in the Sky. From Moab, go northwest 10 miles on U.S. 191, turn left 15 miles on Highway 313 to the junction for Dead Horse Point State Park, then continue straight seven miles.

Shafer Canyon Overlook

Continue one-half mile past the visitors center to this overlook on the left (just before crossing the neck). Shafer Trail Viewpoint, across the neck, provides another perspective one-half mile farther. The neck is a narrow land bridge just wide enough for the road, and it's the only vehicle access to the 40-square-mile Island in the Sky. The overlooks have good views east down the canyon and the incredibly twisting **Shafer Trail Road.** Cattlemen Frank and John Schafer built the trail in the early 1900s to move stock to additional pastures (the "c" in their name was later dropped by mapmakers). Uranium prospectors upgraded the trail to a four-wheel-drive

Viewpoints from Island in the Sky showcase the confluence of the Green and Colorado Rivers.

CANYONLANDS

© W.C. MCRAE

the vertiginous Shafer Trail in Canyonlands National Park

road during the 1950s so that they could reach their claims at the base of the cliffs. Today the Shafer Trail Road connects the mesa top with the White Rim 4WD Road and the Potash Road 1,200 feet and four miles below. High-clearance vehicles should be used on the Shafer, preferably with four-wheel drive if you plan to climb up. Road conditions can vary considerably, so it's a good idea to contact a ranger before starting.

From the neck, follow the paved park road south six miles across prairie-like Grays Pasture, to a junction. The Grand View Point Overlook road continues south while the road to Upheaval Dome turns west.

Grand View Point

Continue south on the park road to a series of incredible vistas over the canyons of the Green and Colorado. The first viewpoint is Buck Canyon Overlook, which looks east over the Colorado River's canyon. Two miles farther is the **Grand View**

> *For many years, Upheaval Dome has kept geologists busy trying to figure out its origin. Strong evidence suggests that a meteorite impact caused the structure. The surrounding ring depression (caused by collapse) and the convergence of rock layers upward toward the center correspond precisely to known impact structures.*

Picnic Area, a handy lunch stop. Continue one mile on the main road past the picnic area to **Grand View Point,** perhaps the most spectacular panorama from Island in the Sky. Monument Basin lies directly below, and countless canyons, the Colorado River, the Needles, and mountain ranges are in the distance. The easy, 1.5-mile **Grand View Trail** continues past the end of the road for other vistas from the point.

Upheaval Dome Road

Return to the road junction and explore more overlooks and geological curiosities in the western portion of Island in the Sky.

The **Green River Overlook** and **Willow Flat Campground** are just west of the junction on an unpaved road. From the overlook, Soda Springs Basin and a section of the Green River (deeply entrenched in Stillwater Canyon) can be seen below. Small Willow Flat Campground is along the way to the overlook; it's open all year (no water or charge).

Continue to the end of the road, 5.3 miles northwest of the road junction, for a look at **Upheaval Dome.** This geologic oddity is a fantastically deformed pile of rock sprawled across a crater about three miles across and 1,200 feet deep. For many years, Upheaval Dome has kept geologists busy trying to figure out its origin. They once assumed that salt of the Paradox Formation pushed the rock layers upward to form the dome. Now, however, strong evidence suggests that a meteorite impact caused the structure. The surrounding ring depression (caused by collapse) and the convergence of rock layers upward toward the center correspond precisely to known impact structures. Shatter cones and microscopic analysis also indicate an impact origin. When the meteorite struck, some time in the last 150 million years, it formed a crater up to five miles across. Erosion removed some of the overlying rock,

CANYONLANDS

perhaps as much as a vertical mile. The underlying salt may have played a role in uplifting the central section.

The easy **Crater View Trail** leads to overlooks on the rim of Upheaval Dome; the first viewpoint is a half-mile round-trip, the second is one mile round-trip. There's also a small **picnic area** here.

White Rim 4WD Road

This driving adventure follows the White Rim below the sheer cliffs of Island in the Sky. A close look at the light-colored surface rock reveals ripple marks and crossbeds laid down near an ancient coastline. The plateau's east side is about 800 feet above the Colorado River. On the west side, the plateau meets the bank of the Green River.

Travel along the winding road presents a constantly changing panorama of rock, canyons, river, and sky. Keep an eye out for desert bighorn sheep. You'll see all three levels of Island in the Sky District, from the high plateaus to the White Rim to the rivers.

Only four-wheel-drive vehicles with high clearance can make the trip. With the proper vehicle, driving is mostly easy but slow and winding; a few steep or rough sections have to be negotiated. The 100-mile trip takes 2–3 days. Allow an extra day to travel all the road spurs.

Mountain bikers find this a great trip, too; most cyclists arrange an accompanying vehicle to carry water and camping gear. Primitive campgrounds along the way provide convenient stopping places. Both cyclists and four-by-four drivers need to obtain reservations and a backcountry permit ($30) for the White Rim campsites from the Island in the Sky visitors center; this can be done in person, by mail, or by phone, 435/259-4351. Demand exceeds supply during the popular spring and autumn seasons, when you should make reservations as far in advance as possible. No services or developed water sources exist anywhere on the drive, so be sure to have plenty of fuel and water with some to spare. Access points are Shafer Trail Road (from near Island in the Sky) and Potash Road (Highway 279 from Moab) on the east and Mineral Bottom Road on the west. White Rim Sandstone forms the distinctive plateau crossed on the drive.

HIKING

Neck Spring Trail

The trail begins near the Shafer Canyon Overlook. A brochure should be available at the trailhead. This moderately difficult hike follows a five-mile loop down Taylor Canyon to Neck and Cabin Springs, formerly used by ranchers, then climbs back to the Island in the Sky Road at a second trailhead one-half mile south of the start. The elevation change is 300 feet. Water at the springs supports maidenhair fern and other water-loving plants. Also watch for birds and wildlife attracted to this spot. Bring water with you because the springs aren't suitable for drinking.

Lathrop Trail

This is the only marked hiking route going all the way from Island in the Sky to the Colorado River. The trailhead is on the left 1.3 miles past the neck. The first 2.5 miles cross Gray's Pasture to the rim, which affords fantastic vistas over the Colorado River. From here, the trail descends steeply, dropping 1,600 feet over the next 2.5

Colorado River Canyon from the Lathrop Trail, Island in the Sky

miles to the White Rim 4WD Road. Part of this section follows an old mining road past several abandoned mines, all relics of the uranium boom. *Don't enter the shafts because they're in danger of collapse and may contain poisonous gases.* From the mining area, the route descends through a wash to the White Rim 4WD Road, follows the road a short distance south, then goes down Lathrop Canyon Road to the Colorado River, another four miles with a descent of 500 feet. Total distance for the strenuous hike is nine miles one-way, with an elevation change of 2,100 feet. The trail has little shade and can be very hot.

Mesa Arch Trail

This easy trail leads to an arch on the rim. The trailhead is on the left 5.5 miles from the neck. On the way, the road crosses the grasslands and scattered juniper trees of Gray's Pasture. A trail brochure available at the start describes the ecology of the mesa. Hiking distance is only one-half mile round-trip with an 80-foot elevation change. The arch, eroded from Navajo Sandstone, frames views of rock formations below and the La Sal Mountains in the distance.

Murphy Point

Three miles south of the Upheaval Dome junction on the main park road, a rough dirt road turns right 1.7 miles to Murphy Point. Hikers can take **Murphy Trail,** which drops from the rim down to the White Rim 4WD Road. This strenuous route forks partway down; one branch follows Murphy Hogback (a ridge) to Murphy Campground on the four-wheel-drive road, and the other branch follows a wash to the road one mile south of the campground. A loop hike along both branches is nine miles round-trip with an elevation change of 1,100 feet.

Grand View Point Area

Two trails begin from the Grand View Picnic Area. **White Rim Overlook Trail** is an easy 1.5-mile hike (round-trip) east along a peninsula to an overlook of Monument Basin and beyond. **Gooseberry Trail** drops off the mesa and descends some extremely steep grades to the White Rim 4WD Road just north of Gooseberry

Campground; the strenuous trip is 2.5 miles one-way with an elevation change of 1,400 feet.

At the overlook, **Grand View Trail** continues past the end of the road for other vistas from the point, which is the southernmost tip of Island in the Sky. The easy hike is 1.5 miles round-trip.

Along Upheaval Dome Road

Aztec Butte is one of the few areas in Island in the Sky with Indian ruins; shortage of water here prevented permanent settlement. The trailhead is on the right one mile northwest of the road junction. An easy trail climbs 200 feet in half a mile to the top of the butte for a good panorama of the Island.

Another easy trail begins on the right 4.4 miles northwest of the road junction. An easy trail climbs **Whale Rock,** a sandstone hump near the outer rim of Upheaval Dome. Distance is one-half mile round-trip with an ascent of 100 feet.

While easy half-mile trails lead to **Upheaval Dome** overviews, energetic hikers can explore this formation from the parking area at the overlook or from White Rim 4WD Road below. **Syncline Loop Trail** makes a strenuous eight-mile circuit completely around Upheaval Dome; the elevation change is 1,200 feet. The trail crosses Upheaval Dome Canyon about halfway around from the overlook; walk east 1.5 miles up the canyon to enter the crater itself. This is the only nontechnical route into the center of the dome. A hike around Upheaval Dome with a side trip to the crater totals 11 miles, and is best done as an overnight trip. Carry plenty of water for the entire trip; this dry country can be very hot in summer. The Green River is the only reliable source of water. From near Upheaval Campsite on White Rim 4WD Road, you can hike four miles on **Upheaval Trail** through Upheaval Canyon to a junction with the Syncline Loop Trail, then another 1.5 miles into the crater; the elevation gain is about 600 feet.

Another hiking possibility in the area, the Alcove Spring Trail leaves the road 1.5 miles before the Upheaval Dome parking area and connects with the White Rim 4WD Road in Taylor Canyon. Total distance is 10 miles one-way (five miles on the trail in Trail Canyon and five miles on a jeep road in Taylor Canyon); the elevation change is about 1,500 feet. Carry plenty of water because the strenuous trail is hot and dry.

CAMPGROUNDS

There is only one developed campground in the Island in the Sky District. **Willow Flat**

Campground has only 12 sites, and is located on the Murphy Point Road. The $5-per-night sites are available on a first-come, first-served basis; no water or services are available. A sign at the park entrance will tell you if the campground is full. Rangers present campfire programs here spring through autumn. Sites often fill except in winter.

Needles

The Needles District showcases some of the finest rock sculptures in Canyonlands National Park. Spires, arches, or monoliths appear in almost any direction you look. Prehistoric ruins and rock art exist in greater variety and quantity than elsewhere in the park. Year-round springs and streams bring greenery to the desert.

While a scenic paved road leads to the park, the park itself has only about a dozen miles of paved roads. Needles District doesn't have a lot to offer travelers who are unwilling to get out of their vehicles and hike; however, even a short hike opens up the landscape and leads to remarkable vistas and prehistoric sites.

To reach the Needles District, go 40 miles south from Moab (or 14 miles north of Monticello) on U.S. 191, turn west on Highway 211, and continue 38 miles.

EXPLORING NEEDLES DISTRICT

BLM Newspaper Rock Historical Monument

Although not in the park itself, Newspaper Rock lies just 150 feet off Highway 211 on the way to the Needles District of Canyonlands National Park. At Newspaper Rock, a profusion of petroglyphs depicts human figures, animals, birds, and abstract designs. These represent 2,000 years of human history during which archaic tribes and Anasazi, Fremont, Paiute, Navajo, and Anglo travelers have passed through Indian Creek Canyon. The patterns on the smooth sandstone rock face stand out clearly, thanks to a coating of dark desert varnish. A quarter-mile nature trail introduces you to the area's desert and riparian vegetation. Picnic areas lie

along Indian Creek across the highway. The park is relatively undeveloped; no drinking water or charge. From U.S. 191 between Moab and Monticello, turn west 12 miles on Highway 211.

Needles Outpost

A general store just outside the park boundary offers a campground ($15 tent or RV without hookups), groceries, ice, gas, propane, a snack bar, showers, jeep rentals and tours, and scenic flights. Call or write ahead, if possible, to arrange for jeep tours and scenic flights: P.O. Box 1107, Monticello, UT 84535, 435/979-4007. The season at Needles Outpost is mid-Mar.–late Oct. The turnoff from Highway 211 is one mile before the Needles visitors center.

the slickrock desert of the Needles District

Newspaper Rock preserves some of the richest and most fanciful prehistoric rock art in Utah.

Visitors Center

Stop here to find out about hiking, back roads, and other aspects of travel in the Needles. The staff has backcountry permits (required for all overnight stays in the backcountry), maps, brochures, and books. Open daily 8 A.M.–5 P.M., 435/259-4711. Outside of office hours, get information at the bulletin board.

Big Spring Canyon Scenic Drive

The main paved park road continues 6.5 miles past the visitors center to Big Spring Canyon Overlook. On the way, you can stop at several nature trails or turn off on four-wheel-drive roads. The overlook takes in a vista of slickrock-edged canyons dropping away toward the Colorado River.

HIKING

The Needles District has about 60 miles of backcountry trails. Many interconnect to provide all sorts of day and overnight trips. Cairns mark the trails; signs point the way at junctions. You can normally find water in upper Elephant Canyon and canyons to the east in spring and early summer, although the remaining water often be-

comes stagnant by midsummer. Always ask the rangers about sources of water; don't depend on its availability. Treat water from all sources, including springs, before drinking. Chesler Park and other areas west of Elephant Canyon are very dry; you'll need to bring all water. Mosquitoes, gnats, and deer flies can be pesky from late spring to midsummer, especially in the wetter places, so be sure to bring insect repellent. To plan your trip, obtain the small hiking map available from the visitors center, Trails Illustrated's Needles District map, or USGS topographic maps. Overnight backcountry hiking requires a $15-per-party permit.

Trails from near the Visitors Center

There are two easy hikes near the visitors center. **Roadside Ruin** is on the left 0.4 mile past the visitors center. A one-third-mile loop trail goes near a well-preserved granary left by Anasazi Indians. A trail guide available at the start tells about the Anasazi and the local plants.

Don't miss the **Cave Spring Trail,** which introduces the geology and ecology of the park and goes to an old cowboy line camp. Turn left 0.7 mile past the visitors center and follow signs about

CANYONLANDS

one mile to the trailhead. Pick up the brochure at the beginning. The 0.6-mile loop goes clockwise, crossing some slickrock; two ladders assist hikers on the steep sections. Native Americans first used these rock overhands for shelter (faint pictographs still decorate the rock walls). Much later, cowboys used these open caves as a line camp from the late 1800s until the park was established in 1964. The park service has re-created the line camp, just 50 yards in from the trailhead, with period furnishings and equipment.

Trails from Big Spring Canyon Overlook Scenic Drive

Pothole Point Nature Trail is on the left of the main road five miles past the visitors center. Highlights of this 0.6-mile loop hike are the many potholes dissolved in the Cedar Mesa Sandstone. A brochure illustrates the fairy shrimp, tadpole shrimp, horsehair worm, snail, and other adaptable creatures that spring to life when rains fill the potholes. You'll also enjoy fine views of distant buttes from the trail.

Slickrock Trail begins on the right 6.2 miles past the visitors center. The trail makes a loop of 2.4 miles round-trip and takes you north to an overlook of the confluence of Big Spring and Little Spring Canyons. Hiking is easy and offers good panoramas. **Big Spring Canyon Overlook,** 6.5 miles past the visitors center, marks the end of the scenic drive but not the scenery.

The **Confluence Overlook Trail** begins here and winds west 5.5 miles to an overlook of the Green and Colorado Rivers 1,000 feet below. The trail crosses Big Spring and Elephant Canyons and follows a jeep road for a short distance. Higher points have good views of the Needles to the south. You might see rafts in the water or bighorn sheep on the cliffs. Except for a few short steep sections, this trail is level and fairly easy. A very early start is recommended in summer because there's little shade. Carry water even if you don't plan to go all the way. This enchanting country has lured many a hiker beyond his or her original goal!

Trails from Squaw Flat Trailhead

A road to **Squaw Flat Campground** and **Elephant Hill** turns left 2.7 miles past the ranger station. The **Squaw Flat Trailhead** sits a short distance south of the campground and is reached by a separate signed road. You can also begin from a trailhead in the campground itself.

re-created cowboy line camp along Cave Spring Trail

Peekaboo Trail winds southeast five miles (one-way) over rugged terrain, including some steep sections of slickrock (best avoided when wet, icy, or covered with snow). There's little shade, so carry water. The trail follows Squaw Canyon, climbs over a pass to Lost Canyon, then crosses more slickrock before descending to Peekaboo Campground on Salt Creek 4WD Road. Look for Anasazi ruins on the way and rock art at the campground. A rockslide took out Peekaboo Spring, which is shown on some maps. Options on this trail include a turnoff south through Squaw Canyon or Lost Canyon to make a loop of 8.75 miles or more.

Squaw Canyon Trail follows the canyon south for 3.75 miles one-way. Intermittent water can often be found until late spring. You can take a connecting trail (Peekaboo, Lost Canyon, and Big Spring Canyon) or cross a slickrock pass to Elephant Canyon.

Lost Canyon Trail, 3.25 miles one-way, is reached via Peekaboo or Squaw Canyon trails and makes a loop with them. Water supports abundant vegetation; you may need to wade. Most of the way is in the wash bottom, except for a section of slickrock to Squaw Canyon.

Big Spring Canyon Trail crosses an outcrop of slickrock from the trailhead, then follows the canyon bottom to the head of the canyon, 3.75 miles one-way. You can usually find intermittent water along the way except in summer. At canyon's end, a climb up steep slickrock (hazardous if covered by snow or ice) takes you to Squaw Canyon Trail and back to the trailhead for a good 7.5-mile loop. Another possibility is to turn southwest to the head of Squaw Canyon, then hike over a slickrock saddle to Elephant Canyon for a 10.5-mile loop.

Trails from Elephant Hill Trailhead

Drive west three miles past the campground turnoff on passable dirt roads to the **Elephant Hill Picnic Area and Trailhead** at the base of Elephant Hill. Sounds of racing engines and burning rubber can often be heard from above as vehicles attempt the difficult four-wheel-drive road that begins just past the picnic area. All of the following destinations can also be reached

by trails from the Squaw Flat Trailhead, although distances will be slightly greater.

Chesler Park is a favorite hiking destination. A lovely desert meadow contrasts with the red and white spires that gave the Needles District its name. An old cowboy line camp is on the west side of the rock island in the center of the park. The distance on **Chesler Park Trail** is about six miles round-trip. The trail winds through sand and slickrock before ascending a small pass through the Needles to Chesler Park. Once inside, you can take the **Chesler Park Loop Trail** (five miles) completely around the park. The loop includes the unusual half-mile **Joint Trail,** which follows the bottom of a very narrow crack. Camping in Chesler Park is restricted to certain areas; check with a ranger.

Druid Arch reminds many people of the massive stone slabs at Stonehenge, which are popularly associated with the druids, in southern England. The arch is an 11-mile round-trip (15 miles if you start at Squaw Flat Trailhead). Follow the Chesler Park Trail two miles to Elephant Canyon, turn up the canyon 3.5 miles, then make a quarter-mile climb to the arch. Upper Elephant Canyon has seasonal water, but the narrow canyon is closed to camping.

Lower Red Lake Canyon Trail provides access to Cataract Canyon of the Colorado River. This long, strenuous trip is best suited for experienced hikers and completed in two days. Distance from the Elephant Hill Trailhead is 19 miles round-trip; you'll be walking on four-wheel-drive roads and trails. If you can drive Elephant Hill 4WD Road to the trail junction in Cyclone Canyon, the hike is only eight miles round-trip. The most difficult trail section is a steep talus slope that drops 700 feet in a half mile into the lower canyon. Total elevation change is 1,000 feet. The canyon has little shade and lacks any water source above the river. Summer heat can make the trip grueling; temperatures tend to be 5–10°F hotter than on other Needles trails. The river level drops between midsummer and autumn, allowing hikers to go along the shore both downstream to see the rapids and upstream to the confluence.

stone pillars near Elephant Hill in the Needles District

Undertows and strong currents make the river dangerous to cross.

Upper Salt Creek Trail

Several impressive arches and many inviting side canyons attract adventurous hikers to the extreme southeast corner of the Needles District. The trail begins at the end of the 13.5-mile four-wheel-drive road up Salt Creek, then goes south 12 miles upcanyon to Cottonwood Canyon/Beef Basin Road near Cathedral Butte, just outside the park boundary. The trail is nearly level except for a steep climb at the end. Water can usually be found. Some wading and bushwhacking may be necessary. The famous "All-American Man" pictograph, shown on some topographic maps (or ask a ranger), is in a cave a short way off to the east at about the midpoint of the trail; follow your map and unsigned paths to the cave, but don't climb in—it's dangerous to both you and the ruins and pictograph inside. Many more archaeological sites can be discovered near the trail, but they're all fragile and great care should be taken when visiting them.

MOUNTAIN BIKING AND FOUR-BY-FOUR EXPLORATION

Visitors with bicycles or four-wheel-drive vehicles can explore the many backcountry roads that lead to the outback. More than 50 miles of challenging roads link primitive campsites, remote trailheads, and sites with ancient cultural remnants. Some roads in the Needles District are rugged and require previous experience in handling four-wheel-drive vehicles on steep inclines and in deep sand.

The best routes for mountain bikers are the Colorado Overlook Road, which leaves from near the visitors center, and the Elephant Hill Road. Horse Canyon, Peekaboo, and Lavender Canyon trails are too sandy for pleasant biking.

All motor vehicles and bicycles must remain on designated roads. Overnight backcountry trips with bicycles or motor vehicles require a $30-per-party permit.

Salt Creek Canyon 4WD Road

This rugged route begins near Cave Spring Trail, crosses sage flats for the next 2.5 miles, then heads deep into a spectacular canyon. Round-trip distance, including a side trip to 150-foot-high Angel Arch, is 26 miles. Agile hikers can follow a steep slickrock route into the window of Angel Arch. You can also explore side canyons of Salt Creek or take the Upper Salt Creek Trail (the "All-American Man" pictograph makes a good day-hike destination of 12 miles round-trip).

Horse Canyon 4WD Road turns off to the left shortly before the mouth of Salt Canyon. Round-trip distance, including a side trip to Tower Ruin, is about 13 miles; other attractions include Paul Bunyan's Potty, Castle Arch, Fortress Arch, and side-canyon hiking. Salt and Horse Canyons can easily be driven in four-wheel-drive vehicles. Salt Canyon is usually closed because of quicksand after flash floods in summer and shelf ice in winter.

Davis and Lavender Canyons

Four-wheel-drive roads enter Davis Canyon and Lavender Canyon from Highway 211 east of the park boundary. Both canyons are accessed through Davis Canyon Road off Highway 211 and contain great scenery, arches, and Indian sites, and both are easily visited with high-clearance vehicles. Davis is about 20 miles round-trip and Lavender is about 26 miles round-trip. Try to allow plenty of time in either canyon because there is much to see and many inviting side canyons to hike. You can camp on BLM land just outside the park boundaries, but not in the park itself.

Colorado Overlook 4WD Road

This popular route begins beside the visitors center and follows Salt Creek to Lower Jump Overlook. Then it bounces across slickrock to a view of the Colorado River (upstream from the confluence). Driving is easy to moderate, although very rough the last 1.5 miles. Round-trip distance is 14 miles.

Elephant Hill 4WD Loop Road

This rugged backcountry road begins three miles past the Squaw Flat Campground turnoff. Only experienced drivers with stout vehicles should attempt the extremely rough and steep climb up Elephant Hill (coming up the back side of Elephant Hill is even worse!). The loop is about 10 miles round-trip. Connecting roads go to the Confluence Overlook Trailhead (the viewpoint is one mile round-trip on foot), the Joint Trailhead (Chesler Park is two miles round-trip on foot), and several canyons. Some road sections on the loop are one-way. The parallel canyons in this area are grabens caused by faulting where a layer of salt has shifted deep underground. In addition

EARLY EXPLORATION OF THE COLORADO RIVER CANYON

The Spanish Dominguez-Escalante Expedition skirted the east edge of the Colorado River canyons in 1776 in an unsuccessful attempt to find a route west to California. Retreating back to New Mexico, the explorers encountered great difficulties in the canyons of southern Utah before finding a safe ford across the Colorado River. This spot, known as the "Crossing of the Fathers," now lies under Lake Powell. Later explorers established the Old Spanish Trail through Utah to connect New Mexico with California. The route crossed the Colorado River near present-day Moab and was used from 1829–1848, when the United States acquired the western territories. Fur trappers also traveled the canyons in search of beaver and other animals during the early 1800s; inscriptions carved into the sandstone record their passage.

Major John Wesley Powell led the first scientific expedition by boat through the Green and lower Colorado river canyons in 1869, then repeated most of the journey in 1871–1872. Cowboys brought in cattle during the 1870s. Some of their camps, corrals, and inscriptions still survive, although grazing no longer takes place in the park. Uranium prospectors swarmed through the area with Geiger counters during the 1950s, staking thousands of claims and opening some mines. Most of the jeep roads in use today date from that time.

CANYONLANDS

Modern camping meets *The Flintstones* at Needles' Squaw Flat Campground.

to Elephant Hill, a few other difficult spots must be negotiated.

This area can also be reached by a long route south of the park using Cottonwood Canyon/ Beef Basin Road from Highway 211, about 60 miles one-way. You'll enjoy spectacular vistas from the Abajo Highlands. Two *very* steep descents from Pappys Pasture into Bobbys Hole effectively make this section one-way; travel from Elephant Hill up Bobbys Hole is possible but much more difficult than going the other way and may require hours of road-building. The Bobbys Hole route may be impassable at times; ask about conditions at the BLM office in Monticello or at the Needles visitors center.

CAMPGROUNDS

The **Squaw Flat Campground,** about six miles from the visitors center, has 26 sites, water, and charges a $10 fee from mid-Mar.–Sept.; it's open the rest of the year with no water or charge (water can be obtained year-round at the visitors center). Rangers present evening programs at the campfire circle on Loop A from spring through autumn.

The Maze

Only adventurous and experienced travelers will want to visit this rugged land west of the Green and Colorado Rivers. Vehicle access wasn't even possible until 1957, when mineral-exploration roads first entered what later became Canyonlands National Park. Today, you'll need a high-clearance four-wheel-drive vehicle, a horse, or your own two feet to get around. The National Park Service plans to keep this district in its remote and primitive condition. An airplane flight, which is recommended if you can't come overland, provides the only easy way to see the scenic features here.

The names of erosional forms describe the landscape—Orange Cliffs, Golden Stairs, the Fins, Land of Standing Rocks, Lizard Rock, the Doll House, Chocolate Bars, the Maze, and Jasper Canyon. The many-fingered canyons of the Maze gave the district its name. Although it is not a true maze, these canyons give that impression.

Getting to the Maze District

Dirt roads to the Hans Flat Ranger Station and Maze District branch off from Highway 24 (across from the Goblin Valley State Park turnoff) and Highway 95 (take the usually unmarked Hite/Orange Cliffs Road between the Dirty Devil and Hite bridges at Lake Powell). The easiest way in is the graded 46-mile road from Highway 24; it's fast, although sometimes badly corrugated. The Hite Road (also called Orange Cliffs Road) is longer, bumpier, and, for some drivers, tedious; it's 54 miles from the turnoff at Highway 95 to the Hans Flat Ranger Station via the Flint Trail. In winter or other times when the Flint Trail is closed, drivers must take the Hite Road to reach the Maze Overlook, Land of Standing Rocks, and the Doll House areas. All roads to the Maze District cross Glen Canyon National Recreation Area (NRA). From Highway 24, two-wheel-drive vehicles with good clearance can travel to Hans Flat Ranger Station and other areas near, but not actually in, the Maze District.

Planning a Maze District Expedition

Although there are very few improvements in the Maze District, explorers will nonetheless need a $15 backcountry permit for overnight backpacking. Note that a backcountry permit in this district is *not* a reservation. You may have to share a site with someone else, especially in the popular spring months. Those using four-by-fours or mountain bikes for overnight expeditions will need a $30 backcountry permit. Also, as in the rest of the park, only designated sites can be used for vehicle camping. You don't need a permit to camp in the adjacent Glen Canyon NRA or on BLM land. *There are no developed sources of water in the Maze District.* Hikers can obtain water from springs in some canyons (check with a ranger to find which are flowing) or from the rivers; purify all water before drinking. The Maze District has nine camping areas (two at Maze Overlook, seven at Land of Standing Rocks) with a 15-person, three-vehicle limit.

The Trails Illustrated topographic map of the Maze District describes and shows the few roads and trails here; some routes and springs are marked on it, too. Agile hikers experienced in desert and canyon travel may want to take off on cross-country routes, which are either unmarked or lightly cairned. Extra care must be taken for preparation and travel in both Glen Canyon NRA and the Maze. Always talk with the rangers beforehand to find out current conditions. Be sure to leave an itinerary with someone reliable who can contact the rangers if you're overdue. Unless the rangers know where to look for you in case of breakdown or accident, a rescue could take weeks!

EXPLORING THE MAZE DISTRICT
North Point

Hans Flat Ranger Station, and this peninsula that reaches out to the east and north, lie at an elevation of about 6,400 feet. Panoramas from

CANYONLANDS

North Point take in the vastness of Canyonlands, including all three districts. From **Millard Canyon Overlook,** just 0.9 mile past the ranger station, you can see arches, Cleopatra's Chair, and features as distant as the La Sal Mountains and Book Cliffs. For the best views, drive out to Panorama Point, about 10.5 miles one-way from the ranger station. A spur road goes left two miles to Cleopatra's Chair, a massive sandstone monolith and area landmark. The trailhead for **North Trail Canyon** begins just down the North Point Road (or 2.4 miles from the ranger station). Two-wheel-drive vehicles can usually reach this spot, where hikers can follow the trail down seven miles (1,000-foot elevation change) through the Orange Cliffs, follow four-wheel-drive roads six miles to the Maze Overlook Trail, then one more mile into a canyon of the Maze. Because North Point belongs to the Glen Canyon NRA, you can camp on it without a permit.

Flint Trail

This narrow, rough, four-wheel-drive road connects the Hans Flat area with the Maze Overlook, Doll House, and other areas below. The road, driver, and vehicle should all be in good condition before attempting this route. Winter snow and mud close the road from late December into March, as can rainstorms anytime. Check conditions first with a ranger. If you're starting from the top, stop at the signed overlook just before the descent to scout for vehicles headed up (the Flint Trail has very few places to pass). The top of the Flint Trail is 14 miles south of Hans Flat Ranger Station; at the bottom, 2.8 nervous miles later, you can turn left two miles to the Golden Stairs Trailhead or 12.7 miles to the Maze Overlook; keep straight 28 miles to the Doll House or 39 miles to Highway 95.

Maze Overlook

Now you're actually in Canyonlands National Park and at the edge of the sinuous canyons of the Maze. You can stay at primitive camping areas (backcountry permit needed) and enjoy the views. **Maze Overlook Trail** drops one mile into the South Fork of Horse Canyon; a rope helps lower packs in a difficult section. Once in the

canyon, you can walk around to the Harvest Scene, a group of prehistoric pictographs, or do a variety of day hikes or backpacks. These canyons have water in some places; check with the ranger when getting your permits. At least four routes connect with the four-wheel-drive road in Land of Standing Rocks (see the Trails Illustrated map). Hikers can also climb Petes Mesa from the canyons or head downstream to explore Horse Canyon (a dry fall blocks access to the Green River, however).

The Golden Stairs

Hikers can descend this steep two-mile (one-way) foot trail to the Land of Standing Rocks Road in a fraction of the time it takes for drivers to follow roads! The trail offers good views of Ernies Country and the Fins but lacks shade or water. The upper trailhead is east two miles from the road junction at the bottom of the Flint Trail.

Land of Standing Rocks

Here, in the heart of the Maze District, strange-shaped rock spires stand guard over myriad canyons. Six camping areas offer scenic places to stay (permit needed). Hikers have a choice of many ridge and canyon routes from the four-wheel-drive road, a trail to a confluence overlook, and a trail that descends to the Colorado River near Cataract Canyon. The well-named Chocolate Bars can be reached by a hiking route from the Wall near the beginning of the Land of Standing Rocks. A good day hike makes a loop from Chimney Rock to the Harvest Scene pictographs; take the ridge route (toward Petes Mesa) one direction and the canyon fork northwest of Chimney Rock the other. Follow your topographic map through the canyons and the cairns between the canyons and ridge. Other routes from Chimney Rock lead to lower Jasper Canyon (no river access) or into Shot and Water Canyons and on to the Green River.

Tall, rounded rock spires near the end of the road reminded early visitors of dolls, hence the name Doll House. The Doll House makes a delightful place to explore in itself, or you can head out on routes and trails. **Spanish Bottom Trail** begins here, then drops steeply to Spanish Bottom beside the Colorado River in 1.2 miles (one-way); a thin trail leads downstream into Cataract Canyon and the first of a long series of rapids. **Surprise Valley Overlook Trail** branches right off the Spanish Bottom Trail after about 300 feet and winds south past some dolls to a T-junction (turn right for views of Surprise Valley, Cataract Canyon, and beyond); the trail ends at some well-preserved granaries, after 1.5 miles one-way. The **Colorado/Green River Overlook Trail** heads north five miles (one-way) from the Doll House to a viewpoint of the confluence. See the area's Trails Illustrated map for routes, trails, and roads.

Getting to the Land of Standing Rocks takes some careful driving, especially on a three-mile stretch above Teapot Canyon. The many washes and small canyon crossings here make for slow going. Short-wheelbase vehicles have the easiest time, as usual. The turnoff for Land of Standing Rocks Road is 6.6 miles from the junction at the bottom of the Flint Trail via a wash shortcut (add about three miles if driving via the four-way intersection). The lower end of the Golden Stairs foot trail is 7.8 miles in; the western end of Ernies Country route trailhead is 8.6 miles in; the Wall is 12.7 miles in; Chimney Rock is 15.7 miles in; and the Doll House is 19 miles in at the end of the road. If you drive from the south on the Hite/Orange Cliffs Road, stop at the self-registration stand at the four-way intersection, about 31 miles in from Highway 95; you can write your own permit for overnights in the park here. This situation may change, however, so check with a ranger for current information.

Horseshoe Canyon Unit

This canyon contains exceptional prehistoric rock art in a separate section of Canyonlands National Park. Ghostly life-size pictographs in the Great Gallery provide an intriguing look into the past. Archaeologists think that the images had religious importance, although the meaning of the figures remains unknown. The Barrier Canyon style of these drawings has been credited to an archaic Indian culture beginning at least 8,000 years ago and lasting until about A.D. 450. Horseshoe Canyon also contains rock art left by the subsequent Fremont and Anasazi people. The relation between the earlier and later prehistoric groups hasn't been determined.

Call the Hans Flat Ranger Station, 435/259-2652, to inquire about ranger-led weekend hikes to the Great Gallery. These are offered as demand justifies on Saturdays and Sundays in spring and early summer.

Great Gallery

Horseshoe Canyon lies northwest of the Maze District. The easiest and most common way to reach Horseshoe Canyon is from the west and Highway 24. In dry weather, cars with good clearance can reach a trailhead on the canyon's west rim. To reach this trailhead from Highway 24, turn east across from the Goblin Valley State Park turnoff, then continue east 30 miles on a dirt road (keep left at the Hans Flat Ranger Station/Horseshoe Canyon turnoff 25 miles in). From the rim and parking area, the trail descends 800 feet in one mile on an old jeep road, which is

© W.C. MCRAE

CANYONLANDS

a panel of the Great Gallery

© W.C. MCRAE

With its wealth of complex rock art, remote Horseshoe Canyon seems to have once served as a sacred meeting place for ancient Native Americans.

now closed to vehicles. At the canyon bottom, turn right two miles upstream to the Great Gallery. The sandy canyon floor is mostly level; trees provide shade in some areas. The hike to the Great Gallery is 6.5 miles round-trip and will take 4–6 hours.

Look for other rock art along the canyon walls on the way to the Great Gallery. Take care not to touch any of the drawings because they're fragile and irreplaceable. (The oil from your hands will remove the paints.) Horseshoe Canyon also offers pleasant scenery and spring wildflowers. Carry plenty of water. Neither camping nor pets are allowed in the canyon, but you can camp on the

rim. Contact the Hans Flat Ranger Station or the Moab office for road and trail conditions.

Horseshoe Canyon can also be reached via primitive roads from the east. A four-wheel-drive road goes north 21 miles from Hans Flat Ranger Station and drops steeply into the canyon from the east side. The descent on this road is so rough that most people prefer to park on the rim and hike the last mile of road. A vehicle barricade prevents driving right up to the rock-art panel, but the 1.5-mile walk is easy. A branch off the jeep road goes to the start of **Deadman's Trail** (1.5 miles one-way), which is less used and more difficult.

CANYONLANDS

The River District

The River District is the name of the administrative unit of the park that oversees conservation and recreation for the Green and Colorado Rivers.

RIVER-RUNNING ABOVE THE CONFLUENCE

The Green and Colorado Rivers flow smoothly through their canyons above the confluence of the two rivers. Almost any shallow-draft boat can navigate these waters: canoes, kayaks, rafts, and powerboats are commonly used. Any travel requires advance planning because of the remoteness of the canyons and the scarcity of river access points. No campgrounds, supplies, or other facilities exist past Moab on the Colorado River or the town of Green River on the Green River. All river-runners must follow park regulations, which include carrying life jackets, using a fire pan for fires, and packing out all garbage and solid human waste. The river flow on both the Colorado and the Green rivers averages a gentle 2–4 mph (7–10 mph mph at high water). Boaters typically do 20 miles per day in canoes and 15 miles per day in rafts.

The Colorado has one modest rapid called the Slide, which is located 1.5 miles above the confluence, where rocks constrict the river to one-third of its normal width; the rapid is roughest during high water levels in May and June. This is the only difficulty on the 64 river miles from Moab. Inexperienced canoeists and rafters may wish to portage around it. The most popular launch points on the Colorado are the Moab Dock (just upstream from the U.S. 191 bridge near town) and the Potash Dock (17 miles downriver on the Potash Road, Highway 279).

On the Green, boaters at low water need to watch for rocky areas at the mouth of Millard Canyon (33.5 miles above the confluence, where a rock bar extends across the river) and at the mouth of Horse Canyon (14.5 miles above the confluence, where a rock and gravel bar on the right leaves only a narrow channel on the left

side). The trip from the town of Green River through Labyrinth and Stillwater Canyons is 120 miles. Launch places include Green River State Park (in Green River) and Mineral Canyon

ENDANGERED FISH OF THE COLORADO RIVER BASIN

Colorado squawfish *(Ptychocheilus lucius):* Native only to the Colorado and its tributaries, this species is the largest minnow in North America. It has been reported as weighing up to 100 pounds and measuring six feet long. Loss of habitat caused by dam construction has greatly curtailed its size and range. Fishers often confuse the smaller, more common **roundtail chub** *(Gila robusta)* with the Colorado squawfish; the chub is distinguished by a smaller mouth extending back only to the front of the eye.

Humpback chub *(Gila cypha):* Scientists first described this fish only in 1946 and know little about its life. This small fish usually weighs less than two pounds and measures less than 13 inches. Today the humpback chub hangs on the verge of extinction; it has retreated to a few small areas of the Colorado River, where the water still runs warm, muddy, and swift. The *bonytail chub (Gila robusta elegans)* has a similar size and shape, but without a hump; its numbers are also rapidly declining.

Humpback or razorback sucker *(Xyrauchen texanus):* This large sucker grows to weights of 10–16 pounds and lengths of about three feet. Its numbers have been slowly decreasing, especially above the Grand Canyon. They require warm, fast-flowing water to reproduce. Mating is a bizarre ritual in the spring: When the female has selected a suitable spawning site, two male fish press against the sides of her body. The female begins to shake her body until the eggs and spermatozoa are expelled simultaneously. One female can spawn three times, but she uses a different pair of males each time.

(52 miles above the confluence; reached on a fair-weather road from Highway 313).

No roads go to the confluence. The easiest return to civilization for nonmotorized craft is a pick-up by jetboat from Moab by Tex's Riverways or Tag-A-Long Tours (see Rafting and Boat Tours under Recreation in the Moab chapter). A far more difficult way out is hiking either of two trails just above the Cataract Canyon Rapids to four-wheel-drive roads on the rim.

Park rangers require that boaters above the confluence obtain a $20 **backcountry permit** either in person from the Moab office or by mail (at least two weeks in advance). River notes on boating the Green and Colorado are available on request from the Moab office, 435/259-3911. Bill and Buzz Belknap's *Canyonlands River Guide* has river logs and maps pointing out items of interest on the Green River below the town of Green River and all of the Colorado from the upper end of Westwater Canyon to Lake Powell. Don Baar's *A River Runner's Guide to Cataract Canyon* also has good coverage.

RIVER-RUNNING THROUGH CATARACT CANYON

The Colorado River enters Cataract Canyon at the confluence and picks up speed. The rapids begin four miles downstream and extend for the next 14 miles to Lake Powell. Especially in spring, the 26 or more rapids give a wild ride equal to the best in the Grand Canyon. The current zips along (up to 16 mph) and forms waves more than seven feet high! When the excitement dies down, boaters have a 34-mile trip across Lake Powell to Hite Marina; most people either carry a motor or arrange for a power boat to pick them up. Because of the real hazards of running the rapids, the National Park Service requires boaters to have proper equipment and a $30 **permit.** Many people go on a commercial trip in which everything has been taken care of (write the park for a list of boat companies or check the list of outfitters in the Moab chapter). Private groups need to contact the Canyonlands River Unit far in advance for permit details at 2282 W. Resource Blvd., Moab, UT 84532, 435/259-3911.

Additional Southeast Utah Sites

In addition to Arches and Canyonlands parks, this corner of Utah contains several scenic and culturally significant sites that deserve a detour. Following are some suggestions on other sites and itineraries to make this part of your journey pleasant and fulfilling.

DEAD HORSE POINT STATE PARK

The land drops away in sheer cliffs from this lofty perch west of Moab. Nearly 5,000 square miles of rugged canyon country lie in the distance. Two thousand feet below, the Colorado River twists through a gooseneck on its long journey to the sea. The river and its tributaries have carved canyons that reveal a geologic layer cake of colorful rock formations. Even in a region of impressive views around nearly every corner, Dead Horse Point stands out for its exceptional-

ly breathtaking panorama. You'll also see below you, along the Colorado River, the result of powerful underground forces: salt, under pressure, has pushed up overlying rock layers into an anticline. This formation, the Shafer Dome, contains potash that is being processed by the Moab Salt Plant. You can see the mine buildings, processing plant, and evaporation ponds (tinted blue to hasten evaporation).

A narrow neck of land only 30 yards wide connects the point with the rest of the plateau. Cowboys once herded wild horses onto the point, then placed a fence across the neck to make a 40-acre corral. They chose the desirable animals from the herd and let the rest go. According to one tale, a group of horses left behind after such a roundup became confused by the geography of the point. They couldn't find their way off and circled repeatedly until they died of thirst within sight of the river below. You may hear other stories of how the point got its name.

Besides the awe-inspiring views, the park also offers a visitors center (with displays), a campground, a picnic area, a group area, a nature trail, and hiking trails. The point has become popular with hang gliders. If you are lucky in timing your visit, you may see one or more crafts gliding back and forth above or below the viewpoint. Dead Horse Point is easily reached by paved road, either as a destination itself or as a side trip on the way to the Island in the Sky District of Canyonlands National Park. From Moab, head northwest 10 miles on U.S. 191, then turn left 22 miles on Highway 313. The drive along Highway 313 climbs through a scenic canyon and tops out on a ridge with panoramas of distant mesas, buttes, mountains, and canyons. Several rest areas are along the road.

Visitors Center and Campground

Stop here for registration ($7 per vehicle for day use) and exhibits about the park. Staff members will answer questions and provide checklists of local flora and fauna. A short slide presentation is given on request. In summer, rangers give talks at the amphitheater behind the visitors center. Books, maps, posters, postcards, film, T-shirts, charcoal, ice, and soft drinks can be purchased. Open daily 8 A.M.–6 P.M. in summer (May 16–Sept. 15) and 9 A.M.–5 P.M. the rest of the year. Contact the park at P.O. Box 609, Moab, UT 84532, 800/322-3770 or 435/259-2614 (reservations). A short nature trail that begins outside introduces the high-desert country and its plants. Continue 1.5 miles on the main road to viewpoints and picnic areas on the point itself. Primitive trails connect the point with several other overlooks, the visitors center, and the campground. Ask for a map at the visitors center.

Kayenta Campground, just past the visitors center, offers sites with electric hookups but no showers; open with water from about mid-March to late October; $14. The campground nearly always fills up during the main season. Either make reservations by calling 800/322-3770, or try to arrive by early afternoon to ensure a space. Winter visitors may camp on the point; no hookups are available, but the restrooms have water.

HOVENWEEP NATIONAL MONUMENT

The Anasazi Indians built many impressive masonry buildings during the early to mid-1200s, near the end of their 1,300-year stay in the area. A drought beginning in A.D. 1274 and lasting 25 years probably hastened their migration from this area. Several centuries of intensive farming, hunting, and woodcutting had already taken their toll on the land. Archaeologists believe the inhabitants retreated south in the late 1200s to sites in northwestern New Mexico and northeastern Arizona. The Ute Indian word *Hovenweep* means "deserted valley," an appropriate name for the lonely high-desert country left behind. The Anasazi at Hovenweep had much in common with the Mesa Verde culture, although the Dakota Sandstone here doesn't form large alcoves suitable for cliff-dweller villages. Ruins at Hovenweep remain essentially unexcavated, awaiting some future archaeologist's trowel.

The Anasazi farmers had a keen interest in the seasons because of their need to know the best time for planting crops. Astronomical stations (alignments of walls, doorways, and tiny openings) allowed the sun priests to determine the

Hovenweep National Monument

© W.C. MCRAE

CANYONLANDS

equinoxes and solstices with an accuracy of one or two days. This precision also may have been necessary for a complex ceremonial calendar. Astronomical stations at Hovenweep have been discovered at Hovenweep Castle and Unit-Type House of Square Tower Ruins and at Cajon Ruins.

Admission to the monument is $6 per vehicle, or $3 per person.

Getting to Hovenweep

One approach from U.S. 191 between Blanding and Bluff is to head east nine miles on Highway 262, continue straight six miles on a small, paved road to Hatch Trading Post, then follow the signs for 16 miles. A good way in from Bluff is to go east 21 miles on the paved road to Montezuma Creek and Aneth, then follow the signs north for 20 miles. A scenic 58-mile route through Montezuma Canyon begins five miles south of Monticello and follows unpaved roads to Hatch and on to Hovenweep; you can stop at the BLM's Three Turkey Ruin on the way. From Colorado, take a partly paved road west and north 41 miles from U.S. 666 (the turnoff is four miles south of Cortez).

The Anasazi farmers had a keen interest in the seasons because of their need to know the best time for planting crops. Astronomical stations allowed the sun priests to determine the equinoxes and solstices with an accuracy of one or two days.

Visitors Center

Hovenweep National Monument protects six groups of villages left behind by the Anasazi. The sites lie near the Colorado border southeast of Blanding. Square Tower Ruins Unit, where the visitors center is located, has the most ruins and the most varied architecture. In fact, you can find all of the Hovenweep architectural styles here. The visitors center has a few exhibits on the Anasazi and photos of local wildlife. A ranger will answer your questions, provide brochures and handouts about various aspects of the monument, and give directions for visiting the other ruin groups. Related books can be purchased.

Hours at the visitors center are 8 A.M.–4:30 P.M. year-round; 970/749-0510; the ruins stay open all the time. There's also a small campground at the monument, $10 per site, no reservations. Mesa Verde National Park administers Hovenweep from Mesa Verde National Park, CO 81330, 970/529-4465.

Square Tower Ruins

This extensive group of Anasazi towers and dwellings lines the rim and slopes of Little Ruin Canyon, which is located a short walk from the visitors center. Obtain a trail guide booklet from the ranger station; the booklet's map shows the several loop trails. You can take easy walks of less than one-half mile on the rim or combine all the trails for a loop of about two miles with only one up-and-down section in the canyon. The booklet has good descriptions of Anasazi life and architecture and of the plants growing along the trail. You'll see towers (D-shaped, square, oval, and round), cliff dwellings, surface dwellings, storehouses, kivas, and rock art. Take care not to disturb the fragile ruins. Keep an eye out for the prairie rattlesnake (a subspecies of the Western rattlesnake), which is active at night in summer and during the day in spring and autumn. Please stay on the trail; don't climb ruin walls or walk on rubble mounds.

Other Ruins

These ruins are good to visit if you'd like to spend more time in the area. You'll need a map and directions from a ranger to find them because they aren't signed. One group, the Goodman Point, near Cortez, Colorado, has relatively little to see except unexcavated mounds.

Holly Ruins group is noted for its Great House, Holly Tower, and Tilted Tower. Most of Tilted Tower fell away after the boulder on which it sat shifted. Great piles of rubble mark the sites of structures built on loose ground. Look for remnants of farming terraces in the canyon below the Great House. A hiking trail connects the campground at Square Tower Ruins with Holly Ruins; the route follows canyon bottoms and is about eight miles round-trip. Ask a ranger for a map and directions. Hikers could also continue to Horseshoe Ruins (one mile farther) and Hackberry Ruins (one-third mile beyond Horseshoe). All of these lie just across the Colorado border and about six miles (one-way) by road from the visitors center.

Horseshoe Ruins and **Hackberry Ruins** are best reached by an easy trail (one mile round-trip) off the road to Holly Ruins. Horseshoe House, built in a horseshoe shape similar to Sun Temple at Mesa Verde, has exceptionally good masonry work. Archaeologists haven't determined the purpose of the structure. An alcove in the canyon below contains a spring and a small shelter. A round tower nearby on the rim has a strategic view. Hackberry House has only one room still intact. Rubble piles and wall remnants abound in the area. The spring under an alcove here still has a good flow and supports lush growths of hackberry and cottonwood trees along with smaller plants.

Cutthroat Castle Ruins were remote even in Anasazi times. The ruins lie along an intermittent stream rather than at the head of a canyon like most other Hovenweep sites. Cutthroat Castle is a large multistory structure with both straight and curved walls. Three round towers stand nearby. Look for wall fragments and the circular depressions of kivas. High-clearance vehicles can go close to the ruins, about 11.5 miles (one-way) from the visitors center. Visitors with cars can drive to a trailhead and then walk to the ruins (1.5 miles round-trip on foot).

Cajon Ruins are at the head of a little canyon on Cajon Mesa in the Navajo Reservation in Utah, about nine miles southwest of the visitors center. The site has a commanding view across the San Juan Valley as far as Monument Valley. Buildings include a large multiroom structure, a round tower, and a tall square tower. An alcove just below has a spring and some rooms. Look for pictographs, petroglyphs, and grooves in rock (used for tool grinding). Farming terraces were located on the canyon's south side.

BETWEEN CANYONLANDS AND CAPITOL REEF

Just south of Blanding, Highway 95—here labeled the "Trail of the Ancients" National Scenic Byway—heads west across a high plateau toward the Colorado River, traversing Comb Ridge, Cedar Mesa, and many canyons. This is remote country, so fill up with gas before leaving Blanding because you can't depend on finding gasoline until Hanksville, which is 122 miles away. Fry Lodge and Hite and the other Lake Powell marinas do have gas and supplies, although their schedules are limited.

Cedar Mesa and its canyons have an exceptionally large number of prehistoric Anasazi Indian sites. Several groups of ruins lie just off the highway. Hikers will discover many more. If you would like to explore the Cedar Mesa area, be sure to drop in at the **Kane Gulch Ranger Station,** located four miles south on Highway 261 from Highway 95. Bureau of Land Management (BLM) staff issues the permits required to explore the Cedar Mesa backcountry at $8 per person for overnight stays in Grand Gulch, Fish Creek Canyon, and Owl Creek Canyon. The number of people permitted to camp at a given time is limited, so you may wish to call ahead; 435/587-1532. BLM people will also tell you about archaeological sites and their values, current hiking conditions, and locations of water. Day hikers will pay a $2 fee to hike certain sections of the monument. Check out the website at www.blm.gov/utah/monticello for current information.

Butler Wash Ruins
Well-preserved pueblo ruins left by the Anasazi lie tucked under an overhang across the wash 11 miles west on Highway 95 (between mileposts 111 and 112) from U.S. 191. At the trailhead on the north side of the highway, follow cairns one-half mile through juniper and piñon pine woodlands and across slickrock to the overlook.

Comb Ridge
Geologic forces have squeezed up the earth's crust in a long ridge running 80 miles south from the

Abajo Peaks into Arizona. Sheer cliff faces plunge 800 feet into Comb Wash on the west side. Engineering the highway down these cliffs took considerable effort. A parking area near the top of the grade offers expansive panoramas across Comb Wash.

Arch Canyon

This tributary canyon of Comb Wash has spectacular scenery and many Indian ruins. Much of the canyon can be seen on a day hike, but 2–3 days are needed to explore the upper reaches. The main streambeds usually have water (purify before drinking). To reach the trailhead, turn north 2.5 miles on a dirt road in Comb Wash (between mileposts 107 and 108 of Highway 95), go past a house and water tank, then park in a grove of cottonwood trees before a stream ford. This is also a good place to camp. The mouth of Arch Canyon lies just to the northwest (it's easy to miss!). Sign in at the register here. Look for an Indian ruin just up Arch Canyon on the right. More ruins lie tucked under alcoves farther upcanyon.

Arch Canyon Overlook

A road and short trail to the rim of Arch Canyon provide a beautiful view into the depths. Turn north four miles on Texas Flat Road (County 263) from Highway 95 between mileposts 102 and 103, park just before the road begins a steep climb, and walk east on an old jeep road about one-quarter mile to the rim. This is a fine place for a picnic, although it has no facilities or guardrails. Texas Flat Road is dirt but okay when dry for cars with good clearance. Trucks can continue up the steep hill to other viewpoints of Arch and Texas Canyons.

Mule Canyon Ruin

Archaeologists have excavated and stabilized this Anasazi village on the gentle slope of Mule Canyon's South Fork. A stone kiva, circular tower, and 12-room structure can be seen, all originally connected by tunnels. Cave Towers, two miles to the southeast, would have been visible from the top of the tower here. Signs describe the ruin and periods of Anasazi development. Turn north

0.3 mile on a paved road from Highway 95 between mileposts 101 and 102. Hikers can explore other Indian ruins in the North and South Forks of Mule Canyon; check with the Kane Gulch Ranger Station for advice and directions. You might see pieces of pottery and other artifacts in this area. Please leave *every* piece in place so that future visitors can enjoy the discovery, too. Federal laws also prohibit removing artifacts.

NATURAL BRIDGES NATIONAL MONUMENT

Streams in White Canyon and its tributaries cut deep canyons, then formed three impressive bridges. Silt-laden floodwaters sculpted the bridges by gouging tunnels between closely spaced loops in the meandering canyons. You can distinguish a natural bridge from an arch because the bridge spans a streambed and was initially carved out of the rock by flowing water. In the monument, these bridges illustrate three different stages of development, from the massive, newly formed Kachina Bridge to the middle-aged Sipapu Bridge, to the delicate and fragile span of Owachomo. All three natural bridges will continue to widen and eventually collapse under their own weight. A nine-mile scenic drive has overlooks of the picturesque bridges, Anasazi ruins, and the twisting canyons. You can follow short trails down from the rim to the base of each bridge or hike through all three bridges on an 8.6-mile trail loop.

Ruins, artifacts, and rock art indicate a long Indian occupation by tribes ranging from archaic groups to the Anasazi. Many fine cliff dwellings built by the Anasazi still stand. In 1883, prospector Cass Hite passed on tales of the huge stone bridges that he had discovered on a trip up White Canyon. Adventurous travelers, including a 1904 *National Geographic* magazine expedition, visited this isolated region to marvel at the bridges. The public's desire for protection of the bridges led President Theodore Roosevelt to proclaim the area a national monument in 1908. Federal administrators then changed the original bridge names from Edwin, Augusta, and Caroline to the Hopi names used today. Although the Hopi never lived here, the Anasazi of White Canyon very likely have descendants in the modern Hopi villages in Arizona.

Visitors Center

From the signed junction on Highway 95, drive in 4.5 miles on Highway 275 to the visitors center (elevation 6,505 feet). Monument Valley Overlook, two miles in, has a panorama south across a vast expanse of piñon pine and juniper trees to Monument Valley and distant mountains. A slide show in the visitors center illustrates how geologic forces and erosion created the canyons and natural bridges. Exhibits introduce the Indians who once lived here, as well as the area's geology, wildlife, and plants. Outside in front, labels identify common plants of the monument.

Rangers will answer your questions about the monument and surrounding area. If asked, staff will provide details on locations of ruins and rock-art sites. You can purchase regional books, topographic and geologic maps, postcards, slides, and film. Checklists of birds, other wildlife, and plants are available, too. Hours at the visitors center are daily 8 A.M.–5 P.M., Mar. 1–May 1 and Oct. 1–Oct. 31; 8 A.M.–6 P.M., May 1–Oct. 1; and 9 A.M.–4:30 P.M. the rest of the year; closed holidays Oct.–Apr. Admission is $6 per vehicle, or $3 per person or bicyclist.

The Bridge View Drive is always open during daylight hours except after heavy snowstorms. A winter visit can be very enjoyable; ice or mud often close the steep Sipapu and Kachina trails, but the short trail to Owachomo Bridge usually stays open. Pets aren't allowed on the trails or in the backcountry at any time.

The address is P.O. Box 1, Natural Bridges, Lake Powell, UT 84533, 435/692-1234. The nearest accommodations and café are at Fry Canyon, 26 miles northwest of the visitors center on Highway 95; the closest gas is available 40 miles east near Blanding or 50 west miles at Hite.

Photovoltaic Array

A large solar electric-power station sits across the road from the visitors center. This demonstration system, the largest in the world when constructed in 1980, has a quarter-million solar cells spread over nearly an acre and produces up to 100 kilowatts. Batteries, located elsewhere, store a two-day supply of power. The monument lies far from the nearest power lines, so the solar cells provide an alternative to continuously running diesel-powered generators.

Natural Bridges Campground

Drive 0.3 mile past the visitors center and turn right into the campground, set in a forest of piñon pine and juniper. Sites stay open all year; $10. Obtain water from a faucet in front of the visitors center. Rangers give talks several evenings each week during the summer season. The campground is often full, but there is a designated overflow area near the intersection of Highway 95 and Highway 261. RVs or trailers more than 21 feet long will also have to use this parking area.

Bridge View Drive

The nine-mile drive begins its one-way loop just past the campground. You can stop for lunch at a picnic area. Allow about 1.5 hours for a quick trip around. To make all the stops and do a bit of leisurely hiking will take most of a day. The cross-bedded sandstone of the bridges and canyons is the 265-million-year-old Cedar Mesa Formation.

Sipapu Bridge viewpoint is two miles from the visitors center. The Hopi name refers to the gateway from which their ancestors entered this world from another world below. Sipapu Bridge has reached its mature or middle-aged stage of development. The bridge is the largest in the monument and has a span of 268 feet and a height of 220 feet. Many people think Sipapu is the most magnificent of the bridges. Another view and a trail to the base of Sipapu are 0.8 mile farther. The viewpoint is about halfway down on an easy trail; allow one-half hour. A steeper and rougher trail branches off the viewpoint trail and winds down to the bottom of White Canyon, which is probably the best place to fully appreciate the bridge's size. Total round-trip distance is 1.2 miles with an elevation change of 600 feet.

Horse Collar Ruin, built by the Anasazi, looks as though it has been abandoned only a few decades, not 800 years. At 3.1 miles from the visitors center, a short trail leads to an overlook. The name comes from the shape of the doorway openings in two storage rooms. Hikers walking in the canyon between Sipapu and Kachina bridges can scramble up a steep rock slope to the site. Like all ancient ruins, these are fragile and must not be touched or entered. Only with such care will future generations of visitors be able to admire the well-preserved structures. Other groups of Anasazi dwellings can be seen in or near the monument, too; ask a ranger for directions.

Kachina Bridge viewpoint and trailhead are 5.1 miles from the visitors center. The massive bridge has a span of 204 feet and a height of 210 feet. A trail, 1.5 miles round-trip, leads to the canyon bottom next to the bridge; the elevation change is 650 feet. Look for pictographs near the base of the trail. Some of the figures resemble Hopi *kachinas* (spirits) and inspired the bridge's name. Armstrong Canyon joins White Canyon just downstream from the bridge; floods in each canyon abraded opposite sides of the rock fin that later became Kachina Bridge.

Owachomo Bridge viewpoint and trailhead are 7.1 miles from the visitors center. An easy walk leads to Owachomo's base—a half-mile round-trip with an elevation change of 180 feet. Graceful Owachomo spans 180 feet and is 106 feet high. Erosive forces have worn the venerable bridge to a thickness of only nine feet. Unlike the other two bridges, Owachomo spans a smaller tributary stream instead of a major canyon. Two streams played a role in the bridge's formation. Floods coming down the larger Armstrong Canyon surged against a sandstone fin on one side while floods in a small side canyon wore away the rock on the other side. Eventually a hole formed, and waters flowing down the side canyon took the shorter route through the bridge. The name *Owachomo* means "flat-rock mound" in the Hopi language; a large rock outcrop nearby inspired the name. Before construction of the present road, a trail winding down the opposite side of Armstrong Canyon provided the only access for monument visitors. The trail, little used now, connects with Highway 95.

Hiking

A canyon hike through all three bridges can be the highlight of a visit to the monument. Un-

maintained trails make an 8.6-mile loop in White and Armstrong canyons and cross a wooded plateau. The trip is easier if you start from Sipapu and come out the relatively gentle grades at Owachomo. Most people take 5–6 hours for this moderately difficult hike. You can save 2.5 miles by arranging a car shuttle between Sipapu and Owachomo trailheads. Another option is to go in or out on the Kachina Bridge Trail midway, cutting the hiking distance about in half. On nearing Owachomo Bridge from below, a small sign points out the trail that bypasses a deep pool. The canyons remain in their wild state; you'll need some hiking experience, water, proper footwear, a compass, and a map (the handout available at the visitors center is adequate). The USGS 71/2-minute topographic maps also cover this area.

When hiking in the canyons, keep an eye out for natural arches and Indian writings. Please don't step on midget faded rattlesnakes or other living entities (such as the fragile cryptobiotic soil). Be aware of flash-flood dangers, especially if you see big clouds billowing in the sky in an upstream direction. You don't need a hiking permit, although it's a good idea to talk beforehand with a ranger to find out current conditions. Overnight camping within the monument is permitted only in the campground. Backpackers, however, can go up or down the canyons and camp outside the monument boundaries. Just be careful to choose high ground in case a flood comes rumbling through! Note that vehicles can't be parked overnight on the loop drive.

CROSSING LAKE POWELL BY FERRY

Eight miles west of the entrance to National Bridges National Monument, travelers will need to make a decision: whether to continue on Highway 95 to cross the Colorado by bridge at Hite or to follow Highway 276 to the Halls Crossing Marina and cross the river—at this point tamed by the Glen Canyon Dam and known as Lake Powell—by car ferry.

Obviously, the ferry is the more exotic choice, and both Halls Crossing and Bullfrog marinas offer lodging and food, which are a relative scarcity in this remote area. Crossing the Colorado on the ferry also makes it easy to access the Bullfrog-Notom Road, a 60-mile partly paved road that climbs through dramatic landscapes on its way to Capitol Reef National Park's otherwise remote Waterfold Pocket. The road ends at Notom, just four miles from the eastern entrance to Capitol Reef park on Highway 24. Alternately, drivers can turn west on the Burr Trail and follow back roads to Boulder, near the Escalante River Canyon.

Glen Canyon National Recreation Area

Lake Powell lies at the center of Glen Canyon National Recreation Area, a vast recreation area that covers 1.25 million acres in Arizona and Utah. When the Glen Canyon Dam was completed in 1964, conservationists deplored the loss of remote and beautiful Glen Canyon of the Colorado River beneath the lake waters. In terms of beauty and sheer drama, Glen Canyon was considered the equal of the Grand Canyon. Today, we have only words, pictures, and memories to remind us of its wonders. On the other hand, the 186-mile-long lake now provides easy access to an area most had not even known existed. Lake Powell is the second-largest human-made lake within the United States. Only Lake Mead, farther downstream, has a greater water-storage capacity. Lake Powell, however, has three times more shoreline—1,960 miles—and holds enough water to cover the state of Pennsylvania one foot deep! Just a handful of roads approach the lake, so access is basically limited to boats—bays and coves offer nearly limitless opportunities for exploration by boaters—or long-distance hiking trails.

Admission to Glen Canyon National Recreation Area is $5 per vehicle or $3 per pedestrian or bicyclist for seven days. There is no charge for passing through Page on Highway U.S. 89. For information on Glen Canyon National Recreation Area, write: Superintendent, P.O. Box 1507, Page, AZ 86040, 520/608-6404, website: www.nps.gpv/glca.

Halls Crossing/Bullfrog Ferry Service

At the junction of Highway 276, a large sign lists the departure times for the ferry; note that these may be different than the times listed in the widely circulated flyer. Confirm the departure times before making the 42-mile journey to Halls Crossing.

The crossing time from Halls Crossing to Bullfrog is 27 minutes (the crossing is only three miles, however). Fares for vehicles smaller than 19 feet 11 inches in length are $12, which includes the driver and all passengers. Bicycles are $3, and motorcycles are $5. Foot passengers are $3 adult. During the high summer season, from May 15–Sept. 14, the ferries run on the hour daily beginning at 8 A.M. The final ferry from Halls Crossing departs at 6 P.M., and the final ferry from Bullfrog departs at 7 P.M. From Apr. 15–May 14, and from Sept. 15–Oct. 31, the Halls Ferry begins operation at 8 A.M. and has sailings every two hours until 4 P.M. The Bullfrog ferry begins at 9 A.M. and has sailings every two hours until 5 P.M. The rest of the year, from Nov. 1–Apr. 14, this same schedule continues, except the final sailings of the day are at 2 P.M. and 3 P.M., respectively.

For reservations and information regarding lodging, tours, boating, and recreation at both Halls Crossing and Bullfrog Marina, contact **Lake Powell Resorts & Marinas** at 100 Lakeshore Drive, Page, AZ 86040, 800/528-6154, website: www.lakepowell.com.

Arriving at **Halls Crossing** by road, you'll first reach a small store offering three-bedroom housekeeping units in trailer houses and an RV park. Coin-operated showers and a laundry room at the RV park are also open to the public. The separate National Park Service **campground,** just beyond and to the left, has sites with a good view of the lake, drinking water, and restrooms; no reservations, $18. Continue one-half mile on the main road to the boat ramp and **Halls Crossing Marina,** 435/684-2261. The marina has a larger store (groceries and fishing and boating supplies), tours to Rainbow Bridge, a boat rental office (fishing, ski, and houseboat), a gas dock, slips, and storage. The **ranger station** is nearby, although rangers are usually out on patrol; look for their vehicle in the area if the office is closed.

Bullfrog Marina has the most extensive visitor facilities of Lake Powell's Utah marinas. It's more like a small town, with a **visitors center,** 435/684-2243, clinic, stores, service station, and a handsome hotel and restaurant. In addition to daily car ferries across to Halls Crossing, the marina offers tours to sights along Lake Powell, including **Rainbow Bridge,** from Apr. 15–Oct. 31, plus boat rentals. Contact the marina at P.O. Box 4055-Bullfrog, Lake Powell, UT 84533, 435/684-2233.

Defiance House Lodge, 800/528-6154 or 435/684-3000, offers comfortable lakeview accommodations and the **Anasazi Restaurant** (open daily in summer for breakfast, lunch, and dinner). Rooms begin at $116 (single or double) in summer (Apr. 1–Oct. 31) and $80 (single or double) in winter. The front desk at the lodge also handles **housekeeping units** (trailers) and an **RV park** Showers, a laundry room, a convenience store, and a post office are at **Trailer Village.** The RV park has showers. Ask the visitors center staff or rangers for directions to primitive camping areas with vehicle access elsewhere along Bullfrog Bay.

Bullfrog Marina can be reached from the north along paved Highway 276. It's 40 miles between Bullfrog and the junction with Highway 95. At Ticaboo, 20 miles north of Bullfrog, is another good lodging option. The **Ticaboo Lodge,** 800/842-2267 or 435/788-2110, is a new hotel, restaurant, and service station complex that pretty much constitutes all of Ticaboo. A double room in summer costs $89.

For more information on the Bullfrog/Notom Road, see the Capitol Reef chapter.

NATURAL BRIDGES TO LAKE POWELL VIA HIGHWAY 95

If the Lake Powell ferry schedule doesn't match your travel plans, Highway 95 will quickly get you across the Colorado River and to the junction with Highway 24 at Hanksville.

Fry Canyon Lodge

The store here originally served uranium mining camps during the 1950s. Today this venerable café and motel, 435/259-5334, website: www.frycanyon.com, offer the only services on

Highway 95 between Blanding and Hite Marina. Comfortable, newly remodeled rooms cost $74–89 (double). In winter, the café may be closed, but accommodations are usually still available. Two Anasazi ruins can be viewed nearby; a road goes to an overlook of one ruin and a short trail goes to the other. Ask for directions. Fry Canyon is 19 miles northwest of the Natural Bridges National Monument turn-off and 24 miles southeast of the Hite Marina turn-off.

Hite

In 1883, Cass Hite came to Glen Canyon in search of gold. He found some at a place later named Hite City and set off a small gold rush. Cass and a few of his relatives operated a small store and post office, which were the only services for many miles. Travelers wishing to cross the Colorado River here had the difficult task of swimming their animals across. Arthur Chaffin, a later resident, put through the first road and opened a ferry service in 1946. The Chaffin Ferry served uranium prospectors and adventurous motorists until the lake backed up to the spot in 1964. A steel bridge now spans the Colorado River upstream from Hite Marina. Cass Hite's store and the ferry site are underwater about five miles downlake from Hite Marina.

Beyond Hite, on the tiny neck of land between the Colorado River bridge and the Dirty Devil bridge, an unmarked dirt road turns north. Called the Hite Road, or the Orange Cliffs Road, this long and rugged road eventually links up with backcountry routes—including the Flint Trail—in the Maze District of Canyonlands National Park.

The uppermost marina on Lake Powell, Hite lies 141 lake miles from Glen Canyon Dam. From here, boats can continue uplake to the mouth of Dark Canyon in Cataract Canyon at low water or into Canyonlands National Park at high water. Hite tends to be quieter than the other marinas and is favored by some anglers and families. Facilities include a small **store** with gas pumps, three-bedroom housekeeping units in trailer houses, and a primitive **campground** (no drinking water; free). Primitive camping is also available nearby off Highway 95 at Dirty Devil,

© W.C. MCRAE

Lake Powell, near Hite

Farley Canyon, White Canyon, Blue Notch, and other locations. A **ranger station** is occasionally open; look for the ranger's vehicle at other times. Contact **Lake Powell Resorts & Marinas** for accommodation and boat rental reservations at 100 Lakeshore Drive, Page, AZ 86040, 800/528-6154; the website is at www.lakepowell.com. Hite Marina can also be contacted at P.O. Box 501, Lake Powell, UT 84533, 435/684-2278.

CANYONLANDS

Capitol Reef

Wonderfully sculptured rock layers in a rainbow of colors put on a fine show here. Although you'll find these same rocks throughout much of the Four Corners region, their artistic variety has no equal outside Capitol Reef National Park. About 70 million years ago, gigantic forces within the earth began to uplift, squeeze, and fold more than a dozen rock formations into the central feature of the park today—Waterpocket Fold, so named for the many small pools of water trapped by the tilted strata. Erosion has since carved spires, graceful curves, canyons, and arches. Waterpocket Fold extends 100 miles between Thousand Lake Mountain in the north and Lake Powell in the south. The most spectacular cliffs and rock formations of Waterpocket Fold form Capitol Reef, located north of Pleasant Creek and curving northwest across the Fremont River toward Thousand Lake Mountain. The reef was named by explorers who found Waterpocket Fold a barrier to travel and likened it to a reef blocking passage on the ocean. The rounded sandstone hills reminded them of the Capitol Dome in Washington, D.C., hence the name Capitol Reef.

Roads and hiking trails in the park provide access to the colorful rock layers and to the plants and wildlife that live here. You'll also see rem-

The pioneer orchards at Fruita still produce fruit beneath the towering walls of Fremont Canyon.

nants of the area's long human history—petroglyphs and storage bins of the prehistoric Fremont Indians, a schoolhouse and other structures built by Mormon pioneers, and several small uranium mines of the 20th century. Legends tell of Butch Cassidy and other outlaw members of the "Wild Bunch" who hid out in these remote canyons in the 1890s.

Even travelers short on time will enjoy a quick look at visitors-center exhibits and a drive on Highway 24 through an impressive cross section of Capitol Reef cut by the Fremont River. You can see more of the park on the Scenic Drive, a narrow paved road that heads south from the visitors center. The drive passes beneath spectacular cliffs of the reef and enters scenic Grand Wash and Capitol Gorge Canyons; allow at least 1.5 hours for the 21-mile round-trip (plus side trips). The fair-weather Notom/Bullfrog Road (paved as far as Notom) heads south along the other side of the reef for almost 80 miles with fine views of Waterpocket Fold. Burr Trail Road (dirt inside the park) in the south actually climbs over the fold in a steep set of switchbacks, connecting Notom Road with Boulder. Only drivers with high-clearance vehicles can explore Cathedral Valley in the park's northern district. All of these roads provide access to viewpoints and hiking trails. A $5-per-vehicle park entrance fee is collected on the Scenic Drive.

Natural History

CLIMATE

Expect hot summer days (highs in the upper 80s and low 90s) and cool nights. Winter brings cool days (highs in the 40s) and night temperatures dropping into the low 20s and teens. Snow accents the colored rocks while rarely hindering traffic on the main highway. Winter travel on the back roads and trails may be halted by snow, but it soon melts when the sun comes out. Annual precipitation averages only seven inches, peaking in the late summer thunderstorm season.

GEOLOGY

Exposed rocks reveal windswept deserts, rivers, mud flats, and inland seas of long ago. Nearly all the layers date from the Mesozoic era (65–230 million years ago), when dinosaurs ruled the earth. Later uplift and twisting of the land, which continues to this day, built up the Colorado

THE WATERPOCKET FOLD

About 65 million years ago, well before the Colorado Plateau uplifted, sedimentary rock layers in south-central Utah buckled, forming a steep-sided monocline, a rock fold with one very steep side in an area of otherwise nearly horizontal layers. A monocline is a "step-up" in the rock layers along an underlying fault. The rock layers on the west side of the Waterpocket Fold have been lifted more than 7000 feet higher than the layers to the east. The 100-mile-long fold was then subjected to millions of years of erosion, slowly removing the upper layers and revealing the warped sedimentary layers at its base. Continued erosion of the sandstone has left many basins, or "waterpockets" along the fold. These seasonal water sources, often called water "tanks" are used by desert animals, and formed a water source for prehistoric Indians. Erosion of the tilted rock layers continues today, forming colorful cliffs, massive domes, soaring spires, stark monoliths, twisting canyons, and graceful arches. Getting a sense of the Waterpocket Fold requires some off-pavement driving. The best viewpoint is along the Burr Trail Road, which climbs up the fold between Boulder and the Notom-Bullfrog Road.

Creation of the Waterpocket Fold

The Ancient Fold

Waterpocket Fold Today

CAPITOL REEF

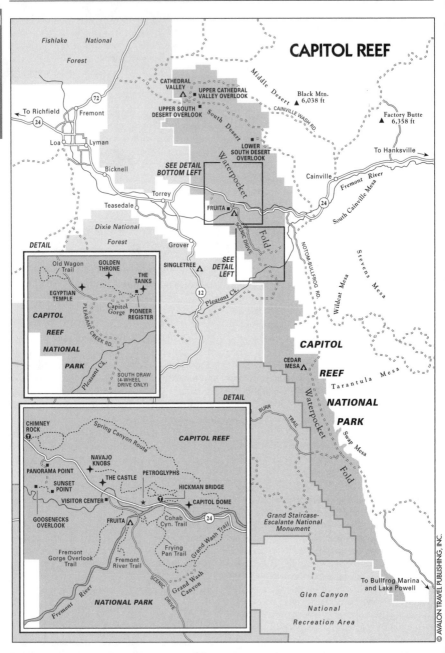

CAPITOL REEF

CAPITOL REEF

Fishlake National Forest

To Richfield
Fremont
72
24
Loa
Lyman
Bicknell
Teasedale
Dixie National Forest
Torrey
Grover

CATHEDRAL VALLEY
UPPER CATHEDRAL VALLEY OVERLOOK
UPPER SOUTH DESERT OVERLOOK
South Desert
Middle Desert
Black Mtn. 6,038 ft
CAINVILLE WASH RD.
Factory Butte 6,358 ft
LOWER SOUTH DESERT OVERLOOK
To Hanksville
Cainville
Fremont River
South Cainville Mesa

Waterpocket

SEE DETAIL BOTTOM LEFT

FRUITA

SCENIC DRIVE

Fold

SEE DETAIL LEFT

Singletree

12
Pleasant Ck.

NOTOM-BULLFROG RD.

Stevens Mesa
Wildcat Mesa

CAPITOL

REEF
CEDAR MESA

Tarantula Mesa

NATIONAL

PARK

Waterpocket

Swap Mesa

DETAIL

Old Wagon Trail
GOLDEN THRONE
THE TANKS
EGYPTIAN TEMPLE
Capitol Gorge
PIONEER REGISTER
CAPITOL
REEF
NATIONAL
PARK
PLEASANT CREEK RD.
Pleasant Ck.
SOUTH DRAW (4-WHEEL DRIVE ONLY)

BURR TRAIL

Fold

DETAIL

CHIMNEY ROCK
Spring Canyon Route
CAPITOL REEF
NAVAJO KNOBS
PANORAMA POINT
THE CASTLE
PETROGLYPHS
SUNSET POINT
HICKMAN BRIDGE
VISITOR CENTER
CAPITOL DOME
GOOSENECKS OVERLOOK
FRUITA
Cohab Cyn. Trail
24
Fremont Gorge Overlook Trail
Frying Pan Trail
Grand Wash Trail
Fremont River Trail
SCENIC DRIVE
Grand Wash Canyon
NATIONAL PARK
Fremont River

Grand Staircase-Escalante National Monument

To Bullfrog Marina and Lake Powell

Glen Canyon National Recreation Area

© AVALON TRAVEL PUBLISHING, INC.

DATURA: A PLANT WITH A PAST

As dusk approaches, the huge white flowers of the datura open, and their sweet smell attracts moths, beetles, and wasps. As intoxicating as the datura's fragrance may be, it doesn't hold a candle to the plant itself, which is a potent hallucinogen. It also contains toxic alkaloids, including nerve toxins capable of killing humans and animals.

Nonetheless, datura (also known as jimsonweed) has a rich history of folk use. Many native peoples in the Americas, including the Zuni, Chumash, and even the Aztecs, were familiar with its uses; some regarded it as a sacred. It's been used as a shamanic ritual drug, as well as a topical analgesic and even as a sort of medieval Mickey Finn. (Pimps in the Middle Ages used datura to make the prostitutes in their employ more compliant.) Accounts from Jamestown, Virginia, one of the earliest British settlements in North America, report a group of soldiers going insane after eating datura in 1676.

Up until 1968, datura was a component of some over-the-counter asthma medicines; it was banned when it gained popularity among American youth and people began using these medications recreationally. Atropine, an anticholinergenic substance often used by ophthalmologists to dilate pupils, is datura's main psychoactive component. It's a central nervous system depressant that mostly causes users to feel drowsy—some report vivid dreams—and also increases heart rate, sometimes to dangerous levels.

In Carlos Castenada's *The Teachings of Don Juan: A Yaqui Way of Knowledge*, Don Juan warns that datura "is as powerful as the best of allies, but there is something I personally don't like about her. She distorts men. She gives them a taste of power too soon without fortifying their hearts and makes them domineering and unpredictable. She makes them weak in the middle of their great power."

Plateau of southern Utah and the Rocky Mountains to the east. Immense forces squeezed the rocks until they bent up and over from east to west in the massive crease of Waterpocket Fold.

FLORA AND FAUNA

Ponderosa pine and other cool-climate vegetation grow on the flanks of Thousand Lake Mountain (7,000–9,000 feet high) in the northwest corner of the park. Most of Waterpocket Fold, however, is at 5,000–7,000 feet, covered with sparse juniper and piñon pine that cling precariously in cracks and thin soils of the slickrock. The soil from each rock type generally determines what will grow. Mancos Shale forms a poor clay soil supporting only saltbush, shadscale, and galleta grass. On Dakota Sandstone you'll see mostly sage and rabbitbrush. Clays of the Morrison Formation repel nearly all plants, while its sandstone nurtures mostly juniper, piñon pine, and cliffrose; uranium prospectors discov-

ered that *astragalus* and prince's plume commonly grow near ore deposits. Sands of the Summerville Formation nourish grasses and four-wing saltbush. The Fremont River and several creeks provide a lush habitat of cottonwood, tamarisk, willow, and other water-loving plants.

Streamside residents include beaver, muskrat, mink, tree lizard, Great Basin spadefoot toad, Rocky Mountain toad, and leopard frog. Spadefoot toads, fairy shrimp, and insects have adapted to the temporary water pockets by completing the aquatic phase of their short life cycles in a hurry. Near water or out in the drier country, you might see mule deer, coyote, gray fox, porcupine, spotted and striped skunks, badger, blacktailed jackrabbit, desert cottontail, yellow-bellied marmot, rock squirrel, Colorado chipmunk, Ord's kangaroo rat, canyon mouse, and five known species of bats. With luck, you may sight a relatively rare mountain lion or black bear.

While you can't miss seeing the many small lizards along the trails, snakes tend to be more secretive; those in the park include the striped whipsnake, Great Basin gopher snake, wandering garter snake, and the rarely seen desert faded pygmy rattlesnake. Some common birds are the sharp-shinned hawk, American kestrel, chukar, mourning dove, white-throated swift, black-chinned and broad-tailed hummingbirds, violet-green swallow, common raven, piñon and scrub jays, canyon and rock wrens, and rufous-sided towhee. Most wildlife, except birds, wait until evening to come out, and they disappear again the following morning.

Exploring the Park

VISITORS CENTER

Start with a 10-minute slideshow, which is shown on request, introducing Capitol Reef's natural wonders and history. A giant relief map gives you a bird's-eye view of the entire park. Rock samples and diagrams illustrate seven of the geologic formations you'll be seeing. Photos identify plants and birds found here. Prehistoric Fremont Indian artifacts on display include petroglyph replicas, sheepskin moccasins, pottery, basketry, stone knives, spear and arrow points, and bone jewelry. Other historic exhibits outline exploration and early Mormon settlement.

Hikers can pick up a map of trails that are near the visitors center and of longer routes in the southern park areas; naturalists will want the checklists of plants, birds, mammals, and other wildlife; history buffs can learn more about the area's settlement and the founding of the park. Rangers offer nature walks, campfire programs, and other special events from Easter to mid-October; the bulletin board outside the visitors center lists what's on. Hours at the visitors center are daily 8 A.M.–7 P.M. June–Sept.; daily 8 A.M.–4:30 P.M. the rest of the year. The visitors center is on Highway 24 at the turn-off for Fruita Campground and the Scenic Drive. For more information, contact Capitol Reef National Park, Torrey, UT 84775, 435/425-3791, website: www.nps.gov/care.

ALONG HIGHWAY 24

From the west, Highway 24 drops from the broad mountain valley near Torrey onto Sulphur Creek, with dramatic rock formations soaring into the horizon. A huge amphitheater of stone rings the basin, with formations such as Twin Rocks, Chimney Rock, and The Castle glowing in deep red and yellow tones. Ahead, the canyon narrows as the Fremont River slips between the cliffs to carve its chasm through Waterpocket Fold. Take in this incredible vista from **Panorama Point,** 2.5 miles west of the visitors center on the south side of the highway. Follow signs south for 0.15 mile to Panorama Point and views of Capitol Reef to the east and Boulder Mountain to the west. A sign explains how glacial meltwaters carried basalt boulders from Boulder Mountain to the reef 8,000–200,000 years ago.

Continue past Panorama Point one mile on a gravel road to the **Goosenecks of Sulphur Creek.** A short trail leads to the Goosenecks Overlook on the rim (elevation 6,400 feet) for dizzying views to the creek below. Canyon walls display shades of yellow, green, brown, and red. Another easy trail leads one-third mile to Sunset Point and panoramic views of the Capitol Reef cliffs and the distant Henry Mountains.

Remnants of the pioneer community of Fruita stretch along the narrow Fremont River Canyon. The **Fruita Schoolhouse** is just east of the visitors center on the north side of the highway. Early settlers completed this one-room log structure in 1896. Teachers struggled at times with rowdy students, but the kids learned their three R's in grades one through eight. Mormon Church meetings, dances, town meetings, elections, and other community gatherings took place here. Lack of students caused the school's closing in 1941. Rangers are on duty some days in summer (ask at the visitors center). At other times, you can peer inside the windows and listen to a recording of a former teacher recalling what school life was like.

Farther down the canyon, 1.2 miles east of the visitors center on the north side of the highway, are several panels of Fremont **petroglyphs**. (Watch for the road signs.) Several human figures with headdresses and mountain sheep decorate the cliff. You can see more petroglyphs by walking to the left and right along the cliff face. Stay on the trail and *do not* climb the talus slope.

Behunin Cabin is located 6.2 miles east of the visitors center on the south side of the highway. Elijah Cutlar Behunin used blocks of sandstone to build this cabin in about 1882. He moved on, though, when floods made life too difficult. Small openings allow a look inside the dirt-floored structure, but no furnishings remain.

Near the end of the narrow sandstone canyon, a small waterfall in the **Fremont River** attracts photographers and impromptu swimming parties. The river twists through a narrow human-made crack in the rock before making its final plunge into a pool below. A sign warns of hazardous footing above the falls, which are dangerous for children. Instead, take the sandy path from the parking area to where you can safely view the falls from below. Use extreme caution if you intend to cool off in the pool at the base of the waterfall because the undertow is strong and dangerous. Parking is 6.9 miles east of the visitors center on the north side of the highway.

ALONG THE SCENIC DRIVE

Turn south from Highway 24 at the visitors center to experience some of the reef's best scenery and to learn more about its geology. An illustrated pamphlet, available on the drive or in the visitors center, has keyed references to numbered stops along the 25-mile (round-trip) drive. Descriptions identify rock layers and explain how they were formed. Just a quick tour takes 1.5 hours, but several hiking trails may tempt you to extend your stay. The scenic drive is paved, although side roads have gravel surfaces.

You'll first pass orchards and several of Fruita's buildings. A **blacksmith shop** (0.7 miles from the visitors center on the right) displays tools, harnesses, farm machinery, and Fruita's first trac-

Fruita Schoolhouse sits at the base of the Fremont Canyon.

© W.C. MCRAE

tor. The tractor didn't arrive until 1940—long after the rest of the country had modernized. In a recording, a rancher tells about living and working in Fruita.

The **Historic Gifford Homestead,** one mile south on the Scenic Drive, is typical of rural Utah farmhouses of the early 1900s. Cultural demonstrations and handmade sales items are available. A picnic area is just beyond; with fruit trees and grass, this makes a pretty spot for lunch. A short trail crosses orchards and the Fremont River to the Fruita Schoolhouse.

The Scenic Drive leaves the Fremont River valley and climbs up a desert slope, with the rock walls of the Waterfold Pocket rising to the east. Turn east into the **Grand Gulch**, a dry channel etched through the sandstone. A dirt road follows the twisting gulch one mile, with sheer rock walls rising along the sandy stream bed. At the road's end, an easy hiking trail follows the gulch 2.5 miles to its mouth along Highway 24.

Past the Slickrock Divide, the rock lining the reef deepens into a ruby red and forms itself into odd columns and spires that resemble statuary. Called the **Egyptian Temple,** this is one of the most striking and colorful areas along the Scenic Drive.

Turn right 8.3 miles from the visitors center, where the Scenic Drive curves east toward Capitol Gorge, onto **Pleasant Creek Road,** which continues south below the face of the reef. After three miles, the sometimes rough dirt road passes Sleeping Rainbow/Floral Ranch (closed to the public) and ends at Pleasant Creek. A rugged four-wheel-drive road continues on the other side but is much too rough for cars. Floral Ranch dates back to Capitol Reef's early years of settlement. In 1939 it became the Sleeping Rainbow Guest Ranch, from the Indian name for Waterpocket Fold. Now the ranch belongs to the park, but the former owners still live here. Pleasant Creek's perennial waters begin high on Boulder Mountain to the west and cut a scenic canyon

completely through Capitol Reef. Hikers can head downstream through the three-mile-long canyon and return, or continue another three miles cross-country to Notom Road.

The **Capitol Gorge** is the end of the Scenic Drive, 10.7 miles from the visitors center. Capitol Gorge is a dry canyon through Capitol Reef much like Grand Wash, although with a somewhat different character. Believe it or not, the narrow, twisting Capitol Gorge was the route of the main state highway through south-central Utah for 80 years! Mormon pioneers laboriously cleared a path so wagons could go through, a task they repeated every time flash floods rolled in a new set of boulders. Cars bounced their way down the canyon until 1962, when the present Highway 24 opened, but few traces of the old road remain today. Walking is easy along the gravel riverbed, but don't enter if storms threaten. An easy one-mile saunter down the gorge will take day hikers past **petroglyphs** and a "register" rockface where pioneers carved their names. For other Capitol Gorge hikes, see following sections.

NORTH DISTRICT

Only the most adventurous travelers get into the remote canyons and desert country of the north. The few roads *cannot* be negotiated by ordinary cars. In good weather, high-clearance vehicles can enter the region from the east, north, and west. The roads lead through stately sandstone monoliths of Cathedral Valley, volcanic remnants, badlands country, many low mesas, and vast sand flats. Foot travel allows closer inspection of these features or lengthy excursions into the canyons of Polk, Deep, and Spring creeks, which cut deeply into the flanks of Thousand Lake Mountain.

Mountain bikers enjoy these challenging roads as well, but they must stay on established roads only. Much of the north district is good for horseback riding, too. **Cathedral Valley Campground's** five sites provide a place to stop for the night; rangers won't permit car camping elsewhere in the district. The **Upper Cathedral Valley Trail,** located just below the campground, is an enjoyable one-mile walk offering excellent views of the Cathedrals. Hikers with a back-

the Egyptian Temple Formation, along Capitol Reef's Scenic Road

country permit must camp at least one-half mile from the nearest road. You can purchase a small guide to this area at the visitors center.

SOUTH DISTRICT
Notom-Bullfrog Road

Capitol Reef is only a small part of Waterpocket Fold. By taking the Notom-Bullfrog Road, you'll see nearly 80 miles of the fold's eastern side. This route crosses some of the younger geologic layers, such as those of the Morrison Formation that form colorful hills. In other places, eroded layers of the Waterpocket Fold jut up at 70-degree angles. The Henry Mountains to the east and the many canyons on both sides of the road add to the memorable panoramas. The road has been paved as far as Notom, and about 25 miles are paved on the southern end near Bullfrog. The rest of the road is good-condition dirt and gravel road. Most cars should have no trouble negotiating this road in good weather. Keep an eye on the weather before setting out, though; the dirt and gravel surface is usually okay for cars when dry but can be too slippery and gooey for *any* vehicle when wet. Sandy spots and washouts may present a problem for low-clearance vehicles; contact the visitors center to check current conditions. Have a full gas tank and carry extra water and food because no services are available between Highway 24 and Bullfrog Marina. Purchase a small guide to this area at the visitors center. Features and mileage along the drive from north to south include the following:

Mile 0.0: The turn-off from Highway 24 is 9.2 miles east of the visitors center and 30.2 miles west of Hanksville (another turn-off from Highway 24 is three miles east).

Mile 2.2: Pleasant Creek; the mouth of the canyon is 5–6 miles upstream, although it's only about three miles by heading cross-country from south of Notom. Hikers can follow the canyon three miles upstream through Capitol Reef to Pleasant Creek Road (off the Scenic Drive).

Mile 4.1: Notom Ranch is to the west; once a small town, Notom is now a private ranch.

Mile 8.1: Burrow Wash; hikers can explore the narrow canyon upstream.

Mile 9.3: Cottonwood Wash; another canyon hike just upstream.

Mile 10.4: Five Mile Wash; yet another canyon hike.

Mile 13.3: Sheets Gulch; a scenic canyon lies upstream here, too.

Mile 14.1: Sandy Ranch Junction; high-clearance vehicles can turn east 16 miles to the Henry Mountains.

Mile 14.2: Oak Creek Access Road to the west; turn here for Oak Creek. The creek cuts a two-mile-long canyon through Capitol Reef that's a good day hike. Backpackers sometimes start upstream at Lower Bowns Reservoir (off Highway 12) and hike the 15 miles to Oak Creek Access Road. The clear waters of Oak Creek flow all year but must be treated for drinking.

Mile 14.4: Oak Creek crossing.

Mile 20.0: Entering Capitol Reef National Park; a small box has information sheets.

Mile 22.3: Cedar Mesa Campground to the west; the small five-site campground is surrounded by junipers and has fine views of Waterpocket Fold and the Henry Mountains. Sites have tables and grills; there's an outhouse but no drinking water; free. **Red Canyon Trail** begins here and heads west into a huge box canyon in Waterpocket Fold; four miles round-trip.

Mile 26.0: Bitter Creek Divide; streams to the north flow to the Fremont River; Halls Creek on the south side runs through Strike Valley to Lake Powell, 40 miles away.

Mile 34.1: Burr Trail Road Junction; turn west up the steep switchbacks to ascend Waterpocket Fold and continue to Boulder and Highway 12 (36 miles). Burr Trail is the only road that actually crosses the top of the fold, and it's one of the most scenic in the park. Driving conditions are similar to the Notom-Bullfrog Road—okay for cars when dry. Pavement begins at the park boundary and continues to Boulder. Although paved, the Burr Trail still needs to be driven slowly because of its curves and potholes. The section of road through Long Canyon has especially pretty scenery.

Mile 36.0: Surprise Canyon Trailhead; a hike into this narrow, usually shaded canyon takes 1–2 hours.

© W.C. MCRAE

Notom-Bullfrog Road climbing up Waterpocket Fold

Mile 36.6: The Post; a small trading post here once served sheepherders and some cattlemen, but today this spot is just a reference point. Park here to hike to Headquarters Canyon. A trailhead for Lower Muley Twist Canyon via Halls Creek lies at the end of a half-mile-long road to the south.

Mile 37.5: Leaving Capitol Reef National Park; a small box has information sheets. Much of the road between here and Glen Canyon National Recreation Area has been paved.

Mile 45.5: Road junction; turn right (south) to continue to Bullfrog Marina (25 miles) or go straight (east) for Starr Springs Campground (23 miles) in the Henry Mountains.

Mile 46.4: The road to the right (west) goes to Halls Creek Overlook. This turn-off is poorly signed and easy to miss; look for it 0.9 mile south of the previous junction. Turn in and follow the road three miles, then turn right at a fork 0.4 mile to the viewpoint. The last 0.3 mile may be too rough for low-clearance cars. A picnic table is the only "facility" here. Far below in Grand Gulch, Halls Creek flows south to Lake Powell. Look across the valley for the double Brimhall Bridge in the red sandstone of Waterpocket Fold. A steep

trail descends to Halls Creek (1.2 miles one-way), and it's possible to continue another 1.1 miles up Brimhall Canyon to the bridge. A register box at the overlook has information sheets on this route. Note, however, that the last part of the hike to the bridge requires difficult rock-scrambling and wading or swimming through pools! Hikers looking for another adventure might want to follow Halls Creek 10 miles downstream to the narrows. Here, convoluted walls as high as 700 feet narrow to little more than arms' length apart. This beautiful area of water-sculpted rock sometimes has deep pools that require swimming.

Mile 49.0: Colorful clay hills of deep reds, creams, and grays rise beside the road. This clay turns to goo when wet, providing all the traction of axle grease.

Mile 54.0: Beautiful panorama of countless mesas, mountains, and canyons. Lake Powell and Navajo Mountain can be seen to the south.

Mile 65.3: Junction with paved Highway 276; turn left (north) for Hanksville (59 miles) or right (south) to Bullfrog Marina (5.2 miles).

Mile 70.5: Bullfrog Marina (see Glen Canyon National Recreation Area in the Canyonlands chapter).

Lower Muley Twist Canyon

"So winding that it would twist a mule pulling a wagon," said an early visitor. This canyon has some of the best hiking in the southern district of the park. In the 1880s, Mormon pioneers used the canyon as part of a wagon route between Escalante and new settlements in southeastern Utah, replacing the even more difficult Hole-in-the-Rock route. Unlike most canyons of Waterpocket Fold, Muley Twist runs lengthwise along the crest for about 18 miles before finally turning east and leaving the fold. Hikers starting from Burr Trail Road can easily follow the twisting bends down to Halls Creek, 12 miles away. Two trailheads and the Halls Creek route allow a variety of trips. You could start from Burr Trail Road near the top of the switchbacks (2.2 miles west of Notom-Bullfrog Road) and hike down the dry gravel streambed. After four miles, you have the options of returning the same way, taking the Cut Off route east 2.5 miles to the Post Trailhead (off Notom-Bullfrog Road), or continuing eight miles down Lower Muley Twist Canyon to its end at Halls Creek. Upon reaching Halls Creek, turn left (north) five miles up the creekbed or the old jeep road beside it to the Post. This section of creek lies in an open, dry valley. With a car shuttle, the Post would be the end of a good two-day, 17-mile hike, or you could loop back to Lower Muley Twist Canyon via the Cut Off route and hike back to Burr Trail Road for a 23.5-mile trip. It's a good idea to check the weather beforehand and avoid the canyon if storms threaten.

Cream-colored cliffs of Navajo Sandstone lie atop the red Kayenta and Wingate formations. Impressively deep undercuts have been carved into the lower canyon. Spring and autumn offer the best conditions (summer temperatures can exceed 100°F). Elevations range from 5,640 feet at Burr Trail Road to 4,540 feet at the confluence with Halls Creek to 4,894 feet at the Post. An in-

> *Lower Muley Twist Canyon was "so winding that it would twist a mule pulling a wagon," said an early visitor. In the 1880s, Mormon pioneers used the canyon as part of a wagon route between Escalante and new settlements in southeastern Utah.*

formation sheet available at the visitors center and trailheads has a small map and route details. Topographic maps of Wagon Box Mesa, Mt. Pennell, and Hall Mesa, and the 1:100,000-scale Escalante and Hite Crossing maps are sold at the visitors center. You'll also find this hike described in Dave Hall's *Hiker's Guide to Utah* and in Michael Kelsey's *Canyon Hiking Guide to the Colorado Plateau* and *Utah Mountaineering Guide*. Carry all water for the trip because natural sources are often dry or polluted.

Upper Muley Twist Canyon

This part of the canyon has plenty of scenery. Large and small natural arches along the way add to its beauty. Upper Muley Twist Road turns north off Burr Trail Road about one mile west from the top of a set of switchbacks. Cars can usually go in one-half mile to a trailhead parking area, while high-clearance four-wheel-drive vehicles can head another 2.5 miles up a wash to the end of the primitive road. Look for natural arches on the left along this last section. **Strike Valley Overlook Trail** (0.75 mile round-trip) begins at the end of the road and leads to a magnificent panorama of Waterpocket Fold and beyond. Return to the canyon, where you can hike as far as 6.5 miles (one-way) to the head of Upper Muley Twist Canyon.

Two large arches lie a short hike upstream; Saddle Arch, the second one on the left, is 1.75 miles away. The **Rim Route** begins across from Saddle Arch, climbs the canyon wall, follows the rim (good views of Strike Valley and the Henry Mountains), and descends back into the canyon at a point just above the narrows, 4.75 miles from the end of the road. (The Rim Route is most easily followed in this direction.) Proceed upcanyon to see several more arches. A narrow section of canyon beginning about four miles from the end of the road must be bypassed to continue; look for rock cairns showing the way around to the right. Continuing up the canyon past the Rim Route sign will take you to several small drainages marking the upper end of Muley Twist Canyon. Climb a high, tree-covered point on the west rim for great views; experienced hikers with a map can follow the rim back to Upper Muley Road (no trail or markers on this route). Bring all the water you'll need because there are no reliable sources in Upper Muley Twist Canyon.

Recreation

Fifteen day-hiking trails begin within a short drive of the visitors center. Of these, only Grand Wash, Capitol Gorge, Sunset Point, and Goosenecks are easy. The others involve moderately strenuous climbs and travel over irregular slickrock. Signs and rock cairns mark the way, but it's all too easy to wander off if you don't pay attention to the route.

Although most hiking trails can easily be done in a day, backpackers and mountain hikers might want to try longer trips in Chimney Rock/Spring Canyons in the north or Muley Twist Canyon and Halls Creek in the south. Obtain the required backcountry permit (free) from a ranger and camp at least one-half mile from the nearest maintained road or trail. (Cairned routes like Chimney Rock Canyon, Muley Twist Canyon, and Halls Creek don't count as trails but are backcountry routes.) Bring a stove for cooking because backcountry users may not build fires. Avoid camping or parking in washes at any time—torrents of mud and boulders can carry away everything!

HIKING TRAILS ALONG HIGHWAY 24

Stop by the visitors center to pick up a map showing hiking trails and trail descriptions. These trailheads are located along the main highway through the park and along the Fremont River. Note that the Grand Wash Trail cuts west through the reef to the Scenic Drive.

Chimney Rock Trail

The trailhead is located three miles west of the visitors center on the north side of the highway. Towering 660 feet above the highway, Chimney Rock is a fluted spire of dark red rock (Moenkopi Formation) capped by a block of hard sandstone (Shinarump Member of the Chinle Formation). A 3.5-mile loop trail ascends 540 feet from the parking lot (elevation 6,100 feet) to a ridge overlooking Chimney Rock; allow 2.5 hours. Panoramic views take in the face of Capitol Reef. Petrified wood along the trail has been eroded from the Chinle Formation (the same rock layer found in Petrified Forest National Park in Arizona). It is illegal to take any of the petrified wood.

Spring Canyon Route

This moderately difficult hike begins at the top of the Chimney Rock Trail. The wonderfully eroded forms of Navajo Sandstone present a continually changing exhibition. The riverbed is normally dry; allow about six hours for the 10-mile (one-way) trip from the Chimney Rock parking area to the Fremont River and Highway 24. (Some maps show all or part of this as "Chimney Rock Canyon.") Check with rangers for the weather forecast before setting off because flash floods can be dangerous, and the Fremont River (which you must wade across) can rise quite high. Normally, the river runs less than knee deep to Highway 24 (3.7 miles east of the visitors center). With luck you'll have a car waiting for you. Summer hikers can beat the heat with a crack-of-dawn departure. Carry water because this section of canyon lacks a reliable source.

From the Chimney Rock parking area, hike Chimney Rock Trail to the top of the ridge and follow the signs for Chimney Rock Canyon. Enter the unnamed lead-in canyon and follow it downstream. A sign marks Chimney Rock Canyon, which is 2.5 miles from the start. Turn right 6.5 miles (downstream) to reach the Fremont River. A section of narrows requires some rock-scrambling (bring a cord to lower backpacks), or the area can be bypassed on a narrow trail to the left above the narrows. Farther down, a natural arch high on the left marks the halfway point.

Upper Chimney Rock Canyon could be explored on an overnight trip. A spring (purify before drinking) is located in an alcove on the right side about one mile up Chimney Rock Canyon from the lead-in canyon. Wildlife use this water source, so camp at least one-quarter mile away. Chimney Rock Canyon, the longest in the park, begins high on the slopes of Thousand Lake Mountain and descends nearly 15 miles southeast to join the Fremont River.

Sulphur Creek Route

This moderately difficult hike begins by following a wash across the highway from the Chimney Rock parking area, descending to Sulphur Creek, then heads down the narrow canyon to the visitors center. The trip is about five miles long (one-way) and takes 3–5 hours. Park rangers sometimes schedule guided hikes on this route. Warm weather is the best time because you'll be wading in the normally shallow creek. Three small waterfalls can be bypassed fairly easily; two falls are just below the goosenecks, and the third is about one-half mile before coming out at the visitors center. Carry water with you. The creek's name may be a mistake because there's no sulphur along it; perhaps outcrops of yellow limonite caused the confusion. You can make an all-day eight-mile hike in Sulphur Creek by starting where it crosses the highway between mileposts 72 and 73, five miles west of the visitors center.

Hickman Natural Bridge, Rim Overlook, and Navajo Knobs Trails

The trailhead is two miles east of the visitors center on the north side of the highway. The graceful Hickman Natural Bridge spans 133 feet across a small streambed. Numbered stops along the self-guided trail correspond to descriptions in a pamphlet available at the trailhead or visitors center. Starting from the parking area (elevation 5,320 feet), the trail follows the Fremont River's green banks a short distance before gaining 380 feet in the climb to the bridge. The last section of trail follows a dry wash shaded by cottonwood, juniper, and piñon pine trees. You'll pass under the bridge (eroded from the Kayenta Formation) at trail's end. Capitol Dome and other sculp-

THE ORCHARDS OF CAPITOL REEF

Capitol Reef remained one of the last places in the West to be discovered by white settlers. First reports came in 1866 from a detachment of Mormon militia pursuing renegade Utes. In 1872, Professor Almon H. Thompson of the Powell Expedition led the first scientific exploration in the fold country and named several park features along the group's Pleasant Creek route. Mormons, expanding their network of settlements, arrived in the upper Fremont Valley in the late 1870s and spread downriver to Hanksville. Junction (renamed Fruita in 1902) and nearby Pleasant Creek (Sleeping Rainbow/Floral Ranch) were settled about 1880. Floods, isolation, and transport difficulties forced many families to move on, especially downstream from Capitol Reef. Irrigation and hard work paid off with prosperous fruit orchards and the sobriquet "the Eden of Wayne County." The aptly named Fruita averaged about 10 families who grew alfalfa, sorghum (for syrup), vegetables, and a wide variety of fruit. Getting the produce to market required long and difficult journeys by wagon. The region remained one of the most isolated in Utah until after World War II.

Although Fruita's citizens have departed, the National Park Service still maintains the old orchards. The orchards are lovely in late April, when the trees are in bloom beneath the towering canyon walls. Visitors are welcome to pick and carry away the cherries, apricots, peaches, pears, and apples during harvest seasons. Harvest times begin in late June or early July and end in October. You'll be charged about the same as in commercial pick-your-own orchards. You may also wander through any orchard and eat all you want on the spot before and during the designated picking season (no charge).

tured features of the Navajo Sandstone surround the site. The two-mile round-trip hike takes about 1.5 hours. Joseph Hickman served as principal of Wayne County High School and later in the state legislature during the 1920s; he and another local man, Ephraim Pectol, led efforts to promote Capitol Reef.

A splendid overlook 1,000 feet above Fruita beckons hikers up the **Rim Overlook Trail.** Take the Hickman Natural Bridge Trail one-quarter mile from the parking area, then turn right two miles at the signed fork. Allow 3.5 hours from the fork for this hike. Panoramic views take in the Fremont River valley below, the great cliffs of Capitol Reef above, the Henry Mountains to the southeast, and Boulder Mountain to the southwest.

Continue another 2.2 miles and more than 500 feet higher from the Rim Overlook to reach **Navajo Knobs.** Rock cairns lead the way over slickrock along the rim of Waterpocket Fold. A magnificent panorama at trail's end takes in much of southeastern Utah.

Cohab Canyon and Frying Pan Trails

Park at Hickman Natural Bridge Trailhead, then walk across the highway bridge. This trail climbs Capitol Reef for fine views in all directions and a close look at the swirling lines in the Navajo Sandstone. After three-quarters of a mile and a 400-foot climb, you'll reach a trail fork: keep right one mile to stay on Cohab Canyon Trail and descend to Fruita Campground or turn left onto Frying Pan Trail to Cassidy Arch (3.5 miles away) and Grand Wash (four miles away). The trail from Cassidy Arch to Grand Wash is steep. All of these interconnecting trails offer many hiking possibilities, especially if you can arrange a car shuttle. For example, you could start up Cohab Canyon Trail from Highway 24, cross over the reef on Frying Pan Trail, make a side trip to Cassidy Arch, descend Cassidy Arch Trail to Grand Wash, walk down Grand Wash to Highway 24, then walk (or car shuttle) 2.7 miles along the highway back to the start (10.5 miles total).

Cohab is a pretty little canyon in the Wingate Sandstone overlooking the campground. Mormon polygamists supposedly used the canyon to escape federal marshals during the 1880s. Hiking the Frying Pan Trail involves an additional 600 feet of climbing from either Cohab Canyon or Cassidy Arch trails. Once atop Capitol Reef, the trail follows the gently rolling slickrock terrain.

Grand Wash

The trailhead is 4.7 miles east of the visitors center on the south side of the highway. One of only five canyons cutting completely through the reef, Grand Wash offers easy hiking and great scenery. There's no trail—just follow the dry gravel riverbed. Flash floods can occur during storms. Canyon walls of Navajo Sandstone rise 800 feet above the floor and close in to as little as 20 feet in width. Cassidy Arch Trailhead (see following description of Grand Wash Road) is two miles away, and parking for Grand Wash from the Scenic Drive is one-quarter mile farther.

HIKING TRAILS ALONG THE SCENIC DRIVE

These hikes begin from trailheads along the Scenic Drive that turns south from the visitors center. There is a $5 entrance fee to travel the Scenic Drive.

Fremont Gorge Overlook Trail

From the start at the Fruita blacksmith shop, the trail crosses Johnson Mesa and climbs steeply to the overlook about 1,000 feet above the Fremont River; round-trip distance is 4.5 miles.

Cohab Canyon Trail

The trailhead is across the road from the Fruita Campground, 1.3 miles from the visitors center. The trail follows steep switchbacks during the first one-quarter mile, then more gentle grades to the top, 400 feet higher and one mile from the campground. You can take a short trail to viewpoints or continue three-quarters of a mile down the other side of the ridge to Highway 24. (See description under Hiking Trails Along Utah 24.) Another option is to turn right at the top on Frying Pan Trail to Cassidy Arch (3.5 miles one-way) and Grand Wash (four miles one-way).

Fremont River Trail

From the trailhead near the amphitheater at the Fruita Campground, 1.3 miles from the visitors center, the trail passes orchards along the Fremont River (elevation 5,350 feet), then begins the climb up sloping rock strata to a viewpoint on

Miner's Mountain. Sweeping views take in Fruita, Boulder Mountain, and the reef. The round-trip distance of 2.5 miles takes about 1.5 hours; the elevation gain is 770 feet.

Grand Wash Road

Turn left off the Scenic Drive 3.6 miles from the visitors center. This side trip follows the twisting Grand Wash for one mile. At road's end, you can continue on foot 2.25 miles (one-way) through the canyon to its end at the Fremont River (see previous description of Grand Wash).

Cassidy Arch Trail begins near the end of Grand Wash Road. Energetic hikers will enjoy good views of Grand Wash, the great domes of Navajo Sandstone, and the arch itself. The 3.5-mile round-trip trail ascends the north wall of Grand Wash (Wingate and Kayenta formations), then winds across slickrock of the Kayenta Formation to a vantage point close to the arch, also of Kayenta. Allow about three hours because the elevation gain is nearly 1,000 feet. The notorious outlaw Butch Cassidy may have traveled through Capitol Reef and seen this arch. Frying Pan Trail branches off Cassidy Arch Trail at the one-mile mark, then wends its way across three miles of slickrock to Cohab Canyon (see previous descriptions of Cohab Canyon and Frying Pan Trails).

Old Wagon Trail

Wagon drivers once used this route as a shortcut between Grover and Capitol Gorge. Look for the trailhead 0.7 mile south of Slickrock Divide, between Grand Wash and Capitol Gorge. The old trail crosses a wash to the west, then ascends steadily through piñon and juniper woodland on Miners Mountain. After 1.5 miles, the trail leaves the wagon road and goes north

DESERT VARNISH

The dark-colored vertical stripes often seen on sandstone cliff faces across the Colorado Plateau are known as desert varnish. They're mostly composed of very fine clay particles, rich in iron and manganese. It's not entirely known how these streaks are formed, but it seems likely that they're at least partly created by mineral-rich water coursing down the cliffs along the varnished areas and wind-blown clay dust sticking to cliff faces. Bacteria and fungi on the rock's surface may help this process along by absorbing manganese and iron from the atmosphere and precipitating it as a black layer of manganese oxide or reddish iron oxide on the rock surfaces. The clay particles in this thin layer of varnish help shield the bacteria against the drying effects of the desert sun. Prehistoric rock artists worked with desert varnish, chipping away the dark varnished surface to expose the lighter underlying rocks.

desert varnish along Lower Calf Creek

one-half mile to a high knoll for the best views of the Capitol Reef area. The four-mile (round-trip) hike climbs 1,000 feet.

Capitol Gorge

Follow the well-maintained dirt road to the parking area in Capitol Gorge to begin these hikes. The first mile downstream is the most scenic: Fremont Indian petroglyphs (in poor condition) appear on the left after 0.1 mile; narrows of Capitol Gorge close in at 0.3 mile; a "pioneer register" on the left at one-half mile consists of names and dates of early travelers and ranchers scratched in the canyon wall; and natural water tanks on the left at three-quarters of a mile are typical of those in Waterpocket Fold. Hikers can continue another three miles downstream to Notom Road.

The **Golden Throne Trail** also begins at the

end of the Scenic Drive. Instead of heading down Capitol Gorge from the parking area, turn left up this trail for dramatic views of the reef and surrounding area. Golden Throne is a massive monolith of yellow-hued Navajo Sandstone capped by a thin layer of red Carmel Formation. The four-mile round-trip trail climbs 1,100 feet in a steady grade to a viewpoint near the base of Golden Throne; allow four hours.

MOUNTAIN BIKING

Cyclists are restricted to existing roads, and because there are so few in the park, Capitol Reef doesn't have much of a reputation as a destination for mountain bikers. One exception is the challenging Cathedral Canyon Loop in the remote northern section of the park. The complete loop is more than 60 miles long and requires that cyclists be experienced and fit. Little water is available along the route, so this ride is best performed in spring or fall, when temperatures are lower. Contact the visitors center for more information on this and other routes.

ROCK CLIMBING

Rock climbing is allowed in the park and is especially popular in the relatively hard Wingate Sandstone formations. Technical rock-climbers should check with rangers to learn about restricted areas; registration is voluntary. Climbers must use "clean" techniques (no pitons or bolts) and keep at least 100 feet from rock-art panels and prehistoric structures. Because of the abundance of prehistoric rock art found there, the section of the rock wall north of Utah Highway 24 between the Fruita Schoolhouse and the east end of the Kreuger Orchard (Mile 81.4) is closed to climbing. Other areas closed to climbing are Hickman Natural Bridge and all other arches and bridges, Temple of the Moon, Temple of the Sun, and Chimney Rock.

CAMPGROUNDS

Fruita Campground stays open all year and has drinking water but no showers or hookups ($10); Nov.–Apr. you have to get water from the visitors center. The surrounding orchards and lush grass make this an attractive spot, situated one mile from the visitors center on the Scenic Drive. Sites often fill by early afternoon in the busy May–Oct. season. One group campground (by reservation only) and a picnic area are nearby. If you're just looking for a place to park for the night, check out the public land east of the park boundary off Highway 24. Areas on both sides of the highway (about nine miles east of the visitors center) may be used for primitive camping; no facilities or charge.

The five-site **Cedar Mesa Campground** is in the park's southern district just off Notom-Bullfrog Road (dirt); campers here enjoy fine views of Waterpocket Fold and the Henry Mountains. Open all year; no water or charge. From the visitors center, go east 9.2 miles on Highway 24, then turn right 22 miles on Notom-Bullfrog Road (avoid this road if wet). **Cathedral Valley Campground** serves the park's northern district; it has five sites (no water or charge) near the Hartnet Junction, about 30 miles north of Highway 24. Take either the Caineville Wash or Hartnet (has a river ford) roads; both are dirt and should be avoided if wet.

Torrey

Torrey (pop. 135) is an attractive little village, with a real Western feel. Only 11 miles west of the Capitol Reef National Park visitors center, it's a friendly and convenient place to stay, with several excellent lodgings and a good restaurant. Because Torrey is at the junction of highways 12 and 24, it's a great hub for exploring the wild country of the Grand Staircase-Escalante National Monument area just to the south and Capitol Reef National Park to the east.

Other little towns lie along the Fremont River, which drains this steep-sided valley. Teasdale is a small community just four miles east, situated in a grove of piñon pines. Bicknell, a small farm and ranch town, is eight miles east of Torrey.

ACCOMMODATIONS

Less than $50

The cabins at the center of town, at the **Torrey Trading Post,** 75 W. Main St., 435/425-3716, are just $35 per night. The **Capitol Reef Inn and Cafe,** 435/425-3271 (closed in winter), has standard motel rooms, a small café serving breakfast and dinner, and a gift shop.

$50–75

The main business in Torrey is its old trading post and country store. Immediately behind it in a grove of trees is the **Chuck Wagon Lodge,** 800/863-3288 or 435/425-3335, with rooms in an older motel (less than $50) or in a brand-new and attractive lodgelike building. There's a pool, a hot tub, and some campsites; open mid-Apr.–mid-Nov.

The **Wonderland Inn,** just east of town near the Hwy. 12 turn-off for Boulder, 800/458-0216 or 435/425-3775, has clean rooms and a restaurant serving breakfast, lunch, and dinner daily. The local **Super 8 Motel** is also just east of town on Hwy. 24, 435/425-3688.

In Teasdale, four miles west of Torrey, **Pine Shadows,** 125 S. 200 West, 800/708-1223 or 435/425-3939, offers new pine bungalows in a piñon forest. Or you can stay in a historic pioneer-era home, also in nearby Teasdale. The

© W.C. MCRAE

Torrey's original one-room school

Cockscomb Inn B&B, 97 S. State St., 800/530-1038 or 435/425-3511, has three guest rooms with queen beds, plus a garden cottage. All rooms have private bathrooms.

In Bicknell, the **Aquarius Motel,** 800/833-5379 or 435/425-3835, offers rooms, some with kitchens. There's also a café open daily for breakfast, lunch, and dinner.

$75–100

The lovely **SkyRidge Bed and Breakfast** is located one mile east of downtown, 435/425-3222. The modern inn has been decorated with high-quality Southwestern art and artifacts; all five guest rooms have private baths. SkyRidge sits on a bluff amid 75 acres; guests are invited to explore the land on foot or on bike.

The **Lodge at Red River Ranch,** between Bicknell and Torrey, 435/425-3322 or 800/20-LODGE (800/205-6343), is located beneath towering cliffs of red sandstone on the banks of the Fremont River. This wonderful wood-beamed lodge sits on a working ranch, but there's nothing rustic or unsophisticated about the accommodations here. The three-story structure is newly built, although in the same grand architectural style of old-fashioned mountain lodges. The great room has a massive stone fireplace, cozy chairs and couches, and a splendid Old West atmosphere. There are 15 guest rooms, most decorated according to a theme, and all have private baths. Guests are welcome to wander ranch paths, fish for trout, or tinker in the gardens and orchards. For information, write P.O. Box 280, Bicknell, UT 84715.

The **Days Inn,** situated at the junction of Hwy. 12 and Hwy. 24, 888/425-3113 or 435/425-3111, has a pool. Just east of Torrey, toward the park, is the **Best Western Capitol Reef Resort,** 800/528-1234 or 435/425-3761, which features luxury accommodations, a pool, and an attractive restaurant (open daily for breakfast, lunch, and dinner). There's also a brand-new **Holiday Inn Express,** east of town toward Capitol Reef, 888/232-4082 or 435/425-3866.

Campgrounds

For campers, **Thousand Lakes RV Park,** located one mile west of town on Hwy. 24, 435/425-3500, has sites with showers, a laundry room, and a store; open Apr. 1–Oct. 31; $16 tents or RVs without hookups, $21 RVs with hookups. Thousand Lakes also has a nightly Western-style cookout in an outdoor pavilion. **Wonderland Resort and RV Park,** one half block south on Hwy. 12 from Hwy. 24 junction, 800/458-0216, has both tenting and RV sites ($15), phone and modem hookups, and laundry facilities. The U.S. Forest Service's **Sunglow Campground** is just east of Bicknell; sites are open mid-May–late October with water and an $8 charge; elevation is 7,200 feet; the surrounding red cliffs really light up at sunset.

FOOD

Several of the motels in town offer American-style food, although it's probably **Cafe Diablo,** 599 W. Main, 435/425-3070, that you'll remember long after you've left Utah. Their specialty is zesty Southwestern cuisine, with excellent dishes like chipotle ribs, shrimp with habañero peppers, and pumpkin seed trout. Because there aren't many restaurants this good in rural Utah, this place is worth taking a detour. Open for lunch and dinner; Closed in winter.

INFORMATION

The **Teasdale Ranger Station** of the Dixie National Forest has information about hiking, horseback riding, and road conditions in the northern and eastern parts of Boulder Mountain and the Aquarius Plateau; books and forest maps are available. The office is located two miles west of Torrey on Hwy. 24, then 1.5 miles south to Main and 138 East (P.O. Box 99, Teasdale, UT 84773), 435/425-3702; open Mon.–Fri. 8 A.M.–4:30 P.M.

Grand Staircase-Escalante

This new national monument contains a vast and wonderfully scenic collection of slickrock canyonlands and desert, prehistoric village sites, Old West ranch land and arid plateaus, and miles of back roads linking stone arches, mesas, and abstract rock formations. The monument even preserves a historic movie set! (Think vintage Westerns.)

The 1.9-million-acre Grand Staircase-Escalante National Monument (GSENM) contains essentially three separate districts: On the eastern third are the narrow wilderness canyons of the Escalante River and its tributaries. In the center of the monument is a vast swath of arid rangeland and canyons called the Kairparowits Plateau, with few developed destinations—before use of all-terrain vehicles (ATVs), dune buggies, and power dirt bikes was limited, these canyons and bluffs were a popular playground for off-road enthusiasts. The western third of the

Calf Creek Trail

monument edges up against the Grey, White, and Pink Cliffs of the Grand Staircase. These thinly treed uplands are laced with former Forest Service roads. The GSENM is the largest land grouping designated as a national monument in the lower 48 states.

There's little dispute that the **Escalante Canyons** are the primary reason people visit the monument. The river and its tributaries cut deep and winding slot canyons through massive slickrock formations, and hiking these canyon bottoms is extremely popular adventure. This multiday trek is a right of passage for many devoted hikers, but you don't have to be a hardened backcountry trekker to enjoy this landscape: two backcountry roads wind through the area, and some day hikes are possible.

The other districts offer less well-defined opportunities for adventure. Backcountry drivers and long-distance mountain bikers will find mile after mile of desert and canyon to explore. **Grosvenor Arch,** with double windows, is a popular back-road destination. At the southern edge of the park, along the Arizona border, is another rugged canyon system that's popular with long-distance hikers. The **Paria River Canyon** is even more remote than the Escalante, and hiking these slot canyons requires experience and preparation.

After an unsteady start, the monument is beginning to feel like a single unit, and not just a cobbled-together assemblage of public land. The basic elements of internal infrastructure, such as consistent signage and helpful maps, are now in place, and with five visitors centers/ranger stations in operation, it now feels like its own entity. It's an evolving project, however, and be sure to inquire at the visitors center or the official website about conditions, restrictions, and new recreational opportunities before setting out.

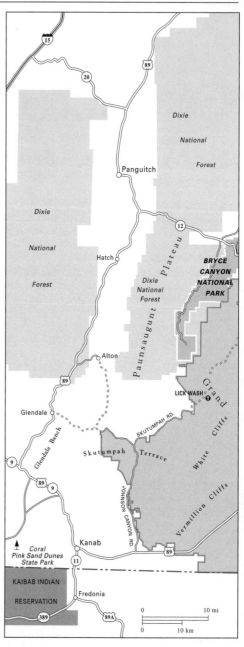

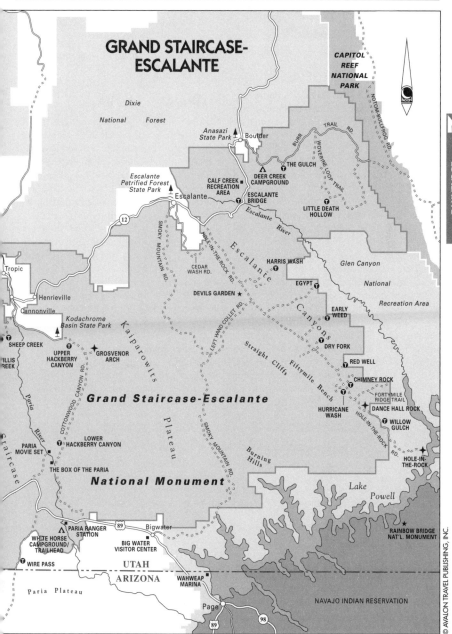

ESCALANTE

Natural History

GEOLOGY

About 300 million years ago, this land was at times a great Sahara-like desert with dunes towering hundreds of feet high. At other times, the land sank below sea level and was covered by water. Thick layers of sediment built up one on top of the other. During the last 50 million years, powerful forces within the earth slowly pushed the entire region one mile upward. The ancestral Colorado River began to carve the deep gorges seen today at the Grand Canyon. In turn, the tributaries of the Colorado, such as the Escalante, were also forced to trench deeper and deeper in order to drain their watershed.

The most characteristic rocks in the monument are the ancient dunes, turned to stone called slickrock, which make up many of the sheer canyon cliffs, arches, and spires of the region. Delicate cross-bedded lines of the former dunes add grace to these features. Forces within the restless plateau have also buckled and folded rock layers into great reefs as long as 100 miles. Weathering then carved them into rainbow-hued rock monuments. The aptly named Cockscomb, visible from the Cottonwood Canyon Road, which cuts through the center of the monument, is an example of these massive rock wrinkles.

FLORA AND FAUNA

The dry conditions and thin or nonexistent soils limit both plant and wildlife in the Escalante region. Annual plants simply wait for a wet year before quickly flowering and spreading their seeds. Piñon pines, junipers, and other plants often adapt by growing in rock cracks that concentrate moisture and nutrients. Small mammals such as mice, wood rats, rock squirrels, and chipmunks find food and shelter in these outposts of vegetation. Even meager soils permit growth of hardy shrubs like blackbrush, greasewood, sagebrush, rabbitbrush, and Mormon tea. Prickly pear and other types of cacti do well in the desert, too.

Perhaps the most unusual plant communities are the cryptobiotic crusts found on sandy soils. Mosses, lichens, fungi, algae, and diatoms live together in a gray-green to black layer up to several inches thick. Microclimates surrounding canyon seeps and springs provide a haven for hanging gardens of grasses, ferns, orchids, columbines, mosses, and other water-loving plants. River and stream banks have their own

DOWN THE GRAND STAIRCASE

The broad, tilted terraces of the Grand Staircase step down through time. Some 200 million years of sedimentation are visible here: pink in the north, then traveling through gray, white, and into vermilion cliffs.

A freshwater lake deposited the limey siltstones that became the Pink Cliffs (see these same rocks in Bryce National Park). This layer formed on top of the shales of the Gray Cliffs, deposited when an ocean covered the area, and rich with marine fossils and coal, formed from ancient wetland plants. The next older stairstep, the White Cliffs, is composed of Navajo sandstone, one of the main rocks seen in Zion National Park. On the bottom step, the bright Vermilion Cliffs (visible around Kanab) are also sandstone, laden with fossils of fish and dinosaurs. At the base of the whole staircase, the striped, brick-colored Chinle badlands form the bed for the Paria River.

These sandstone steps are stacked like pancakes. As in much of the Colorado Plateau region, the erosional activity of water and wind produces amazing geological displays, including the intricate network of deep canyons, uplifted plateaus, sheer cliffs, beautiful sandstone arches and natural bridges, water pockets, sandstone monoliths, pedestals and balanced rocks, domes and buttes.

vegetation, including river willows, cattails, tamarisks, and cottonwoods.

Wildlife you might see in the semiarid desert are mule deer, desert bighorn sheep, pronghorns, coyotes, bobcats, foxes, skunks, porcupines, and many species of rodents. Ravens, eagles, hawks, owls, falcons, magpies, and smaller birds fly overhead. Watch out for the poisonous rattlesnakes and scorpions, although these shy creatures won't attack unless provoked.

Exploring the Park

VISITORS CENTERS

The headquarters of the GSENM is in Kanab, quite distant from the heart—or even the boundaries—of the monument itself. This is the best office to contact by mail or phone before you set out. Contact the **GSENM Headquarters** at 318 North 100 East, Kanab, UT 84741, 435/644-4600, website: www.ut.blm/monument. The office is open daily Mar. 15–Nov. 15, 7:30 A.M. to 5:30 P.M. In winter, the office is open Mon.–Fri., 8 A.M.–4:30 P.M.

The regional visitors centers are good to stop by for information and advice before setting out. These include the following:

Escalante Interagency Visitors Center
755 West Main
Escalante, UT 84726
435/826-5499
Open daily 7:30 A.M.–5:30 P.M.; winter hours are Mon.–Fri., 8 A.M.–4:30 P.M.

Cannonville Visitors Center
10 Center St.
Cannonville, UT 84718
435/679-8981
Open daily Mar. 15–Nov. 15, 8 A.M.–4:30 P.M.

Anasazi State Park
460 N. Highway 12
Boulder, UT
435/335-7382
Open daily 9 A.M.–5 P.M.

Paria Contact Station
Highway 89
44 miles east of Kanab, UT
Open daily Mar. 15–Nov. 15, 8:30 A.M.–4:15 P.M.

Another visitors center will open in 2003 near Big Water, Utah, along U.S. 89 at the southern edge of the monument.

PARK ACCESS

There is currently no entrance fee for visiting the monument. Free permits are required for all overnight backcountry camping or backpacking. There is a fee to camp in the monument's three developed campgrounds.

Hikers in the Paria Wilderness area are required to buy a permit (this includes Paria Canyon and Coyote Buttes), as are hikers at the Calf Creek Recreation Area.

Only two paved roads pass through the monument, both in an east-west trajectory. Highway 12, on the northern border of the park, links Bryce Canyon and Capitol Reef National Parks with access to the Escalante canyons. This is one of the most scenic roads in Utah—in fact, *Car and Driver* magazine rates this route as one of the 10 most scenic in all of the United States. Its innumerable swallow-your-gum vistas and geologic curiosities will keep you on the edge of your car seat.

U.S. 89, which travels along the southern edge of the monument between Kanab and Lake Powell, is not exactly a slouch when it comes to scenery either. It is also the access road for the North Rim of the Grand Canyon in Arizona. Three fair-weather dirt roads, each with a network of side roads and trails, cut through the rugged heart of the monument, linking the two paved roads. Before heading out on these back roads, check with a visitors center for conditions; high-clearance vehicles are recommended.

ESCALANTE

THE POLITICS OF ESTABLISHING THE NATIONAL MONUMENT

In September 1996, President Bill Clinton declared 1.9 million acres of south central Utah a national monument, ending a decades-old debate about preserving the wilderness canyons in this part of the Southwest. The federal government's move sought to prevent the establishment of coal mines in the area, which had been planned by a Dutch resource-extraction consortium. The monument was formed by combining existing public land into a single administrative unit: the land now preserved as Grand Staircase-Escalante National Monument consists of land formerly supervised by the Bureau of Land Management (BLM), the Forest Service, and the state of Utah. The responsibility for administering the new monument was assigned to the BLM.

Preservation of the canyons as a national monument angered the Republican Utah legislative delegation and many others in this deeply conservative state. They were angry that they were not consulted about the formation of the monument, and they argued that the federal government should not interfere with local agriculture and the existing community. The move pleased environmentalists and backcountry recreationalists, however, who feared that the existence of a mining operation, no matter how environmentally sound, would destroy the area's unique scenic splendor and ancient Anasazi art and ruins.

Feelings pro and con about the monument can still run deep around Escalante and southern Utah, but a whole new breed of business is springing up to address the needs of the tourists and recreationalists who flock here. For people who have adapted to the changing economic and environmental forces, hostility to the monument and the crowds it attracts is subsiding.

The irony in all of this is that so far, in terms of land usage, very little has changed for either the farmers and ranchers who have leased these federal lands for generations or for the hikers and bikers who want to explore the wilds of this canyon country. The BLM has moved slowly to reassess access to the land and is trying to preserve the land's tradition as a multiuse area (with ranchers retaining grazing leases on federal land). Certain restrictions are in place, but these mostly affect the use of all-terrain vehicles (ATVs) and non-street-legal vehicles (off-road vehicles, dune buggies, and certain kinds of dirt bikes). Certain primitive roads will not receive regular maintenance. You will hear rumors aplenty about other restrictions being considered, but drastic changes do not seem imminent.

As has always been the case, the major considerations in planning a trip to this area remain the weather and the condition of the roads, not the anger of the locals or the machinations of the federal government.

SIGHTS ALONG HIGHWAY 12

This tour proceeds west to east, from Bryce Canyon National Park and Tropic along the north edge of the monument to the towns of Escalante and Boulder. Stop at the **Canyonville Visitors Center,** 10 Center St., 435/679-8981, for information about backroad conditions and hikes in this part of the monument. Two backcountry roads depart from Canyonville, leading to remote corners of the monument.

Johnson Canyon/Skutumpah Road

This route links Canyonville with U.S. 89 just east of Kanab (46 miles one-way). The unpaved portions of this road are usually in good condition, except after rains, when the bentonite soils that comprise the roadbed turn to goo. In good weather, cars can usually make the journey. The road follows the Pink and White Cliff terraces of the Grand Staircase, with access to some excellent and comparatively undersubscribed-to hiking trails. Several steep slot canyons make for excellent canyoneering. At the junction of Glendale Bench Road, turn west to reach Glendale, farther north on U.S. 89. The lower 16 miles of Johnson Canyon Road are paved.

Cottonwood Canyon Scenic Backroad

This 46-mile route also connects Cannonville with

U.S. 89, but passes through quite different terrain and landscapes. One of the most scenic backcountry routes in the monument, the Cottonwood Canyon road not only offers access to dramatic Grosvenor Arch, but it also passes along The Cockscomb, a soaring buckle of rock that divides the Grand Staircase and the Kairparowits Plateau. Cottonwood Creek, which this road parallels, is a normally dry streambed that cuts through the angular rock beds of The Cockscomb. Several excellent hikes lead into the canyons and narrows, where the Paria River, Hackberry Canyon, and Cottonwood Creek all meet, about 20 miles south of Canyonville. Check at the Canyonville visitors center for information about road conditions. Although the road is sometimes passable for cars, several road crossings are liable to washouts after rainstorms, and the northern portion is impassable even to four-wheel-drives when wet because of the extremely unctuous nature of the roadbed. Check conditions before setting out if you plan to go beyond Grosvenor Arch.

An article, "Motoring into Escalante Land," by Jack Breed in the September 1949 issue of National Geographic, *brought attention to the scenery and renamed the area "Kodachrome Flat," for the then-experimental kind of Kodak film used by the expedition.*

Kodachrome Basin State Park

Visitors come to this basin southeast of Bryce Canyon National Park to see not only colorful cliffs but also strange-looking rock pillars that occur nowhere else in the world. Sixty-seven rock pillars (here called "sand pipes") found in and near the park range in height from six to nearly 170 feet. One theory of their origin is that earthquakes caused sediments deep underground to be churned up by water under high pressure. The particles of calcite, quartz, feldspar, and clay in the sand pipes came from underlying rock formations, and the pipes appeared when the surrounding rock eroded away. Most of the other rocks visible in the park are Entrada Sandstone: the lower orange layer is the Gunsight Butte Member, and the white layer with orange bands is the Cannonville Member.

Signs name some of the rock features. "Big Stoney," the phallus-shaped sand pipe overlooking the campground, is so explicit that it doesn't need a sign! An article, "Motoring into Escalante Land," by Jack Breed in the September 1949 issue of *National Geographic,* brought attention to the scenery and renamed the area "Kodachrome Flat," for the then-experimental kind of Kodak film used by the expedition. The state park makes a worthwhile stop, both as a day trip to see the geology and as a pleasant spot to camp. A $4 per-vehicle day-use fee is charged. The park also offers several good half-day hiking trails.

To reach the park, drive to Cannonville and follow signs to Cottonwood Canyon Road for nine miles on paved roads. Adventurous drivers can also approach the park from U.S. 89 to the south via the Cottonwood Canyon road (35 miles) or the Skutumpah road through Bull Valley Gorge and Johnson Canyon (48 miles). These routes may be impassable in wet weather but may be okay for cars with good clearance in dry weather.

Scenic Safaris operates **guided horseback and horse-drawn coach rides** in the park. You can arrange rides at **Trailhead Station,** a small store in the park that sells groceries and camping supplies from about early April to late October, or contact P.O. Box 278, Cannonville, UT 84718, 435/679-8536 or 435/679-8787.

The state park's **campground** sits in a natural amphitheater at an elevation of 5,800 feet. It's open all year, has restrooms, showers, a dump station, and sites for $14. During the winter, restrooms and showers may close, but pit toilets are available. The campground usually has room except on summer holidays. For information or reservations, contact the park at P.O. Box 238, Cannonville, UT 84718, 800/322-3770 or 435/679-8562 (reservations).

Grosvenor Arch

Just one mile off the Cottonwood Canyon, a side road leads to the magnificent Grosvenor

Arch. In fact, there are two arches here, jutting like flying buttresses out of a soaring cliff. The larger of the two openings is 99 feet across. The 1949 National Geographic Society Expedition named the double arch in honor of the society's president. The turn-off is 10 miles from the state park turn-off and 29 miles from U.S. 89. This is a good spot for a picnic.

Escalante Petrified Forest State Park

This pleasant park just northwest of Escalante offers camping, boating, fishing, picnicking, hiking, a visitors center with displays of petrified wood and dinosaur bones, and a chance to see petrified wood along trails. Rivers of 140 million years ago carried trees to the site of present-day Escalante and buried them in sand and gravel. Burial prevented decay as crystals of silicon dioxide gradually replaced the wood cells. Mineral impurities added a rainbow of colors to the trees as they turned to stone. Weathering has exposed this petrified wood and the water-worn pebbles and sand of the Morrison Formation. For a look at some colorful petrified wood, follow the **Petrified Forest Trail** from the campground up a hillside wooded with piñon pine and juniper. At the top of the 240-foot-high ridge, continue on a loop trail to the petrified wood; allow 45–60 minutes for the one-mile round-trip. **Rainbow Loop Trail** (three-quarters of a mile) branches off the Petrified Forest Trail to more areas of petrified wood.

The **campground** stays open all year, offering drinking water and showers but no hookups. The adjacent 139-acre Wide Hollow Reservoir offers fishing, boating, and bird-watching. Canoe rentals are $5 per hour, or $20 per day. The park is 1.5 miles west of town on Highway 12, then 0.7 mile north on a gravel road; $4 per vehicle for day use, $16 per vehicle to camp. Contact P.O. Box 350, Escalante, UT 84726, 435/826-4466 (ranger) or 800/322-3770 (reservations).

Escalante

The town of Escalante, 38 miles east of Bryce Canyon and 23 miles south of Boulder, has all services and is headquarters for explorations of the Escalante River Canyons. The Escalante

Interagency Office, 755 W. Main St., 435/826-5499, provides information on local hikes and road conditions. For more information on lodging and services in Escalante, see following section.

Smoky Mountain Road

From Escalante, it's 78 miles south to Big Water, just shy of Lake Powell, along the Smoky Mountain Road. This road is in rougher condition than other cross-monument roads. Be sure to check out conditions before setting out; four-wheel-drive vehicles are required. As this route passes across the Kaiparowits Plateau, the landscapes are bleak and arid. Then, the road drops precipitously down onto a bench where side roads lead through badlands to Lake Powell beaches. Big Water is 19 miles from Page, Arizona, and 57 miles from Kanab.

Hole-in-the-Rock Road

The building of this road by determined Mormons was one of the great epics in the colonization of the West. Church leaders organized the

Peek-a-boo Canyon, off Hole-in-the-Rock Road

© JUDY JEWELL

A PIONEER ACCOUNT OF ESCALANTE TRAVEL

Mormon pioneer Elizabeth Morris Decker described the descent from Hole-in-the-Rock Road in a letter to her parents on February 22, 1880:

If you ever come this way it will scare you to death to look down it. It is about a mile from the top down to the river and it is almost strait [sic] down, the cliffs on each side are five hundred feet high and there is just room enough for a wagon to go down. It nearly scared me to death. The first wagon I saw go down they put the brake on and rough locked the hind wheels and had a big rope fastened to the wagon and about ten men holding back on it and then they went down like they would smash everything. I'll never forget that day. When we was walking down Willie looked back and cried and asked me how we would get back home.

Hole-in-the-Rock Expedition to settle the wild lands around the San Juan River of southeastern Utah, believing that a Mormon presence would aid in ministering to the Indians there and prevent non-Mormons from moving in. In 1878, the Parowan Stake issued the first call for a colonizing mission to the San Juan, even before a site had been selected.

Preparations and surveys took place the following year as the 236 men, women, and children received their calls. Food, seed, farming and building tools, 200 horses, and more than 1,000 head of cattle would be taken along. Planners ruled out lengthy routes through northern Arizona or eastern Utah in favor of a straight shot via Escalante that would cut the distance in half. The expedition set off in the autumn of 1879, convinced that they were part of a divine mission.

Yet hints of trouble to come filtered back from the group as they discovered the Colorado River crossing to be far more difficult than first be-

lieved. Lack of springs along the way added to their worries. From their start at Escalante, road builders progressed rapidly for the first 50 miles, then slowly over rugged slickrock for the final six miles to Hole-in-the-Rock. A 45-foot sheer drop below this narrow notch was followed by three-quarters of a mile of extremely steep slickrock to the Colorado River. The route looked impossible, but three crews of workers armed with picks and blasting powder worked simultaneously to widen the notch and to construct a precarious wagon road down to the river and up cliffs on the other side.

The job took six weeks. Miraculously, all of the people, animals, and wagons made it down and were ferried across the Colorado River without a serious accident. Canyons and other obstacles continued to block the way as the weary group pressed on. Only after six months of exhausting travel did they stop at the present-day site of Bluff on the San Juan River.

Today, on a journey from Escalante, you can experience a bit of the same adventure the pioneers knew. Except for scattered signs of ranching, the land remains unchanged. If the road is dry, vehicles with good clearance can drive to within a short distance of Hole-in-the-Rock. The rough conditions encountered past Dance Hall Rock require more clearance than most cars allow. Bring sufficient gas, food, and water for the entire 126-mile round-trip from Escalante.

The turn-off from Highway 12 is five miles east of Escalante. In addition to rewarding you with scenic views, Hole-in-the-Rock Road passes many side drainages of the Escalante River to the east and some remote country of the Kaiparowits Plateau high above to the west. Staff members at the information center just west of Escalante can give current road conditions and suggest hikes.

Metate Arch and other rock sculptures decorate **Devil's Garden,** 12.5 miles down Hole-in-the-Rock Road. Turn west 0.3 mile at the sign to the parking area because you can't really see the "garden" from the road. Red- and cream-colored sandstone formations sit atop pedestals or tilt at crazy angles. Delicate bedding lines run through the rocks. There are no trails or markers—just wander about at your whim. The Bureau of Land

ESCALANTE

Management (BLM) has provided picnic tables, grills, and outhouses for day use. No overnight camping is permitted at Devil's Garden.

Dance Hall Rock (38 miles down Hole-in-the-Rock Road) jumped to the fiddle music and lively steps of the expedition members in 1879. Its natural amphitheater has a relatively smooth floor and made a perfect gathering spot when the Hole-in-the-Rock group had to wait three weeks at nearby Fortymile Spring for road work to be completed ahead. Dance Hall Rock is an enjoyable place to explore and only a short walk from the parking area. Solution holes, left from water dissolving in the rock, pockmark the Entrada Sandstone structure.

At road's end (57 miles from Highway 12), continue on foot across slickrock to the notch and views of the blue waters of Lake Powell below. Rockslides have made the descent impossible for vehicles, but hikers can scramble down to the lake and back in about one hour. The elevation change is 600 feet. The half-mile round-trip is strenuous. After a steep descent over boulders, look for steps of Uncle Ben's Dugway at the base of the notch. Below here the grade is gentler. Drill holes in the rock once held oak stakes against which logs, brush, and earth supported the outer wagon wheels. The inner wheels followed a narrow rut 4–6 inches deep. About two-thirds of the route down is now under water, although the most impressive road work can still be seen.

Calf Creek Recreation Area

This stunning canyon and park offers the most accessible glimpse of what the Escalante Canyon country is all about. The trailhead to 126-foot **Lower Calf Creek Falls** is here, and you should definitely make plans for the half-day hike, especially if you have no time for further exploration of this magical landscape. Otherwise, stop here to picnic in the shade of willows and cottonwoods. This is also the most convenient and attractive **campsite** for dozens of miles. The 13 campsites have water, fire pits, and picnic tables.

The Million-Dollar Road

Highway 12 between Escalante and Boulder was only completed in 1935, by workers in the Civil-

Lower Calf Creek Falls

© JUDY JEWELL

ian Conservation Corps. The cost was a budget-busting $1 million. Before then, mules carried supplies and mail across this wilderness of slickrock and narrow canyons. The section of Highway 12 between Calf Creek and Boulder is extraordinarily scenic—even jaded travelers used to the wonders of Utah will have to pull over and ogle the views from the **Hog's Back,** where the road crests a fin of rock above the canyons of the Escalante. Be here for sunset on a clear evening and you'll have a memory to carry for the rest of your life.

Boulder

Boulder is a tiny community in a lovely location at the base of Boulder Mountain, where the alpine air mixes with the desert breezes. The single best lodging choice in the Escalante region—the Boulder Mountain Lodge—is here, so plan accordingly. See following sections for more information.

Anasazi State Park

Museum exhibits, an excavated village site, and a

pueblo replica provide a look into the life of these ancient people. The Anasazi stayed here for 50–75 years some time between A.D. 1050 and 1200. They grew corn, beans, and squash in fields nearby. Village population peaked at about 200, with an estimated 40–50 dwellings. Why the Anasazi left or where they went isn't known for sure, but a fire swept through much of the village before the Anasazi abandoned it. Perhaps they burned the village on purpose, knowing they would move on. University of Utah students and faculty excavated the village, known as the Coombs Site, in 1958 and 1959. You can view pottery, axe heads, arrow points, and other tools found at the site in the museum, along with more perishable items like sandals and basketry that came from more protected sites elsewhere. A diorama shows how the village might have appeared in its heyday. You can see video programs on the Anasazi and modern tribes upon request.

The self-guided tour of the ruins begins behind the museum, which is located on Highway 12, 28 miles northeast of Escalante and 38 miles south of Torrey, 435/335-7308. You'll see a whole range of Anasazi building styles—a pit house, masonry walls, *jacal* walls (mud reinforced by sticks), and combinations of masonry and jacal. Replicas of habitation and storage rooms behind the museum show complete construction details. The park is open daily mid-May–mid-Sept., 8 A.M.–6 P.M.; 9 A.M.–5 P.M. the rest of the year. Admission is $3 per person, or $6 per vehicle (whichever is the least). Books, videos, T-shirts, and postcards are sold.

Burr Trail Road

The Burr Trail Road, originally a cattle trail blazed by stockman John Atlantic Burr, extends from the town of Boulder on Highway 12 to the Notom-Bullfrog Road, which runs between Highway 24 near the eastern entrance to Capitol Reef National Park and Bullfrog Marina on Lake Powell, off Highway 276. Starting at Boulder, roughly the first third of this scenic 36-mile road is now paved. Pavement ends at the boundary of Capitol Reef National Park, where the route traverses the Circle Cliffs, as well as spectacular canyon areas such as Long Canyon and The Gulch. As

the route meets the Waterpocket Fold, in Capitol Reef National Park, a breathtaking set of switchbacks rise some 800 feet in only one-half mile. These switchbacks are not considered suitable for RVs or vehicles towing trailers. The unpaved sections of the road are subject to changes caused by weather conditions. Visitors should inquire about road and weather conditions before setting out. Also inquire about hiking trails down into the Escalante canyons that depart from side roads to the Burr Trail.

The Burr Trail Road joins the Notom-Bullfrog Road just before exiting Capitol Reef park. For information on the Notom-Bullfrog Road, see the Capitol Reef chapter.

SIGHTS ALONG HIGHWAY 89

This tour proceeds from Kanab to the Utah–Arizona border. From Kanab to Page, Arizona, at the Colorado River's Glen Canyon Dam, is 80 miles. For information on Kanab, see the following section.

Johnson Canyon Road

Eight miles east of Kanab, Johnson Canyon Road heads north along the western border of the monument before joining the Skutumpah Road and the Glendale Bench Road. This road system links up with several more remote backcountry roads in the monument, and eventually leads to Canyonville along Highway 12. From U.S. 89, the Johnson Canyon Road is paved for its initial miles. The road passes an abandoned movie set, where the TV series *Gunsmoke* was sometimes filmed. These old sets are on BLM land and can usually be visited on foot. The road them climbs up through the Vermilion and then the White Cliffs of the Grand Staircase. This portion of the route is quite scenic. The road then passes over the Skutumpah Terrace, a rather featureless plateau covered with scrub. The northerly portions of this route near Highway 12 are described previously.

Pariah Townsite Road

This road has several names, including Paria Valley Road. It turns north off U.S. 89 at

Milepost 31. This five-mile-long dirt road is passable to cars when dry. It passes some towering and colorful canyons and mesas, among which the remains of a **1930s Western movie set** are slowly decaying. From the parking area, walking trails lead out to the abandoned bleached wood buildings, which make for great photo opportunities against the rugged backdrop. Farther along the road, as it approaches the Paria River, is the remains of the actual ghost town of Pareah, although there's not much left to see.

Paria Canyon and the Vermilion Cliffs National Monument

The Paria Canyon—a set of magnificent slot canyons that drain from Utah down through northern Arizona to the Grand Canyon—is the focus of popular multiday canyoneering expeditions. The Paria Canyon and 293,000 acres of surrounding desert grasslands are now protected as the **Vermilion Cliffs National Monument.** Although the monument spreads south from the Utah–Arizona border, access to the monument's most famous sites is through from backroads in Utah. In addition to the long Paria Canyon backpacking route, some shorter but strenuous day hikes explore this area; see following sections under Recreation. For more information, contact the Kanab monument headquarters or stop at the Paria Ranger Station, near Milepost 21 on U.S. 89.

Cottonwood Canyon Road

A few miles east of the ranger station, the Cottonwood Canyon Road leads north. The unpaved road's lower portions, usually passable with cars in dry weather, pass through scenic landscapes as the road pushes north. The route climbs up across a barren plateau before dropping down onto the Paria River. Several good hikes lead off from roadside trailheads into steep side canyons. The route continues north along The Cockscomb, a long wrinkle of rock ridges that run north and south across the desert. At the northern end of this route are Grosvenor Arch, Kodachrome State Park, and Highway 12 (46 miles).

Smoky Mountain Road

At the little crossroads of **Big Water,** the GSENM is building a new visitors center to serve the needs of travelers to the monument and to Glen Canyon National Recreation Area (NRA), which is immediately adjacent to this area. The center is supposed to open in 2003. Joining Highway 89 at Big Water is the **Smoky Mountain Road.** This long and rugged road links Big Water to Highway 12 at Escalante, 78 miles north. The southern portions of the route pass through the Glen Canyon NRA, and side roads lead to remote beaches and flooded canyons. The original *Planet of the Apes* film was shot here, before this area was inundated by Lake Powell.

From Big Water, it's 19 miles to Page, Arizona, on U.S. 89.

Recreation

The monument preserves some of the best long-distance hiking trails in the American Southwest. Since the monument was established and the consequent increase in tourism, shorter day hikes have also been developed to serve travelers who want to sample the wonderful slot canyons and backcountry of this vast desert landscape without venturing too far afield.

Be sure to check at local visitors centers for road and trail conditions, and to get up-to-date maps. Many of the following hikes require extensive travel on backcountry roads, which can be

impassable after rains and rough the rest of the time. In summer, these trails are hot and exposed: Always carry plenty of water and sunscreen and wear a hat.

Hiking the **Escalante River Canyon** is recognized worldwide as one of the great wilderness treks. Most people devote 4–6 days to exploring these slickrock canyons, which involve frequent scrambling (if not rock-climbing), stream fording (if not swimming), and exhausting detours around rock falls and log jams. Some day hikes are possible along the Escalante River drainage. Hikers without a week to spare can sample the landscape along the Dry Fork Coyote Gulch trail, which links two fascinating and beautifully constricted slot canyons.

The **Paria Canyon** is another famed long-distance slickrock canyon hike that covers 37 miles between the border of Utah and the edge of the Colorado River's Marble Canyon. Several long day hikes leave from trailheads on the Paria Plateau, along the border with Arizona.

Other areas with developed hiking trails include the Skutumpah Road area and Cottonwood Canyon, in the center of the park. Otherwise, hiking in the monument is mostly on unmarked routes. Although the park is developing more day-hiking options, the rangers also encourage hearty adventurers to consider extended hikes across the rugged and primitive outback, beyond the busy canyon corridors. Call one of the visitors centers and ask for help from the rangers to plan a hiking adventure where there are no trails.

The monument preserves some of the best long-distance hiking trails in the American Southwest. Since the monument was established, day hikes have also been developed to serve travelers who want to sample the wonderful slot canyons and backcountry of this vast desert landscape without venturing too far afield.

HIKES ALONG JOHNSON CANYON ROAD/ SKUTUMPAH ROAD

The northern portions of this road pass through the White Cliffs area of the Grand Staircase, and several steep and narrow canyons are trenched into these terraces. Rough hiking trails explore these slot canyons. The **Willis Creek Narrows** trailhead is nine miles south of Cannonville along Skutumpah Road. The relatively easy trail follows a small stream as it etches a deep and narrow gorge through the Navajo Sandstone. From the parking area, where Skutumpah Road crosses Willis Wash, walk downstream along the wash. Follow the streambed, which quickly descends between slickrock walls. The canyon is at times no more than 6–10 feet across, while the walls rise

up 200–300 feet. The trail follows the (usually dry) streambed through the canyon for nearly 2.5 miles. To return, backtrach up the canyon.

Approximately 1.5 miles farther south on Skutumpah Road, a narrow bridge vaults over the **Bull Valley Gorge.** Like the Willis Creek Narrows, this is a steep and narrow cleft in the slickrock; however, scrambling along the canyon bottom is a greater challenge, part of the reward for which is viewing a wrecked automobile wedged between the canyon walls. From the bridge, walk upstream along a faint trail on the north side of the crevice until the walls are low enough to scramble down. From here, the canyon deepens quickly, and you'll have to negotiate several dry falls along the way (a rope will come in handy). When you reach the area below the bridge, look up to see a 1950s-model pickup truck trapped between the canyon walls. Three men died in this 1954 mishap; their bodies were recovered, but the pickup was left in place. The canyon continues another mile from this point; there is no loop trail out of the caynon, so turn back when you've seen enough.

Twenty miles south of Canyonville, the Skutumpah Road crosses **Lick Wash,** from which trails lead downstream into slot canyons to a remote *arroyo* (dry river bed) surrounded by rock-topped mesas. One of these lofty perches contains a preserve of now-rare native grasses. Although this area can be reached from a day hike, this is also a good place to base a multiday camping trip. The trail starts just below the road crossing on Lick Wash and follows the usually dry streambed as it plunges down into a narrow slot canyon. The canyon bottom is mostly level and easy to hike. After one mile, the canyon begins to widen, and after four miles, Lick Wash joins Park Wash, a larger desert canyon.

Looming above this canyon junction are mesas topped with deep sandstone terraces that are part of the White Cliffs of the Grand Staircase. Rising to the east is **No Mans Mesa,** skirted on all sides by steep-sided cliffs. The 1,788 acres atop the mesa were grazed by goats for six months in the 1920s, but before or since then has never been grazed by herbivores. This pristine grassland is protected by the BLM as an Area of Critical Environmental Concern. Hardy hikers can scramble up a steep trail—used by the aforementioned goats—to visit this wilderness preserve. The ascent of No Mans Mesa is best considered an overnight trip from the Lick Wash trailhead.

HIKES ALONG COTTONWOOD CANYON ROAD

The northerly portions of this route pass by **Kodachrome Basin State Park** (see previous description), with a fine selection of hiking trails through colorful rock formations. The short **Nature Trail** introduces the park's ecology. The **Panorama Trail** loops through a highly scenic valley with sand pipes and colorful rocks; the easy trail is three miles round-trip and takes about two hours. **Angel's Palace Trail** begins just east of the group campground and makes a three-quarter-mile loop with fine views; the elevation gain is about 300 feet. The **Grand Parade Trail** makes a 1.5-mile loop with good views of rock pinnacles; begin from the concession stand or group campground. **Eagles View Trail,** a historic cattle trail, climbs nearly 1,000 feet up steep cliffs above the campground, then drops into Henrieville, two miles away; the highest overlook is a steep half-mile ascent from the campground. **Arch Trail** is a half-mile round-trip hike to a natural arch; access the trailhead by a signed dirt road or a two-mile (round-trip) trail; a brochure and numbered stops identify local plants.

Continue south on Cottonwood Canyon Road for 7.5 miles from the state park to the crossing of Round Valley Draw. From here, turn south on BLM Rd. 422 toward **Hackberry Canyon.** Hikers can travel the 22-mile length of this scenic canyon in three days or make day hikes from either end of the trail. The lower canyon meets Cottonwood Canyon at an elevation of 4,700 feet just above the mouth of the

Paria River. The Cottonwood Canyon Road provides access to both ends. A small spring-fed stream flows down the lower half of Hackberry. Many side canyons invite exploration. One of them, Sam Pollock Canyon, is on the west about 4.5 miles upstream from the junction of Hackberry and Cottonwood Canyons; follow it 1.75 miles up to **Sam Pollock Arch** (60 feet high and 70 feet wide). Available topographic maps include the metric 1:100,000 Smoky Mountain or the 7½-minute Slickrock Bench and Calico Peak. Michael Kelsey's *Hiking and Exploring the Paria River* contains trail and trailhead information and a history of the Watson homestead, located a short way below Sam Pollock Canyon.

The confluence of the Paria, Hackberry, and the Cottonwood Canyons provide the backdrop to an excellent, although strenuous day hike. The **Box of the Paria River** involves some steep climbs up rocky slopes as it traverses a tongue of slickrock between the mouth of the Hackberry and Paria Canyons. The route then follows the Paria River through its "box" or cliff-sided canyon in The Cockscomb formation. The trail returns to the trailhead by following Cottonwood Canyon upstream to the trailhead. The round-trip hike is about seven miles long. Inquire at visitors centers for maps and about conditions.

HIKES ALONG THE ESCALANTE RIVER

The maze of canyons that drain the Escalante River presents exceptional hiking opportunities. You'll find everything from easy day hikes to challenging backpacking treks. The Escalante's canyon begins just downstream from the town of Escalante and ends at Lake Powell about 85 miles beyond. In all this distance, only one road (Highway 12) bridges the river. Many side canyons provide additional access to the Escalante, and most are as beautiful as the main gorge. The river system covers such a large area that you can find solitude even in spring, the busiest hiking season. The many eastern canyons remain virtually untouched.

The Escalante canyons preserve some of the quiet beauty once found in Glen Canyon, which is now lost under the waters of Lake Powell. Prehistoric Anasazi and Fremont Indians have left ruins, petroglyphs, pictographs, and artifacts in many locations. These archaeological resources are protected by federal law. *Please don't collect or disturb them.*

Before setting out, visit the rangers at the information center on the west edge of Escalante for the required free permit to backpack overnight in the GSENM, and to check on the latest trail and road conditions before setting out. Restrictions on group size may be in force on some of the more popular trails. You can also obtain topographic maps and literature that show trailheads, mileages, and other information that may be useful in planning trips. Some of the more popular trailheads have self-registration stations for permits.

The best times for a visit are early March to early June and mid-September to early November. Summertime trips are possible, too, but be prepared for higher temperatures and greater flash-flood danger in narrow canyons. Travel along the Escalante River involves frequent crossings, and there's always water in the main canyon, usually ankle to knee deep. Pools in the "Narrows" section between Scorpion Gulch and Stevens Canyon can be up to chest deep in spots (which you can bypass), but that's the exception. All this wading can destroy leather boots, so it's best to wear canvas shoes or boots. High-topped boots, available at surplus stores, work well and prevent gravel from getting inside. Occasional springs, some tributaries, and the river itself provide drinking water. Always purify it first; the BLM warns of the unpleasant disease giardiasis, which is caused by an invisible protozoan. Don't forget insect repellent—mosquitos and deer flies seek out hikers in late spring and summer. Long-sleeved shirts and long pants also discourage biting insects and protect against the brush.

Escalante Canyon Trailheads

The many approaches to the area allow all sorts of trips. Besides the road access at Escalante and the Highway 12 bridge, hikers can reach the Escalante River through western side canyons from Hole-in-the-Rock Road or eastern side canyons from Burr Trail Road. The western-canyon trailheads on Hole-in-the-Rock Road can be more easily reached by car, thus facilitating vehicle shuttles. To reach eastern-canyon trailheads, with the exceptions of Deer Creek and the Gulch on Burr Trail Road, you'll need lots of time and, if the road is wet, a four-wheel-drive vehicle. You'll also need to carry water for these more remote canyons. With the exception of Deer Creek, they're usually dry.

Town of Escalante to Highway 12 Bridge

(15 miles) This first section of canyon offers easy walking and stunning canyon scenery. Tributaries and sandstone caves invite exploration. You'll find good camping areas all along. Usually the river here is only ankle deep. Either enter Escalante River at the bridge next to the sawmill, or go one mile east of town on Highway 12 and turn north past the cemetery (visible from highway) and town dump. Almost immediately, the river knifes its way through the massive cliffs of the Escalante Monocline, leaving the broad valley of the upper river behind. Although there is no maintained trail along this stretch of the east-flowing river, it's relatively easy to pick your way along the river bank.

Death Hollow, which is far prettier than the name suggests, comes in to the Escalante from the north after 7.5 miles. Several good swimming holes carved in rock lie a short hike upstream from the Escalante; watch for poison ivy among the greenery. Continue farther up Death Hollow to see more pools, little waterfalls, and outstanding canyon scenery. You can bypass some pools, but some you'll have to swim—bring a little inflatable boat, air mattress, or waterproof bag to ferry packs.

Sand Creek, on the Escalante's north side 4.5 miles downstream from Death Hollow, is also worth exploring; deep pools begin a short way up from the mouth. After another one-half mile down the Escalante, a natural arch appears high on the canyon wall. Then the Escalante Natural Bridge comes into view about one-half mile farther, just two miles from the Highway 12 bridge. In fact, Escalante Natural Bridge makes a good day-hike destination upstream from the highway.

ESCALANTE

Highway 12 Bridge to Harris Wash

(26.5 miles) This is where many long-distance trekkers begin their exploration of the Escalante canyons. In this section, the Escalante Canyon offers a varied show: in places the walls close in to make constricted narrows, at other places they step back to form great valleys. Side canyons filled with lush greenery and sparkling streams contrast with dry washes of desert, yet all can be fun to explore. A good hike of 4–6 days begins at the highway bridge, goes down the Escalante to Harris Wash, then up Harris to a trailhead off Hole-in-the-Rock Road (37 miles total).

From the Highway 12 bridge parking area, a trail leads to the river. Canyon access goes through private property; cross the river at the posted signs to avoid barking dogs at the ranch just downstream. **Phipps Wash** comes in from the south (right side) after 1.5 miles and several more river crossings. Turn up its wide mouth one-half mile to see Maverick Bridge in a drainage to the right. To reach Phipps Arch, continue another three-quarters of a mile up the main wash, turn left into a box canyon, and scramble up the left side (see 7½-minute Calf Creek topographic map).

Bowington (Boynton) Arch is an attraction of a north side canyon known locally as Deer Creek. Look for this small canyon on the left one mile beyond Phipps Wash; turn up it one mile past three deep pools and then turn left a short way into a tributary canyon. In 1878, gunfire resolved a quarrel between local ranchers John Boynton and Washington Phipps. Phipps was killed, but both their names live on.

Waters of **Boulder Creek** come rushing into the Escalante from the north in the next major side canyon, 5.75 miles below the Highway 12 bridge. The creek, along with its Dry Hollow and Deer Creek tributaries, provides good canyon walking; deep areas may require swimming or climbing up on the plateau. (You could also start down Deer Creek from the Burr Trail Road where they meet, 6.5 miles southeast of Boulder at a primitive BLM campground; starting at the campground, follow Deer Creek 7.5 miles to Boulder Creek, then 3.5 miles down Boulder to the Escalante.)

Deer and Boulder creeks have water year-round.

High, sheer walls of Navajo Sandstone constrict the Escalante River in a narrow channel below Boulder Creek, but the canyon widens again above **The Gulch** tributary, 14 miles below the highway bridge. Hikers can head up The Gulch on a day hike.

Alternately, hikers can descend The Gulch from the Burr Trail Road to join the Escalante Canyon at this point (The Gulch trailhead is 10.8 miles southeast of Boulder). The hike from the road down to the Escalante is 12.5 miles, but there's one difficult spot: a 12-foot waterfall in a section of narrows about halfway down has to be bypassed. When Rudi Lambrechtse, author of *Hiking the Escalante,* tried friction climbing around the falls and the pool at their base, he fell 12 feet and broke his foot. That meant a painful three-day hobble out. Instead of taking the risk, Rudi recommends backtracking about 300 feet from the falls and friction climbing out from a small alcove in the west wall (look for a cairn on the ledge above). Climb up Brigham Tea Bench, walk south, then look for cairns leading back east to the narrows, and descend to the streambed (a rope helps to lower packs in a small chimney section).

Most springs along the Escalante are difficult to spot. One that's easy to find is in the first south bend after the Gulch; water comes straight out of the rock a few feet above the river. The Escalante Canyon becomes wider as the river lazily meanders along. Hikers can cut off some of the bends by walking in the open desert between canyon walls and riverside willow thickets. A bend cut off by the river itself loops to the north just before Horse Canyon, three miles below the Gulch. Along with its tributaries **Death Hollow** and **Wolverine Creek, Horse Canyon** drains the Circle Cliffs to the northeast. Floods in these mostly dry streambeds wash down pieces of black petrified wood. (Vehicles with good clearance can reach the upper sections of all three canyons from a loop road off Burr Trail Road.) Horse and Wolverine Creek Canyons offer good easy-to-moderate hiking, but if you really want a challenge, try Death Hollow (sometimes called "Little

Death Hollow" to distinguish it from the larger one near Hell's Backbone Road). Starting from the Escalante River, go about two miles up Horse Canyon and turn right into Death Hollow; rugged scrambling over boulders takes you back into a long section of twisting narrows. Carry water for Upper Horse Canyon and its tributaries; Lower Horse Canyon usually has water.

About 3.5 miles down the Escalante from Horse Canyon, you'll enter Glen Canyon NRA and come to Sheffield Bend, a large, grassy field on the right. Only a chimney remains from Sam Sheffield's old homestead. Two grand amphitheaters lie beyond the clearing and up a stiff climb in loose sand. Over the next 5.5 river miles to Silver Falls Creek, you'll pass long bends, dry side canyons, and a huge slope of sand on the right canyon wall. Don't look for any silver waterfalls in **Silver Falls Creek**—the name comes from streaks of shiny desert varnish on the cliffs. You can approach Upper Silver Falls Creek by a rough road from Burr Trail Road, but a car shuttle between here and any of the trailheads on the west side of the Escalante River would take all day. Most hikers visit this drainage on a day hike from the river. Carry water with you.

When the Hole-in-the-Rock route proved so difficult, pioneers figured there had to be a better way to the San Juan Mission. Their new wagon road descended Harris Wash to the Escalante River, climbed part of Silver Falls Creek, crossed the Circle Cliffs, descended Muley Twist Canyon in the Waterpocket Fold, then followed Hall's Creek to Hall's Crossing on the Colorado River. Charles Hall operated a ferry there from 1881–1884. Old maps show a jeep road through Harris Wash and Silver Falls Creek Canyons, used before the National Park Service closed off the Glen Canyon NRA section. Harris Wash lies just one-half mile downstream and across the Escalante from Silver Falls Creek.

Harris Wash

(10.25 miles one-way from trailhead to river) Clear, shallow water glides down this gem of a canyon. High cliffs streaked with desert varnish are deeply undercut and support lush hanging gardens. Harris Wash provides a beautiful route

to the Escalante River, but it can also be a destination in itself; tributaries and caves invite exploration along the way. The sand and gravel streambed makes for easy walking. Reach the trailhead from Highway 12 by turning south 10.8 miles on Hole-in-the-Rock Road, then left 6.3 miles on a dirt road (keep left at the fork near the end). Don't be dismayed by the drab appearance of upper Harris Wash. The canyon and creek appear a few miles downstream. The Harris Wash Trailhead now has a restriction of 12 persons per group.

Harris Wash to Lake Powell

(42.75 miles) The Escalante continues its spectacular show of wide and narrow reaches, side canyons to explore, and intriguing rock formations. A trip all the way from Harris Wash Trailhead to the Escalante, down the Escalante to near Lake Powell, then out to the Hurricane Wash Trailhead is 66.25 miles, taking 8–10 days. Many shorter hikes using other side canyons are possible, too.

Still in a broad canyon, the Escalante flows past **Fence Canyon** (on the west), 5.5 miles from Harris Wash. Fence Canyon has water and is a strenuous 3.5-mile cross-country route out to the end of Egypt Road. Get trail directions from a ranger and bring a topographic map. (Adventurous hikers could do a three-day, 20-mile loop via Fence Canyon, the Escalante River, and the northern arm of Twentyfive Mile Wash.) To reach the trailheads, take Hole-in-the-Rock Road 17.2 miles south of Highway 12, then turn left (east) 3.7 miles on the Egypt Road for Twentyfive Mile Wash Trailhead or 9.1 miles for Egypt Trailhead.

Twentyfive Mile Wash, on the west side 11.5 miles below Harris Wash, is a good route for entering or leaving the Escalante River. The moderately difficult hike is 13 miles one-way from trailhead to river. Scenery transforms from an uninteresting dry wash in the upper part to a beautiful canyon with water and greenery in the lower reaches. To get to the trailhead, take Hole-in-the-Rock Road 17.2 miles south of Highway 12, then turn left 3.7 miles on Egypt Road.

Moody Creek enters the Escalante six meandering river miles below Twentyfive Mile Wash (or just 2.25 miles as the crow flies). A rough road off Burr Trail Road gives access to Moody Creek, Purple Hills, and other eroded features. The distance from trailhead to river is seven miles one-way (moderately strenuous), although most hikers find it more convenient to hike up from the Escalante. **Middle Moody Creek** enters Moody Creek three miles above the Escalante. Moody and Middle Moody Canyons feature colorful rock layers, petrified wood, a narrows, and solitude. Carry water because springs and waterpockets cannot be counted on. Canyons on the east side of the Escalante tend to be much drier than those on the west side.

East Moody Canyon enters the Escalante 1.5 miles downstream from Moody Canyon, and it, too, makes a good side trip. There's often water about one-half mile upstream. Continuing down the Escalante, look on the left for a *rincon,* a meander cut off by the river. **Scorpion Gulch** enters through a narrow opening on the right, 6.5 miles below Moody Canyon. A strenuous eight-mile climb up Scorpion Gulch over rockfalls and around deep pools brings you to a trailhead on Early Weed Bench Road. Experience, directions from a ranger, and a topographic map are needed. A challenging four-day, 30-mile loop hike uses Fox Canyon, Twentyfive Mile Wash, the Escalante River, and Scorpion Gulch. Water is found only in lower Twentyfive Mile Wash, the river, and lower Scorpion Gulch. The Early Weed Bench turn-off is 24.2 miles south on Hole-in-the-Rock Road from Highway 12; head in 5.8 miles to Scorpion Gulch Trailhead.

In the next 12 miles below Scorpion Gulch, Escalante Canyon is alternately wide and narrow. Then the river plunges into the **Narrows,** a five-mile-long section choked with boulders; plan on spending a day picking a route through. Watch out for chest-deep water here! Remote and little-visited, **Stevens Canyon** enters from the east near the end of the Narrows. Stevens Arch stands guard 580 feet above the confluence; the opening measures 225 feet wide and 160 feet high. The upper and lower parts of Stevens Canyon usually have some water.

Coyote Gulch, on the right 1.5 miles below Stevens Canyon, marks the end of the Escalante for most hikers. In some seasons, Lake Powell comes within one mile of Coyote Gulch and occasionally floods the canyon mouth. Coyote can stay flooded for several weeks, depending on the release flow of Glen Canyon Dam and water volume coming in. The river and lake don't have a pretty meeting place—quicksand and dead trees are found here. Logjams make it difficult to travel in from the lake by boat.

Coyote Gulch has received more publicity than other areas of the Escalante, and you're more likely to meet other hikers here. Two arches, a natural bridge, graceful sculpturing of the streambed and canyon walls, deep undercuts, and a cascading creek make a visit well worthwhile. The best route in starts where Hole-in-the-Rock Road crosses Hurricane Wash, 34.7 miles south of Highway 12. It's 12.5 miles one-way from the trailhead to the river, and the hike is moderately strenuous. For the first mile, you follow the dry, sandy wash without even a hint of being in a canyon. Water doesn't appear for three more miles. You'll reach Coyote Gulch, which has water, at 5.25 miles from the trailhead. Another way into Coyote Gulch begins at the Red Well Trailhead; it's 31.5 miles south on Hole-in-the-Rock Road, then 1.5 miles east (keep left at the fork). A start from Red Well adds three-

surveying Dry Fork Coyote Gulch and its maze of canyons

quarters of a mile more to the hike than the Hurricane Wash route, but it is also less crowded.

Dry Fork of Coyote Gulch

Twenty-six miles south on the Hole-in-the-Rock Road is a series of narrow, scenic, and exciting-to-explore slot canyons reached by a moderate day hike. The canyons feed into the Dry Fork of Coyote Gulch, reached from the Dry Fork trailhead. These three enchanting canyons are named **Peek-a-boo, Spooky,** and **Brimstone.** Exploring these slot canyons requires basic canyoneering or scrambling skills. From the trailhead parking lot, follow cairns down into the sandy bottom of Dry Fork Coyote Gulch. The slot canyons all enter the gulch from the north; watch for cairns and trails because the openings can be difficult to notice. The slots sometimes contain deep pools of water; chokestones and pour-offs can make access difficult. No loop trail links the three slot canyons; follow each until the canyon becomes to narrow to continue, then come back out. To make a full circuit of these canyons requires about 3.5 miles of hiking.

HIKES IN THE CALF CREEK RECREATION AREA

The hike to **Calf Creek Falls** is, for many people, the highlight of their first trip to the Escalante area. It's the dazzling enticement that brings peo-

© JUDY JEWELL

ESCALANTE

Calf Creek Trail

ple back for longer and more remote hiking trips. From the trailhead and park just off Highway 12, the trail winds between high cliffs of Navajo Sandstone streaked with desert varnish, where you'll see beaver ponds, Indian ruins and pictographs, and the misty 126-foot-high **Lower Calf Creek Falls.** A brochure available at the trailhead next to the campground identifies many of the desert and riparian plant species along the way. Round-trip is 5.5 miles with only a slight gain in elevation; bring water and perhaps a

WALKING SOFTLY

Only great care and awareness can preserve the pristine canyons of the Escalante. You can help if you pack out all trash, avoid trampling on the fragile cryptobiotic soils (dark areas of symbiotic algae and fungus on the sand), travel in groups of 12 or fewer, don't disturb Indian artifacts, and protect wildlife by leaving your dogs at home. Most important, bury human waste well away from water sources, trails, and camping areas; unless there's a fire hazard, burn toilet paper to aid decomposition. Campfires in developed or designated campgrounds are allowed only in fire grates, fire pits, or fire pans.

Wood collection in these areas is not permitted. The use of backpacker stoves is recommended by the National Parks Service and the Bureau of Land Management. Visitors are encouraged to maximize efforts to "leave no trace" of their passage in the area.

Leave No Trace, Inc. is a national organization dedicated to awareness, appreciation, and respect for our wildlands. The organization also promotes education about outdoor recreation that is environmentally responsible. More information about Leave No Trace is available at its website: www.lnt.org.

lunch. Summer temperatures can soar, but the falls and the crystal-clear pool beneath stay cool. Sheer cliffs block travel farther upstream.

Calf Creek Campground, near the road, has 13 sites with drinking water from early April–late October ($7). Reserve group sites through the Escalante visitors center.

HIKES IN THE PARIA CANYON/VERMILION CLIFFS

The wild and twisting canyons of the Paria River and its tributaries offer a memorable experience for experienced hikers. Silt-laden waters have sculpted the colorful canyon walls, revealing 200 million years of geologic history. *Paria* means "muddy water" in the Paiute language. You enter the 2,000-foot-deep gorge of the Paria in southern Utah, then hike 37 miles downstream to Lee's Ferry in Arizona, where the Paria empties into the Colorado River. A handful of shorter, but rugged day hikes lead to superb scenery and geologic curiosities.

Ancient petroglyphs and campsites show that Pueblo Indians traveled the Paria more than 700 years ago. They hunted mule deer and bighorn sheep while using the broad, lower end of the canyon to grow corn, beans, and squash. The Dominguez-Escalante Expedition stopped at the mouth of the Paria in 1776, and these were the first white men to see the river. John D. Lee and three companions traveled through the canyon in 1871 to bring a herd of cattle from the Pahreah settlement to Lee's Ferry. After Lee began a Colorado River ferry service in 1872, he and others farmed the lower Paria Canyon. Prospectors came here to search for gold, uranium, and other minerals, but much of the canyon remained unexplored. In the late 1960s, the BLM organized a small expedition whose research led to protection of the canyon as a primitive area. The Arizona Wilderness Act of 1984 designated Paria Canyon a wilderness, along with parts of the Paria Plateau and Vermilion Cliffs. In 2000, the Vermilion Cliffs National Monument was created. For more information, check out the website at www.az.blm.gov/vermilion/vermilion.htm. The **BLM Paria Canyon Ranger Station** is in

Utah, 43 miles east of Kanab on U.S. 89 near Milepost 21. It's on the south side of the highway, just east of the Paria River. Permits are required for hiking in the Paria Canyon and to visit other sites in the Vermilion Cliffs National Monument.

Hiking Paria Canyon

Allow 4–6 days to hike Paria Canyon because of the many river crossings and because you'll want to make side trips up some of the tributary canyons. The hike is considered moderately difficult. Hikers should have enough backpacking experience to be self-sufficient because help may be days away. Flash floods can race through the canyon, especially July–Sept. Rangers close the Paria if they think a danger exists. Because the upper end has the most narrow passages (between miles 4.2 and 9.0), rangers require that all hikers start here in order to have up-to-date weather information.

The actual trailhead is two miles south of the ranger station on a dirt road near a campground and old homestead site called White House Ruins. The exit trailhead is in Arizona at Lonely Dell Ranch of Lee's Ferry, 44 miles southwest of Page via U.S. 89 and 89A (or 98 miles southeast of Kanab on U.S. 89A).

You must register at a trailhead or the visitors center, or the Kanab BLM office at 318 N. 100 East in Kanab, UT 84741, 435/644-2672; open Mon.–Fri. 8 A.M.–4:30 P.M. year-round. Permits to hike the canyon are $5 per day per person and per dog. The visitors center and the office both provide weather forecasts and brochures with map and hiking information. The visitors center always has the weather forecast posted at an outdoor information kiosk.

All visitors need to take special care to minimize their impact on this beautiful canyon. Check the BLM "Visitor Use Regulations" for the Paria before you go. Regulations include no campfires in the Paria and its tributaries, a pack-in/pack-out policy, and that latrines be made at least 100 feet away from river and campsite locations. Also, remember to take some plastic bags to carry out toilet paper; the stuff lasts years and years in this desert climate. You don't want to haunt future hikers with TP flowers!

The Paria ranger recommends a group size of six maximum; regulations specify a 10-person limit. No more than 20 people per day can enter the canyon for overnight trips. The best times to travel along the Paria are from about mid-Mar.–June and Oct.–Nov. May, especially Memorial Day weekend, tends to be crowded. Winter hikers often complain of painfully cold feet. Wear shoes suitable for frequent wading; canvas shoes are better than heavy leather hiking boots. You can get good drinking water from springs along the way (see the BLM hiking brochure for locations); it's best not to use the river water because of possible chemical pollution from farms and ranches upstream. Normally the river's only ankle deep, but in spring or after rainy spells, it can become waist deep. During thunderstorms, levels can rise to more than 20 feet deep in the Paria Narrows, so heed weather warnings! Quicksand, which is most prevalent after flooding, is more a nuisance than a danger—usually it's just knee deep. Many hikers carry a walking stick to probe the opaque waters for good crossing places.

Wrather Canyon Arch

One of Arizona's largest natural arches lies about one mile up this side canyon of the Paria. The massive structure has a 200-foot span. Turn right (southwest) at Mile 20.6 on the Paria hike. (The mouth of Wrather Canyon and other points along the Paria are unsigned; you need to follow your map.)

Shuttle Services

You'll need to make a 150-mile round-trip car shuttle for this hike or make arrangements for someone else to do it for you, using either your car (about $75) or theirs ($125–150). Contact the GSENM headquarters for a current list of authorized shuttle operators.

Buckskin Gulch and Wire Pass

Buckskin Pass is an amazing tributary of the Paria, with convoluted walls reaching hundreds of feet high. Yet the canyon narrows to as little as four feet in width. In places the walls block out so much light that it's like walking in a cave. Be

very careful to avoid times of flash-flood danger. Hiking this 20-mile-long gulch can be strenuous, with rough terrain, deep pools of water, and log and rock jams that may require the use of ropes. Conditions vary considerably from one year to the next.

Day hikers can get a taste of this incredible canyon country by driving to the Wire Pass Trailhead, 8.5 bumpy miles down BLM Rd. 700 (also called Rock House Valley Rd.), between mileposts 25 and 26, about 37 miles east of Kanab. From the trailhead, a relatively easy trail leads into **Wire Pass,** a narrow side canyon that joins Buckskin Gulch. The 3.5 mile in-and-out round-trip travels the length of Wire Pass to its confluence with Buckskin Gulch. From here, you can explore this exceptionally narrow canyon, or follow Buckskin Gulch to its appointment with Paria Canyon (12.5 miles).

For the full experience of Buckskin Gulch, long-distance hikers can begin at Buckskin Gulch trailhead, 4.5 miles south of U.S. 89 off BLM Rd. 700. From here, it's 16.3 miles (one-way) to the Paria Canyon. Hikers can continue down the Paria or turn upstream and hike six miles to exit at the White House trailhead near the ranger station.

Coyote Buttes

You've probably seen photos of these dramatic rock formations: towering sand dunes frozen into rock. These much-photographed buttes are located on the Paria Plateau, just south of Wire Pass. Access is strictly controlled, and you can only enter the area with advanced reservation and by permit. The number of people allowed into the area is also strictly limited; however, the permit process, fees, and restrictions are exactly the same as for Paria Canyon; see the Vermilion Cliffs monument website for information (www.az.blm.gov/vermilion/vermilion.htm).

The BLM has divided the area into Coyote North and Coyote South, with a limit of 10 people per day in each. The Wave—the most photographed of the buttes—is in the north, so this region is the most popular (and easiest to reach from Utah). Coyote North is reached from Wire Pass Trailhead (see previous entry); BLM staff members will give you a map and directions when you get your permit. After the trailhead, you're on your own because the wilderness lacks signs. Permits are more difficult to obtain in spring and autumn—the best times to visit—and on weekends. The fragile sandstone can break if climbed on, so it's important to stay on existing hiking routes and wear soft-soled footwear.

MOUNTAIN BIKING

Mountain bikes are allowed on all roads in the monument, but not on hiking trails. They are not allowed to travel cross country off roads, or to make their own route across slickrock; however, there are hundreds of miles of primitive road in the monument, with dozens of loop routes possible to cyclists on multiday camping trips. In addition to following the scenic **Burr Trail** from Boulder to Waterpocket Fold in Capitol Reef National Park, cyclists can loop off this route and follow the Circle Cliffs/Wolverine trail. This 45-mile loop traverses the headwaters of several massive canyons as they plunge to meet the Escalante River.

The **Hole-in-the-Rock Road** is mostly a one-way-in, one-way-out kind of road, but cyclists can follow side roads to hiking trailheads and big vistas over the Escalante Canyons. Popular side roads are the 10-mile round-trip to the area known as Egypt, and the Fifty Mile Bench Road, a 27-mile loop trail from the Hole-in-the-Rock Road that explores landscapes above Glen Canyon. The Left Hand Collet Road, a rough jeep trail that a mountain bike can bounce through easily enough, links Hole-in-the-Rock Road with the Smoky Mountain Road system, with links to both Escalante in the north and Big Water in the south.

Other popular routes in the **Big Water area** include the Nipple Butte loop and the steep loop around Smoky Butte and Smoky Hollow, with views down onto Lake Powell. The **Cottonwood Canyon Road,** which runs between U.S. 89 and Cannonville, is another long-distance back road with access to a network of lesser traveled trails.

Request more information on mountain biking from the visitors centers. They have handouts and maps and can help cyclists plan backcountry bike adventures. This country is remote and primitive, and cyclists will need to take everything with them that they are likely to need. Also, there are no treated water sources in the monument, so cyclists will need to transport all their drinking water or be prepared to purify it.

RAFTING

Most of the year, shallow water and rocks make boat travel impossible on the Escalante River, but for 2–3 weeks during spring runoff, river levels rise high enough, peaking between early April and late May. (In some years there may not be enough water in any season.) Keep in touch with the information center in Escalante to hit the river at its highest. Shallow draft and maneuverability are essential, so inflatable canoes or kayaks work best (also because they are easier to carry out at trip's end or if water levels drop too low for floating). Not recommended are rafts (too wide and bulky) and hard-shelled kayaks and canoes (they get banged up on the many rocks). The usual launch is the Highway 12 bridge; Coyote Gulch—a 13-mile hike—is a good spot to get out, as are the Crack in Wall route (a 2.75-mile hike on steep sand from the junction of Coyote and Escalante Canyons to Forty-Mile Ridge Trailhead; four-wheel drive needed; a rope is required to negotiate the vessel over the canyon rim) and Hole-in-the-Rock (a 600-foot ascent over boulders; rope suggested). You could also arrange for a friend to pick you up by boat from the Halls Crossing or Bullfrog Marina. River boaters need a free backcountry permit from either the BLM or the National Park Service.

FOUR-BY-FOUR AND OFF-ROAD EXPLORATION

Without a mountain bike or a pair of hiking boots, the best way to explore the backcountry of the GSENM is with a four-wheel-drive high-clearance vehicle; however, the scale of the monument, the primitive quality of many of the roads, and the extreme weather conditions common in the desert mean that you shouldn't head into the backcountry unless you are confident in your skills as a mechanic and driver. Choose roads that match your vehicle's capacity and your driving ability, and you should be okay. Some roads that appear on maps are slowly going back to nature: rather than close some roads, park officials are letting the desert reclaim them. Other roads are being closed, so it's best to check on access and road conditions before setting out. Remember that many of the roads in the monument are *very* slow going. If you've got somewhere to be in a hurry, these corrugated, boulder-dodging roads may not get you there in time. Be sure to take plenty of water—not just for you to drink but also for your overheated radiator.

There are still some areas in the monument where non-street-legal vehicles, such as dirt bikes and all-terrain vehicles, are allowed. Check with rangers to verify.

Escalante

The outstanding scenery of the countryside surrounding the town of Escalante has been discovered, and the town is being dragged, kicking and screaming, into a new reality: as a major center for ecotourism. Escalante is a natural hub for exploration of the new GSENM. Even if you don't have the time or the inclination to explore the rugged canyon country that the monument protects, you'll discover incredible scenery just by traveling Highway 12 through the Escalante country.

At first glance, Escalante looks like a town that time has passed by. Only 950 people live here, in addition to the resident cows, horses, and chickens that you'll meet just one block off Main Street. Yet this little community is the biggest place for more than 60 miles around and a center for ranchers and travelers. Escalante (elevation 5,813 feet) has the neatly laid-out streets and trim little houses typical of Mormon settlements. The former Latter-Day Saints' Tithing Office (behind the Griffin grocery store) dates from 1884. Pioneers had little cash then and paid their tithes in potatoes, fruit, and other produce. The building now has historic exhibits on the Daughters of Utah Pioneers; open by appointment (phone numbers of volunteers are listed on the door).

The outstanding scenery of the countryside surrounding the town of Escalante has been discovered, and the town is being dragged, kicking and screaming, into a new reality: as a major center for ecotourism.

ACCOMMODATIONS
Less than $50
The following are pretty basic, but perfectly acceptable: The **Moqui Motel,** 480 W. Main, 435/826-4210, has rooms and some kitchenettes and an RV park ($15 with hookups; no tents). The **Circle D Motel,** 475 W. Main, 435/826-4297, has a restaurant, and pets are welcome in some rooms. In addition to regular rooms, there's one two-bedroom unit ($80) and one four-bedroom ($105).

The following close in winter and are generally open Mar.–Oct. The **Padre Motel,** 20 E. Main, 435/826-4276, 800/462-7923, or 800/733-8824, has regular motel rooms and five mini-suites with two bedrooms each. Bunkhouse-style cabins sleeping two are available at **Escalante Outfitters,** 310 W. Main, 435/826-4266.

$50–75
You can enjoy staying at the pleasant and modern **Rainbow Country B&B,** 586 E. 300 South, 435/826-4567 or 800/252-UTAH (800/252-8824), and also avail yourself of their custom tours. The B&B's four guest rooms share 2.5 baths; guests have the use of a hot tub, a pool table, and a TV lounge. The hosts offer several

ESCALANTE

© JUDY JEWELL

sunset at Escalante State Park

tour itineraries featuring your choice of hiking, back-road four-wheel-drive exploring, or even camping trips. You can also arrange personalized tours to suit your interests. The **Prospector Inn,** 380 W. Main, 435/826-GOLD (435/826-4653), is Escalante's newest motel; there's a restaurant and lounge on premises. Open year-round; children 12 and under stay free.

Campgrounds
In addition to the Escalante Petrified Forest State Park campground described in the Sights Along Highway 12 section, you can stay at **Broken Bow RV Camp,** 495 W. Main St., 888/241-8785 or 435/826-4959, which has cabins (starting at $20), sites for tents ($12) and RVs ($17 with hookups), plus showers and a laundromat; closed in winter.

Calf Creek Recreation Area lies in a pretty canyon 15.5 miles east of Escalante on Highway 12; sites run $7 and are open early Apr.–late Oct.; you can reserve group sites through the BLM office. **Calf Creek Falls Trail** (5.5 miles round-trip) begins at the campground and follows the creek upstream to the 126-foot-high falls.

Campgrounds at **Posey Lake** (16 miles north) and **Blue Spruce** (19 miles north) sit atop the Aquarius Plateau in Dixie National Forest. Sites ($7) open around Memorial Day weekend and close in mid-September. Take the dirt Hell's Backbone Road from the east edge of town.

FOOD

The **Ponderosa Restaurant,** 45 N. 400 West, 435/826-4658, offers Escalante's best food, in a large log lodge in the center of town. The menu focuses on steaks, chicken, burgers, and other American fare. Alcohol is served. The **Cowboy Blues Diner and Bakery,** 530 W. Main, 435/826-4251, serves Western-style food and bakery goods. The **Circle D Restaurant,** 425 W. Main, 435/826-4251, serves American and Mexican food. The **Golden Loop Cafe,** 39 W. Main, 435/826-4433, has standard American fare. All are open daily for breakfast, lunch, and dinner. The **Trailhead Café,** at the corner of Main Street and 100 East, has good coffee and Internet access. The **Esca-Latte Coffee Shop and Pizza Parlor,** 310 W. Main St, 435/826-4266, has espresso coffee, handmade pizza, and microbrewed beer.

INFORMATION AND SERVICES

The Escalante Interagency office at 755 West Main on the west edge of town has an **information center** for visitors to Forest Service, BLM, and National Park Service areas around Escalante; this is also one of the best spots for information on the GSENM; open Mon.–Fri. (daily from early Mar.–late Oct.) 8 A.M.–5 P.M. Write P.O. Box 246, Escalante, UT 84726, 435/826-5499.

Hikers or bikers headed for overnight trips in the monument system can obtain permits at the information center. Normally it's best to contact the information center first, but you can also communicate directly with the **Dixie National Forest office,** P.O. Box 246, Escalante, UT 84726, 435/826-5400; the **Bureau of Land Management office,** P.O. Box 225, Escalante, UT 84726, 435/826-4291; or the **National Park Service office,** P.O. Box 511, Escalante, UT 84726, 435/826-4315.

THE PETRIFIED FOREST

Trees fall into water, are washed downstream, and are buried by mud, silt, and ash. Minerals and elements, like silica (from volcanic ash), enter the wood either from water or the ground, filling in the "pores." When the pores of the wood have been filled, its color changes, depending on the minerals present. This mineral-loaded wood is resistant to rotting and is often quite beautiful, displaying the original cellular structure and grain of the wood.

Two especially good places to see petrified wood are along Huber Wash, in the western section of Zion National Park just west of Springdale, and at Escalante Petrified Forest State Park, just west of the town of Escalante.

Although it should go without saying that the petrified wood in these places should stay there—and not travel home in a hiker's pack or pocket—this general ethical guideline is backed up by a potent mythology of misfortune befalling people who steal petrified wood. Posted on a bulletin board at the base of the Petrified Forest Trail in the state park are many letters from people who decided to return bits of petrified wood they'd secreted away from the park, and the tales of how their lives went down the tubes after they'd stolen the wood.

Kazan-Ivan Memorial Clinic, on Center Street behind Bob Munson's Grocery, 435/826-4374, offers medical care on Mondays and Thursdays. The **Municipal Park** on the west edge of town has covered picnic tables, restrooms with water (except in winter), grills, and a small playground. **Escalante Outfitters,** 310 W. Main, 435/826-4266, probably has that camping item you forgot as well as topographic maps and books. For **guided tours** of the monument, contact **Escalante Outback Adventures,** 325 W. Main St, 435/826-4967 or 877/777-7988, website: www.escalante-utah.com.

HELL'S BACKBONE

This scenic 38-mile drive climbs high into the forests north of Escalante with excellent views of Death Hollow and Sand Creek Canyons and the distant Navajo, Fiftymile, and Henry Mountains.

Hell's Backbone Road reaches an elevation of 9,200 feet on the slopes of Roger Peak before descending to Hell's Backbone, 25 miles from town. Mule teams used this narrow ridge, with precipitous canyons on either side, as a route to Boulder until the 1930s. At that time, a bridge built by the Civilian Conservation Corps allowed the first vehicles to make the trip. You can still see the old mule path below the bridge. After 38 miles, the road ends at Highway 12; turn right 24 miles to return to Escalante or turn left three miles to Boulder. Cars can usually manage the gravel and dirt Hell's Backbone Road when it's dry. Snows and snowmelt, however, block the way until about late May. Check with the Interagency office in Escalante for current conditions. Trails and rough dirt roads lead deeper into the backcountry to more vistas and fishing lakes.

Posey Lake Campground (elevation 8,700 feet) offers sites amid aspen and ponderosa pines; open with drinking water from Memorial Day weekend to mid-September ($7). Rainbow and brook trout swim in the adjacent lake. A hiking trail (two miles round-trip) begins near space number 14 and climbs 400 feet to an old fire lookout tower, with good views of the lake and surrounding country. Posey Lake is 14 miles north of Escalante, then two miles west on a side road.

Blue Spruce Campground (elevation 7,860 feet) is another pretty spot, but it has only six sites. Anglers can try for pan-sized trout in a nearby stream. The campground, surrounded by blue spruce, aspen, and ponderosa pine, has drinking water from Memorial Day weekend to mid-September ($7); go north 19 miles from town, then turn left and drive one-half mile.

Boulder

About 150 people live in this farming community at the base of Boulder Mountain. Ranchers began drifting in during the late 1870s, although not with the idea of forming a town. By the mid-1890s, Boulder had established itself as a ranching and dairy center. Remote and hemmed in by canyons and mountains, Boulder remained one of the last communities in the country to rely on pack trains for transportation. Motor vehicles couldn't drive in until the 1930s. Today Boulder is worth a visit to see an excavated Anasazi village and the spectacular scenery along the way. Take paved Highway 12 either through the canyon and slickrock country from Escalante or over the Aquarius Plateau from Torrey (near Capitol Reef National Park). Burr Trail Road connects Boulder with Capitol Reef National Park's southern district via Waterpocket Fold and Circle Cliffs. A fourth way in is from Escalante on the dirt Hell's Backbone Road, which comes out three miles west of Boulder at Highway 12.

TOURS AND EXCURSIONS

Red Rock 'n Llamas, P.O. Box 1304, Boulder, UT 84716, 435/559-7325, offers a variety of fully outfitted hiking adventures in the Escalante Canyon area. Llamas will carry most of the gear, leaving you to explore in comfort. Most trips are four days and cost between $500–650. Write for a schedule.

If llamas don't strike you as Western enough for your backcountry adventure, **Escalante Canyon Outfitters,** P.O. Box 1330, Boulder, UT 84716, 888/326-4453 or 435/335-7311, website: www.ecohike.com, offers a selection of full-service guided tours of the Escalante country with pack horses.

ACCOMMODATIONS
$50–75
Poole's Place (closed in winter), across the road from the state park, 800/730-7422 or

Boulder Mountain Lodge adjoins a small wetland.

© W.C. MCRAE

435/335-7422, has a well-maintained motel, café, and gift shop.

$75–100

You wouldn't expect to find one of Utah's nicest places to stay in tiny Boulder, but the **Boulder Mountain Lodge,** along Highway 12 right in town, 800/556-3446 or 435/355-7460, offers the kinds of facilities and setting that make this one of the few destination lodgings in the state. The lodge's buildings are grouped around the edge of a private, 15-acre pond that serves as an ad hoc wildlife refuge. You can sit on the deck or wander paths along the pond, watching and listening to the amazing variety of birds that make this spot their home. The guest rooms and suites are in a handsome and modern Western-style lodge facing the pond; rooms are nicely decorated with quality furniture and beddings, and there's a central Great Room with a fireplace and library.

Campgrounds

Hall's Store, next to Anasazi State Park, 435/335-7304, runs a small RV park ($13; self-contained; no tents). Otherwise, there are several Forest Service campgrounds on nearby Boulder Mountain (follow Highway 12 north from town).

Guest Ranches

Cowboy up at the **Boulder Mountain Ranch,** seven miles from Boulder on the Hell's Backbone Rd., 435/355-7480, website: www.boulderutah .com/bmr. Guests have a choice of simple B&B accommodations in the lodge or free-standing cabins ($55–65), horseback riding, or multiday pack trips along the Great Western Trail. There are also two- to five-day riding and lodging packages based out of the ranch. Contact the ranch at P.O. Box 1373, Boulder, UT 84716.

FOOD

The Boulder Mountain Lodge restaurant, the **Hell's Backbone Grill,** 800/556-3446 or 435/355-7460, offers just about the only fine dining in all of southern Utah. You'll find fresh fish and seafood, adventurous game and meat preparations, and excellent desserts; open for three meals daily. For simpler fare, the **Burr Trail Cafe** (open Memorial Day weekend–autumn) is at the intersection of Highway 12 and Burr Trail Road, 435/335-7432.

INFORMATION AND SERVICES

Look for a **visitor information** booth in the center of town; usually it's in front of the Burr Trail Cafe. Open daily May–Oct. about 9 A.M. 6 P.M. The two gas stations in Boulder sell groceries and snack food.

AROUND BOULDER
Boulder Mountain Scenic Drive

Utah 12 climbs high into forests of ponderosa pine, aspen, and fir on Boulder Mountain between the towns of Boulder and Torrey. The modern highway replaces what used to be a rough dirt road. Travel in winter is usually possible now, although heavy snows can close the road. Viewpoints along the drive offer sweeping panoramas of the Escalante Canyon country, Circle Cliffs, Waterpocket Fold, and the Henry Mountains. Hikers and anglers can explore the alpine country of Boulder Mountain and seek out the 90 or so trout-filled lakes. The Dixie National Forest map (Escalante and Teasdale Ranger District offices) shows the back roads, trails, and lakes.

The U.S. Forest Service has three developed campgrounds about midway along this scenic drive: **Oak Creek** (18 miles from Boulder, elevation 8,800 feet), **Pleasant Creek** (19 miles from Boulder, elevation 8,700 feet), and **Singletree** (24 miles from Boulder, elevation 8,600 feet). The season with water lasts from about late May–mid-Sept.; sites cost $8. Campgrounds may also be open in spring and autumn without water for $3. **Lower Bowns Reservoir** (elevation 7,400 feet) has primitive camping (no water or fee) and fishing for rainbow and some cutthroat trout; turn east five miles on a rough dirt road (not recommended for cars) just south of Pleasant Creek Campground.

Contact the **Teasdale Ranger District office,** near Torrey, 435/425-3702, for recreation information in the northern and eastern parts of

ESCALANTE

Boulder Mountain; contact the **Escalante Ranger District office,** Escalante, 435/826-5499 or 435/826-5400, for the southern and western areas. **Wildcat Information Center,** near Pleasant Creek Campground, has forest information; open in the summer with irregular hours.

Kanab

Striking scenery surrounds this small town in Utah's far south. The Vermilion Cliffs to the west and east glow with a fiery intensity at sunrise and sunset. Streams have cut splendid canyons into surrounding plateaus. The Paiute Indians knew the spot as *Kanab* (place of the willows), which still grow along Kanab Creek. Mormon pioneers arrived in the mid-1860s and tried to farm along the unpredictable creek. Irrigation difficulties culminated in the massive floods of 1883, which in just two days gouged a section of creekbed 40 feet below its previous level. Ranching proved better suited to this rugged and arid land.

Hollywood discovered this dramatic scenery in the 1920s and has filmed more than 150 movies and TV series here since. Famous films shot hereabouts include movies as different as *My Friend Flicka, The Lone Ranger,* and *The Greatest Story Ever Told.* The TV series *Gunsmoke* and *F Troop* were shot locally. Film crews have constructed several Western sets near Kanab, but most lie on private land and are difficult to visit. The Paria set

east of town, however, is on BLM land and open to the public.

While most park visitors see Kanab (pop. 5,500) as a handy stopover on trips to Bryce, Zion, and Grand Canyon National Parks and the southern reaches of the GSENM, there are a few interesting sites around town that may warrant more than a sleep–eat–dash out of town visit.

SQUAW TRAIL

This well-graded trail provides a close look at the geology, plantlife, and animals of the Vermilion Cliffs just north of town. Allow about one hour on the moderately difficult trail to reach the first overlook (two miles round-trip with a 400-foot elevation gain) or 1.5 hours to go all the way up (three miles round-trip with an 800-foot elevation gain). Views to the south take in Kanab, Fredonia, Kanab Canyon, and the vast Kaibab Plateau. At the top, look north to see the White, Gray, and Pink Cliffs of the Grand Staircase. The trailhead

near Kanab, a set for the *Gunsmoke* TV series

© W.C. MCRAE

BEST FRIENDS ANIMAL SANCTUARY

If anybody else owned these 35,000 acres in the canyon north of town, there would be expensive McMansions sprawling across the hills. Instead, there are giant octagonal doghouses filled with animals no one else wants: former research animals, aggressive dogs, old dogs, sick dogs, dogs who have been abused or neglected. There are also plenty of cats, rabbits, birds, pot-bellied pigs, and horses (including one that's over 40 years old).

Best Friends Animal Sanctuary, the largest no-kill animal shelter in the country, takes in unwanted or abused animals and provides whatever rehabilitation is possible. Many animals are adopted out, but even the unadoptable ones are given homes for life, with plenty of care and attention from the sanctuary's fleet of employees and volunteers.

The shelter's origins date back to the 1970s, when a group of animal-lovers began trying to prevent the euthanization of unadoptable animals. They began rescuing animals who were about to be put to sleep by shelters, re-

© PAUL LEVY

habilitated them as necessary, and found them homes. In the early 1980s, this group of dedicated rescuers bought land in Angel Canyon just north of Kanab and, with their motley crew of unadoptable animals, established this sanctuary. Now, some 1,800 animals live here at any given time, and the shelter is the county's largest employer, with over 200 staff members caring for the animals and the grounds.

But even this large staff can't take care of all of the animals' needs. The shelter's fleet of volunteers is constantly changing; each volunteer spends anywhere from a couple of days to a couple of months feeding, walking, petting, and cleaning up after the animals. Volunteers also give the animals the attention and socialization necessary for them to become good companions.

Best Friends runs tours several times a day. Call 435/644-2001 for reservations or to learn more about volunteering at the shelter. There's no charge for a tour, although donations are gladly accepted.

is at the north end of 100 East near the city park. Pick up a trail guide at the information center (brochures may also be available at the trailhead or BLM office). Bring water with you. Try to get a very early start in summer.

MOQUI CAVE

This natural cave has been turned into a tourist attraction with a large collection of Indian artifacts. Most of the arrowheads, pottery, sandals, and burial items on display have been excavated locally. A diorama re-creates an Anasazi ruin located five miles away in Cottonwood Wash. Fossils, rocks, and minerals are exhibited, too, including what's claimed to be one of the largest fluorescent mineral displays in the country.

The collections and a gift shop lie within a spacious cave that stays pleasantly cool even in the hottest weather. Open daily except Sunday from early March to mid-November; summer hours are 9 A.M.–7 P.M., with shorter hours in spring and autumn; $4 adults, $3.50 seniors, $3 ages 13–17, and $2 children 6–12. The cave is five miles north of Kanab on U.S. 89, 435/644-2987.

CORAL PINK SAND DUNES STATE PARK

Churning air currents funneled by surrounding mountains have deposited huge sand dunes in this valley west of Kanab. The ever-changing dunes reach heights of several hundred feet and

ESCALANTE

cover about 2,000 of the park's 3,700 acres. Different areas in the park have been set aside for hiking, off-road vehicles, and a campground. If you see what looks like a family reunion, it might be just a man and his wives from the nearby polygamist settlements of Colorado City or Hildale!

From Kanab, the shortest drive is to go north eight miles on U.S. 89 (to between mileposts 72 and 73), turn left 9.3 miles on the paved Hancock Road to its end, then turn left (south) one mile on a paved road into the park. From the north, you can follow U.S. 89 3.5 miles south of Mount Carmel Junction, then turn right (south) 11 miles on a paved road. The back road from Cane Beds in Arizona has about 16 miles of gravel and dirt with some sandy spots; ask a park ranger for current conditions. Entrance fees are $4 per vehicle for day use, $12 per vehicle for camping. Contact the park at P.O. Box 95, Kanab, UT 84741, 800/322-3770 or 435/648-2800 (reservations).

The canyon country surrounding the park has good opportunities for hiking and off-road vehicle travel; the BLM office in Kanab can supply maps and information. Drivers with four-wheel-drive vehicles can turn south on Sand Springs Road (1.5 miles east of Ponderosa Grove Campground) and go one mile to Sand Springs and another four miles to the South Fork Indian Canyon Pictograph Site in a pretty canyon. Visitors may not enter the Kaibab-Paiute Indian Reservation, which is south across the Arizona state line, from this side.

ENTERTAINMENT AND EVENTS

In summer, free musical concerts are held at the city park gazebo, at the center of town. Wednesdays bring an ongoing local talent show. One of summer's largest events is the **Southern Utah Fiddle Championship,** which is held annually in mid-July. An even more unique Kanab event is the **Greyhound Gathering** in mid-May, when hundreds of greyhound owners converge on the town. Events include a parade, a race, and a howl-in. The Greyhound Gang, a nonprofit organization dedicated to

the rescue, rehabilitation, and adoption of ex-racing greyhounds, hosts this unlikely festival. Contact the visitors center for more information.

Shopping

Alderman & Son Photo, 19 W. Center, 435/644-5981, supplies film and camera needs (including repairs) beyond what you would expect in a town of this size. The shop almost qualifies as an antique camera museum.

Find a good selection of books, camping gear, and clothing, along with a little coffee bar at **Willow Creek Books & Coffee,** 263 S. 100 East, 435/644-8884.

Denny's Wigwam, 78 E. Center, 435/644-2452, is a landmark Old West trading post with lots of quality Western jewelry, cowboy hats and boots, and souvenirs. Danny's also hosts elaborate chuck wagon meals and entertainment, but usually only for bus tours. If a shindig is already scheduled, you can sometimes join the festivities by paying for an individual ticket.

ACCOMMODATIONS

Lodging reservations are a good idea during the busy summer months. All of the motels and campgrounds are on U.S. 89, which follows 300 West, Center, 100 East, and 300 South through town.

Less than $50

The **Canyonlands International Youth Hostel,** one-half block off U.S. 89 at 143 E. 100 South, 435/644-5554. is a small, motel-like complex, with rooms converted to simple dorm-style accommodations. Facilities include a kitchen, a laundry room, a TV room, a patio, a lawn, locked storage, and a reference library of regional maps and books. Open year-round; check-in is 9 A.M.–11 P.M. No hostel card is required.

Riding's Quail Park Lodge, 125 U.S. 89 North, 800/644-5094 or 435/644-5094, has a pool and accepts pets. The same people own the nearby **Bob-Bon Inn,** 236 U.S. 89 North,

800/644-5094 or 435/644-5094, a nicely renovated motel.

Aiken's Lodge National 9 Inn is at 79 W. Center, 800/524-9999 or 435/644-2625, and has a pool; closed Jan. and Feb. The **Sun-N-Sand Motel**, 347 S. 100 East, 800/654-1868 or 435/644-5050, has a pool, a spa, and kitchenettes. The **Brandon Motel**, 223 W. Center, 800/839-2631 or 435/644-2631, has a pool, kitchenettes, and accepts pets.

$50–75

The one lodging in Kanab that varies from the usual motor-court formula is the **Parry Lodge**, 89 E. Center, 800/748-4104 or 435/644-2601. Built during Kanab's heyday as a movie-making center, the Parry Lodge was where the stars stayed; 60 years later, this is still a pleasant place to spend the night. At the very least, you'll want to stroll through the lobby, where lots of photos of the celebrities who once stayed here are displayed. There are several two-bedroom units, a pool, and a good restaurant.

The **Treasure Trail Motel**, 150 W. Center, 800/603-2687 or 435/644-2687, has basic, clean rooms and a pool. The **Four Seasons Motel**, 36 N. 300 West, 435/644-2635, has a pool and accepts pets. The **Super 8**, 70 S. 200 West, 435/644-5500, has a heated pool.

$75–100

The **Best Western Red Hills Motel**, 125 W. Center, 800/830-2675 or 435/644-2675, has comfortable rooms and a pool, and is within a short walk of restaurants. (Rates drop substantially during spring, fall, and winter.) The **Holiday Inn Express**, one mile east of downtown at 815 E. U.S. 89, 435/644-8888 or 800/HOLIDAY (800/465-4329) offers a nine-hole golf course, a free breakfast bar, a pool, and a hot tub.

Campgrounds

The **Kanab RV Corral**, 483 S. 100 East, 435/644-5330, has sites with hot showers, a pool, and a laundromat open all year. The **Hitch'n Post RV Park**, 196 E. 300 South, 800/458-3516 or 435/644-2681, has sites with

showers open all year. The **Crazy Horse Campark**, 625 E. 300 South, 435/644-2782, has sites with a pool, a store, a game room, and showers; open mid-Apr.–late Oct.

Near the east entrance to Zion National Park, the **Zican Indian Store**, 435/648-2154, has a campground with hot showers, restrooms, and sites for tents and RVs.

The campground at **Coral Pink Sand Dunes State Park** has restrooms with showers, paved pull-through sites, and a dump station. It's a pleasant, shady spot, but it can hum with ATV traffic. Open all year, but the water is shut off from late October until Easter; winter campers need to bring their own. Reservations are recommended for the busy Memorial Day–Labor Day season.

Just north of the state park, the BLM maintains **Ponderosa Grove Campground** on the north edge of the dunes; no water. From Kanab, head eight miles north on U.S. 89, turn west on Hancock Rd. (between mileposts 72 and 73) and continue 7.3 miles to the campground.

FOOD

The **Vermillion Café**, 4 E. Center, 435/644-3886, is the place for espresso drinks, pastries, and deli sandwiches. You can find a good selection of organic and natural foods, including deli items, at **Wildflower Health Foods**, 18 E. Center, 435/644-3200. The setting is casual and the food is simple but sophisticated, with a modern Southwest flair, at **Rocking V Café**, 97 W. Center, 435/644-8001.

The **Parry Lodge**, 89 E. Center, 435/644-2601, has a homey dining room featuring steak, seafood, and some international dishes; open daily for breakfast, lunch, and dinner (closed 2–6 P.M.). Photos of former movie-star guests decorate the walls. The **Chef's Palace Restaurant**, 176 W. Center, 435/644-5052, offers steak, prime rib, and seafood; open daily for breakfast, lunch, and dinner.

For good, unfussy Mexican and American cooking, try the friendly **Nedra's Too**, 300 S. 100 East in the Heritage Center, 435/644-2030;

open daily for breakfast, lunch, and dinner; or **Houston's Trail's End Restaurant,** 32 E. Center, 435/644-2488; open daily for breakfast, lunch, and dinner.

The **Wok Inn,** 86 S. 200 West, 435/644-5400, has Hunan and Szechuan cuisine; open weekdays for lunch and dinner and weekends for dinner only; closed in winter. The best place for Mexican food is **Escobar's,** 373 E. 300 South, 435/644-3739. Beer is served; closed Saturday.

INFORMATION

Staff members at the **information center,** 70 S. 100 East (Kanab, UT 84741), 435/644-5033, offer literature and advice for services in Kanab and travel in Kane County; open year-round Mon.–Sat. 8 A.M.–8 P.M. The **Grand Staircase-Escalante National Monument** has an information center at 318 N. 100 East, 435/644-2672; open Mon.–Fri. 7:45 A.M.–4:30 P.M.

Bryce Canyon

Note: Please see color map of
Bryce Canyon *on pages vi–vii.*

A geologic fairyland of rock spires rises beneath the high cliffs of the Paunsaugunt Plateau. This intricate maze, eroded from a soft limestone, now glows with warm shades of reds, oranges, pinks, yellows, and creams. The rocks provide a continuous show of changing color through the day as the sun's rays and cloud shadows move across the landscape.

Looking at these rock formations is like looking at the sky on a cloudy day; it's easy to find images in the shapes of the rocks. Some see the natural rock sculptures as Gothic castles, others as Egyptian temples, subterranean worlds inhabited by dragons, or vast armies of a lost empire. The Paiute Indian tale of the Legend People relates how various animals and birds once lived in a beautiful city built for them by Coy-

ote; when the Legend People began behaving badly toward Coyote, he transformed them all into stone.

Bryce Canyon isn't a canyon at all, but the largest of a series of massive amphitheaters cut into the Pink Cliffs. In Bryce Canyon National Park, you can gaze into the depths from viewpoints and trails on the plateau rim or hike down moderately steep trails and wind your way among the spires. A 17-mile scenic drive traces the length of the park and passes many overlooks and trailheads. Off-road, the nearly 36,000 acres of Bryce Canyon National Park offers many opportunities to explore spectacular rock features, dense forests, and expansive meadows.

The park's elevation ranges from 6,600–9,100 feet, so it's usually much cooler here than at Utah's other

Bryce Canyon

© JUDY JEWELL

national parks. Expect pleasantly warm days in summer, frosty nights in spring and autumn, and snow in winter. The visitors center, scenic drive, and a campground stay open throughout the year. Allow a full day to see the visitors center exhibits, enjoy the viewpoints along the scenic drive, and take a few short walks. Photographers usually obtain the best results early and late in the day when shadows set off the brightly colored rocks. Memorable sunsets and sunrises reward visitors who stay overnight. Moonlit nights reveal yet another spectacle.

Natural History

GEOLOGY

As the top step of the Grand Staircase, Bryce's rocks are young by geologic standards. The park's Pink Cliffs lay on top of older rock layers, which are exposed in stairstep form as you head south toward the Grand Canyon.

This fantastic landscape got its start about 60 million years ago as sediments dropped to the bottom of a large body of water—named Lake Flagstaff by geologists. Silt and calcium carbonate and other minerals settled on the lake bottom, then consolidated and became the Claron Formation—a soft, silty limestone with some shale and sandstone.

Lake Flagstaff had long since disappeared when the land began to rise as part of the Colorado Plateau uplift about 16 million years ago. Uneven pressures beneath the plateau caused it to break along fault lines into a series of smaller plateaus at different levels known as the "Grand Staircase." Bryce Canyon National Park occupies part of one of these plateaus—the Paunsaugunt.

The spectacular Pink Cliffs on the east edge of the Paunsaugunt Plateau contain the famous erosional features known as the "hoodoos," carved in the Claron Formation. Variations in hardness of the rock layers result in these strange features, which seem almost alive. Water flows through cracks, wearing away softer rock around

HOODOOS

Though many visitors assume that wind shaped Bryce Canyon's hoodoos, they were, in fact, formed by water, ice and gravity, and the way that these forces interact on rocks of varying hardness.

When the Colorado Plateau uplifted, vertical breaks—called joints—formed in the plateau. Joints allowed water to flow into the rock. As water flowed through these joints, erosion widened them into rivulets, gullies, and eventually, deep slot canyons. Even more powerful than water, the action of ice freezing, melting, then freezing again (as it does about 200 days a year at Bryce) causes ice wedges to form within the rock joints, eventually breaking the rock.

Bryce Canyon is composed of layers of limestone, siltstone, dolomite and mudstone. Each rock type erodes at different rates, carving the strange shapes of the hoodoos. The word *hoodoo* derives from the same sources as *voodoo*; both words are sometimes used to describe folk beliefs and practices. Early Spanish explorers transferred the mystical sense of the word to the towering, vaguely humanoid rock formations that rise above Southwestern landscapes. The Spaniards believed that Native Americans worshipped these statue-like "enchanted rocks." In fact, while early Indians considered many hoodoo areas sacred, there is no evidence that they worshiped the stones themselves.

© JUDY JEWELL

hard, erosion-resistant caps. Finally, a cap becomes so undercut that the overhang allows water to drip down, leaving a "neck" of rock below the harder cap. Traces of iron and manganese provide the distinctive coloring. The hoodoos continue to change—new ones form and old ones fade away. Despite appearances, wind plays little role in creation of the landscape; it's the freezing and thawing, snowmelt, and rainwater that dissolve weak layers, pry open cracks, and carve out the forms. The plateau cliffs, meanwhile, recede at a rate of about one foot every 50–65 years; look for trees on the rim that now overhang the abyss. Listen, and you might hear the sounds of pebbles falling away and rolling down the steep slopes.

FLORA AND FAUNA

Bryce's plant life changes considerably with elevation; higher elevations are moister than the lowlands and can support relatively lush vegetation. The warm, dry slopes beneath the canyon's rim, below about 7,000 feet, are dominated by piñon pine, Utah juniper, and Gambel oak.

Between 7,000–8,500 feet, Ponderosa pines rise majestically over greenleaf manzanita and other shrubs. You'll find these species in the area around the visitors center, campground, and lodge.

Blue spruce, white fir, Douglas fir, limber pine, bristlecone pine, and aspen thrive in the cool, moist conditions above 8,500 feet. It's easy to see these trees at Rainbow and Yovimpa Points, which are just above 9,100 feet.

Wildflowers put on a showy display from spring to early autumn. Springs and seeps below the rim support pockets of water birch, bigtooth maple, willows, and narrow-leaf cottonwood.

Larger wildlife visit the higher elevations in summer, then move down out of the park as winter snows arrive. It's no shock that mule deer frequent Bryce's meadows, especially in morning and evening, but it's a little more surprising to see wild turkeys grazing there. Other residents include mountain lion, black bear, coyote, bobcat, gray fox, striped skunk, badger, porcupine, Utah prairie dog, yellow-bellied marmot, Uinta chipmunk, and golden-mantled ground squir-

GREENLEAF MANZANITA

One of the easiest plants to identify at Bryce is greenleaf manzanita. The leaves on this low-lying shrub are dark green and leathery; the bark is cinnamon-colored. Look closely, and you may see fine hairs on the stems. Pink urn-shaped flowers dangle from the stems in May, followed in late summer by fruit that resembles tiny cream-colored apples (*manzanita* is a Spanish word for little apple). Manzanita, which is common in California and the inland Pacific Northwest, easily survives snowy winters, though parts of the plant that aren't covered by an insulating blanket of snow may die from the cold. In order to conserve water during the hot summers, manzanita leaves stand straight up in a vertical position, reducing the surface area exposed to the sun and slowing transpiration.

Native Americans brewed a diuretic tea from manzanita leaves, and made cider from its ripe fruits. They also used the crushed leaves and fruit as a poultice for poison ivy. Patient (or lucky) visitors may spot wildlife browsing on the manzanita—both mule deer and wild turkeys are fond of it.

rel. Beaver live near the park on the East Fork of the Sevier River. (*Paunsaugunt* is Paiute for "home of the beaver.") Despite the cool climate, you can find a few reptiles; look for the short-horned lizard, skink, and Great Basin rattlesnake.

Birds appear in greatest numbers from May–Oct. Violet-green swallows and white-throated swifts dive and career among the hoodoos in hot pursuit of flying insects. Other summer visitors are the golden eagle, red-tailed hawk, Western tanager, and mountain bluebird. Year-round residents include woodpeckers, owls, raven, Steller's jay, Clark's nutcracker, and blue grouse.

Bryce's cliffs have become home to a thriving population of California condors. Six condors were released in the Vermilion Cliffs south of Bryce in 1996, and the population has grown to about 100. Peregrine falcons are another avian success story here; at least two pairs of these raptors nest in the park. Look for them from Paria View.

BRYCE CANYON

Although some wild creatures may seem quite tame, they must not be fed or handled—rodents may have diseases, and young deer contaminated with human scent might be abandoned by their mothers. Also, animals who become dependent on humans may die in winter when left to forage for themselves after the summer crowds have left.

Exploring the Park

VISITORS CENTER

From the turn-off on Highway 12, follow signs past Ruby's Inn to the park entrance; the visitors center is a short distance farther on the right. A brief slideshow, shown every half hour, introduces the park. Geologic exhibits illustrate how the land was formed and how it has changed. Historic displays interpret the Paiute Indians, early explorers, and the first settlers. Trees, flowers, and wildlife are identified. Rangers present a variety of naturalist programs, including short hikes, from mid-May–early September; see the posted schedule. Open daily all year (except Christmas) 8 A.M.–4:30 P.M., with extended hours during the warmer months. Contact the park at Bryce Canyon, UT 84717, 435/834-5322, website: www.nps.gov/brca.

Special hazards you should be aware of include crumbly ledges and lightning strikes. People who have wandered off trails or gotten too close to the drop-offs have had to be pulled out by rope. Avoid cliffs and other exposed areas during electrical storms, which are most common in late summer.

Entrance fees are $20 per vehicle. This includes park admission and unlimited shuttle use. Admission is good for seven days. Admission on foot or bicycle is $10.

From Bryce Junction (at the intersection of U.S. 89 and Highway 12, seven miles south of Panguitch), head 14 miles east on Highway 12, then south three miles on Highway 63. Or, from Torrey (near Capitol Reef National Park), head 103 miles south and west on Highway 12, then turn south onto Highway 63 for the final three

© JUDY JEWELL

The design of Bryce Canyon's new visitors center echoes the park's older structure.

miles into the park (winter snows occasionally close this section). Both approaches have spectacular scenery.

TOURS

Ruby's Inn, a hotel, restaurant, and recreation complex at the park entrance, is a good place to take measure of the opportunities for organized recreation and sight-seeing excursions in and around Bryce Canyon. The lobby is filled with outfitters who are anxious to take you out on the trail; you'll find each of the following there, along with other vendors who organize hayrides, barn dances, and chuck wagon dinners. **Red Canyon Horseback Rides,** 435/468-8660, has horseback riding near Bryce Canyon from May–Oct. There's a choice of half ($40) and whole ($75 including lunch) day trips. Shorter rides (as well as half- and full-day trips) are offered by **Scenic Rim Trail Rides,** 435/834-5341 ext. 217, which also operates out of Ruby's. An hour-long ride is $19. Ruby's also sponsors a rodeo nightly Mon.–Sat. at 7 P.M. across from the inn.

You can also explore the area around Bryce Canyon on a noisier steed. Guided all-terrain vehicle (ATV) tours of Red Canyon are offered by **Great Western ATV,** 800/432-5383 or 435/834-5200. A one-hour trip is $28, a three-hour trip is $69.

If you'd like to get a look at Bryce and the surrounding area from the air, you can choose to take a scenic flight-seeing tour from **Bryce Canyon Airlines,** 435/834-5341, which offers both plane and helicopter tours. There's quite a range of options, from a 15-minute trip to a nearby mesa ($35) to a 2.5-hour trip that takes in the Grand Canyon ($295).

BRYCE CANYON SHUTTLE

When rangers and visitors alike began to complain seriously about the "Bryce Canyon national parking lot," park administrators took note, but bigger parking lots obviously weren't the environmentally friendly solution.

In 2000, the National Park Service (NPS) instituted a shuttle service through Bryce Canyon Park. Buses run during the peak summer season from the Shuttle Parking and Boarding Area at the intersection of highways 12 and 63 to the visitors center, with stops at Ruby's Inn and Ruby's Campground. From the visitors center, the bus travels to the park's developed areas, including all the main amphitheater viewpoints, Sunset Campground, and the Bryce Canyon Lodge. Passengers can take as long as they like at any viewpoint, and catch a later bus. The shuttle bus service also makes it easier for hikers, who don't need to worry about car shuttles between trailheads.

Use of the shuttle bus system is not mandatory; you can still bring in your own vehicle. However, even if you do drive into the park, don't plan to pull a trailer all the way to Rainbow Point. Trailers aren't allowed past Sunset Campground. Trailer parking is available at the visitors center.

SCENIC DRIVE

From elevations of about 8,000 feet near the visitors center, the park's scenic drive gradually winds 1,100 feet higher to Rainbow Point. About midway you'll notice a change in the trees from largely ponderosa pine to spruce, fir, and aspen. On a clear day, you can enjoy vistas of more than 100 miles from many of the viewpoints. Because of parking shortages on the drive, trailers must be left at the visitors center or campsite. Visitors wishing to see the rest of the viewpoints may choose to walk on the Rim Trail.

Fairyland Point

To reach the turn-off (just inside the park boundary), go north 0.8 mile from the visitors center, then east one mile. Whimsical forms line Fairyland Canyon a short distance below. You can descend into the "fairyland" on the **Fairyland Loop Trail** or follow the **Rim Trail** for other panoramas.

Sunrise and Sunset Points

These overlooks are off to the left about one mile past the visitors center; they're connected by a half-mile paved section of the **Rim Trail.** Panoramas from each point take in large areas of Bryce Amphitheater and beyond. The lofty Aquarius and Table Cliff Plateaus rise along the skyline to the northeast; you can recognize the same colorful Claron Formation in cliffs that faulting has raised about 2,000 feet higher. A short walk down either the **Queen's Garden Trail** or the **Navajo Loop Trail** from Sunset Point can bring you up close to Bryce's hoodoos and provide a totally different experience from what you get atop the rim.

Inspiration Point

It's well worth the three-quarters of a mile walk south along the **Rim Trail** from Sunset Point to see a fantastic maze of hoodoos in the "Silent City." (It's also accessible by car, from a spur road near the Bryce Point turn-off.) Weathering along vertical joints has cut many rows of narrow gullies, some more than 200 feet deep.

Bryce Point

This overlook at the south end of Bryce Amphitheater has expansive views to the north and east. It's also the start for the **Rim, Peekaboo Loop,** and **Under-the-Rim trails.** From the turn-off two miles south of the visitors center, follow signs 2.1 miles in.

Paria View

Cliffs drop precipitously into the headwaters of Yellow Creek, a tributary of the Paria River. You can see a section of Under-the-Rim Trail winding up a hillside near the mouth of the amphitheater below. Distant views take in the Paria River Canyon, White Cliffs (of Navajo Sandstone), and Navajo Mountain. The plateau rim in the park forms a drainage divide. Precipitation falling west of the rim flows gently into the East Fork of the Sevier River and the Great Basin; precipitation landing east of the rim rushes through deep canyons in the Pink Cliffs to the Paria River and on to the Colorado River and the Grand Canyon. Take the turn-off for Bryce Point, then keep right at the fork.

Farview Point

This sweeping panorama takes in a lot of geology. You can see levels of the Grand Staircase

that include the Aquarius and Table Cliff Plateaus to the northeast, Kaiparowits Plateau to the east, and White Cliffs to the southeast. Look beyond the White Cliffs to see a section of the Kaibab Plateau that forms the north rim of the Grand Canyon in Arizona. The overlook is on the left nine miles south of the visitors center.

Natural Bridge

This large feature lies just off the road on the left, 1.7 miles past Farview Point. The span is 54 feet wide and 95 feet high. Despite its name, this is an arch, formed by weathering from rain and freezing, rather than by stream erosion like a true natural bridge. Once the opening reached ground level, runoff began to enlarge the hole and to dig a gully through it.

Agua and Ponderosa Canyons

You can admire sheer cliffs and hoodoos from the Agua Canyon overlook on the left, 1.4 miles past Natural Bridge. With a little imagination, you might be able to pick out the Hunter and the Rabbit below. Ponderosa Canyon overlook, on the left 1.8 miles farther, offers a panorama similar to that at Farview Point.

Yovimpa Point and Rainbow Point

The land drops away in rugged canyons and fine views at the end of the scenic drive, 17 miles south of the visitors center. At an elevation of 9,115 feet, this is the highest area of the park. Yovimpa and Rainbow points lie only a short walk apart yet offer different vistas. The **Bristlecone Loop Trail** is an easy one-mile loop from Rainbow Point to ancient bristlecone pines along the rim. The **Riggs Spring Loop Trail** makes a good day hike; you can begin from either Yovimpa Point or Rainbow Point and descend into canyons in the southern area of the park. the **Under-the-Rim Trail** starts from Rainbow Point and winds 22.5 miles to Bryce Point; day-hikers could make a 7.5-mile trip by using the Agua Canyon Connecting Trail and a car shuttle.

Recreation

HIKING

Hikers enjoy close-up views of the wonderfully eroded features and gain a direct appreciation of Bryce's geology. Because almost all of the trails head down off the canyon's rim, they're moderately difficult, with many ups and downs, but the paths are well graded and signed. Hikers not accustomed to the 7,000- to 9,000-foot elevations will find the going relatively strenuous and should allow extra time. Be sure to carry water and drink frequently—staying well hydrated will give you more energy.

Wear a hat and sunscreen to protect against sunburn, which can be a problem at these elevations. Don't forget rain gear because storms can come up suddenly. Always carry water for day trips because only a few natural sources exist. Ask at the visitors center for current trail conditions and water sources; you can also pick up a free hiking map at the visitors center. Snow may block some trail sections in winter and early spring. Horses are permitted only on Peekaboo Loop. Pets must stay above the rim; they're allowed on the Rim Trail only between Sunset and Sunrise points.

Overnight hikers can obtain the required $5 backcountry permit at the visitors center (camping is allowed only on the Under-the-Rim and Riggs Spring loop trails). Backpack stoves must be used for cooking; wood fires are prohibited. Although there are several isolated springs in Bryce's backcountry, it's prudent to carry at least one gallon of water per person per day. Ask about the location and flow of springs when you register for the backcountry permit.

Don't expect much solitude during the summer on the popular Rim, Queen's Garden, Navajo, and Peekaboo loop trails. Fairyland Loop Trail is less used, and the backcountry trails are al-

most never crowded. September and October are the choice hiking months—the weather is best and the crowds smallest, although nighttime temperatures in late October can dip well below freezing.

Rim Trail

This easy trail follows the edge of Bryce Amphitheater for 5.5 miles between Fairyland and Bryce points; the elevation change is 540 feet. Most people walk just sections in leisurely strolls or use the trail to connect with five others. The half-mile section near the lodge between Sunrise and Sunset points is paved and nearly level; other parts are gently rolling.

Because almost all of the trails head down off the canyon's rim, they're moderately difficult, with many ups and downs, but the paths are well graded and signed. Hikers not accustomed to the 7,000- to 9,000-foot elevations will find the going relatively strenuous.

Fairyland Loop Trail

This trail winds in and out of colorful rock spires in the northern part of Bryce Amphitheater, a somewhat less-visited area one mile off the main park road. Although the trail is well graded, remember the 900-foot climb you'll make when you exit. You can take a loop hike of eight miles from either Fairyland Point or Sunrise Point by using a section of the **Rim Trail;** a car shuttle saves three hiking miles. The whole loop is too long for many visitors, who enjoy short trips down and back to see this "fairyland."

Queen's Garden Trail

A favorite of many people, this trail drops from Sunrise Point through impressive features in the middle of Bryce Amphitheater to a hoodoo resembling a portly Queen Victoria. The hike is 1.5 miles round-trip and has an elevation change of 320 feet, which you'll have to climb on the way back. This is the easiest excursion below the rim and takes about 1.5 hours. Queen's Garden Trail also makes a good loop hike with the **Navajo** and **Rim** trails; most people who do the loop prefer to descend the steeper Navajo and climb out on Queen's Garden Trail for a 3.5-mile hike. Trails also connect with the **Peekaboo Loop Trail** and go to the town of Tropic.

Navajo Loop Trail

From Sunset Point, you'll drop 520 feet in three-quarters of a mile through a narrow canyon. At the bottom, the loop leads into deep, dark **Wall Street**—an even narrower canyon one-half mile long—then returns to the rim; the total distance is about 1.5 miles. Other destinations from the bottom of Navajo Trail are **Twin Bridges, Queen's Garden Trail, Peekaboo Loop Trail,** and the town of Tropic. The 1.5-mile trail to Tropic isn't as scenic as the other trails, but it does provide another way to enter or leave the park; ask at the visitors center or in Tropic for directions to the trailhead.

Peekaboo Loop Trail

This enchanting walk is full of surprises at every turn—and there are lots of turns! The trail is in the southern part of Bryce Amphitheater, which has some of the most striking rock features. You can start from Bryce Point (6.5 miles round-trip), from Sunset Point (5.5 miles round-trip via Navajo Trail), or from Sunrise Point (seven miles round-trip via Queen's Garden Trail). The loop itself is 3.5 miles long with many ups and downs and a few tunnels. The elevation change is 500–800 feet, depending on the trailhead you choose. This is the only trail in the park where horses are permitted; remember to give horseback travelers the right-of-way and, if possible, to step to higher ground when you allow them to pass.

Under-the-Rim Trail

The longest trail in the park winds 22.5 miles below the Pink Cliffs between Bryce Point in the north and Rainbow Point in the south. Allow at least two days to hike the entire trail; the elevation change is about 1,500 feet with many ups and downs. Four connecting trails from the scenic drive allow you to travel the Under-the-Rim Trail as a series of day hikes, too. Another option is to combine the Under-the-Rim and **Riggs Spring Loop** trails for a total of 31.5 miles.

Though Bryce is most popular during the summer months, it is especially beautiful and other-worldly during the winter, when the rock formations are topped with snow. Because Bryce is so high (the elevation ranges from 8,000–9,000 feet), winter lasts a long time, often into April.

The main park roads and most viewpoints are plowed, and the Rim Trail is an excellent, easy snowshoe or cross-country ski route. **Paria Ski Trail** (five-mile loop) and **Fairyland Ski Trail** (2.5-mile loop) are marked for snowshoers and cross-country skiers. Whenever snow depth measures 18 inches or more, snowshoes are loaned free-of-charge at the visitor center (the deposit of a credit card is required). Rent cross-country ski equipment just outside the park at Ruby's Inn, 888/279-2304 or 435/834-5180, website: www.bryceviewlodge.com. Miles of snowmobile trails are groomed outside the park.

During the winter, most of the businesses around the park entrance shut down. The notable exception is Ruby's Inn, which is a wintertime hub of activity. During the winter months, rates drop precipitously—most rooms go for less than $50 from Jan–March.

Ruby's Inn hosts the Bryce Canyon Winter Festival during Presidents Day weekend in February. The 3-day festival includes free cross-country skiing and snowshoeing clinics, demos and tours. This is also the time and place to pick up tips on ski archery and winter photography.

The **Hat Shop,** an area of delicate spires capped by erosion-resistant rock, makes a good day-hiking destination; begin at Bryce Point and follow the Under-the-Rim Trail for about two miles. Most of this section is downhill (elevation change of 900 feet), which you'll have to climb on the way out.

Bristlecone Loop Trail

The easy one-mile loop begins from either Rainbow or Yovimpa Point and goes to viewpoints and ancient bristlecone pines along the rim. These hardy trees survive fierce storms and extremes of hot and cold that no other tree can. Some of the bristlecone pines here are 1,700 years old.

Riggs Spring Loop

One of the park's more challenging day hikes or a leisurely overnighter, this trail begins from Rainbow Point and descends into canyons in the southern area of the park. The loop is about nine miles long, with an elevation change of 1,625 feet. Of the three backcountry campgrounds along the trail, the Riggs Spring site is most conveniently located, about halfway around the loop. Great views of the hoodoos, lots of aspen trees, a couple of pretty meadows, and great views off to the east are some of the highlights of this hike. Day hikers may want to take a shortcut bypassing Riggs Spring, saving three-quarters of a mile.

Mossy Cave Trail

This easy trail is not on the main park road; it's just off Highway 12, northwest of Tropic, near the east edge of the park. Hike up Water Canyon to a cool alcove of dripping water and moss. Sheets of ice and icicles add beauty to the scene in winter. The hike is only one mile round-trip with a small elevation gain. A side trail, just before the cave, branches right a short distance to a little waterfall; look for several small arches in the colorful canyon walls above. Although the park lacks perennial natural streams, the stream in Water Canyon flows even during dry spells. Mormon pioneers labored three years to channel water from the East Fork of the Sevier River through a canal and down this wash to the town of Tropic. Without this irrigation, the town might not even exist. From the visitors center, return to Highway 12 and turn east 3.7 miles toward Escalante; the parking area is on the right just after a bridge (between mileposts 17 and 18). Rangers schedule guided walks to the cave and the waterfall during the main season.

MOUNTAIN BIKING

Although mountain biking is prohibited on trails inside the national park, just a few miles west of the park entrance, Red Canyon's bike trails are spectacularly scenic and exhilarating to ride. For information on Red Canyon, see the following section.

Ruby's Inn provides a shuttle service for Red Canyon mountain bikers.

HORSEBACK RIDING

If you'd like to get down among the hoodoos, but aren't sure that you have the energy to hike back up to the rim, consider letting a horse help you along. The park offers guided rides near Sunrise Point, and both two-hour ($30) and half-day ($45) trips are offered. Both rides descend to the floor of the canyon; the longer ride follows the Peek-a-Boo Loop Trail. Riders must be at least seven years old, and no more than 220 pounds, and the horses and wranglers are all used to novices.

BRYCE CANYON

BRISTLECONE PINE

Somewhere on earth, a bristlecone pine tree may be the planet's oldest living organism. The trees here, although not the world's oldest, are up to 1,700 years old. (A bristlecone in California is nearly 4,800 years old.) These twisted, gnarly trees are easy to spot in the area around Rainbow Point because they *look* their age.

What makes a bristlecone live so long? For one, its dense, resinous wood protects it from insects, bacteria, and fungi that kill many other trees. It grows in a harsh, dry climate, where there's not a lot of competition from other plants. During droughts that would kill most other plants, the bristlecone can slow down its metabolism until it's practically dormant, then spring back to life when conditions are less severe. Although the dry desert air poses its own set of challenges, it also keeps the tree from rotting.

Besides its ancient look, a bristlecone pine can be recognized by its distinctive needles—they're packed tightly, five to a bunch, with the bunches running along the length of a branch, giving it a bottle-brush-like appearance.

Accommodations and Food

Travelers can have a hard time finding accommodations and campsites from Apr.–Oct. in both the park and nearby areas. Advance reservations at lodges and motels are a good idea; otherwise, plan to arrive by late morning. Bryce Canyon Lodge is the only lodging in the park itself—you'll need to make reservations months in advance to get a room in this historic landmark. Other motels are clustered near the park entrance road. A larger selection of lodgings and dining options is found in Tropic, 11 miles east on Highway 12.

The park's two campgrounds operate on a first-come, first-served basis; arrive by noon in the main season to be assured of a spot.

Reach the **Bryce Canyon Information Line,** an area motel reservation service, at 435/444-6689.

LESS THAN $50

In order to find lodgings for less than $50 during the high summer season, head about 17 miles west of the park, to the U.S. 89 and Highway 12 junction, where the **Bryce Junction Inn,** 800/437-4361 or 435/676-2221, is a standard motel with rooms topping out at about $50.

$50–75

Other hotels are clustered on Highway 12, right outside the park boundary. Many of these have seen a lot of use over the years, usually without a lot of attendant upkeep. The **Foster's Motel** has plain vanilla motel rooms for right around $50. It's located four miles west of the park entrance at 1150 Hwy. 12, 800/372-4750 or 435/834-5227, website: www.fostersmotel.com.

One of the newest lodgings, and a good value for the area, is the **Bryce View Lodge,** near the park turn-off and across the road from Ruby's Inn, 888/279-2304 or 435/834-5180, website: www.bryceviewlodge.com. Rooms in the handsome lodge-like buildings start at about $55. Six miles west of the park turn-off, the **Bryce Canyon Pines Motel,** 800/892-7923 or 435/

834-5441, website: www.brycecanyonmotel.com, has rooms and cottages ranging from $65–95, a seasonal covered pool, horseback rides, and a restaurant open daily for breakfast, lunch, and dinner from early April to late October.

$75–100

At **Bryce Canyon Resort,** near the junction of Hwy. 12 and Hwy. 63, 800/834-0043 or 435/834-5351, recently renovated rooms start at about $85 per night. Rooms in the old building are $69, with simple cabins running about $50.

$100–125

Set among ponderosa pines a short walk from the rim, the **Bryce Canyon Lodge** was built in 1923 by a division of the Union Pacific Railway; a spur line once terminated at the front entrance. The lodge has lots of charm and is listed on the National Register of Historic Places. It also has by far the best location of any Bryce-area accommodation; it's the only lodging in the park itself.

Hotel rooms start at $99 and run to $123 for a suite; Western cabins are $110. The lodge is open Apr. 1–Oct. 31. Activities include horseback rides, park tours, evening entertainment, and ranger talks; a gift shop sells souvenirs. Try to make reservations for accommodations as far in advance as possible (eight months advised) with Xanterra Parks & Resorts, 14001 E. Iliff Ave., Ste. 600, Aurora, CO 80014, 800/834-5351 or 650/372-1705 (Bryce Canyon Lodge), in-season. You can also make reservations at this website: www.xanterra.com.

The large, resort-like **Best Western Ruby's Inn** offers many year-round services on Hwy. 63 just north of the park boundary (Bryce, UT 84764), 800/468-8660 or 435/834-5341, website: www.rubysinn.com. The hotel features two indoor pools and a spa; rooms start just under $100. Kitchenettes and family rooms are also available; pets are okay. Ruby's Inn is more than just a place to stay, however. This is

© JUDY JEWELL

Bryce Canyon Lodge

one of the area's major centers for all manner of recreational outfitters, dining, entertainment, and shopping.

The **general store** has a large stock of groceries, camping and fishing supplies, film and processing, Indian crafts, books, and other souvenirs. The **Bryce post office** is at the store, too. Horseback rides, helicopter tours, and airplane rides are arranged in the lobby (see Recreation section). In winter, cross-country skiers can rent gear and use trails located near the inn as well as in the park. Snowmobile trails are available (snowmobiles may not be used within the park). Western-fronted shops across from Ruby's Inn offer trail rides, chuck wagon dinners, mountain-bike rentals, souvenirs, and a petting farm. **Rodeos** take place in the nearby arena nightly Mon.–Sat. in-season.

CAMPGROUNDS

The park's two campgrounds both have water, some pull-through spaces, and cost $10. Try to arrive early for a space during the busy summer season because both campgrounds usually fill by 1 or 2 P.M., and only group areas may be reserved.

The **North Campground** is on the left just past the visitors center. The best sites here are just a few yards downhill from the Rim Trail, with easy hiking access to other park trails. The **Sunset Campground** is about 2.5 miles farther on the right, across the road from Sunset Point. Sunset has campsites accessible to people with disabilities.

Groceries, camping supplies, and coin-operated showers and a laundry room are available from mid-Apr.–late Sept. at the **General Store,** between North Campground and Sunrise Point. During the rest of the year, you can go outside the park to Ruby's Inn for these services.

The Dixie National Forest has three Forest Service **campgrounds** located in scenic settings among ponderosa pines. Often they'll have room when campgrounds in the park have filled. Group sites can be reserved, but the rest are available on a first-come, first-served basis. All sites have water and cost $8–10. The **Pine Lake Campground** lies at 7,700 feet just east of Pine Lake in a forest of ponderosa pine, spruce, and juniper. Sites are open mid-June–mid-Sept. From the highway junction north of the park, head northeast 11 miles on Highway 63 (gravel), then turn southeast six miles.

King Creek Campground is located on the west shore of the Tropic Reservoir, which has a boat ramp and fair trout fishing. Sites are at 8,000 feet and are usually open May–late Sept. Head seven miles south of Highway 12 down the gravel East Fork Sevier River Road, located 2.8 miles west of the park turn-off. To reach the **Red Canyon Campground,** turn off Highway 12 four miles east of U.S. 89. It's located at 7,400 feet, below brilliantly colored cliffs, and stays open from late May–late Sept. Contact the Powell Ranger District office in Panguitch, 435/676-8815, for more information on Kings and Red Canyon campgrounds and at the Escalante Ranger District office in Escalante, 435/826-5400, for Pine Lake.

Private campgrounds in the area are $20 and up per night. The **Ruby's Inn Campground,** at the park junction, 435/834-5301, is open from early Apr.–late Oct., with spaces for tents and RVs; showers and a laundry room are open all year. They've also got a few tipis ($23 per day) and bunkhouse-style cabins ($40 per day, no bedding provided). All of the considerable facilities at Ruby's are available to camping patrons. The **Bryce Canyon Pines Campground,** four

miles west of the park entrance, 800/892-7923 or 435/834-5441, has an indoor pool, a game room, groceries, and shady sites.

FOOD

The dining room at the **Bryce Canyon Lodge,** 435/586-9476, offers a varied menu with moderate prices; open daily in season for breakfast, lunch, and dinner (reservations advised for dinner). With 12 hours advance notice, you can order a box lunch.

The Ruby's Inn **Canyon Diner,** 435/834-5341, is one of Bryce Canyon's better restaurants; open for breakfast, lunch, and dinner daily. Casual lunch and dinner fare is served in the inn's snack bar from Apr.–Oct. Also check at Ruby's for seasonal chuck wagon meals, accompanied by singers and Western entertainment.

Bryce Canyon Resort, near the turn-off for the park, 800/834-0043 or 435/834-5351, has an on-site restaurant that features steak and barbecue and is open daily for breakfast, lunch, and dinner. Two miles west of the park turn-off is **Foster's,** 435/834-5227, a long-standing institution with old-fashioned diner food.

Additional Bryce Canyon–Area Sights

RED CANYON

The drive on Highway 12 between U.S. 89 and the turn-off for Bryce Canyon National Park passes through this well-named canyon. You may think that it should have been included in the national park because the brightly colored rocks belong to the same Claron Formation that's exposed at Bryce; however, because it's not part of the park, the trails at Red Canyon are open to the kinds of recreation that is prohibited in the park, principally mountain biking and ATV riding. In fact, this canyon is becoming very popular as other Utah mountain-biking destinations become overpopularized; however, many trails are restricted to foot traffic.

Staff members at the **Red Canyon Visitors Center** can tell you about the trails, as well as

scenic backcountry roads, that wind through the area; books and maps are sold; open daily about 8 A.M.–6 P.M. during the warmer months; located between mileposts 3 and 4 on Highway 12, one-quarter mile west of Red Canyon Campground. You can contact the Powell Ranger District office in Panguitch for information year-round, 435/676-8815. (For details about Red Canyon Campground, see the Campgrounds section under Accommodations.)

Hiking

The U.S. Forest Service maintains many scenic hiking trails that wind back from the highway to give you a closer look at the geology. The following are open to hikers only. **Pink Ledges Trail,** the easiest and most popular, loops one-half mile past intriguing erosional features from the Red Canyon Visitors Center. Signs identify some of the trees and plants; the elevation gain is 100 feet. The **Birdseye Trail** winds through formations and connects the visitors center with a parking area on Highway 12 just inside the forest boundary, 0.8 mile away. **Buckhorn Trail** begins from Site number 23 in Red Canyon Campground and climbs one mile for views of erosional forms and Red Canyon; the campground is on the south side of Highway 12 between mileposts 3 and 4. The **Tunnel Trail** ascends 300 feet in 0.7 mile for fine views of the canyon. The trail begins from a pullout on the south side of Highway 12 just west of a pair of tunnels, crosses the streambed, then climbs a ridge to viewpoints on the top. Ask at the visitors center for other good area trails worth exploring.

Mountain Biking

For tame pedalers, a spanking new, paved bike trail parallels Highway 12 for five miles through Red Canyon. Parking lots are located at either end of the trail.

True mountain bikers will eschew the pavement and head to **Casto Canyon Trail,** a 17-mile one-way trail that winds through a variety of red-rock formations and forest. The route starts and ends along Highway 12. If you don't have a shuttle vehicle at each of the trailheads, you'll need to peddle back another eight miles along the paved roadside trail to retrieve your vehicle. Start at Tom Best Road, just east of Red Canyon. You'll climb up through forest, turning onto Berry Spring Creek Road and then Cabin Hollow Road. When the trail starts heading into Casto Canyon, you'll have five downhill miles of wonderful red-rock scenery. When you reach the Casto Canyon Trailhead, you can choose to return to Highway 12, or you can pedal out to Highway 89 and Panguitch. Much of the trail is strenuous, and you'll need to take water along because there's no source along the way. There are several side trails along the way to

make this into a shorter ride; see the Forest Service brochure on Red Canyon trails.

CEDAR BREAKS NATIONAL MONUMENT

If you're taking a meandering drive between Zion and Bryce National Parks, you may want to pay a visit to Cedar Breaks. But take note: this is high country, and the road is closed by snow from mid-Oct.–late May.

Cedar Breaks is much like Bryce Canyon, but it's on a different high plateau. While Bryce's amphitheater was eroded from the Paunsaugunt Plateau, here it's the west edge of the Markagunt Plateau that's been eroded, carving a giant amphitheater 2,500 feet deep and more than three miles across. A fairyland of forms and colors appears below the rim. Ridges and pinnacles extend like buttresses from the steep cliffs. Cottony patches of clouds often drift through the craggy landscape. Traces of iron, manganese, and other minerals have tinted the normally white limestone a rainbow of warm hues. The intense colors blaze during sunsets and glow even on a cloudy day. Rock layers look much like those at Bryce Canyon National Park and, in fact, are the same Claron Formation, but here they're 2,000 feet higher. Elevations range from 10,662 feet at the rim's highest point to 8,100 feet at Ashdown Creek below. In the distance beyond the amphitheater, you can see Cedar City and the desert's valleys and ranges. Dense forests broken by large alpine meadows cover the rolling plateau country away from the rim. More than 150 species of wildflowers brighten the meadows during summer; the colorful display peaks during the last two weeks in July.

A five-mile scenic drive leads past four spectacular overlooks, each with a different perspective. Avoid overlooks and other exposed areas

A fairyland of forms and colors appears below the rim. Ridges and pinnacles extend like buttresses from the steep cliffs. Minerals have tinted the normally white limestone a rainbow of warm hues. The intense colors blaze during sunsets and glow even on a cloudy day.

during thunderstorms, which are common on summer afternoons. Heavy snows close the road most of the year. You can drive in only from about late May until the first big snowstorm of autumn, usually some time in October. Winter visitors can come in on snowmobiles (unplowed roads only), skis, or snowshoes from Brian Head (two miles north of the monument) or from Highway 14 (2.5 miles south). Cedar Breaks National Monument is 24 miles east of Cedar City, 17 miles south of Parowan, 30 miles southwest of Panguitch, and 27 miles northwest of Long Valley Junction. The nearest accommodations and restaurants are two miles north in Brian Head.

Visitors Center and Campground

A log cabin contains exhibits and an information desk. The exhibits provide a good introduction to the Markagunt Plateau and identify local rocks, wildflowers, trees, animals, and birds. Related books, topographic and forest maps, posters, slides, and camera film are sold. Staff members offer nature walks, geology talks, and campfire programs; see the schedules posted in the visitors center and at the campground. Open daily Jun. 1–mid-Oct. 8 A.M.–6 P.M. A $4 per-vehicle entrance fee is collected near the visitors center; there's no charge if you're just driving through the monument without stopping. The small campground to the east has water and a $9 fee; camping is first-come, first-served. The campground is open from about Jun. 1–mid-Sept. There's a picnic area near the campground. Contact the monument at 2390 West Highway 56, Suite #11, Cedar City, UT 84720-4151, 435/586-9451, or www.nps.gov/cebr.

Hiking Trails

Two easy trails near the rim give an added appreciation of the geology and forests here. Allow extra time while on foot—it's easy to get out of breath at these high elevations! Regulations prohibit pets on the trails. The **Spectra Point/Wasatch Rampart Trail** begins at the visitors center, then follows the rim along the south edge of the amphitheater to an overlook. The hike is four miles round-trip with some ups and downs. Weather-beaten bristlecone pines grow at Spectra Point, about halfway down the trail.

The **Alpine Pond Trail** forms a two-mile loop that drops below the rim into one of the few densely wooded areas of the amphitheater. The trail winds through enchanting forests of aspen, subalpine fir, and Engelmann spruce. You can cut the hiking distance in half with a car shuttle between the two trailheads or by taking a connector trail that joins the upper and lower parts of the loop near Alpine Pond. Begin from either Chessmen Ridge Overlook or the trailhead pullout 1.1 miles farther north. A trail guide is available at the start or at the visitors center.

Tropic

Mormon pioneer Ebenezer Bryce homesteaded near the town site of Tropic in 1875, but the work of scratching a living from the rugged land became too hard. He left five years later for more promising areas in Arizona. The name of the park commemorates his efforts. He is remembered as saying of the area, "Well, it's a hell of a place to lose a cow." Other pioneers settled six villages near the upper Paria River between 1876–1891. The towns of Tropic, Cannonville, and Henrieville still survive. Tropic lies just 11 miles east of Bryce Canyon National Park, visible from many of the park's viewpoints. Travelers think of Tropic primarily for its cache of motels lining Main Street (Highway 12); several pleasant B&Bs also grace the town. A **log cabin** built by Ebenezer Bryce has been moved to a site beside the Bryce Pioneer Village Motel; ask to see the cabin's small collection of pioneer and Indian artifacts. A **tourist booth** in the center of town is open daily from early May–late Oct., about 11 A.M.–7 P.M.

ACCOMMODATIONS

$50–75

The basic motel rooms at **Doug's Place Country**

Inn, 800/993-6847 or 435/679-8600, website: www.dougsplace.net, are part of a complex that includes a restaurant and a store. Rooms top out at $65 during the peak summer season. In the same price range, **Bryce Valley Inn,** 800/442-1890 or 435/679-8811, website: www.brycevalleyinn.com, has rooms in an attractive wood-fronted, Western-look motel. Pets are okay for a fee. On the south end of town, the **Bryce Pioneer Village Motel,** 800/222-0381 or 435/679-8546, website: www.bpvillage.com, has motel rooms and several cabins (one with kitchen); there's also a campground.

At the **Bryce Canyon Inn,** 800/592-1468 or 435/679-8502, the tidy new cabins are nicely furnished and cost $65 during high season. Also new are the **Bryce Country Cabins,** 80 S. Main St., 888/679-8643 or 435/679-8643, website: www.brycecountrycabins.com. The cabins overlook a meadow, and each has a private bath. One-half mile south of town is the log-cabin style **Francisco's Farm Bed & Breakfast,** 51 Francisco Ln., 800/642-4136 or 435/679-8721, which offers rooms in a farmhouse, all with private baths.

$75–100

Located a few blocks from the highway, the **Bryce Point Bed & Breakfast,** 61 N. 400 West, 888/200-4211 or 435/679-8629, website: www.brycepointlodging.com, is a large home with very nice rooms, all with private baths, TVs and VCRs, and views out every window. All rooms have private entrances. There's also a guest cabin. The attractive **Bullberry Inn B&B,** 800/249-8126 or 435/679-8820, website: www.bullberryinn.com, has wraparound porches, and guest rooms with private baths and rustic-style furniture. At **Canyon Livery B&B,** 660 W. 50 South, 888/889-8910 or 435/679-8780, every room has a private bath, balcony, and views of Bryce Canyon.

More than $100

The **Stone Canyon Inn** 435/679-8611 or 866/489-4680, website: www.stonecanyoninn.com, just west of Tropic with views onto Bryce, has comfortable, uncluttered rooms starting at about $100.

FOOD

Hoo Doos Restaurant is part of Doug's Place Country Inn, 435/679-8632, and serves Mexican food, Texas-style barbecue, and steaks. It's open for breakfast, lunch, and dinner daily, and is licensed to sell liquor. The **Hungry Coyote Restaurant,** at the Bryce Valley Inn, 435/679-8811, has a liquor-licensed restaurant with an outdoor mesquite barbecue area. Open for three meals daily.

Panguitch

Pioneers arrived here in 1864, but hostile Ute Indians forced evacuation just two years later. A second attempt by settlers in 1871 succeeded, and Panguitch (the Paiute word for "big fish") is now the largest town in the area.

Panguitch is one of the more pleasant towns in this part of Utah, and there are an abundance of reasonably priced motels, and a couple of good places to eat. It's also a good stopover on the road between Zion and Bryce National Parks.

The early 20th-century commercial buildings downtown have some of their original facades. On side streets you can see sturdy brick houses built by the early settlers. Stop by the **Daughters** of Utah Pioneers Museum in the old bishop's storehouse at 100 East and Center to see historic exhibits of Panguitch; open Mon.–Sat. about 4–8 P.M. in summer and by appointment the rest of the year; phone numbers of volunteers are on the door.

The **Paunsagaunt Wildlife Museum,** 250 East Center St., 435/676-2500, in the old Panguitch public school, is a taxidermy collection of more than 400 animals from western North America displayed in dioramas resembling their natural habitats. There are also displays of stuffed animals from Africa, India, and Europe. It's actually quite well done, and kids seem to love it. There's also a good collection of Native American artifacts. Admission is $4 adults, $2.50 children 6–12.

The **city park** on the north edge of town has picnic tables, a playground, tennis courts, and a tourist information cabin. A **swimming pool** is at 250 E. Center by the high school, 435/676-2259.

ACCOMMODATIONS

Less than $50

The **Adobe Sands,** 390 N. Main St., 800/497-9261 or 435/676-8874, is a perfectly acceptable budget motel, open May–Oct. The **Blue Pine Motel,** 130 N. Main St., 800/299-6115 or 435/676-8197, is an attractive place that permits pets.

$50–75

The **Bryce Way Motel,** 429 N. Main St., 800/225-6534 or 435/676-2400, has a heated indoor pool. The **Color Country Motel,** 526 N. Main St., 800/225-6518 or 435/676-2386, has an outdoor pool and clean, well-maintained rooms. The **Bryce Canyon Motel,** 308 N. Main St., 435/676-8441, is well-kept and has kitchenette rooms. The **Panguitch Inn Motel,** an old downtown hotel at 50 N. Main St., 800/331-7407 or 435/676-8871, is open seasonally May–Oct.

Along U.S. 89, the **Best Western New Western,** 180 E. Center St., 800/528-1234 or 435/676-8876, has a swimming pool and hot tub, plus laundry facilities. Rooms here hover around $75 during the high summer season.

$75–100

Seven miles south of Panguitch, at the junction of highways 89 and 12 is a large faux-Western complex called the **Western Town Resort,** 888/687-4339 or 435/676-8770, website: www.westerntownresort.com. The resort looks like a vintage frontier town, with trading posts, country stores, and stables, but most of the buildings, in fact, offer motel accommodations. Western Town, which is gradually evolving toward being a full-service resort, offers a saloon and dance hall (complete with a huge display

of *The Book of Mormon,* free for the taking), a restaurant, guided horseback rides, and a variety of cowboy-style activities.

Campgrounds

Open year-round, **Hitch-N-Post Campground,** 420 N. Main, 435/676-2436, offers spaces for tents and RVs and has showers and a laundry room. The **Big Fish KOA Campground,** 555 S. Main, 435/676-2225, on the road to Panguitch Lake, is open Apr. 15–Oct. 15 with a pool, a recreation room, a laundry room, and showers; $20 tents, $25 for RVs, and $46 for cabins. The closest public campground is on Highway 12 in Red Canyon.

FOOD

Buffalo Java, 47 N. Main St., 435/767-8900, serves pastries, bagels, ice cream, and espresso drinks during the summer months. The **Flying M Restaurant,** 580 N. Main, 435/676-8008, is a favorite for hearty breakfast and standard American fare. For mesquite-grilled meats, try **Cowboy's Smokehouse Bar-B-Q,** 95 N. Main St., 435/676-8030. Traditional Italian favorites, with several vegetarian options, are dished up at **Grandma Tina's Spaghetti House,** 523 N. Main St., 435/676-2377. Tina also serves breakfast, including espresso and deep-fried scones (actually like tasty, not-too-sweet doughnuts).

Believe it or not, there's a tavern in Panguitch! The **Trails End Saloon,** 535 N. Main St., 435/676-2235, serves beer (including local microbrews) and wine coolers. During the summer, there's often live music on weekend evenings.

INFORMATION AND SERVICES

The **information center** in the city park, 800/444-6689 or 435/676-8131 (Bryce Canyon Information Line), offers brochures and suggestions for services in Panguitch and travel to Bryce Canyon National Park and other scenic destinations nearby; open daily early May–late Oct., 9 A.M.–5 P.M.; closed in winter. Contact the **Garfield County Travel Council** year-round at P.O. Box 200, Panguitch, UT 84759,

435/676-8421. The **Powell Ranger District office** of the U.S. Forest Service has information on campgrounds, hiking trails, fishing, and scenic drives in the forest and canyons surrounding Bryce Canyon National Park; open Mon.–Fri. 8 A.M.–4:30 P.M. at 225 E. Center (U.S. 89) or write P.O. Box 80, Panguitch, UT 84759, 435/676-8815.

The **post office** is at 65 N. 100 West, 435/676-8853. **Garfield Memorial Hospital** provides medical services at 224 N. 400 East, 435/676-8811 (hospital), 435/676-8842 (clinic).

BRYCE CANYON

Zion

Note: Please see color map of Zion on page iv–v.

Zion is a magnificent park, with stunning, soaring scenery. The canyon's naming is credited to Isaac Behunin, who believed this spot to be a refuge from religious persecution. When Brigham Young later visited the canyon, however, he found tobacco and wine in use and declared the place "not Zion"—which some dutiful followers then began calling it!

But the story here is really just all about rocks and water. Little trickles of water, percolating through massive chunks of sandstone, have created both dramatic canyons and markedly un-desert-like habitats, enabling an incredible variety of plants to find niches here.

When you visit Zion, the first thing you'll notice are the sheer cliffs and great monoliths of Zion Canyon reaching high into the heavens. Energetic streams and other forces of erosion created this land of finely sculptured rock. The large park spreads across 147,000 acres and contains eight geologic formations and four major vegetation zones. Elevations range from 3,666 feet, in lower Coalpits Wash, to 8,726 feet, atop Horse Ranch Mountain.

The highlight for most visitors is Zion Canyon, which is approximately 2,400 feet deep. Zion Canyon Scenic Drive winds through the canyon along the North Fork of the Virgin River past some of the most spectacular scenery in the park. (During the spring, summer, and early fall, a shuttle bus ferries visitors along this route.) Hiking trails branch off to lofty viewpoints and narrow side canyons. Adventurous souls can continue on foot past the road's end into the eerie depths of the Virgin River Narrows in upper Zion Canyon.

© JUDY JEWELL

the Three Patriarchs

The spectacular Zion–Mt. Carmel Highway, with its switchbacks and tunnels, provides access to the canyons and high plateaus east of Zion Canyon. Two other roads enter the rugged Kolob section northwest of Zion Canyon. The *Kolob,* a Mormon name meaning "the brightest star, next to the seat of God," includes wilderness areas rarely visited by humans.

Zion's grandeur extends all through the year. Even rainy days can be memorable as countless waterfalls plunge from every crevice in the cliffs above. Spring and autumn are the choice seasons for the most pleasant temperatures and the best chances of seeing wildlife and wildflowers. From about mid-Oct.–early Nov., cottonwoods and other trees and plants blaze with color. Summer temperatures in the canyons can be uncomfortably hot, with highs hovering above 100°F. It's also the busiest season. In winter, nighttime temperatures drop to near freezing and weather tends to be unpredictable, with bright sunshine one day and freezing rain the next. Snow-covered slopes contrast with colorful rocks. Snow may block some of the high-country trails and the road to Lava Point, but the rest of the park is open and accessible year-round.

Natural History

GEOLOGY

The rock layers at Zion began as sediments of oceans, rivers, lakes, or sand dunes deposited 65–240 million years ago. The soaring Navajo Sandstone cliffs that form such distinctive features as the Great White Throne and the Three Patriarchs were originally immense sand dunes. Look for the slanting lines in these rock walls, which result from shifting winds as the sand dunes formed. Calcium carbonate in the sand piles acted as a glue to turn the dunes into rock, and it's also responsible for the white color of many of the rocks. The reddish rocks are also Navajo Sandstone, but they've been stained by iron oxides—essentially rust.

Kayenta shale is the other main rock you'll see in Zion. For an up-close look, check out the streambed at Middle Emerald Pool. The rippled gray rock is Kayenta shale. This shale, which lays beneath Navajo Sandstone, is much less permeable than the sandstone. Water can easily trickle through the relatively porous sandstone, but when it hits the impermeable Kayenta shale, it runs along the top surface of the rock and seeps out on the side of the nearest rock face. Weeping Rock, with its lush cliffside springs, is a good place to see the junction between Navajo Sandstone and Kayenta shale.

A gradual uplift of the Colorado Plateau, which continues today, has caused the formerly lazy rivers on its surface to pick up speed and knife through the rock layers. You can really appreciate these erosive powers during flash floods, when the North Fork of the Virgin River or other streams roar through their canyons. Erosion of some of the Virgin River's tributaries couldn't keep up with the main channel, and they were left as "hanging valleys" on the canyon walls. A good example is Hidden Canyon, which is reached by trail in Zion Canyon.

Faulting has broken the Colorado Plateau into a series of smaller plateaus. At Zion you are on the Kolob Terrace of the Markagunt Plateau, whose rock layers are younger than those of the Kaibab Plateau at the Grand Canyon National Park and older than those exposed on the Paunsaugunt Plateau at Bryce Canyon National Park.

Although some erosive forces, like flash floods, are dramatic, the subtle freezing and thawing of water and the slow action of tree roots are responsible for most of the changes. Water seeps into the Navajo Sandstone, accumulating especially in the long, vertical cracks in the cliffs. The dramatic temperature changes, especially in the spring and fall, cause regular freezing and thawing, slowly enlarging the cracks and setting the stage for more dramatic rock falls. Erosion and rock fall continue to shape Zion Canyon. In 1995 a huge rockslide blocked Zion Canyon Scenic Drive and left hundreds of people trapped at the lodge for several days until crews were able to clear a path.

ZION

NAVAJO SANDSTONE

Take a look anywhere along Zion Canyon, and you'll see 1,600–2,200-foot cliffs of Navajo Sandstone. The big walls of Zion were formed from sand dunes deposited during a hot, dry period about 200 million years ago. Shifting winds blew the sand from one direction, then another—a careful inspection of the sandstone layer reveals the diagonal lines resulting from this "cross-bedding." Recent studies by researchers at the University of Nebraska-Lincoln, printed in *Nature* magazine conclude that the vast dunes of southern Utah were formed when the landmass on which they sit was about 15 degrees north of the equator, about the same location as today's Honduras. The shift patterns apparent in the sandstone—the slanting striations easily seen in cliff-faces—were caused in part by intense monsoon rains, which served to compact and move the dunes each rainy season.

Eventually, a shallow sea washed over the dunes. Lapping waves left shells behind, and as the shells dissolved, their lime seeped down into the sand and cemented it into sandstone. After the Colorado Plateau lifted, rivers cut deeply through the sandstone layer. The formation's lower layers are stained red from iron oxides.

FLORA AND FAUNA

Many different plant and animal communities live in the rugged terrain of deep canyons and high plateaus. Because the park lies near the meeting place of the Colorado Plateau, the Great Basin, and the Mojave Desert, species representative of all three regions can be found here.

Only desert plants can endure the long, dry spells and high temperatures found at Zion's lower elevations; they include cacti (prickly pear, cholla, and hedgehog), blackbrush, creosote bush, honey mesquite, and purple sage. Cacti and yucca are common throughout the park. Pygmy forests of piñon pine, Utah juniper, live oak, mountain mahogany, and cliffrose grow between about 3,900–5,600 feet.

Once you get above the canyon floor, Zion's plants are not so different from what you'd find in the Pacific Northwest. Trees such as ponderosa pine and Douglas fir can thrive here thanks to the moisture they draw from the Navajo sandstone. White fir and aspen are also common on high, cool plateaus. Permanent springs and streams support a profusion of greenery such as cottonwood, box elder, willow, red birch, horsetail, and ferns. Watch out for poison ivy in moist, shady areas.

Colorful wildflowers pop out of the ground—indeed even out of the rocks—at all elevations from spring through autumn. In early spring, look for the Zion shooting star, a plant in the primrose family found only in Zion. Here, its nodding pink flowers are easily spotted along the Emerald Pools trails and at Weeping Rock. You're also likely to see desert phlox, a low plant covered with pink flowers and, by mid-May, golden columbine.

Mule deer are common throughout the park. Also common is a type of beaver called a "bank beaver," which lives along the banks of the Virgin River rather than in log lodges, which would be too frequently swept away by flash floods. (Even though these beavers don't build log lodges, they still gnaw like crazy on trees—look near the base of riverside trees near Zion Lodge for their work.) Other wildlife includes elk, mountain lion, bobcat, black bear, bighorn sheep (reintroduced), coyote, gray fox, porcupine, ringtail cat, black-tailed jackrabbit, rock squirrel, cliff chipmunk, beaver, and many species of mice and bats.

Birders have spotted more than 270 species in and near the park, but most common are red-tailed hawk, turkey vulture, quail, mallard, great horned owl, hairy woodpecker, raven, scrub jay, black-headed grosbeak, blue-gray gnatcatcher, canyon wren, Virginia's warbler, white-throated swift, and broad-tailed hummingbird. Zion's high cliffs are good places to look for peregrine falcons; try spotting them from the cliffside at Angel's Rest trail.

Hikers and campers will undoubtedly see northern sagebrush lizards, and hikers need to watch for Western rattlesnakes, although these relatively rare reptiles are unlikely to attack unless provoked.

Exploring the Park

Zion National Park is 43 miles northeast of St. George, 60 miles south of Cedar City, 41 miles northwest of Kanab, and 86 miles southwest of Bryce Canyon National Park.

Large RVs and bicycles must heed special regulations for the long tunnel on the Zion–Mt. Carmel Highway (see the following section, East of Zion Canyon). Visitors short on time usually drop in at the visitors center and ride the shuttle along Zion Canyon Scenic Drive, stopping for short walks on the Weeping Rock or Riverside Walk trails. A stay of two days or longer is better to take in more of the grand scenery and hike other inviting trails.

Kolob Canyons Road, in the extreme northwestern section of the park, begins just off I-15 Exit 40 at the **Kolob Canyons Visitors Center** and climbs to an overlook for great views of the Finger Canyons of the Kolob; the drive is 10 miles round-trip. Motorists with more time may also want to drive the Kolob Terrace Road to Lava Point for another perspective of the park; this drive is about 44 miles round-trip from Virgin (on Highway 9) and has some unpaved sections.

VISITORS CENTER

The park's sprawling new visitors center opened in 2000 between Watchman and South campgrounds. The plaza outside the building features several interpretive plaques, including some pointing out environmentally sensitive design features of the visitors center. Inside, a large area is devoted to backcountry information; staff

ZION

© JUDY JEWELL

Zion National Park's new visitors center

ZION CANYON SHUTTLE

By the late 1990s, visitors to Zion remembered the traffic nearly as vividly as they remembered the Great White Throne; throughout much of the summer, the canyon road was simply a parking lot for enormous RVs. In order to relieve the congestion, the National Park Service has instituted an Apr.–Oct. **shuttle bus service** through the canyon.

There are actually two separate bus lines: one line travels between Springdale and the park entrance, stopping within a short walk of every Springdale motel and near several large visitor parking lots; the other bus line starts just inside the park entrance at the visitors center and runs the length of the Zion Canyon Road, stopping at scenic overlooks, trailheads, and Zion Lodge. Lodge guests may obtain a pass authorizing them to drive to the lodge, but in general, private vehicles are no longer allowed to drive up Zion Canyon.

This is less of a pain than it might seem. It's still fine to drive to the campgrounds; in fact, the road between the park entrance and the Zion–Mt. Carmel Highway junction is open to all vehicles. Buses run frequently, so there's rarely much of a wait, and most of the bus drivers are friendly and

well-informed, offering an engaging commentary on the sights that they pass (even pointing out rock climbers on the canyon's big walls).

If you get to Zion before 10 A.M. or after 3 P.M., there may be parking spaces available in the visitors center lot. Midday visitors should just park in Springdale (at your motel or in a public lot) and catch a shuttle bus to the park entrance.

Riding the bus is free; its cost of operation is included in the park admission fee. Buses run as often as every six minutes from 5:30 A.M.–11 P.M. (less frequently early in the morning and in the evening). No pets are allowed on the buses. From Nov.–Mar., private vehicles are allowed on all roads, and the buses are out of service.

Zion Canyon Scenic Drive is a six-mile road that follows the North Fork of the Virgin River upstream. Impressive natural formations along the way include the Three Patriarchs, Mountain of the Sun, Lady Mountain, Great White Throne, Angels Landing, and Weeping Rock. The bus stops at eight points of interest along the way; you can get on and off the bus as often as you wish at these stops. The road ends at Temple of Sinawava and the beginning of the Riverside Walk Trail.

members can answer your questions about various trails, give you updates on the weather forecast, and help you arrange a shuttle to remote trailheads.

The busiest part of the visitors center is its bookstore, which is stocked with an excellent selection of books covering natural history, human history, and regional travel. Topographic and geologic maps, posters, slides, postcards, and film are sold here, too.

The best way by far to get a feel for Zion's impressive geology and variety of habitats is to take a hike with a park ranger. Many nature programs and hikes are offered from late Mar.–Nov.; check the posted schedule. From Memorial Day to Labor Day, children's programs are held at Zion Nature Center near South Campground; ask at the visitors center for details. A Backcountry Shuttle Board allows hikers to coordinate transportation between trailheads.

The Zion Canyon Visitors Center is open daily 9 A.M.–5 P.M. in winter and 8 A.M.–8 P.M. in summer. For up-to-date information on the park, check out this website: www.nps.gov/zion, or call 435/772-3256. The mailing address is Zion National Park, Springdale, UT 84767.

An entry fee of $20 ($10 for bus passengers and bicyclists), which is good for seven days, is charged at the East and South entrance stations year-round.

ZION MUSEUM

The old visitors center reopened in 2002 as a museum of southern Utah's cultural history, with exhibits focusing on Native American and Mormon history. The museum is open daily 8 A.M.–7 P.M. in summer, with shorter winter hours. It's at the first shuttle stop after the visitors center.

EAST OF ZION CANYON

The east section of the park is a land of sandstone slickrock, hoodoos, and narrow canyons. You can see much of the dramatic scenery along the Zion–Mt. Carmel Highway (Highway 9) between the East Entrance Station and Zion Canyon. Most of this region invites exploration on your own. Try hiking a canyon or heading up a slickrock slope (the pass between Crazy Quilt and Checkerboard Mesas is one possibility). Highlights on the plateau include views of the White Cliffs and Checkerboard Mesa (both near the East Entrance Station) and a hike on the Canyon Overlook Trail (it begins just east of the long tunnel). Checkerboard Mesa's distinctive pattern is caused by a combination of vertical fractures and horizontal bedding planes, both accentuated by weathering. The highway's spectacular descent into Zion Canyon goes first through a 530-foot tunnel, then a 5,600-foot tunnel, followed by a series of six switchbacks to the canyon floor. Because the tunnel (completed in 1930) is narrow, any vehicle more than 7 feet 10 inches wide, 11 feet 4 inches high, or 40 feet long (50 feet with trailer) must go through in one-way traffic; a $10 fee (good for two passages) is charged at the tunnel to do this. Bicycles must be carried through the long tunnel (it's too dangerous to ride).

KOLOB CANYONS

North and west of Zion Canyon lies the remote backcountry of the Kolob. This area became a second Zion National Monument in 1937, then was added to Zion National Park in 1956. You'll see all but one of the rock formations present in the park and evidence of past volcanic eruptions. Two roads lead into the Kolob. The paved five-mile Kolob Canyons Road begins at the Kolob Canyons Visitors Center just off I-15 and ends at an overlook and picnic area; it's open all year. Kolob Terrace Road is paved from the town of Virgin (15 miles west on Highway 9 from the South Entrance Station) to the turn-off for Lava Point; snow usually blocks the way in winter.

Kolob Canyons Visitors Center

Although it is small and has just a handful of exhibits, this visitors center is a good place to stop for information on exploring the Kolob region. Hikers can learn current trail conditions and obtain the permits required for overnight trips and Zion Narrows day trips. Books, topographic and geologic maps, posters, postcards, slides, and film are sold. Open daily 8 A.M.–4:30 P.M. (to 5 P.M. in summer); 435/586-9548. The visitors center and the start of the Kolob Canyons Road lie just off I-15 Exit 40.

Kolob Canyons Road

This five-mile scenic drive winds past the dramatic Finger Canyons of the Kolob to Kolob Canyons Viewpoint and a picnic area at the end of the road. The road is paved and has many pullouts

---

THE ZION–MT. CARMEL TUNNEL

If your vehicle is 7 feet 10 inches wide, 11 feet 4 inches tall, or larger, you will need a traffic control escort through the narrow, mile-long Zion-Mt. Carmel Tunnel. Vehicles this size are too large to stay in their lane while traveling through the tunnel, which was built in the 1920s, when autos were not only small, but few and far between. Nearly all RV's, buses, trailers, fifth-wheels, and some camper shells will require an "escort."

Visitors requiring an escort must pay a $10 fee per vehicle in addition to the entrance fee. Pay this fee at either park entrance before proceeding to the tunnel. The fee is good for two trips through the tunnel for the same vehicle during a 7-day period.

Though the park service persists in using the term "escort," you're really on your own through the tunnel. Rather than following an escort vehicle, park staff will stop oncoming traffic, allowing you enough time to drive down the middle of the tunnel. From April 1 through late October, traffic control staff is present at the tunnel 8 A.M.–8 p.m. daily. During the winter season, oversized vehicle passage must be arranged at the entrance stations, Zion Canyon Visitor Center, Zion Lodge, or by phoning 435/772-3256. Bicycles and pedestrians are not allowed in the tunnel.

© JUDY JEWELL

fault uplift in Kolob Canyons

where you can stop to admire the scenery. The first part of the drive follows the 200-mile-long Hurricane Fault that forms the west edge of the Markagunt Plateau. Look for the tilted rock layers deformed by friction as the plateau rose nearly one mile. **Taylor Creek Trail,** which begins two miles past the visitors center, provides a close look at the canyons (see Taylor Creek Trail in the Hiking Trails in Kolob Canyons section). Lee Pass, four miles beyond the visitors center, was named after John D. Lee of the infamous Mountain Meadows Massacre; he's believed to have lived nearby for a short time after the massacre. **La Verkin Creek Trail** begins at Lee Pass Trailhead for trips to Kolob Arch and beyond. Signs at the end of the road identify the points, buttes, mesa, and mountains. The salmon-colored Navajo Sandstone cliffs glow a deep red at sunset. **Timber Creek Overlook Trail** begins from the picnic area at road's end and climbs one-half mile to the overlook (elevation 6,369 feet); views encompass the Pine Valley Mountains, Zion Canyons, and distant Mt. Trumbull.

Lava Point

The panorama from Lava Point (elevation 7,890 feet) takes in the Cedar Breaks area to the north, the Pink Cliffs to the northeast, Zion Canyon Narrows and tributaries to the east, the Sentinel and other monoliths of Zion Canyon to the southeast, and Mt. Trumbull on the Arizona Strip to the south. Signs help identify features. Lava Point, which sits atop a lava flow, is a good place to cool off in summer—temperatures are about 20°F cooler than in Zion Canyon. Aspen, ponderosa pine, Gambel oak, and white fir grow here. A small, primitive **campground** near the point offers sites during warmer months; no water or charge.

Kolob Reservoir

This high-country lake north of Lava Point has good fishing for rainbow trout. An unpaved boat ramp is at the south end near the dam. People sometimes camp along the shore, although there are no facilities. Most of the surrounding land is private. To reach the reservoir, continue north 3.5 miles on Kolob Terrace Road from the Lava Point turn-off. The fair-weather road can also be followed past the reservoir to the Cedar City area. Blue Springs Reservoir, near the turn-off for Lava Point, is closed to the public.

Recreation

HIKING IN ZION CANYON

The trails in Zion Canyon provide perspectives of the park that are not available from the roads. Many of the hiking trails require long ascents but aren't too difficult at a leisurely pace. Carry water on all but the shortest walks. Descriptions of the following trails are given in order from the mouth of Zion Canyon to the Virgin River Narrows.

Experienced hikers can do countless off-trail routes in the canyons and plateaus surrounding Zion Canyon; rangers can suggest areas. Rappelling and other climbing skills may be needed to negotiate drops in some of the more remote canyons. Groups cannot exceed 12 hikers per trail or drainage. Overnight hikers must obtain backcountry permits ($5) from either the Zion Canyon or Kolob Canyons visitors centers. Some areas of the park—mainly those near roads and major trails—are closed to overnight use. Zion Lodge offers shuttle services for hikers, or you can check the Backcountry Shuttle Board at the visitors center.

Pa'rus Trail
Shuttle stops: Visitors Center and Canyon Junction

This two-mile paved trail runs from the South Campground to the Canyon Junction shuttle bus stop. For most of its distance, it skirts alongside the Virgin River and makes for a nice early morning or evening stroll. Listen for the trilling song of the canyon wren, then try to spot the small bird in the bushes. The accessible Pa'rus Trail is the only trail in the park that's open to bicycles and pets.

Watchman Trail
Shuttle stop: Visitors Center

From a trailhead north of Watchman Campground, the trail climbs 370 feet to a bench below Watchman Peak, the prominent mountain southeast of the visitors center. You'll enjoy views of lower Zion Canyon and the town of Springdale. The well-graded trail follows a side canyon past some springs, then ascends to the overlook; the distance is 2.4 miles round-trip and takes about two hours. A wide variety of trees and plants lines the way. In summer, it's best to get an early start. Rangers lead nature walks during the main season.

Court of the Patriarchs Viewpoint
Shuttle stop: Court of the Patriarchs

A short trail from the parking area leads to the viewpoint. The Patriarchs, a trio of peaks to the west, overlook Birch Creek; they are (from left to right) Abraham, Isaac, and Jacob. Mount Moroni, the reddish peak on the far right, partly blocks the view of Jacob. Although the official viewpoint is a beautiful place to relax and enjoy the view, you can get an even better view by crossing the road and heading about one-half mile up the Sand Bench Trail.

Sand Bench Trail
Shuttle stops: Court of the Patriarchs or Zion Lodge

This easy loop has good views of the three Patriarchs, the Streaked Wall, and other monuments of lower Zion Canyon. The trail is 1.7 miles long with a 500-foot elevation gain; allow about three hours. During the main season, Zion Lodge organizes three-hour horseback rides on the trail. (The horses churn up dust and leave an uneven surface, though, so hikers usually prefer to go elsewhere.) The trail soon leaves the riparian forest along Birch Creek and climbs onto the dry benchland. Piñon pine, juniper, sand sage, yucca, prickly pear cactus, and other high-desert plants and animals live here. Hikers can get off the shuttle at the Court of the Patriarchs Viewpoint, walk across the scenic drive, then follow a service road to the footbridge and trailhead. A 1.2-mile trail along the river connects the trailhead with Zion Lodge. In warmer months, try to hike in early morning or late afternoon.

Emerald Pools Trails
Shuttle stop: Zion Lodge

Three spring-fed pools, small waterfalls, and views of Zion Canyon make this climb worthwhile. You have a choice of three trails. The easiest is the paved trail to the Lower Pool; cross the footbridge near Zion Lodge and turn right 0.6 mile. The Middle Pool can be reached by continuing 0.2 mile on this trail or by taking a totally different trail from the footbridge at Zion Lodge (after crossing the bridge, turn left, then right up the trail). Together these trails make a 1.8-mile round-trip loop. A third trail begins at the Grotto Picnic Area, crosses a footbridge and turns left 0.7 mile; the trail forks left to the Lower Pool and right to the Middle Pool. A steep 0.4-mile trail leads from the Middle Pool to Upper Emerald Pool. This magical spot has a white-sand beach and towering cliffs rising above. Allow 1–3 hours to visit the pools, and don't expect to find solitude; these relatively easy trails are quite popular.

West Rim Trail
Shuttle stop: The Grotto

This strenuous trail leads to some of the best views of Zion Canyon. Backpackers can continue on the West Rim Trail to Lava Point and other destinations in the Kolob region. Start from Grotto Picnic Area (elevation 4,300 feet) and cross the footbridge, then turn right along the river. The trail climbs the slopes and enters the cool and shady depths of Refrigerator Canyon. Walter's Wiggles, a series of 21 closely spaced switchbacks, wind up to Scout Lookout and a trail junction—four miles round-trip and a 1,050-foot elevation gain. Scout Lookout has fine views of Zion Canyon. The trail is paved and well graded to this point. Turn right one-half mile at the junction to reach the summit of Angels Landing.

Angels Landing rises as a sheer-walled monolith 1,500 feet above the North Fork of the Virgin River. Although the trail to the summit is rough, chains provide security in the more exposed places. The climb is safe with care and good weather, but don't go if the trail is covered with snow or ice or if thunderstorms threaten. Children must be closely supervised, and people who are afraid of heights should skip this trail. Once on top, you'll see why Angels Landing got its name—the panorama makes all the ef-

fort worthwhile. Average hiking time for the round-trip between Grotto Picnic Area and Angels Landing is four hours, best hiked during the cooler morning hours.

Energetic hikers can continue 4.8 miles on the main trail from Scout Lookout to West Rim Viewpoint, which overlooks the Right Fork of North Creek. This strenuous 12.8-mile round-trip from Grotto Picnic Area has a 3,070-foot elevation gain. West Rim Trail continues through Zion's backcountry to Lava Point (elevation 7,890 feet), where there's a primitive campground. A car shuttle and one or more days are needed to hike the 13.3 miles (one-way) from Grotto Picnic Area. You'll have an easier hike by starting at Lava Point and hiking down to the picnic area; even so, be prepared for a *long* day hike. The trail has little or no water in some seasons.

Weeping Rock Trail
Shuttle Stop: Weeping Rock

A favorite with visitors, this easy trail winds past lush vegetation and wildflowers to a series of cliffside springs above an overhang. Thousands of water droplets glisten in the afternoon sun. The springs emerge where water seeping through more than 2,000 feet of Navajo Sandstone meets a layer of impervious shale. The paved trail is a half-mile round-trip with a 100-foot elevation gain. Signs along the way identify some of the trees and plants.

Observation Point Trail
Shuttle stop: Weeping Rock

This strenuous trail climbs 2,150 feet in 3.6 highly scenic miles to Observation Point (elevation 6,507 feet) on the edge of Zion Canyon. Allow about six hours for the round-trip. Trails branch off along the way to Hidden Canyon, upper Echo Canyon, East Entrance, East Mesa, and other destinations. The first of many switchbacks begins a short way up from the trailhead at Weeping Rock parking area. You'll reach the junction for Hidden Canyon Trail (see the following entry for Hidden Canyon) after 0.8 mile. Several switchbacks later, the trail enters sinuous Echo Canyon. This incredibly narrow chasm can be explored for short distances upstream and downstream to deep pools and pour-offs. **Echo Canyon Trail** branches to the right at about the halfway point; this rough trail continues farther up the canyon and connects with trails to Cable Mountain, Deertrap Mountain, and the East Entrance Station (on Zion–Mt. Carmel Highway). The East Rim Trail then climbs slickrock slopes above Echo Canyon with many fine views. Parts of the trail are cut right into the cliffs (work was done in the 1930s by the Civilian Conservation Corps). You'll reach the rim at last after three miles of steady climbing. Then it's an easy 0.6 mile through a forest of piñon pine, juniper, Gambel oak, manzanita, sage, and some ponderosa pine to Observation Point. Impressive views take in Zion Canyon below and mountains and mesas all around. The **East Mesa Trail** turns right about 0.3 mile before Observation Point and follows the plateau northeast to a dirt road outside the park.

Hidden Canyon
Shuttle stop: Weeping Rock

See if you can spot the entrance to Hidden Canyon from below! Inside the narrow canyon are small sandstone caves, a little natural arch, and diverse plantlife. The high walls, rarely more than 65 feet apart, block sunlight except for a short time at midday. Hiking distance on the moderately difficult trail is about three miles round-trip between the Weeping Rock parking area and the lower canyon; follow the East Rim Trail 0.8 mile, then turn right 0.7 mile on Hidden Canyon Trail to the canyon entrance. Footing can be a bit difficult in places because of loose sand, but chains provide handholds on the more exposed sections. Steps chopped into the rock just inside Hidden Canyon help bypass some deep pools. Allow 3–4 hours for the round-trip; the elevation change is about 1,000 feet. After heavy rains and spring runoff, the creek forms a small waterfall at the canyon entrance. The canyon is about one mile long and mostly easy walking, although the trail fades away. Look for the arch on the right about one-half mile up the canyon.

Riverside Walk
Shuttle stop: Temple of Sinawava

This is one of the most popular hikes in the park and, except for the Pa'rus, it's the easiest. The nearly level paved trail begins at the end of Zion Canyon Scenic Drive and winds one mile upstream along the river to the Virgin River Narrows. Allow about two hours to take in the scenery—it's a good place to see Zion's lovely hanging gardens. Countless springs and seeps on the canyon walls support luxuriant plant growth and swamps. Most of the springs occur at the contact between the porous Navajo Sandstone and the less permeable Kayenta Formation below. The water and vegetation attract abundant wildlife; keep an eye out for birds and animals and their tracks. At trail's end, the canyon is wide enough for only the river. Hikers continuing upstream must wade and sometimes even swim (see following entry for The Narrows). Late morning is the best time for

© JUDY JEWELL

Riverside Walk

photography. In autumn, cottonwoods and maples display bright splashes of color.

The Narrows
Shuttle stop: Temple of Sinawava

Upper Zion Canyon is probably the most famous backcountry area in the park, yet it's also one of the most strenuous. There's no trail and you'll be wading much of the time in the river, which is usually knee to chest-deep. In places, the high, fluted walls of the upper North Fork of the Virgin River are only 20 feet apart, and very little sunlight penetrates the depths. Mysterious side canyons beckon.

Hikers should be well prepared and in good condition—river hiking is more tiring than that over dry land. The major hazards are flash floods and hypothermia. Finding the right time to go

In places, the high, fluted walls of the upper North Fork of the Virgin River are only 20 feet apart, and very little sunlight penetrates the depths. Mysterious side canyons beckon.

through can be tricky: spring runoff is too high, summer thunderstorms bring hazardous flash floods, and winter is too cold. That leaves just part of early summer (mid-June–mid-July) and early autumn (mid-Sept.–mid-Oct.) as the best bets. You can get through the entire 16-mile (one-way) Narrows in about 12 hours, although two days is best to enjoy the beauty of the place. Children under 12 shouldn't attempt hiking the entire canyon.

Don't be tempted to wear river sandals or sneakers up the Narrows because it's easy to twist an ankle on the slippery rocks. If you have a pair of hiking boots that you don't mind drenching, they'll work, but an even better solution is available from the Zion Adventure Company, in Springdale at 36 Lion Blvd., 435/772-1001, website: www.zionadventures.com. They rent specially designed river hiking boots, along with neoprene socks, walking sticks, and, in cool weather, dry suits. They also provide a valuable orientation to hiking the Narrows. Boots, socks, and sticks rent for $16 per day, $25 for two days; with a dry suit the package costs $35 per day, $55 for two days.

Talk with rangers at the Zion Canyon Visitors Center before starting a trip; they also have a handout with useful information on planning a Narrows hike. You'll need a permit for hikes all the way through the Narrows—even on a day trip. No permit is needed if you're just going partway in and back in one day, although you must first check conditions and the weather forecast with rangers. Permits are required for overnight hikes; get them from the backcountry desk at the visitors center the day before you plan to hike or the morning of your hike (from 8 A.M.–noon). Only one-night stays are allowed. No camping is permitted below Big Springs. Group size for hiking and camping is limited to 12 (of the same affiliation, family, etc.) on the *entire* route.

A hike downstream saves not only climbing but also the work of fighting the river currents. In

© JUDY JEWELL

entering the Narrows, Zion National Park

ZION

fact, the length of the Narrows should only be hiked downstream. The upper trailhead is near Chamberlain's Ranch, reached by an 18-mile dirt road that turns north from Highway 9 east of the park. The lower trailhead is at the end of the Zion Canyon Scenic Drive. The elevation change is 1,280 feet.

A good half-day trip begins at the end of the Gateway to the Narrows Trail and follows the Narrows 1.5 miles upstream to Orderville Canyon, then back the same way. Orderville Canyon makes a good destination in itself; you can hike quite a ways up from Zion Canyon.

During the summer, Springdale Cycles offers a daily shuttle to Chamberlain's Ranch, leaving from the Mean Bean Coffee House at 6:30 A.M. Make shuttle reservations between 9 A.M.–6 P.M. on the day before you want to ride. The fee is $25 per person; a flat rate of $100 applies if fewer than four people are signed up. Call 800/776-2099 for information and reservations.

HIKING TRAILS EAST OF ZION CANYON

Canyon Overlook Trail

You can't take the shuttle bus to this fun hike; it starts on the road east of Zion Canyon and features great views from the heights without the stiff climbs found on most other Zion trails. Allow about one hour for the one-mile round-trip; elevation gain is 163 feet. A booklet available at the start or at the Zion Canyon Visitors Center describes the geology, plantlife, and clues to the presence of wildlife. The trail winds in and out along the ledges of Pine Creek Canyon, which opens into a great valley. Panoramas at trail's end take in lower Zion Canyon in the distance. A sign at the viewpoint identifies Bridge Mountain, Streaked Wall, East Temple, and other features. The Great Arch of Zion—termed a "blind arch" because it's open on only one side—lies below; the arch is 580 feet high, 720 feet long, and 90 feet deep. The Canyon Overlook Trail begins across from the parking area just east of the longer (west) tunnel on the Zion–Mt. Carmel Highway.

HIKING TRAILS IN THE SOUTHWEST DESERT

Huber Wash

From the parking area on Highway 9, this trail heads 2.5 miles up Huber Wash, through painted desert and canyons. One of the highlights of hiking in this area, besides the desert scenery, is the abundance of petrified wood. There's even a logjam of petrified wood at the 2.5-mile mark, where the trail ends in a box canyon, decked with a hanging garden. If you're up to a tricky climb over the petrified logjam, you can climb up and catch the Chinle Trail, then hike five miles back to the road on that trail. The Chinle Trail emerges onto Highway 9 about 2.5 miles east of the Huber Wash trailhead.

During the summer, this area of the park can be extremely hot, and in the early spring, it's often too muddy to hike. Thus, this is the ideal autumn hike. Even then, it'll be quite warm. Remember to bring plenty of water.

The Huber Wash trailhead is about six miles west of the park entrance on Highway 9, near a power substation. Because the trail starts outside the park, it's not necessary to pay the park entrance fee if all you want to do is hike in this area.

HIKING TRAILS IN KOLOB CANYONS

Taylor Creek Trail

This is an excellent day hike from Kolob Canyons Road. The easy-to-moderate trail begins on the left two miles from the Kolob Canyons Visitors Center and heads upstream into the canyon of the Middle Fork of Taylor Creek. Double Arch Alcove is 2.7 miles from the trailhead; a dry fall 0.2 mile farther blocks the way (water flows over it during spring runoff and after rains). A giant rockfall occurred here in June 1990. From this trail you can also explore the North Fork of Taylor Creek. A separate trail along the **South Fork of Taylor Creek** leaves the drive at a bend 3.1 miles from the visitors center, then goes 1.2 miles upstream beneath steep canyon walls.

ZION

Hiking to Kolob Arch

Kolob Arch vies with Landscape Arch in Arches National Park as the world's longest natural rock span. Differences in measurement techniques have resulted in a controversy regarding which is longer: Kolob Arch's span has been measured variously at 292–310 feet, while Landscape Arch's measures at 291–306 feet. Kolob probably takes the prize because its 310-foot measurement was done with an accurate electronic method. Kolob's height is 330 feet and its vertical thickness is 80 feet. The arch makes a fine destination for a backpacking trip. Spring and autumn are the best seasons to go; summer temperatures rise into the 90s and winter snows make the trails hard to follow.

You have a choice of two moderately difficult trails. **La Verkin Creek Trail** begins at Lee Pass (elevation 6,080 feet) on Kolob Canyons Scenic Drive, four miles beyond the visitors center. The trail drops into Timber Creek (intermittent flow), crosses over hills to La Verkin Creek (flows year-round; some springs, too), then turns up side canyons to the arch. The 14-mile round-trip can be done as a long day trip, but you'll enjoy the best lighting for photos at the arch if you camp in the area and see it the following morning. Carry plenty of water for the return trip; the 800-foot climb to the trailhead can be hot and tiring.

You can also hike to Kolob Arch on the **Hop Valley Trail,** reached from Kolob Terrace Road. The Hop Valley Trail is seven miles one-way to Kolob Arch with an elevation drop of 1,050 feet; water is available in Hop Valley and La Verkin Creek. You may have to do some wading in the creek, and the trail crosses private land (don't camp there).

HIKING TRAILS FROM LAVA POINT

Two trails—West Rim and Wildcat Canyon—begin from Lava Point Trailhead in the remote West Rim area of the park. You can reach the trailhead via the Kolob Terrace Road or by hiking the one-mile **Barney's Trail** from Site 2 in the Lava Point campground.

The **West Rim Trail** goes southeast to Zion Canyon, 13.3 miles one-way with an elevation drop of 3,600 feet (3,000 of them in the last six miles). Water can normally be found along the way at Sawmill, Potato Hollow, and Cabin springs.

The **Wildcat Canyon Trail** heads southwest five miles to a trailhead on Kolob Terrace Road (16 miles north of Virgin); the elevation drop is 450 feet. This trail lacks a reliable water source. You can continue north and west toward Kolob Arch by taking the four-mile **Connector Trail** to **Hop Valley Trail.**

Snow blocks the road to Lava Point for much of the year; the usual season is May or June–early Nov. Check road conditions with the Zion Canyon or Kolob Canyon visitors centers. From the South Entrance Station in Zion Canyon, drive west 15 miles on Highway 9 to Virgin, turn north 21 miles on Kolob Terrace Road (signed Kolob Reservoir), then turn right 1.8 miles to Lava Point.

A special hike for strong swimmers is the **Left Fork of North Creek,** a.k.a. "The Subway." This challenging nine-mile day hike involves, at the very least, lots of route-finding and many stream crossings.

Like the Narrows, the Left Fork can be hiked either part-way up, then back down (starting and ending at the Left Fork Trailhead) or, with a shuttle, from an upper trailhead at the Wildcat Canyon Trailhead downstream to the Left Fork Trailhead. The "top-to-bottom" route requires rappelling skills and at least 60 feet of climbing rope or webbing. It also involves swimming through several deep sections of very cold water.

Obviously, the Left Fork is not for everyone. Even though it is in a day-use-only zone, the Park Service requires a special permit, which,

> *Kolob Arch vies with Landscape Arch in Arches National Park as the world's longest natural rock span. Differences in measurement techniques have resulted in a controversy regarding which is longer. Kolob probably takes the prize because its 310-foot measurement was done with an accurate electronic method.*

unlike other Zion backcountry permits, is available ahead of time through a somewhat convoluted lottery process. Prospective hikers should visit the park's website, www.nps.gov/zion, click the "In Depth" button, then click the "Backcountry" link. From there you will be instructed to email or fax (435/772-3426) information about your planned trip, including the size of your party and three choices of dates when you would like to hike. Trip dates are awarded by lottery. Only 50 permits are issued per day. If you're planning this hike at the last minute, try calling 435/772-0170 to see if there are any openings. The Left Fork trailhead is on the Kolob Terrace Road 8.1 miles north of Virgin.

BIKING

One of the fringe benefits of the Zion Canyon shuttle bus is the great bicycling that's resulted from the lack of automobile traffic. It used to be way too scary to bike along the narrow, traffic-choked Zion Canyon Scenic Drive, but now it's a joy.

On the stretch of road where cars are permitted—between the visitors center and Canyon Junction (where the Zion–Mt. Carmel road meets Zion Canyon Scenic Drive)—the two-mile, paved Pa'rus Trail is open to bikers as well as pedestrians, and makes for easy, stress-free pedaling.

If you decide you've had enough cycling, every shuttle bus has a rack that can hold two bicycles. Bike parking is plentiful at the visitors center, Zion Lodge, and most trailheads.

Bike rentals are available in Springdale at Springdale Cycles, 932 Zion Park Blvd., 800/776-2099 or 435/772-0575; and at Bike Zion, 1458 Zion Park Blvd., 800/475-4576 or 435/772-3929.

ROCK CLIMBING

Rock-climbers come to scale the high Navajo Sandstone cliffs; after Yosemite, it's the nation's most popular big-wall climbing area. For route descriptions, pick up a copy of *Desert Rock,* by Eric Bjørnstad or *Rock Climbing Utah,* by Stewart M. Green. Both books are sold at the Visitors Center bookstore. Check to make sure your climbing area is open—some are closed to protect wildlife.

If watching the climbers at Zion gives you a hankering to scale a wall, the Zion Adventure Company, in Springdale at 36 Lion Blvd., 435/772-1001, website: www.zionadventures.com, runs day-long climbing clinics for beginning and experienced climbers. Because no outfitters are permitted to operate inside the park, these classes are held near St. George.

HORSEBACK RIDING

Trail rides leave from the corral near Zion Lodge and head down the Virgin River. A one-hour trip ($20) goes to the Court of the Patriarchs, and a half-day ride ($45) follows the Sand Bench Trail. Riders must be at least seven years old and weigh no more than 220 pounds.

Accommodations

ZION LODGE

The rustic lodge, 435/586-9476, sits in the heart of Zion Canyon, three miles up Zion Canyon Scenic Drive. Zion Lodge provides the only accommodations and dining places within the park. It's open year-round; reservations for rooms should be made as far in advance as possible. During high season, all rooms are booked months ahead. Double rooms begin at $107; cute cabins are $116.

The moderately priced restaurant offers a varied American menu daily for breakfast, lunch, and dinner. Picnic lunches can be ordered in advance by calling 435/772-3213, ext. 160. A snack bar serves fast food (closes in winter). Zion Lodge organizes horseback rides along the Virgin River (one hour) and Sand Bench Trail (three hours). Tours in open-air vehicles provide narrated sight-seeing trips in Zion Canyon; they run several times daily between Memorial Day and Labor Day weekends. The lodge also has evening programs, a post office counter (open Mon.–Sat.), and a gift shop. Make reservations for Zion Lodge by writing Xanterra Parks & Resorts, 1400 E. Iliff Ave., Ste. 600, Aurora CO, 80014, or call 303/297-2757. Reserve online at www.xanterra.com.

CAMPGROUNDS

Zion Canyon Campgrounds

Campgrounds in the park often fill up on Easter and other major holidays. During the summer, they're often full by early afternoon, so it's best to arrive early in the day. The **South** and **Watchman** campgrounds, both just inside the South Entrance, have sites for $14 with water but no showers; Watchman has some sites with electrical hookups for $16. Reservations can be made in advance for Watchman Campground at 800/365-2267 or http://reservations.nps.gov. One of the campgrounds stays open in winter.

South Campground is a bit smaller and more oriented to tent camping than Watchman, and it has easy access to the Pa'rus Trail, but tenters shouldn't eschew Watchman; loops C and D are for tents, and sites D-20 and D-33 are two of the nicest campsites you'll find in the park.

Some of the pioneers' fruit trees in the campgrounds are still producing; you're free to pick your own. Additional campgrounds lie just outside the park in Springdale (see following section on Springdale).

Kolob Canyons Campgrounds

The Kolob section of the park doesn't have a campground. The nearest one within the park is Lava Point Campground (see Lava Point section under Kolob Canyons). The **Redledge Campground,** in Kanarraville, is the closest commercial campground to the Kolob Canyons area; go two miles north on I-15, take Exit 42, and continue 4.5 miles into downtown Kanarraville, 435/586-9150. The campground is open year-round with a store, showers, and a laundry room; $14 tents or RVs without hookups, $17.50 RVs with hookups, and campers cabins or a tipi for $12. The tiny agricultural community was named after a local Paiute chief. A low ridge south of town marks the southern limit of prehistoric Lake Bonneville. Hikers can explore trails in Spring and Kanarra Canyons within the **Spring Canyon Wilderness Study Area** just east of town.

ZION

Springdale and Vicinity

Mormons settled this tiny town (pop. 470) in 1862, but with its location just outside the park's south entrance, Springdale is geared more toward serving park visitors than the typical Mormon settlement. Its many high-quality motels and B&Bs, as well as frequent shuttle bus service into the park, make Springdale an appealing base for a visit to Zion. Farther down the road toward Hurricane are the little towns of Rockville and Virgin, both of which are quickly becoming B&B suburbs of Springdale.

ZION CANYON GIANT SCREEN THEATRE

You *know* you should be in the park itself, not looking at movies of it on a six-story-tall screen. But, assuming you've been out hiking all day and need a little rest, come here to meet the Anasazi, watch Spanish explorers seek golden treasure, witness the hardships of pioneer settlers, enter remote slot canyons, and join rock-climbers hundreds of feet up vertical cliff faces. The feature program is *Treasure of the Gods,* but there's nearly always a big-screen version of a Hollywood movie showing as well (don't expect to see current hits; all the movies are a few years old). Shows start on the hour 9 A.M.–9 P.M. from May 1–Oct. 31 and on the odd hours between 11 A.M.–7 P.M. the rest of the year; $7.50 adults, $4.50 children under 12. Call 435/772-2400 or 888/256-FILM (888/256-3456) for more information.

O. C. TANNER AMPHITHEATER

The summer highlight at this open-air theater is a series of musical concerts held on Saturday evenings throughout the summer. The amphitheater is located just outside the park entrance; call 435/652-7994 for information.

ACCOMMODATIONS

$50–75
The most reasonably priced lodgings in Springdale

are the motel rooms at the **Zion Canyon Campground,** 479 Zion Park Blvd., 435/772-3237. Budget travelers should also consider the **Zion Park Motel,** 865 Zion Park Blvd., 435/772-3251, with clean basic rooms and a small pool. The **Canyon Ranch Motel,** 668 Zion Park Blvd., 435/772-3357, is another good value, with individual cottages—some with kitchenettes—scattered around a grassy, shaded courtyard.

The **El Río Lodge,** 995 Zion Park Blvd., 888/772-3205 or 435/772-3205, offers rooms in a green, shady location with a sundeck.

There are several good B&Bs springing up around Zion. Most ask for two-night minimums on holiday weekends.

In Springdale, **O'Toole's Under the Eaves B&B,** 980 Zion Park Blvd., 435/772-3457, features homey guest rooms, two with shared bath, in a vintage home. It's also possible to pay a bit more and get a kitchenette room here. Children over 10 welcome.

The Blue House Bed & Breakfast Inn sits in a pretty country setting in the small community of Rockville, five miles from the park entrance, 125 E. Main, 800/869-3912 or 435/772-3912. Also in Rockville, the **Handcart House Bed & Breakfast,** 244 W. Main, 435/772-3867, is a handsome modern home that looks like a pioneer landmark but offers all modern comforts. All guest rooms have private baths.

$75–100
Flanigan's Inn, 428 Zion Park Blvd., 800/765-7787 or 435/772-3244, is a very comfortable place to stay, with a restaurant, a pool, and a complimentary breakfast buffet. The **Pioneer Lodge Motel,** 838 Zion Park Blvd., 435/772-3233, has a restaurant, a pool, and a spa. A variety of room styles are available, including a three-bed unit and a deluxe suite. The **Driftwood Lodge,** 1515 Zion Park Blvd., 800/528-1234 or 435/772-3262, has a pool and a spa.

Harvest House B&B, 29 Canyonview Dr., 435/772-3880, is an expertly run B&B in the center of Springdale with an old-fashioned porch and a hot tub. The four guest rooms, all with private baths, are nicely decorated. **Red Rock Inn,** 998 Zion Park Blvd., 435/772-3139, $74–79 (single or double), offers lodgings in newly constructed individual cabins, all with canyon views. Full-breakfast baskets are delivered to your door.

For a B&B with a Western difference, try the **Snow Family Guest Ranch,** 633 E. Hwy. 9, in Virgin. Located on 12 acres, the ranch raises horses and offers nine guest rooms to travelers. Children are accepted with prior arrangement only; no pets.

$100–125

Probably the nicest place to stay in Springdale is the new **Desert Pearl Inn,** 707 Zion Park Blvd., 888/828-0898 or 435/772-8888, a very handsome lodgelike hotel perched above the Virgin River. Much of the wood used for the beams and the finish moldings was salvaged from a railroad trestle made of century-old Oregon fir and redwood that once spanned the north end of the Great Salt Lake. The rooms are all large and beautifully furnished, with a modern look.

The new **Best Western Zion Park Inn,** 1215 Zion Park Blvd., 800/934-7275 or 435/772-3200, is an attractive complex with a good restaurant, a swimming pool, a gift shop, and some of the nicest rooms in Springdale. In addition to regular rooms, there are also various suites and kitchen units available.

Just outside the south gates to Zion, the **Cliffrose Lodge,** 281 Zion Park Blvd., 800/243-8824 or 435/772-3234, sits in five acres of lovely, well-landscaped gardens with riverfront access. The rooms are equally nice, and there's a pool and a laundry room.

The **Novel House Inn at Zion,** 73 Paradise Rd., 800/711-8400 or 435/772-3650, is a newly constructed B&B with 10 guest rooms, each decorated with a literary theme and named after an author (including Mark Twain, Rudyard Kipling, and Louis L'Amour). All rooms have private baths and great views, and are in the $95ñ110 range.

Campgrounds

The **Zion Canyon Campground,** 479 Zion Park Blvd., 435/772-3237, offers cabins, new motel rooms, tent sites (no dogs allowed in tent sites), and RV sites; facilities include a store, pizza parlor, game room, laundry room, and showers.

FOOD

Just outside the park entrance, near the Springdale shuttle stop, **Sol Foods,** 435/772-0277, is a short walk from either park campground and a good place for a salad or sandwich. There's also a computer with Internet access.

Mean Bean Coffee, 932 Zion Park Blvd., 435/772-0654, is the hip place to hang in the morning. Besides coffee drinks, they serve a few pastries. For a more substantial breakfast, or lunch to go, head across the way to **Oscar's Café,** 948 Zion Park Blvd., 435/772-3232. **Tsunami Juice and Java,** just outside the park at 180 Zion Park Blvd., 435/772-3818, has what their name implies and that little something extra—showers! (Showers are $4.)

Panda Garden Chinese Restaurant, 805 Zion Park Blvd., 435/772-3535, serves surprisingly good Chinese cuisine daily for lunch and dinner. Also good, and reasonably priced, is **Zion Pizza and Noodle,** 868 Zion Park Blvd., 435/772-3815, a fun place with a good selection of microbrews. The American-style menu at the **Bumbleberry Inn,** 897 Zion Park Blvd., 435/772-3224, includes bumbleberry pies and pancakes; open Mon.–Sat. for breakfast, lunch, and dinner.

The following restaurants all offer full liquor service: **Flanigan's Inn,** 428 Zion Park Blvd., 435/772-3244, has varied Southwestern and traditional American offerings; open daily for breakfast, lunch, and dinner. The **Pioneer Restaurant,** 828 Zion Park Blvd., 435/772-3009, serves American food, with vegetarian specialties; open daily for breakfast, lunch, and dinner.

Find Springdale's best meals at the **Bit & Spur Restaurant,** 1212 Zion Park Blvd., 435/772-3498, a Mexican restaurant with a menu that goes far beyond the usual south-of-the-border concoctions. (Keep your fingers crossed that sweet-potato tamales will be the evening's special!) Open for dinner only. Across the street, the **Switchback Grille,** 1215 Zion Park Blvd.,

435/772-3200, offers wood-fired pizza, rotisserie chicken, and steaks and seafood in a pleasantly bland atmosphere. There's patio seating in good weather; open for three meals daily.

INFORMATION AND SERVICES

Just off Zion Park Boulevard, the folks at **Zion Adventure Company,** 36 Lion Blvd., 435/772-1001, offer an incredibly valuable service to people who want to explore Zion to its fullest. Their rental packages (most notably water hiking boots and drysuits) and their advice have made hiking the Virgin River Narrows safer and more accessible. They also offer rock-climbing and canyoneering classes and try to teach people to learn how to explore safely and adventurously on their own.

If you're looking to rent a bike or go on a guided bike tour (outside the park boundaries), stop by **Springdale Cycle Tours,** 932 Zion Park Blvd., 800/776-2099 or 435/772-0575. **Bike Zion,** 1458 Zion Park Blvd., 435/772-3929, also rents mountain bikes, including some fancy full-suspension models.

People traveling with their dogs are in a bit of a dilemma when it comes to visiting Zion. No pets are allowed on the shuttle buses, and it's absolutely unconscionable to leave a dog inside a car here in the warmer months. Fortunately, the **Doggy Dude Ranch,** 435/772-3105, provides high-quality daytime and overnight boarding on Highway 9 in Rockville.

The **Zion Canyon Medical Clinic,** 435/772-3226, provides emergency services from about May–Oct.; take the turn-off for the O.C. Tanner Amphitheater. The **post office** is in the center of town on Zion Park Boulevard, 435/772-3950. You may also want to check out the many art galleries, rock shops, and gift shops along Zion Park Boulevard. Campers who left that crucial piece of equipment at home should visit **Zion Outdoors,** downstairs at 868 Zion Park Blvd., 435/772-0630.

HURRICANE

Although it's not as conveniently located as Springdale, there are a couple of places worth knowing about in Hurricane, which is located 19 miles from Zion National Park.

Budget travelers, take note: the **Dixie Hostel,** situated in a gracious old stucco building downtown at 73 S. Main St., 435/635-9000, offers inexpensive dorm-style lodgings and private rooms; guests have access to a laundry and kitchen. Linens and a light breakfast are included. Across the street at **New Garden Cafe,** 138 S. Main St,, 435/635-9825, the emphasis is on vegetarian sandwiches and entrées. Open Mon.–Sat. for breakfast, lunch, and dinner, and Sunday for brunch.

One of Hurricane's main attractions, **Pah Tempe Hot Springs,** has an uncertain future. The springs supplying this lovely, down-home hot springs resort have lost their oomph since the local water conservation district's nearby pipeline damaged the aquifer. The resort owners are hoping to reopen, so it's worth calling 435/635-2879 to see if the problems have been solved. The resort is on Enchanted Way just off Highway 9, one mile north of Hurricane.

ZION

St. George

Southern Utah's largest town lies between lazy bends of the Virgin River on one side and rocky hills of red sandstone on the other. In 1861, more than 300 Mormon families in the Salt Lake City area answered the call to go south to start the Cotton Mission, of which St. George became the center (hence the frequently used term "Dixie" to describe the area). The settlers overcame great difficulties to farm and to build an attractive city in this remote desert. Brigham Young chose the city's name to honor George A. Smith, who had served as head of the Southern (Iron) Mission during the 1850s. (The title "Saint" means simply that he was a Mormon—a Latter-day Saint.) Visits to some of the historic sites will add to your appreciation of the city's past; ask for the brochure *St. George Historic Walking Tour* at the chamber of commerce. The warm climate, dramatic setting, and many year-round recreation opportunities have helped make St. George (pop. about 50,000) the fastest-growing city in the state.

Visitors can look at the **St. George Temple** from the outside, and stop in its visitors center, 250 E. 400 South, 435/673-5181, or tour **Brigham Young's winter home,** 67 W. 200 North, 435/673-2517, but if your eye is set on Zion, you'll most likely just use St. George as a jumping-off point.

A group of dinosaur trackways documents the passage of at least two different species more than 200 million years ago. The well-preserved tracks may have been made by a 20-foot-long herbivore weighing an estimated 8–10 tons and by a carnivore half as long.

THE DINOSAUR TRACKWAYS AND OLD FORT PEARCE

Both of these sites illustrate periods of Utah's past. They're easily visited on a scenic back-road drive through the desert between St. George and Hurricane—just a bit of a detour on the way to Zion. Most of the road is unpaved and has some rough and sandy spots, but it should be okay for cautiously driven cars in dry weather. From Hurri-

cane, drive south eight miles on 700 West, then turn west 8.5 miles to the dinosaur trackways turn-off and another two miles to the Fort Pearce turn-off. From St. George, head east on 700 South and follow the road as it turns south; turn left (east) 2.1 miles on a paved road immediately after crossing the Virgin River, turn left 3.5 miles on another paved road after a curve, then turn left (east) 5.6 miles on an unpaved road to the Fort Pearce turn-off (or another two miles to the dinosaur trackways turn-off). Signs for Warner Valley and Fort Pearce point the way at many, but not all, of the intersections.

A group of dinosaur trackways documents the passage of at least two different species more than 200 million years ago. The well-preserved tracks, in the Moenave Formation, may have been made by a 20-foot-long herbivore weighing an estimated 8–10 tons and by a carnivore half as long. No remains of the dinosaurs themselves have been found here.

The name of Old Fort Pearce honors Captain John Pearce, who led Mormon troops of the area during the Black Hawk War with Ute Indians from 1865–1869. In 1861, ranchers had arrived in Warner Valley to run cattle on the desert grasslands. Four years later, however, Indian troubles threatened to drive the settlers out. The Black Hawk War and periodic raids by Navajo Indians made life precarious. Springs in Fort Pearce Wash—the only reliable water for many miles—proved the key to domination of the region. In December 1866, work began on a fort overlooking the springs. The stone walls stood about eight feet high and were more than 30 feet long. No roof was ever added. Much of the fort and the adjacent corral (built in 1869) have survived to the present. Local cattlemen still use the springs for their herds. Petroglyphs can be seen one-quarter mile downstream from the fort along ledges on the north side of the wash.

SNOW CANYON STATE PARK

If St. George's outlet stores and chain restaurants threaten to close in on you, head a few miles north of town to the red-rock canyons, sand dunes, volcanoes, and lava flows of Snow Canyon. Walls of Navajo Sandstone 50–750 feet high enclose the five-mile-long canyon. Hiking trails trace the canyon bottom and lead into the backcountry for a closer look at the geology, flora, and fauna. Common plants are barrel, cholla, and prickly pear cacti, yucca, Mormon tea, shrub live oak, cliffrose, and cottonwood. Delicate wildflowers bloom mostly in the spring and autumn, following the wet seasons, but cactus and the sacred datura (see sidebar in Capitol Reef chapter) can flower in the heat of summer.

Wildlife includes sidewinder and Great Basin rattlesnakes, Gila monster, desert tortoise, kangaroo rat, squirrel, cottontail, kit fox, coyote, and mule deer. You may find some Indian rock art, arrowheads, bits of pottery, and ruins. Many of the place names in the park honor Mormon pioneers. Snow Canyon was named for Lorenzo and Erastus Snow—not for the rare snowfalls.

Summers are too hot for comfortable hiking except in early morning. Highway 18 leads past an overlook on the rim of Snow Canyon and to the paved park road (Highway 300) that drops into the canyon and follows it to its mouth and the small town of Ivins. Snow Canyon is about 12 miles northwest of St. George. It's reached either by Highway 18—the faster way—or via Santa Clara and Ivins. Each vehicle is charged a $5 day-use fee.

TOURS

Southern Utah Scenic Tours, 888/404-8687 or 435/867-8690, website: www.utahscenic tours.com, runs guided tours of Zion, Bryce, and the Grand Canyon, departing from either Cedar City or St. George.

GOLF

With one private and eight public golf courses in the area, St. George enjoys a reputation as Utah's winter golf capital. Red sandstone cliffs serve as the backdrop for **Dixie Red Hills,** 1250 N. 645 West, on the northwest edge of town, 435/634-5852, a nine-hole, par-34 municipal course. **Green Spring Golf Course,** 588 N. Green Spring Dr. (just west of I-15 Washington Exit 10), 435/673-7888, has 18 holes (par 71) and a reputation as one of the finest courses in Utah. The nine-hole **Twin Lakes Golf Course,** 660 N. Twin Lakes Dr. on the northeast edge of town (take the I-15 west frontage road, Highland Dr.), 435/673-4441, is one of the area's most picturesque courses.

Professionals favor the cleverly designed **Sunbrook Golf Course,** 2240 Sunbrook Dr. off Dixie Downs Rd., between Green Valley and Santa Clara, 435/634-5866: 27 holes, par 72. The **St. George Golf Club** has a popular 18-hole, par-73 course south of town in Bloomington Hills, 435/634-5854. The **Southgate Golf Course,** 1975 S. Tonaquint Dr. on the southwest edge of town, 435/628-0000, has 18 holes and a 70 par. The adjacent Southgate Game Improvement Center, 435/674-7728 can provide golfers with computerized golf swing analysis plus plenty of indoor practice space and lots of balls. **Entrada,** 2511 W. Entrada Trail, 435/674-7500, is a new 18-hole course that's fast on its way to becoming St. George's most respected. The Johnny Miller-designed course is located northwest of St. George and incorporates natural lava flows, rolling dunes, and *arroyos* (dry river beds) into its design. The 18-hole course, **Sky Mountain,** is located northeast of St. George in nearby Hurricane.

ACCOMMODATIONS

St. George offers many places to stay and eat. Motel prices stay about the same year-round, although they may drop if business is slow in summer. Considering the popularity of this destination, prices are reasonable and quality is high. Golfers should ask about golf-and-lodging packages. You'll find most lodgings along the I-15 business route of St. George Boulevard (Exit 8) and Bluff Street (Exit 6). As for food, you'll find almost every fast-food place known to humanity just off the interstate on St. George Boulevard.

ZION

Less than $50

Many of St. George's less expensive lodging choices operate at Exit 8 off I-15 or on St. George Boulevard as it heads west to downtown. Right at the freeway exchange you'll find **Motel 6,** 205 N. 1000 East, 800/466-8356 or 435/628-7979, with a pool; pets are okay. The **Travelodge East,** 175 N. 1000 East, 800/574-8552 or 435/673-4621, has some kitchenettes and a pool; small pets are okay.

Heading toward downtown, the **Sunbird Inn,** 750 E. St. George Blvd., 888/628-9081 or 435/628-9000, offers a pool and a spa; pets are okay in designated rooms. Rooms hover around $50. The **Sun Time Inn,** 420 E. St. George Blvd., 800/237-6253 or 435/673-6181, has kitchenettes and a pool.

Near Exit 6 off I-15, the **Budget 8 Motel,** 1230 S. Bluff St., 800/275-3494 or 435/628-5234, offers a pool and a spa.

$50–75

East of the Exit 8 interchange is the **Ramada Inn,** 1440 E. St. George Blvd. (right beside the Factory Outlet Mall), 800/713-9435 or 435/628-2828; facilities include an outdoor pool and a hot tub, and a complimentary continental breakfast is included. Rooms are close to $75. The **Days Inn Thunderbird,** 150 N. 1000 East, 800/527-6543 or 435/673-6123, has a pool, hot tub, sauna, fitness center, free continental breakfast, and pets are okay.

The **Best Western Travel Inn,** 316 E. St. George Blvd., 800/528-1234 or 435/673-3541, has an outdoor pool and an indoor spa; children under 12 stay free. The **Singletree Inn,** 260 E. St. George Blvd., 800/528-8890 or 435/673-6161, has a pool, a hot tub, and free continental breakfast; pets are okay with $5 fee. Special golf package rates are available.

Close to downtown is one of St. George's best, the **Best Western Coral Hills,** 125 E. St. George Blvd., 800/542-7733 or 435/673-4844, a very attractive property with indoor and outdoor pools and two spas, an exercise room, and a complimentary continental breakfast. Children under 12 stay free. Also near downtown, The **Chalet Motel,** 664 E. St. George Blvd.,

888/628-6272 or 435/628-6272, offers some efficiency kitchens, two three-bed rooms, and a pool. **Weston's Econolodge,** 460 E. St. George Blvd., 435/673-4861, has a pool and a spa, and small pets are okay.

Leave the freeway at Exit 6 off I-15 to find another selection of motels. Most rooms at **The Bluffs Motel,** 1140 S. Bluff St., 800/832-5833 or 435/628-6699, are suites with efficiency kitchens. Facilities include a pool and a spa; pets are okay. A two-night minimum is required for stays during Easter weekend and some special events.

The **Ranch Inn,** 1040 S. Main, 800/332-0400 or 435/628-8000, offers a number of suite-like rooms with efficiency kitchens; there's a guest laundry room, a pool, and an indoor hot tub.

$75–100

The **Holiday Inn Resort Hotel & Convention Center,** 850 S. Bluff St., 800/457-9800 or 435/628-4235, is a large complex with a "Holidome" complete with indoor and outdoor pools, whirlpool, recreation/fitness facilities, tennis court, and putting green. Children under 18 stay free. The **Best Western Abbey Inn,** 1129 S. Bluff St., 888/222-3946 or 435/652-1234, is brand new, and all rooms have microwaves and refrigerators. There's an outdoor pool, an indoor spa, recreation/fitness facilities, and a free hot breakfast. Both of these lodgings are near Exit 6 off I-15.

The most prestigious address in St. George is the **Sheraton Four Points Inn,** 1450 S. Hilton Inn Dr., 800/662-2525 or 435/628-0463. Located on a golf course, the hotel has beautiful public areas and nicely appointed guest rooms. Facilities include a pool, a sauna, and private tennis courts.

Just across from Brigham Young's winter home, the **Seven Wives Inn Bed & Breakfast,** 217 N. 100 West, 800/600-3737 or 435/628-3737, offers rooms in two historic homes. All guest rooms have private baths and are decorated with antiques. Children and pets are welcome, and guests can get free passes to a local gym.

Also in St. George's historic district is **An Olde Penny Farthing Inn,** 278 N. 100 West, 435/673-7755. Built in the 1870s as a pioneer home, the handsome structure has been beautifully restored as an inn with five guest rooms, each individually decorated with period furnishings and fine art; all have private baths. Although most of the rooms here run more than $75, the cozy Sego Lily room is perfect for a single traveler, and only $45 single, $55 double.

You'll find an entire compound of pioneer-era homes at the **Greene Gate Village Historic Bed & Breakfast Inn,** 76 W. Tabernacle, 800/350-6999 or 435/628-6999. Nine beautifully restored homes offer a variety of lodging options—groups or families can rent an entire home. Many rooms come with kitchens and private baths, some with private whirlpools; there's a pool for the enjoyment of all guests. Some pets are okay, and children are welcome.

Campgrounds

The best camping in the area is at **Snow Canyon State Park,** 800/322-3770 or 435/628-2255 (reservations), in a pretty canyon setting, with showers. Go 12 miles north on Highway 18, then left two miles; $14 without hookups, $17 with hookups.

Right in St. George, **McArthur's Temple View RV Resort,** 975 S. Main, 800/776-6410 or 435/673-6400, is located near the temple district and has a pool, a laundry room, and showers. East of town is **Settlers RV Park,** 1333 E. 100 South (near I-15 Exit 8), 435/628-1624, with a pool and showers; RVs only.

Farther north, near I-15 Washington Exit 10, you'll find **St. George Campground & RV Park,** 2100 E. Middleton Dr., 435/673-2970, with tent sites, a pool, a laundry room, and showers; and **Redlands RV Park,** 650 W. Telegraph, 800/553-8269 or 435/673-9700, with a pool, a store, a laundry room, and showers.

Spas

St. George is home to two large spa resorts and recreation centers in gorgeous natural settings. The **Green Valley Spa,** 1871 West Canyon View Dr., 800/237-1068 or 435/628-8060, website: www.greenvalleyspa.com, is a fitness, sports, health, and beauty spa resort with all-inclusive rates. Facilities include three pools, racquetball courts, a fully equipped gym with an array of fitness classes, tennis instruction, golf club privileges, plus hiking and climbing in neighboring canyons. There's also a whole catalog of beauty and rejuvenation treatments, ranging from massage, wraps, and aromatherapy to Native American medicine ceremonies and Shamanic card divination. Lodging is in the Coyote Inn, a luxury condominium development that flanks a park-like pool and garden area. Three spa meals daily are included in the rates. The Green Valley Spa requires a three-night minimum stay, with seven-day packages also available. Rates, which include all meals and most recreation and treatments, start at about $1,500 for a three-night stay.

Slightly less swanky, the **Red Mountain Spa,** 202 N. Snow Canyon Rd., 800/407-3002, website: www.redmountainspa.com, focuses on outdoor adventure and fitness. Facilities include numerous swimming and soaking pools, a fitness center and gym, tennis courts, a salon, a spa, conference rooms, plus access to lots of hiking and biking trails. Prices, which include all meals, lodging, and use of most spa facilities and recreation, start at about $230 per person per day, with special deals often available online. Spa services, including massage, facials, body polishing, and aromatherapy, cost extra.

FOOD

For a major recreation and retirement center, St. George is curiously lacking in unique places to eat. Almost every chain restaurant can be found here, but don't expect a bevy of local fine-dining houses. Some exceptions are listed as follows. You'll also find it bizarrely difficult to find restaurants that stay open late; even in high season, most restaurants close by 9 P.M.

The best place to head for lunch or dinner is Ancestor's Square, a trendy shopping development at the intersection of St. George Boulevard and Main Street. **Painted Pony,** 435/634-1700, has good Southwestern food. Dine Chinese at **J.J. Hunan Chinese Restaurant,** 435/628-7219. Pick up pizza at **Pizza Factory,** 435/628-1234.

Just across St. George Boulevard, **Bear Paw Coffee,** 75 N. Main St., 435/634-0126, is one of the few places in town to hang out and drink coffee. Breakfasts are large and delicious.

Unless noted, all of the following serve wine and cocktails. **Pancho & Lefty's,** 1050 S. Bluff St., 435/628-4772, serves Mexican lunch and dinners in a semiformal atmosphere. For Mexican food with a view, try **Paula's Cazuela,** 745 W. Ridgeview Dr. on the northwest edge of town, 435/673-6568, a hilltop restaurant serving fine Mexican fare for lunch and dinner.

For formal dining and spectacular views, head west toward the airport for **Sullivan's Rococo Inn & Steak House,** 511 Airport Rd., 435/628-3671; prime rib, steak, and seafood are the specialties. At **Scaldoni's Gourmet Grill,** in the Phoenix Plaza Mall, 929 W. Sunset Blvd., 435/674-1300, you can mix and match pastas with a wide variety of sauces.

INFORMATION AND SERVICES

The **St. George Chamber of Commerce** can tell you about the sights, events, and services of southwestern Utah; it has brochures of accommodations, restaurants, a historic walking tour, and area ghost towns; open Mon.–Fri. 9 A.M.–5 P.M. and Sat. 9 A.M.–1 P.M. The office is in the old county courthouse (built 1866–1876) at 97 E. St. George Boulevard (St. George, UT 84770), 435/628-1658, website: www.ezeeee.com.

For recreation, see the **Pine Valley Ranger District office,** 196 E. Tabernacle (St. George, UT 84770), 435/652-3100, for information on fishing, hiking, and camping in the Dixie National Forest north of town; maps of the forest and Pine Valley Wilderness are available; open Mon.–Fri. 8 A.M.–5 P.M. The **Bureau of Land Management** oversees vast lands in Utah's southwest corner and the Arizona Strip; open Mon.–Fri. 7:45 A.M.–4:30 P.M.; the offices for Dixie Resource Area, 435/688-3200, and the Shivwits and Vermilion Resource Areas of the Arizona Strip, 435/628-4491, are at 345 E. Riverside.

The **post office** is at 180 N. Main, 435/673-3312. The **Dixie Regional Medical Center** provides hospital care at 544 S. 400 East, 435/634-4000 (physician referral number is 801/628-6688). You can exchange foreign currency at **First Security Bank,** 410 E. Tabernacle, 435/574-6600.

Transportation

Skywest Airlines, 800/453-9417, has direct flights to Salt Lake City six times daily and to Las Vegas twice daily.

Rent automobiles in town from **Budget,** 116 W. St. George Blvd., 800/527-0700 or 435/673-6825; or Enterprise, 652 E. St. George Blvd., 435/634-1556. **National,** 800/227-7368 or 435/673-5098, and **Avis,** 800/230-4898 or 435/627-2002, are at the airport.

Greyhound buses depart from McDonald's Restaurant at 1235 S. Bluff Street for Salt Lake City, Denver, Las Vegas, and other destinations; 435/673-2933. The **St. George Shuttle** will take you to Las Vegas in a 15-passenger van for $20 from 850 S. Bluff Street (Holiday Inn); call 435/628-8320 for schedule.

Cedar City

Cedar City (pop. 18,953), known for its scenic setting and its summertime Utah Shakespearean Festival, is a handy base for exploring a good chunk of southern Utah. Just east of town rise the high cliffs of the Markagunt Plateau—a land of panoramic views, colorful rock formations, desolate lava flows, extensive forests, and flower-filled meadows. Also on the Markagunt Plateau is the Cedar Breaks National Monument, an immense amphitheater eroded into the vividly hued underlying rock. Within an easy day's drive are Zion National Park to the south and Bryce Canyon National Park and Grand Staircase-Escalante to the east. Cedar City is just east of I-15, 52 miles northeast of St. George and 253 miles southwest of Salt Lake City; take I-15 Exit 57, 59, or 62.

UTAH SHAKESPEAREAN FESTIVAL

Cedar City's lively festival presents three Shakespearean plays each season, choosing from both well-known and rarely performed works. Most of the action centers on the Adams Shakespeare Theatre, an open-air theatre in the round, which is closely designed after the original Globe Theatre from Elizabethan London. The indoor Randall Jones Theatre presents the "Best of the Rest"—works by other great playwrights such as Chekhov, Molière, and Arthur Miller. A total of eight plays are staged each from late June–mid-Oct.

Costumed actors stage the popular Greenshow each day before the performances with a variety of Elizabethan comedy skits, Punch and Judy shows, period dances, music, juggling, and other good natured 16th-century fun. Another activity, the Royal Feaste, presents a pre-performance Elizabethan-style dinner (a feast with no silverware!) and entertainment from Tudor times ($30 per person, reservations required). Backstage tours of the costume shop, makeup room, and stage show you how the festival works. At literary seminars each morning, actors and Shakespearean scholars discuss the previous night's play. Production seminars, held daily except Sunday, take a close look at acting, costumes, stage props, special effects, and other details of play production.

The Greenshow and seminars are free, but you'll have to pay for most other events. Tickets cost $15–40, and it's wise to purchase them well in advance; however, last-minute theatregoers can usually find tickets to *something;* call 435/586-7790 for more information. Detailed brochures listing activities and dates of performances are available by mail from the Utah Shakespearean Festival, Cedar City, UT 84720, 435/586-7878 or 800/PLAYTIX (800/752-9849) (box office) and online at www.bard.org.

The theaters are on the Southern Utah University campus near the corner of Center and 300 West. Rain occasionally dampens the performances (the Elizabethan theater is open to the sky), and plays may move to a conventional theater next door, where the box office is located.

SCENIC DRIVES
Parowan Gap

Ten miles west of the small I-15 town of Parowan is a pass where Indians have pecked many designs into the rocks. Indians and wildlife hunting the Red Hills commonly passed through this gap, and it may have served as an important site for hunting rituals. The rock art's meaning hasn't been deciphered, but it probably represents the thoughts of many different Indian tribes over the past 1,000 or more years. Geometric designs, snakes, lizards, mountain sheep, bear claws, and human figures are all still recognizable. You can get here on a good gravel road from Parowan by going north on Main and turning left 10.5 miles on the last street (400 North). Or, from Cedar City, go north on Main (or take I-15 Exit 62), follow signs for Highway 130 north 13.5 miles, then turn right 2.5 miles on a good gravel road (near Milepost 19). You'll find an interpretive brochure and map at the Bureau of Land Management (BLM) offices in Cedar City.

Markagunt Scenic Byway (Highway 14)

Starting at Cedar City's eastern boundary, Highway 14 plunges into a narrow canyon flanked by steep rock walls before climbing up to the top of the Markagunt Plateau. This is a scenic route, passing dramatic rock cliffs and pink-rock hoodoos that echo the formations at Zion and Bryce Canyon National Parks. Although it's not a quick drive—especially if you get caught behind a lumbering RV—the scenic qualities of the canyon and the incredible vistas, which extend across Zion and down into Arizona, will amply repay your patience. The route also passes several wooded campgrounds and small mountain resorts. Because of their elevations—mostly 8,000–9,000 feet—these high mountain getaways are popular when the temperatures in the desert basin towns begin to bake. The route ends at the Long Valley Junction, at Highway 89, 41 miles east of Cedar City.

ACCOMMODATIONS

Cedar City is popular with visitors, so it's best to reserve a room at least a day or two in advance during the summer. There are two major concentrations of motels. A half dozen large chain hotels cluster around I-15 exits, together with lots of fast-food restaurants and strip malls. Downtown, along Main Street, are even more motels, ranging from classy new resort-like hotels to well-maintained budget motels. You can easily walk from most of the downtown motels to the Shakespeare Festival. Most of Cedar City's B&Bs are also within a stroll of the festival grounds.

Note that the following prices are for the high summer festival season. Outside of high season, expect rates to drop about one-third.

Less than $50

Downtown the **Zion Inn**, 222 S. Main, 435/586-9487, is one of Cedar City's best budget choices, with kitchenettes in some rooms. The **Super 7 Motel**, 190 S. Main, 435/586-6566, has a free continental breakfast, and accepts pets.

$50–75

The following motels string along Main Street in downtown Cedar City. The **Travelodge Motel**, 2555 N. Main, 800/348-8216 or 435/586-7435, is a good deal with a pool and spa; pets are okay. The **Cedar Rest Motel**, 479 S. Main, 435/586-9471, offers basic rooms; small pets are okay. The **Rodeway Inn**, 281 S. Main, 800/424-4777 or 435/586-9916, has a pool, a sauna, and a spa; pets are okay.

The **Best Western El Rey Inn**, 80 S. Main, 800/528-1234 or 435/586-6518, offers suites, a restaurant, a pool, a sauna, and a spa. All rooms at the **Stratford Court Hotel**, 18 S. Main, 435/586-2433 or 877/688-8884, are nonsmoking; this nice hotel has an outdoor pool, free passes to a local gym, and a complimentary continental breakfast.

Out at I-15 Exit 59, the **Comfort Inn**, 250 N. 1100 West, 800/627-0374 or 435/586-2082, has a pool, a spa, some kitchenettes, and a complimentary continental breakfast. Near the same exit, the **Holiday Inn**, 1575 W. 200 North, 800/432-8828 or 435/586-8888, also offers a pool, a good restaurant, a spa, and a sauna; pets are okay.

At I-15 exit 57, the **Days Inn**, 1204 S. Main, 888/556-5637 or 435/867-8877, has an indoor pool and complimentary continental breakfast.

At I-15 exit 52, a new **Econolodge**, 333 N. 1100 West, 888/326-6613 or 435/867-4700, has an outdoor pool and a hot tub.

$75–100

One of the best places to stay in Cedar City is the **Best Western Town & Country Inn**, 200 N. Main, 435/586-9911. It is a sprawling complex with nicely furnished rooms and suites, indoor and outdoor pools, and spas. Rooms have microwaves and refrigerators; several restaurants are adjacent. The **Abbey Inn**, 940 W. 200 North, 800/325-5411 or 435/586-9966, offers a pool and kitchenettes.

Bed-and-breakfast inns and Shakespeare seem to go hand-in-hand. The **Bard's Inn Bed & Breakfast**, 150 S. 100 West, 435/586-6612, two blocks from the Shakespearean Festival, has seven guest rooms, all with private bath, plus there's a two-bedroom cottage. Open during the festival season only. The **Paxman Summer House Bed & Breakfast**, 170 N. 400 West, 888/586-3755 or 435/586-3755, is an antique-furnished Victorian home with four guest rooms, all with private baths. A two-night minimum is required on summer weekends in July and August; located two blocks from the Shakespearean Festival. The **Desert Blossom Bed and Breakfast Inn,** 140 S. 100 West, 435/867-4691, has four rooms all with private bathrooms in a restored early 20th-century cottage. The inn is just around the corner from the festival grounds.

For a more rural touch, the **Willow Glen Inn Bed & Breakfast,** 3308 N. Bulldog Rd., 435/586-3275, offers a three-bedroom inn plus two cottages (with a total of six guest rooms); located on a 10-acre farm five miles north of downtown Cedar City, I-15 Exit 62; some shared baths.

$100–125

The **Baker House Bed & Breakfast,** 1800 Royal Hunte Dr., 888/611-8181 or 435/867-5695, website: www.bakerhouse.net, is a few minutes' drive from the festival, but the rooms here are some of the most luxurious in Cedar City and most have great views. There are five guest rooms in this modern Queen Anne mansion, all with private baths, fireplaces, and TVs.

Campgrounds

Cedar City KOA, 1121 N. Main, 800/562-9873 or 435/586-9872, is open all year with cabins, showers, a playground, and a pool, and can accommodate tents as well as RVs. **Country Aire RV Park,** 1700 N. Main, 435/586-2550, is open all year with showers and a pool; no tent sites. The **Town and Country RV Park,** 50 W. 200 North, 435/586-9900, is close to downtown; no tent sites.

East of Cedar City on Highway 14 are a handful of campgrounds in the Dixie National Forest. The closest, **Cedar Canyon,** is 12 miles from town, in a pretty canyon along Cow Creek. It's at 8,100 feet and open with water from early June–mid-Sept.; $8.

FOOD

Family restaurants dominate Cedar City's cuisine. **Sullivan's Cafe,** 301 S. Main, 435/586-

6761, is a favorite for casual family dining. **Boomer's,** 5 N. Main St., 435/865-9665, serves burgers, shakes, fries, and American standards. Upstairs is **Boomer's Pasta Garden,** a sister restaurant with a selection of pasta dishes.

At the **Pastry Pub,** 86 W. Center, 435/867-1400, you'll find pastries, sandwiches, and coffee; it's as close to a coffee shop as you'll find in Cedar City.

For Cantonese-style food, there's **Hunan Restaurant,** 501 S. Main, 435/586-8952, and **China Garden Restaurant,** 64 N. Main, 435/586-6042, whose giant sign you surely won't miss in downtown Cedar City. You can have a drink with your Mexican food at **Pancho and Lefty's,** 2107 N. Main, 435/586-7501, and **La Fiesta,** 900 N. Main, 435/586-4646. For pizza, try the **Pizza Factory,** 124 S. Main, 435/586-3900, open Mon.–Sat.; or **Godfather's Pizza,** 241 N. Main, 435/586-1111, located in the old train station.

The following fine-dining restaurants each serve wine and cocktails. **Adriana's Restaurant,** 164 S. 100 West, 435/865-1234, has an English atmosphere with fine dining and is open in summer Mon.–Sat. for lunch and dinner; call for hours off-season. East of Cedar City on Highway 14 is a dramatic desert canyon with two of the area's finest restaurants; both open for dinner only. Five miles east of town is the Western-style **Milt's Stage Stop,** 435/586-9344, serving steak, prime rib, and seafood. The steak house atmosphere is a bit more formal at **Rusty's Ranch House,** two miles east on Highway 14, 435/586-3839, a new restaurant in a dramatic canyon setting.

INFORMATION AND SERVICES

The **Iron County Travel Council** has literature and advice on travel in the area; open Mon.–Fri. 8 A.M.–7 P.M. and Sat. 9 A.M.–1 P.M. in summer; Mon.–Fri. 8 A.M.–5 P.M. the rest of the year; located at 581 N. Main (P.O. Box 1007, Cedar City, UT 84720), 435/586-5124. The **Cedar City Ranger District office** of the Dixie National Forest has information on recreation and travel on the Markagunt Plateau; at 82 N. 100

East (P.O. Box 627, Cedar City, UT 84721-0627), 435/865-3200. The Dixie National Forest **supervisor's office,** in the same building, provides general information for the entire forest; P.O. Box 580, Cedar City, UT 84721-0580, 435/865-3700.

The **BLM's Cedar City District office** is just off Main at 176 E. DL Sargeant Drive on the north edge of town (Cedar City, UT 84720), 435/586-2401; open Mon.–Fri. 7:45 A.M.–4:30 P.M. For more specific information on the southern Wah Wah Mountains and other desert areas around town, visit the **BLM's Beaver River Resource Area office;** open Mon.–Fri. 7:45 A.M.–4:30 P.M.; at 365 S. Main (Cedar City, UT 84720), 435/586-2458.

The **Mountain West Bookstore,** 77 N. Main, 435/586-3828, offers a selection of Utah history, travel, general reading, and LDS titles.

Transportation

Skywest Airlines has flights between the Cedar City Municipal Airport and Salt Lake City, 800/453-9417. Rent a car from **National,** at the airport, 435/586-4004, or at National's office at the Town and Country Inn, 200 N. Main, 435/586-9900. **Speedy Rentals,** 650 N. Main, 435/586-7368, rents vans, cars, pickups and motorhomes.

Greyhound Bus, 1355 S. Main (the C-Mart Texaco station near the south I-15 interchange), 435/586-1204, offers service twice daily to Salt Lake City, Denver, St. George, Las Vegas, and other destinations.

Resources

Suggested Reading

Guidebooks and Travelogues

Barnes, F.A. *Canyon Country Off-Road Vehicle Trails.* Moab, UT: Arch Hunter Books. A series of backcountry driving guides to the canyon areas of southern and eastern Utah. This series originally had more than 25 slim volumes, but only seven are currently in print (many are still available locally in Utah bookstores). Current volumes cover Arches and La Sal areas, the Maze, Needles, Island and Canyon Rims areas in Canyonlands National Park (three books), and a volume dedicated to the Moab area. Prices are usually $8 per book.

Benchmark Maps. *Utah Road & Recreation Atlas.* Medford, OR: Benchmark Maps, 2002; 95 pages, $19.95. Shaded relief maps emphasize landforms, and recreational information is abundant. Use it to locate campgrounds, backroads, and major trailheads, although there's not enough detail to rely on it for hiking.

Casey, Robert L. *A Journey to the High Southwest.* Old Saybrook, CT: Globe Pequot Press, 2000; 464 pages, $19.95. Introduction, history, and travel in southern Utah and adjacent Arizona, New Mexico, and Colorado.

Huegel, Tony. *Utah Byways: 65 Backcountry Drives for the Whole Family, Including Moab, Canyonlands, Arches, Capitol Reef, San Rafael Swell and Glen Canyon.* Wilderness Press, 2000; 208 pages, $16.95. If you're looking for off-highway adventure, this is your guide. The book includes detailed directions, human and natural history, outstanding photography, full-page maps for each of the 65 routes, and an extensive how-to chapter for beginners.

Sierra Club. *Desert Southwest: The Sierra Club Guides to the National Parks.* New York: Random House, 1996; 352 pages, $17.95. Beautiful color photos illustrate the wildlife and scenic beauties of Utah's five national parks. The other parks described are Mesa Verde in Colorado, Grand Canyon and Petrified Forest in Arizona, Carlsbad Caverns in New Mexico, and Guadalupe Mountains and Big Bend in Texas. The text tells of the history, geology, wildlife, and flora. Maps and trail descriptions show hiking possibilities.

Zwinger, Ann. *Wind in the Rock: The Canyonlands of Southeastern Utah.* Tucson: University of Arizona Press, 1986; 258 pages, $9.50. Well-written accounts of hiking in the Grand Gulch and nearby canyons. The author tells of the area's history, archaeology, wildlife, and plants.

Outdoor Activities

Adkison, Ron. *Best Easy Day Hikes Grand Staircase-Escalante and the Glen Canyon Region.* Helena, MT: Falcon Publishing, 1998; 120 pages, $6.95. Features 19 hikes in south central Utah Canyon Country, including the newly created Grand Staircase Monument; also includes Paria Canyon.

Adkison, Ron. *Hiking Grand Staircase-Escalante and the Glen Canyon Region.* Helena, MT: Falcon Publishing, 1998; 320 pages, $14.95. The vast Escalante/Glen Canyon area of southern Utah is nearly roadless, and hiking is about the only way you'll have a chance to visit these beautiful and austere canyons. This guide includes detailed information on 59 hikes, including Paria Canyon and Grand Gulch, in addition to the new Grand Staircase Monument.

Allen, Steve. *Canyoneering 3.* Salt Lake City: University of Utah Press, 1997; 328 pages, $21.95. This book provides excellent, detailed descriptions of a variety of hikes in the Grand Staircase-Escalante National Monument, ranging from day hikes to multiday treks.

Barnes, F.A. *Canyon Country Hiking and Natural History.* Salt Lake City: Wasatch Publishers, 1977; 176 pages, $7. An introduction to the delights of hiking among the canyons and mountains in southeastern Utah.

Barnes, F.A. *Canyon Country Slickrock Hiking and Biking.* Moab, UT: Canyon Country Publications, 1990; 289 pages, $14. "An illustrated guide to a completely different kind of hiking and mountain biking in the canyon country of southeastern Utah." A good introduction, areas to explore, personal anecdotes, and many black-and-white photos make this book fun to read and use.

Barnes, F.A. *Hiking the Historic Route of the 1859 Macomb Expedition.* Moab, UT: Canyon Country Publications, 1989; 49 pages, $8. Captain John Macomb led the first expedition to explore and write about what's now Canyonlands National Park. Adventurous hikers can retrace part of Macomb's route, thanks to the descriptions, maps, and photos in this little guide.

Barnes, F.A., and Tom Kuehne. *Canyon Country Mountain Biking.* Moab, UT: Canyon Country Publications, 1988; 145 pages, $11. Authors tell how to get the most out of biking the canyon country of southeastern Utah. Trail descriptions take you through Arches and Canyonlands National Parks, the La Sal Mountains, and Canyon Rims Recreation Area.

Bicycle Vacation Guides. *Bicycle Utah.* Bicycle Vacation Guides, Inc. (P.O. Box 738, Park City, UT 84060; 801/649-5806); $5. This series of booklets describes 20 mountain-bike routes, one booklet for each of Utah's nine travel districts. The booklets are *Bridgerland, Canyonlands, Castle Country, Color Country, Dinosaurland, Golden Spike Empire, Great Salt Lake Country, Mountainland,* and *Panoramaland.* Each book gives locations of trails on a map and full trail descriptions, including a graph of the trail's vertical component. Booklets are found at many visitors' centers and bookstores.

Bjørnstad, Eric. *Desert Rock I: Rock Climbs in National Parks.* Evergreen, CO: Chockstone Press, 1996; 242 pages, $25. This is a classic climbing guide by one of Utah's most respected climbers.

Brereton, Thomas, and James Dunaway. *Exploring the Backcountry of Zion National Park: Off Trail Routes.* Natural History Association, 1988; 112 pages, $7.50. Leave the crowds behind and discover Zion's backcountry.

Campbell, Todd. *Above and Beyond Slickrock.* Salt Lake City: Wasatch Publishers, 1999; 281 pages, $19.95. Exploring the slickrock country of Southeastern Utah.

Crowell, David. *Mountain Biking Moab.* Helena, MT: Falcon Publishing, 1997; 232 pages, $10.95. A guide to the many trails around Moab, from the most popular to the little explored, in a handy size: small enough to take on the bike with you.

Green, Stewart M. *Rock Climbing Utah.* Helena, MT: Falcon Publishing, 1998; 538 pages, $26.95. Good detail on climbs in all of Utah's national parks, including many line drawings and photos with climbing routes highlighted.

Kals, W.S. *Land Navigation Handbook.* San Francisco: Sierra Club Books, 1983; 288 pages, $15. This handy pocket guide will enable you to confidently explore Utah's extensive backcountry. Explains not only how to use a map and compass but also other navigation methods such as altimeter and using the sun and stars.

Kelsey, Michael R. *Canyon Hiking Guide to the Colorado Plateau*. Provo, UT: Kelsey Publishing, 1999; 288 pages, $15.95. One of the best guides to hiking in southeastern Utah's canyon country. Geologic cross sections show the formations you'll be walking through. The book has descriptions and maps for 64 trips in Utah, 38 hikes in adjacent Arizona, 13 in Colorado, and two in New Mexico. The author is ahead of his time in using just the metric system, but the book is otherwise easy to follow.

Kelsey, Michael R. *Hiking, Biking and Exploring Canyonlands National Park and Vicinity*. Provo, UT: Kelsey Publishing, 1992; 320 pages, $14.95. The author's newest guide emphasizes hiking and local history. He used his mountain bike and hiking boots to explore the backcountry, rather than a four-wheel-drive vehicle. Uses metric system.

Kelsey, Michael R. *River Guide to Canyonlands National Park*. Provo, UT: Kelsey Publishing, 1991; 256 pages, $11.95. Explains how to do a trip on the Green and Colorado rivers and the many hikes and things to see along the way, including lots of local lore. Begins at the town of Green River on the Green and Moab on the Colorado; coverage ends at the confluence area (there's not much on Cataract Canyon). Uses metric system.

Lambrechtse, Rudi. *Hiking the Escalante*. Salt Lake City: Wasatch Publishers, 1999; 189 pages, $11.95. "A wilderness guide to an exciting land of buttes, arches, alcoves, amphitheaters, and deep canyons." Introduction to history, geology, and natural history of the Escalante region in southern Utah. Contains descriptions and trailhead information for 42 hiking destinations. The hikes vary from easy outings suitable for children to a highly challenging four-day backpack trek.

Schneider, Bill. *Best Easy Day Hikes Canyonlands and Arches*. Helena, MT: Falcon Publishing, 1997; 74 pages, $6.95. Twenty-one hikes in this popular vacation area, geared to travelers who are short on time or aren't able to explore the canyons on more difficult trails.

Schneider, Bill. *Exploring Canyonlands and Arches National Parks*. Helena, MT: Falcon Publishing, 1997; 202 pages, $14.95. A hiking guide to these two Moab-area parks. Includes 63 easy and more difficult hikes.

Trails Illustrated. *Moab Bike Routes*. Evergreen, CO: Trails Illustrated, 1995; $7. Handy plasticized topographic map with Moab-area routes. Trails Illustrated also produces trail guides to the various national forests in Utah ($8.99).

Utesch, Peggy. *The Utah-Colorado Mountain Bike Trail System, Route I—Moab to Loma: Kokopelli's Trail*. Moab, UT: Canyon Country Publications, 1990; 81 pages, $9. Learn about desert bicycling, then take off with the detailed descriptions in this well-illustrated guide. The 130-mile trail twists over spectacular terrain between Moab, Utah, and Loma, Colorado.

Utesch, Peggy, and Bob Utesch. *Mountain Biking in Canyon Rims Recreation Area*. Moab, UT: Canyon Country Publications, 1992; 89 pages, $8. An illustrated mountain-bikers' guide to exploring this vast and beautiful area south and east of Canyonlands National Park. You'll need the separate map *Canyon Country Off-Road Vehicle Trail Map: Canyon Rims Recreation Area* by F.A. Barnes.

Waterman, Laura, and Guy Waterman. *Backwoods Ethics: Environmental Issues for Hikers and Campers*. Woodstock, VT: Countryman Press, 1993; 280 pages, $14. Thoughtful commentaries on how the hiker can visit the wilderness with the least impact. Case histories dramatize the need to protect the environment.

Zwinger, Ann. *Run, River, Run: a Naturalist's Journey Down One of the Great Rivers of the*

American West. Tucson: University of Arizona Press, 1984; 317 pages, $17.95. An excellent description of the author's experiences along the Green River from its source in the Wind River Range of Wyoming to the Colorado River in southeastern Utah. The author weaves geology, Indian ruins, plants, wildlife, and her personal feelings into the text and drawings.

Memoirs

Abbey, Edward. *Desert Solitaire.* New York: Ballantine Books, 1991; 337 pages, $6.99. A meditation on the Red Rock Canyon country of Utah. Abbey brings his fiery prose to the service of the American outback, while excoriating the commercialization of the West.

Loeffler, Jack. *Adventures with Ed: A Portrait of Abbey.* Albuquerque: University of New Mexico Press, 2002; 308 pages; $24.95. This memoir by Abbey's good friend helps readers see the person behind the icon.

Melloy, Ellen. *Raven's Exile.* New York: Henry Holt & Company, 1994; 256 pages, $25. Throughout a summer of Green River raft trips, Melloy reflects on natural and human history of the area.

History and Current Events

Cahalan, James M. *Edward Abbey: A Life.* Tucson: University of Arizona Press, 2001; 357 pages; $27.95. A biography of environmentalist and writer Edward Abbey.

Dellenbaugh, Frederick S. *A Canyon Voyage: The Narrative of the Second Powell Expedition.* Tucson: University of Arizona Press, 1984; 277 pages, $16.95. A well-written account of John Wesley Powell's second expedition down the Green and Colorado rivers, from 1871–1872. The members took the first Grand Canyon photographs and obtained much valuable scientific knowledge.

Powell, John Wesley. *The Exploration of the Colorado River and its Canyons.* Mineola, NY: Dover Publications, reprinted 1997 (first published in 1895); 400 pages, $10.95. Powell's 1869 and 1871–1872 expeditions down the Green and Colorado rivers. His was the first group to navigate through the Grand Canyon. A description of the 1879 Uinta Expedition is included, too.

Archaeology

Lister, Robert, and Florence Lister. *Those Who Came Before.* Southwest Parks and Monuments, 1983; 184 pages, $16.95. A well-illustrated guide to the history, artifacts, and ruins of prehistoric Southwest Indians. The author also describes parks and monuments containing archaeological sites.

Slifer, Dennis. *Guide to Rock Art of the Utah Region: Sites with Public Access.* Albuquerque: University of New Mexico Press, 2000; 245 pages, $15.95. The most complete guide to rock-art sites, with descriptions of more than 50 sites in the Four Corners region. Complete with maps and directions, and with an overview of rock-art styles and traditions.

Natural Sciences

Baars, Donald L. *The Colorado Plateau: A Geologic History.* Albuquerque: University of New Mexico Press, 1994; 279 pages, $14.95. Written for the layperson, this book takes you on a tour of the Four Corners area geology from the ancient twisted rocks at the bottom of the Grand Canyon to the fiery volcanism and icy glaciations of the Pleistocene epoch.

Chronic, Halka. *Roadside Geology of Utah.* Mountain Press Publishing, 1990; 325 pages, $16. This layperson's guide tells the story of the state's fascinating geology as seen by following major roadways.

Fagan, Damian. *Canyon Country Wildflowers.* Helena, MT: Falcon Publishing, 1998; 192 pages, $17.95. A comprehensive field guide to the diverse flora of the Four Corners area.

Fleischner, Thomas Lowe. *Singing Stone: A Natural History of the Escalante Canyons.* University of Utah Press, 1999; 237 pages, $17.95. A former Outward Bound instructor who has guided many city people through the Escalante Canyons, Fleischner knows the area well and lends firsthand vitality to his information on the area's plants, animals, ecology, geology, and prehistory.

Halfpenny, James, and Elizabeth Biesiot. *A Field Guide: Mammal Tracking in Western America.* Boulder, CO: Johnson Books, 1988; 163 pages, $14.95. No need to guess what animal passed by. This well-illustrated guide shows how to read trails of large and small wildlife. More determined detectives can study the scatology chapter.

Hamilton, Wayne L. *The Sculpturing of Zion: Guide to the Geology of Zion.* Springdale, UT: Zion Natural History Association, 1984; 132 pages, $14.95. This outstanding book explains geologic forces and history. Clear graphs, drawings, and beautiful color photography illustrate the nontechnical text.

Williams, David. *A Naturalist's Guide to Canyon Country.* Helena, MT: Falcon Publishing, 2000; 188 pages, $22.95. If you want to buy just one field guide, this is the one to get. It's well-written, beautifully illustrated, and a delight to use.

Suggested Reading

Internet Resources

Although a virtual visit to Utah cannot replace the real thing, you'll find an enormous amount of helpful information on the World Wide Web. Thousands of websites interlink to cover everything from ghost towns to the latest community news.

Travel

www.utah.com
The Utah Travel Council is a one-stop shop for all sorts of information on Utah. It takes you around the state to sights, activities, events, maps, and offers links to local tourist offices. The accommodations listings are the most up-to-date source for current prices and options.

www.yahoo.com
The well-organized Yahoo site will take you almost anywhere in Utah. Select Regional, U.S. States, then Utah.

utah.citysearch.com
City Search sites are great for finding a community's news, arts, entertainment, and Internet links.

officialcitysites.org/utah.htm
Official City Sites will take you directly to you place of interest for the links there.

www.state.ut.us
The official State of Utah website has travel information, agencies, programs, and what the legislature is up to.

www.skiutah.com
If you're thinking snow, glide over to Ski Utah, where you'll also find summer activities at the ski resorts.

The Great Outdoors

www.nps.gov
The National Park Service offers pages for all their areas at this site, where a click-on map will take you to Utah's parks. You can also enter this address followed by a slash and the first two letters of the first two words of the place (first four letters if there's just a one-word name); for example, www.nps.gov/brca takes you to Bryce Canyon National Park and www.nps.gov/zion leads to Zion National Park.

www.gorp.com/gorp/location/ut/ut.htm
The Great Outdoor Recreation Pages offers lots of hiking and other outdoor information, including specifics on national forests and wilderness areas.

parks.state.ut.us
The Utah State Parks site offers details on the large park system.

www.desertusa.com
Desert USA's Utah section discusses places to visit and what plants and animals you might meet there.

www.americansouthwest.net/utah
Utah Guide provides an overview of national parks, national recreation areas, and some state parks.

Index

Index

Index

RUINS

SCENIC DRIVES

Index

Acknowledgments

I'd like to thank Judy Jewell for all of her help with this first edition. It's great to be working together again. I'd also like to thank Andrea and Corey for sharing their frequent-flier status with me while I was working on this book. It was fun sharing Utah (and Georgia) adventures that even the duties of high-tech ghostwriting couldn't overcome.

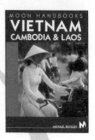

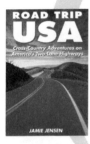

U.S.~Metric Conversion

1 inch	=	2.54 centimeters (cm)
1 foot	=	.304 meters (m)
1 yard	=	0.914 meters
1 mile	=	1.6093 kilometers (km)
1 km	=	.6214 miles
1 fathom	=	1.8288 m
1 chain	=	20.1168 m
1 furlong	=	201.168 m
1 acre	=	.4047 hectares
1 sq km	=	100 hectares
1 sq mile	=	2.59 square km
1 ounce	=	28.35 grams
1 pound	=	.4536 kilograms
1 short ton	=	.90718 metric ton
1 short ton	=	2000 pounds
1 long ton	=	1.016 metric tons
1 long ton	=	2240 pounds
1 metric ton	=	1000 kilograms
1 quart	=	.94635 liters
1 US gallon	=	3.7854 liters
1 Imperial gallon	=	4.5459 liters
1 nautical mile	=	1.852 km

To compute celsius temperatures, subtract 32 from Fahrenheit and divide by 1.8. To go the other way, multiply celsius by 1.8 and add 32.

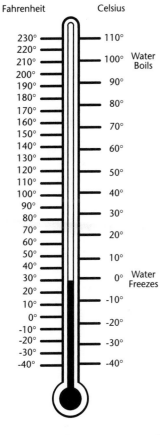

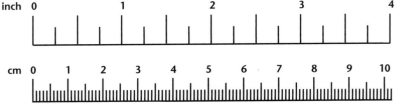